1 'Durham Cathedral'
Manchester University, Whitworth Art Gallery $16\frac{1}{8} \times 20\frac{7}{8}$: 410×530 *Water-colour*
Thomas GIRTIN (1775–1802)

Water-colour Painting in Britain

II   The Romantic Period

Martin Hardie

Edited by Dudley Snelgrove *with*
Jonathan Mayne *and* Basil Taylor

B. T. BATSFORD LTD   LONDON

First published 1967

Printed and bound in Great Britain
by William Clowes and Sons, Limited, London and Beccles,
Collotype plates printed by L. Van Leer and Co. N.V.,
London and Amsterdam,
for the publishers B. T. BATSFORD LTD
4 Fitzhardinge Street, Portman Square, London W1

CONTENTS

ACKNOWLEDGMENT

The Editors are indebted to the following for assistance in the preparation of the present volume: Mr. Evelyn Joll for assistance with the Turner chapter; Dr. Miklos Rajnai and Mr. Alec Cotman for kindly reading the chapters concerned with the Norwich School; Dr. Marion Spencer for her assistance on the Bonington chapter; Miss Margot Holloway who has again given valuable help in checking the typescript, reading the proofs and making the index of artists.

We are also greatly indebted to all those Museums and private collectors who have assisted us in connection with works in their ownership mentioned or illustrated in the text. As in the case of the preceding volume, an index of artists mentioned in the text is included. A complete index of the entire work as well as a substantial bibliography of water-colour painting will be published in the third and final volume of the work.

The Publishers wish to thank the owners of the paintings reproduced in this book, and whose names are given beneath the illustrations. In particular they wish to thank the Trustees of the British Museum; the Courtauld Institute of Art, Witt Collection; The Syndics of the Fitzwilliam Museum, Cambridge; Leeds City Art Gallery and Temple Newsam House; Herbert Powell Bequest (National Art-Collections Fund); the Trustees of the Victoria and Albert Museum (Crown Copyright); the Trustees of the Wallace Collection, London.

ABBREVIATIONS

B.M.   British Museum
Diary   Joseph Farington's Diary, ed. James Greig. 8 vols. 1922–1928
L.B.   Laurence Binyon: Catalogue of Drawings by British Artists in the British Museum. 4 vols. 1898–1907
Oppé Coll.   Collection of Mr. D. L. T. Oppé
Roget   J. L. Roget: History of the 'Old Water-colour' Society. 2 vols. 1891
V.A.M.   Victoria and Albert Museum
Whitley 1700–1799 I and II   W. T. Whitley: Artists and their Friends in England 1700–1799. 2 vols. 1928
Whitley 1800–1820   W. T. Whitley: Art in England 1800–1820. 1928
Whitley 1821–1837   W. T. Whitley: Art in England 1821–1837. 1930

THE ILLUSTRATIONS

THE ILLUSTRATIONS

THE ILLUSTRATIONS

THE ILLUSTRATIONS

CHAPTER I

Thomas Girtin

William Pearson

In his brief life of twenty-seven years, Thomas Girtin (1775–1802) won an undisputed place among the great masters of water-colour painting. He ranks with Turner and Constable, Cotman and De Wint, and Turner himself is said to have said—'Had Girtin lived I should have starved'; the close association between them in their student days gives added weight to the remark. Girtin and Turner were more than topographers. Between them they did much to alter the technique and development of water-colour painting, and to found a school which was specifically English. They tried the old patterns, then discarded them for new.

Girtin's own contemporaries and immediate successors, slow to recognise and adequately to analyse the characteristics of his genius, were none the less aware that a new force had arisen and gave it a full share of discriminating praise.[1] Three entries in Farington's *Diary* are of special interest as showing contemporary valuation of Girtin and Turner:

> Jan. 21, 1799. 'He [Northcote] said He could not think Daniell had much power in the art . . . whereas in those of Turner & the drawings of Girtin, there is evidently genius & feeling, from which much may be expected.'

> Feb. 9, 1799. 'Hoppner told me Mr. Lascelles as well as Lady Sutherland are disposed to set up Girtin against Turner—who they say effects his purpose by industry—the former more genius—Turner finishes too much.'

> Jan. 26, 1803. 'Turner has a great deal of painter's feeling, but his works too much made up from pictures, not enough of original observation of nature: Girtin had more of it [said by Northcote].'

Contemporary esteem is also shown by the fact that about 1800 Sir George Beaumont owned some thirty drawings in water-colour by Girtin, and Constable's study of these drawings is apparent in his earliest water-colours made about 1805 to 1810. In the *Introductory Lessons for Painting in Water-Colours*, 1800, James Roberts advises the beginner to 'consult and dwell on the exquisite drawings of Turner and Girtin. The castigated purity of the one, and the magic splendour of the former, will teach him to view Nature with the eye of a master.'

[1] For contemporary appreciation in newspaper criticisms, Whitley, 1700–1799, II, 235.

Few facts are recorded about Girtin's short life. He was born in Southwark on February 18, 1775, and the register of St. Saviour's, Southwark, a month later, records the baptism of 'Thomas, son of John Girtin, Brushmaker, and Rose Hannah'. In most biographies his father, who died in 1778, is described as a rope-maker, owning a Thames-side business. Probably he dealt in both brushes and cordage, a usual combination even in recent years. What is more important is that, two months later, on the other bank of the Thames, above a small barber's shop in Maiden Lane, Strand, Joseph Mallord William Turner was born.

An elder son of John Girtin's, John, baptised on April 19, 1773, became an engraver. Thomas first had drawing lessons from a certain Mr. Fisher of Aldersgate Street, and then became a pupil of Edward Dayes. There is a tradition that the relationship between Dayes and Girtin was a stormy one, but on this point the evidence is far from clear. The chief authority is a note in the manuscript of John Pye, the engraver, written probably between 1850 and 1860, and quoted for the first time by Roget[1]:

> Young Girtin, he tells me, soon excelled his master, which 'this jealous & small-minded person' never forgave him. The praise bestowed upon his pupil was gall to him & increased his hatred. In order to check his progress, he employed him to colour prints week after week & month after month. This was his employment till, feeling himself designed for better things, he expostulated with Dayes, telling him he was placed with him to learn to draw, not to colour prints. His tyrant insisted on obedience. Girtin refused; on which Dayes committed him to prison as a refractory apprentice. The Earl of Essex, hearing of his imprisonment, went to see him, & saw that he had covered the walls of his room with spirited sketches. Pleased with the young man's frank & open manner, he released him from confinement & from the tyranny of Dayes by buying up his indentures; & from that time to the day of Girtin's death, the Earl continued to be one of his kindest friends and patrons.

This story, however, will not hold. Thornbury says that Girtin was committed to Bridewell,[2] but this would have been impossible unless his master were a freeman of the City of London, and the records of Bridewell Prison up to the end of 1795 contain no mention of Girtin's name.[3] Girtin's obituary notice in the *Gentleman's Magazine*[4] merely says that Girtin 'was, for a short time, the pupil of Mr. Dayes', but when we take into consideration Dayes' fretful and conceited mind, and his natural, though not necessarily overwhelming, mortification that his pupil should so greatly outshine him, we can easily postulate a feeling of strain between them, which, nevertheless, did not interfere to any great extent with their relationship as master and pupil. Girtin, in association with James Moore, who was his first patron, was certainly in close touch with Dayes as late as 1794. His early work is so perfectly in the style of Dayes that clearly he had learnt all that he could teach him, though apparently the only contemporary recognition of what Girtin owned to his master is contained in a note by the editor of Dayes' works[5]: 'Girtin was a pupil of Mr. Dayes, under whose tuition he made considerable progress in his profession'.

The influence of Dayes—his use of very liquid washes of colour, over a drawing with

[1] Roget, I, p. 84.
[3] Randall Davies, *Thomas Girtin's Water-colours*, 1924, p. 11.
[4] *Gentleman's Magazine*, February LXXIII, 1803, pt. 1, p. 188.
[5] E. W. Brayley, ed. *Works of the Late Edward Dayes*, 1805, p. 329.
[2] W. Thornbury, *Life of Turner*, 1862, p. 62.

2

flat shadows painted in a pale bluish grey, with touches of warmer and darker colour indicating details of brick and stone with all their joins and interstices—is seen in all of Girtin's work up to 1795. It is almost impossible to differentiate between a drawing such as *Manorbier Castle, Pembroke*, with its signature, *Jas Moore Delt. Girtin Pinx*, and others by Dayes after James Moore, in the Ashmolean Museum.

At the close of his apprenticeship with Dayes (which started May 15, 1789 and ended in 1791 or 1792), Girtin was employed in colouring prints in the workshop of John Raphael Smith. It was here that he met Turner, who was engaged in the same occupation. It was possibly here also that both Girtin and Turner first encountered Dr. Monro. Between 1788 and 1790 the two young artists were both employed by architects to wash in skies and add backgrounds, as well as to lay flat tints.

Girtin's work first appeared before the public in 1792, when the fourth number of the *Copper Plate Magazine* contained an engraving after one of his drawings of Windsor Castle. In the following year he was again represented in the same publication. In 1794 he made his *début* at the Royal Academy with *Ely Minster*,[1] a drawing based on a sketch by James Moore, (1766–1799). Moore, an enthusiastic amateur of the arts, carried on the business of a wholesale linen-draper in Cheapside, but seems to have spent most of his time touring England in search of information for his antiquarian publications. In 1786 he had produced *A List of the Abbies, Priories & other Religious Houses, Castles, etc. in England & Wales, collected from Dugdale etc. etc.*, and in 1791 he began work on *Monastic Remains & Ancient Castles in England & Wales. Drawn on the Spot by James Moore, Esq. F.A.S. & executed in aquatint by G. I. Parkyns Esq.* The first volume of this work was published in 1792. In pursuit of his material, Moore set out for Scotland in May 1792, accompanied by John Charles Brooke, of the College of Heralds. Moore, who was not himself an accomplished draughtsman, usually got a professional artist to work over his sketches before they were sent to the engraver, and it is generally accepted that Girtin was employed in making drawings from Moore's Scottish sketches, published in 1794 with the title *Twenty-five Views in the Southern Part of Scotland from a Collection of Drawings made by James Moore, Esq., F.A.S., in the year 1792*. Some accounts among Moore's papers show that Girtin was paid at the rate of 6s. for a full day's work. But in this case the question arises whether Girtin did not actually accompany the party to Scotland. The *Gentleman's Magazine*[2] states definitely that he did so: 'Mr. Moore was his first patron, and with him he went a tour into Scotland. The prospects he saw in that country gave that wildness of imagery to the scenery of his drawings by which they are so pre-eminently distinguished. He also went with Mr. Moore to Peterborough, Lichfield and Lincoln, and indeed to many other places remarkable for their rich scenery, either in nature or architecture.' The principal reason alleged for the rejection of this plain statement is that until 1797 Girtin did not exhibit any Scottish subjects at the Royal

[1] The drawing was acquired by James Moore. C. F. Bell, *Fresh Light on some Water-colour Painters of the Old British School*, Walpole Soc., V, 1917.
[2] 1799, LXIX, part 1, p. 446.

Academy, but this is scarcely conclusive. It is unlikely that the *Gentleman's Magazine* can be altogether wrong on such an easily verifiable point, which Thornbury also accepts; but the only alternative, i.e. that the passage quoted refers to 1796, and not to 1792, cannot stand in view of the facts that one series of Scottish drawings is unmistakably in Girtin's 1792–1793 manner; that, if Moore travelled to Scotland in 1796 he made no sketches himself, for there are none in the portfolios of his drawings, some of which, with his note-books, came into the possession of the Ashmolean Museum in 1912; and, finally, that Moore's last-known sketches were made in 1795, and his health was probably already failing (he died in 1799 of pulmonary trouble). In the absence of definite evidence to the contrary, Bell[1] maintains that these early Scottish sketches are Girtin's own records, and are not transcripts of Moore's. While Dayes re-drew or re-touched some of the sketches made by Moore on this journey of 1792, there is nothing to support the tradition that he was one of the party. Drawings by Dayes and Girtin, which were apparently based upon the result of this tour, were exhibited at the Leicester Galleries in July 1913. Girtin's work showed extraordinary precocity for a youth of seventeen, and it was almost impossible to distinguish between his drawings and those of his master. If Dayes, working from Moore's sketches, made good water-colours of *Castleacre Priory, Norfolk*,[2] and *Pluscardine Abbey, Elgin*,[3] Girtin made even better of *Warkworth Castle*[4], *Helmsley Castle, Yorks*[5] and *Dumbarton Rock and Castle*[6]. From a stylistic approach, however, I feel that *Edinburgh, The Castle Rock*[7] engraved in the *Twenty-five Views*, was painted in the Dayes manner by Girtin from a sketch by Moore, and was not by a Girtin who had seen with his own eyes the majesty of the castle and the stark grandeur of its rocky setting. The case for a visit to Scotland with Moore in 1792 is 'not proven'.

In 1794 Girtin made a Midland tour which included a visit to Lincoln with Moore,[8] and his three exhibits at the Royal Academy in 1795—*Warwick Castle*,[9] *Peterborough Cathedral*[10] and *Lichfield Cathedral*[11]—were the fruits of this journey. It is almost certain that in 1795 he was with Moore in Sussex. After this time the relationship seems to have lapsed.

C. F. Bell considers that Girtin's early drawings of Welsh scenery were transcripts of Moore's sketches, for they have all the characteristics of the style in which Girtin was working about 1792–4, the period during which he was employed by Moore, and Moore's last journey to Wales was made in 1791, when Girtin was only sixteen. On the other hand, Farington[12] wrote: 'Girtin told us he had been on a tour through Wales with a young man from Norwich of the name of Moss—Girtin had no money, so Moss advanced him £20, & afterwards £5 more, all which he had expended, as he bore half expences with Moss, excepting for carriage horses & servant.' This account is so circumstantial that it must be

---

[1] C. F. Bell, 1, *op. cit.*, p. 50. See also Thomas Girtin and David Loshak, *The Art of Thomas Girtin*, 1954, p. 27.
[2] Oxford, Ashmolean Museum.   [3] Oxford, Ashmolean Museum.
[4] Oxford, Ashmolean Museum.   [5] Coll. Mr. and Mrs. Tom Girtin.
[6] Coll. Mr. and Mrs. Tom Girtin.   [7] Cambridge, Fitzwilliam Museum.
[8] Some of his Lincoln drawings were engraved in B. Howlett's *Selection of Views, in the County of Lincoln*, 1805.
[9] Oxford, Ashmolean Museum.   [10] Oxford, Ashmolean Museum.
[11] Coll. Mr. and Mrs. Tom Girtin.   [12] *Diary*, October 24, 1798.

accepted as correct. There is no evidence for the date at which this journey took place, but there is a tradition that it was in 1794.[1] Laurence Binyon,[2] referring to *near Beddgellert*,[3] thinks that Girtin was in Wales after 1796, and the fine *Carnarvon Castle*[4] (Pl. 3), and the slightly smaller version of it belonging to the artist's great grandson, were certainly not painted before 1798. It must be remembered, however, that these pictures could have been worked up from earlier sketches.

An unfinished drawing of *Richmond Castle*[5] is in perfect preservation and is of great interest as showing Girtin's methods at a transitional period, about 1795–1796. More than half of it remains as a pencil drawing, and the handling of the pencil shows all those characteristic traits to which reference will be made later. Then, at the top and on some rocks and water below, Girtin has begun to add colour, timidly, daintily, like a miniaturist. There is no effect of light and shade carried all over the drawing in sepia or Indian ink, as one would expect; and though the buildings are tinted with yellow over an underlying shadow, there are already hints in this drawing of the direct application of local colour. Girtin was beginning to break away from Dayes.

The year 1795 was of great importance in Girtin's artistic development, for by then he had come under the notice of Dr. Monro, whose helpful encouragement of young artists has already been mentioned. It has been generally accepted that Girtin's association with the doctor began earlier than this date, and that he received definite instruction in his art at Adelphi Terrace. Roget writes[6]: 'And so we find Tom Girtin at seventeen or eighteen selected to make topographic drawings for *Walker's Magazine*, and one of the young artists at work at Dr. Monro's.' The accounts of Girtin's connection with Dr. Monro are probably based on the article in the *Library of Fine Arts*,[7] 1832, but the discovery of Farington's *Diary* and of James Moore's portfolios puts another aspect on the matter. It was some years later that Varley, De Wint and others met at Dr. Monro's for mutual instruction and improvement, and there is no evidence that at this date, 1795, there was anyone else but Turner there. Moreover, it appears that Turner and Girtin received from the Doctor employment, and not instruction. Farington's remarks are illuminating[8]: 'Turner and Girtin told us they had been employed by Dr. Monro three years to draw at his house in the evening.' 'Dr. Monro[9] wishes to obtain admission to the Royal Academy for Girtin, a young man of 20 years of age, as a Student. I told him I would undertake to obtain it if he is sufficiently advanced in drawing the human figure.' Some of the joint labours of Turner and Girtin under the aegis of Dr. Monro survive in Swiss and Italian drawings, in the Turner Bequest, most of which are undoubtedly copies of drawings by Cozens. Finberg has

[1] Roget, I, p. 88.
[2] L. Binyon, *Thomas Girtin*, 1900.
[3] B.M. 1855. 2.14.52.
[4] V.A.M. P.30–1932.
[5] Huntington Library, San Marino; the finished version is in Coll. of Mr. and Mrs. Tom Girtin.
[6] Roget, p. 86.
[7] *Recollections of the late Thomas Girtin*, 1832, III, p. 307.
[8] *Diary*, October 24, 1798.
[9] *Diary*, November 26, 1795. There is no mention of Girtin's name in the records of the Royal Academy Schools, although Thornbury says he was for three years a student there.

ascribed these drawings to Girtin alone, and though the question still remains to be solved, it is at least certain that Girtin had the main share in them. Roget says that Cornelius Varley told Joseph J. Jenkins on January 1, 1858, that Girtin made a great number of outlines, some of which the Doctor employed Turner to tint in grey and afterwards colour and that Girtin complained of this as not giving him the same chance of learning to paint. The fact that their employment consisted principally of copying Cozens, who had become insane in 1794, and was under the care of Dr. Monro, is of great importance. We can only speculate as to the Doctor's motives in thus employing the two young men, especially when his own predilection, as a collector of drawings, was for Laporte and Hearne. Did he, A. P. Oppé suggests, wish to have copies of drawings 'which he could borrow but not acquire', or did he wish to give the two most promising artists of the younger generation the inestimable benefit of studying the methods of the greatest master of water-colour painting who had hitherto appeared? Whatever the Doctor's motive may have been—and surely it was entirely altruistic—its effect on Girtin's artistic development was immense.

Until this time, Girtin had been working altogether in the manner of Dayes: that is to say, as a careful and supremely competent topographical draughtsman, but about 1796 he developed suddenly into an interpreter rather than a recorder of the aspects of nature. His association with Turner has also to be considered. They were of the most opposite characters conceivable, as Binyon has pointed out: 'Girtin open, vivacious, generous and joyous; Turner close, inscrutable and taciturn.'[1] In early days they were in very close touch, working together at Dr. Monro's and at the house of John Henderson, a neighbour of Dr. Monro in Adelphi Terrace, and also on their sketching expeditions, as is proved by the existence of their many drawings of the same subject; for example, a drawing of *Dover*, by Girtin, in Mr. and Mrs. Tom Girtin's collection, and a similar drawing by Turner in the Whitworth Art Gallery, Manchester. It is after 1796 that Girtin breaks away from Turner and develops a distinct manner of his own.

In 1796 Girtin, now of age, made a tour in the north of England, getting as far into Scotland as Jedburgh. He probably visited York, Durham and other places on the way, gaining material which was to be used in later drawings. Such, for instance, is the black and white study of *Durham Cathedral*,[2] which he afterwards used for his splendid water-colour in the Victoria and Albert Museum.[3] A sketch of 1796 must also have provided the material for two later drawings of *Durham*, obviously of common origin, belonging to Mr. J. R. Roget and the Whitworth Art Gallery, Manchester.[4] Evidence of the Scottish journey is a pencil sketch in the British Museum signed *Jedborough Scotd. T. Girtin 1796*.[5] Other Jedburgh drawings belong to Mr. R. Skinner and the National Gallery of Ireland; and yet another, a nearer view of the village, was shown at Walker's Galleries in 1932. In

[1] L. Binyon, *op. cit.*, p. 12.
[3] V.A.M. P.33–1928.
[4] The *Durham* drawings belonging to Sir Edmund Bacon, Mr. J. R. Roget and the Whitworth Art Gallery are reproduced by Randall Davies, *op. cit.*, pls. 20, 76, 77.
[5] B.M. 1889, 6.3.256.

[2] Coll. Sir Edmund Bacon, Bt.

1797 he exhibited ten drawings at the Royal Academy, including five of *York*, two of *Jedburgh* and two of *St. Cuthbert's, Holy Island*, worked up from the sketches of his tour in the previous year. From 1797 onwards he is at his zenith. In 1798 he exhibited nine drawings (including two of Rievaulx Abbey), and six in 1799. In 1799 he was in negotiation with Lord Elgin to accompany him on a journey to Constantinople, but this project fell through, because Lord Elgin would not pay what the artist considered a reasonable salary. It may be said here that Girtin never lacked distinguished patronage. He often stayed at Cassiobury with the Earl of Essex, and it was probably there that he made the lovely, silvery drawing of *Lake with Herons*[1] (Pl. 7)—so unlike anything that had preceded it in British art. Sir George Beaumont bought many of his drawings and the Hon. Spencer Cowper 'had the largest and finest collection of Girtin's drawings of any gentleman of that day.' The Earl of Hardwicke and the Earl of Buchan were friends as well as buyers, and a faithful patron was the Earl of Harewood's eldest son Edward Lascelles, who is said to have set aside a room for Girtin's use at Harewood, where the artist lived for long periods.

In 1800 Girtin exhibited at the Royal Academy three drawings, *Bristol Hot Well, York* and *Jedburgh*. In that year he was living at 11 Scott's Place, Islington, the house of Phineas Borrett, a freeman of the Goldsmiths' Company, and he married Borrett's daughter on October 16, 1800. They moved into a house in St. George's Row, Bayswater, a few doors from the residence of Paul Sandby, who, though now old, was to survive his youthful neighbour by seven years. In the following year the asthma, from which Girtin had always suffered, became much worse, and he spent the winter of 1801 in Paris, while his wife, owing to her approaching confinement, returned to her father's home. There has always been a hint that Paris was a curious and unsuitable alternative to London for a victim of asthma; but his great-grandson, the late Thomas Girtin said there was a tradition that he was on his way to Madeira. A letter of June 27, 1801, from Lord Harewood, says, 'I am sorry to hear that you are under the necessity of going to another climate for the benefit of your health.' A visit to Madeira was again projected in 1802. In October of 1802 Girtin received a letter from Sir George Beaumont which said: 'The pleasure I feel at your successful labours is much alloyed by the indifferent account you give of your health. You must take care of yourself, and I hope that you will be able to settle your concerns that you may pass the winter in Madeira. Lady Beaumont joins with me in best wishes for your success, & the return of your health. I am, dear Sir, your sincere well-wisher, G. H. Beaumont.'[2] This is not the kind of letter to be written to a man who, as we shall see, was said to be suffering from the penalty of his own excesses.

In 1801, Girtin, already known for his views and panorama of London, was, no doubt, being urged on every side to visit Paris. To anyone who had studied London and its river so exhaustively as Girtin, Paris and the Seine must have made a strong and exhilarating appeal. In Paris for better or worse as regards his health, he stayed for the production of

[1] Birmingham, City Art Gallery. [2] Roget, I, p. 113.

7

some of his most vigorous and outstanding work. To this period belong two superb drawings, the *Porte St. Denis*,[1] (Pl. 11) in the Victoria and Albert Museum, and the *La Rue St. Denis* (Pl. 10), belonging to Sir Edmund Bacon; and the Museum also possesses the small and charming *Street Scene, near Paris*,[2] dated 1802. His principal work, however, was his set of Paris views, published in 1803 by John Girtin, with the title '*A Selection of Twenty of the most Picturesque Views in Paris, and its environs, Drawn & Etched in the year 1802, by the late Thomas Girtin; being the Only Etchings of that Celebrated Artist: and Aquatinted in exact imitation of the original Drawings, In the Collection of the Rt. Hon*^{ble} *the Earl of Essex.*'

The *Gentleman's Magazine*'s obituary says that: 'These views were taken at different times of the day; and as the Parisians are rather jealous of any person, especially a foreigner, taking view of their metropolis, he, on these occasions, usually took a coach for a given number of hours, and stopped opposite to the place of which he intended to make a design; and he was so anxious to get the tints of Nature that he frequently remained in it the whole day. He etched all the places in the soft ground, so that they have all the effects of drawing.' Roget[3] states that 'the drawings' were bought by the Earl of Essex and were afterwards presented by him to the Duke of Bedford. It is true that there is a set of touched proofs at Woburn Abbey, but it is much more probable that 'the original drawings', referred to by John Girtin in the title of the publication, and by Roget, are a set of the etchings which were inherited from the Earl of Essex by Captain Richard Ford. They are washed over with bistre, the skies being occasionally touched with blue, and they have some alterations made in pen. We are inclined to think that, apart from a series of pencil sketches in the British Museum, there never were any original drawings. The artist, using the soft-ground method of etching, makes his drawing in pencil on a thin sheet of paper strained over a copper plate prepared with a specially soft and tacky ground which the pressure of the pencil lifts from the plate at every touch. Pencil studies, such as those in the British Museum, were the natural preliminary. A series of trial proofs of the soft-ground etchings belongs to the Victoria and Albert Museum, among them one or two showing discarded plates. Some of them bear pencil notes in Girtin's writing. The procedure undoubtedly was for Girtin to tint the proofs with washes of sepia or bistre, and the aquatints in the published work were produced with the aid of the washed proofs, and not of finished drawings, by F. C. Lewis and other engravers. It is in the etched states—the trial proofs at the Victoria and Albert Museum and elsewhere, and a complete set of the finished etchings at the British Museum—that the real power and beauty of Girtin's work appears. The aquatints, fine though they are in technique, are but a secondhand interpretation of Girtin's art. In the etchings we find the full beauty of his broken, tremulous, irregular line which seems to touch every piece of a landscape, every corner of a building, with the lightness of a caress; suggesting, just by a dot or a nervous pressure, the little varieties of form and accent which the untrained eyesight would hardly see.

[1] V.A.M. 37–1886. [2] V.A.M. 1087–1884.
[3] Roget, I, 112.

The publication of the Paris aquatints was still in prospect when Girtin died suddenly on November 9, 1802. He was buried in the churchyard of St. Paul's Covent Garden, and among those who followed his remains to the grave were Sir William Beechey, Sir George Beaumont, Hearne, Edridge and Turner. Edridge made the portrait, now in the British Museum[1], showing Girtin seated on a camp-stool, sketching. He seems to have been a dandy in his day, for his tall figure and elegant limbs are clad in the height of fashion, a cutaway long coat, buckskin breeches and Hessian boots.

At the time of his death he was exhibiting at Spring Gardens a Panorama of London, entitled *Eidometropolis*, said to have been painted in oil, but more probably in distemper.[2] This Panorama was executed in 1800 and 1801, and one might think that another reason for the Paris visit may have been connected with a project for its exhibition in Paris, as well as for bringing home a panorama of Paris for exhibition in London. The latter idea, which never came to fruition, is noted by Whitley in connection with a letter of April 1802 from Paris to Girtin's brother John; but it has not apparently been realised that Girtin's 'I think the Panorama here does not answer', may well refer to a proposal for the exhibition in France of his already completed London Panorama. Further evidence is supplied by Farington's[3] entry: 'Lord Mulgrave spoke with much regard of the memory of *Girtin* the artist, who was with him a little time at Mulgrave Castle. . . . Girtin having a desire to carry to *Paris* a *Panorama View of London* with a view to exhibit it there, Lord Mulgrave procured him a Passport;[4] but when He arrived at Paris He was not permitted.'

It was not till after his return to London that the Panorama was exhibited at Spring Gardens, and it does not seem to have had particular success, coming as it did, too soon after Robert Barker's similar panorama. The Panorama, however, concerns us here only for the fact that six water-colour studies for the finished work are in the British Museum (Pls. 1 and 2), and that the final result supplies another instance of the extraordinary energy and industry which filled Girtin's short life of twenty-seven years.

He was one of the founders in 1799 of a Sketching Club which met in the evenings,[5] and it is seen that Turner was not of the party. On the back of a *Landscape Composition, Moonlight*,[6] by Francia, in the Victoria and Albert Museum is the following inscription:

This drawing was made on Monday May the 20th 1799 at the room of Robert Ker Porter of No. 16 Great Newport Street, Leicester Square, in the very painting room, that formerly was Sir Josuah [sic] Reynolds's, and since has been Dr. Samuel Johnson's; and for the first time on the above day convened a small and select society of Young Painters under the title (as I give it)

---

[1] B.M. 1845. 8.18.1.
[2] For accounts of this Panorama see: Roget, I, pp. 103–108; W. T. Whitley, 'Girtin's Panorama', *The Connoisseur*, LXIX, 1924, p. 13; and J. Mayne, *Thomas Girtin*, 1949, pp. 60–64. Girtin and Loshak, *op. cit.*, p. 36, date it two or three years earlier.
[3] *Diary*, March 24, 1807.
[4] According to Roget the passport was procured through Sir Charles Long, then Under-Secretary of State; Lady Long was Girtin's favourite pupil.
[5] F. H. H. Guillemard, 'Girtin's Sketching Club', *The Connoisseur*, LXIII, 1922, p. 190; A. P. Oppé, 'Cotman and the Sketching Society', *The Connoisseur*, LXVII, 1923, p. 189.
[6] V.A.M. 477–1883.

of the Brothers; met for the purpose of establishing a school of Historic Landscape, the subjects being designs from poetick passages;

L⁵. Francia.

The Society consists of—Worthington, J. C⁵. Denham—Treas ͬ,
R ͭ. K ͬ. Porter, T⁵. Girtin, T⁵. Underwood, G ͤ. Samuel & L⁵, Francia, Secret ͭ.

One would think that in such a hard-working, honest, fruitful life there was no action on which scandal might seize. Nevertheless, Girtin's memory has to be vindicated against a charge which, originating with Edward Dayes, subsequently gained much credence. Dayes[1] wrote as follows:

> This artist died November the 9th, 1802, after a long illness, in the twenty-eight year of his age. Biography is useful to stimulate to acts of industry and virtue; or, by exhibiting the contrary, to enable us to shun the fatal consequences of vice. While our heart bleeds at the premature death of the subject of this paper, it becomes equally an act of justice to caution young persons against the fatal effects of suffering the passions to overpower their reason, and to hurry them into acts of excess, that may, in the end, render life a burden, destroy existence, or bring on a premature old age. Though his drawings are generally too slight, yet they must even be admired as the off-spring of a strong imagination. Had he not trifled away a vigorous constitution, he might have arrived at a very high degree of excellence as a landscape painter.

Edwards repeats the slander,[2] ending his note on Girtin with the cruel and sententious remark: 'Girtin died . . . at the early age of twenty-seven years: but intemperance and irregularity have no claim to longevity.' This harsh statement is embroidered with inventive touches in the *Somerset House Gazette*:[3]

> But that vicious course which makes a wreck of the body, cannot fail to ruin the mind: the continued sensual indulgence of this extraordinary young man, enfeebled his mental powers, and the distinguished competitor of Turner, the thoughtless, kind-hearted Girtin, by a premature death, haply, alas but saved his posthumous fame from the imputation of his sinking into a mannerist.

Evidence is all against the charge and the tale has been exploded by Roget, and, in recent days, by Hugh Stokes and the artist's great-grandson.[4] In fact there is reason to believe that Girtin—delicate, a constant sufferer from bronchitis and asthma—burned himself out.

Girtin's work falls into two well-defined periods, the dividing line being the year 1796. As, in that year he reached the age of twenty-one, the first period is merely that of his studentship, although the brief span of his life gives it an interest and importance which it would perhaps not otherwise deserve. There is no clumsy, immature period in his work. He seems to have been born with the artist's wondering mind, intensely sensitive, intensely responsive to beauty, and with an inborn natural gift for recording what he saw and felt. His natural gifts were fortified by the zeal with which he worked, for, besides practising at

[1] *Op. cit.*, p. 329.   [2] E. Edwards, *Anecdotes of Painters*, 1808, p. 280.
[3] *Somerset House Gazette*, I, 1824, p. 82. The account of Girtin in the *Library of Fine Arts*, 1832, is clearly based upon this article.
[4] *Walker's Monthly*, April and May 1930.

Dr. Monro's, he frequented the house of John Henderson, of Adelphi Terrace and copied Canaletto, Piranesi, Hearne, Marlow, Morland and Malton. 'He early made Nature his model; but the first master that struck his attention forcibly was Canaletti', says the obituary notice in the *Gentleman's Magazine*.[1] The *Library of Fine Arts*[2] also stresses the importance of Canaletto: 'Much of the knowledge which Girtin obtained in the display of contrast of colour in open landscape was derived from the study of [Richard] Wilson, whose bold and effective pictures in oil, Girtin might be said to have translated into water-colour. The vigour and richness of his architectural subjects, which were no less striking, was alike ascribable to his contemplation of the pictures of Canaletti; indeed, he was alternately designated by his admirers, when he first evinced that power in his works which had never been before seen in drawings, the Wilson or the Canaletti of water-colours.' Laurence Binyon,[3] in his critical study of Girtin, rightly accepts that Canaletto was by far the most important of the influences which moulded Girtin's style, and emphasises in particular what he must have learnt from Canaletto's *View of Venice*, belonging to Sir George Beaumont, which Girtin must have had many opportunities for studying. In Binyon's opinion the romantic-classical tradition of Claude and Poussin yielded in Girtin's mind to the integrity of vision, unerringness of hand and sobriety of temper, which are the fundamental qualities of Canaletto. But it should be clear that it is the spirit of Wilson and Canaletto, their selective simplicity and restraint, which informs Girtin's works, for even as a boy he was no mere imitator. The copies he made at John Henderson's house of architectural subjects by artists such as Malton, Piranesi and Canaletto show clearly how his personal vision insisted on its own expression. Typical of his fine monochrome work of this period is the *Ruins of the Savoy Palace*.[4] Very many of his early drawings, like this, are architectural in subject, but his real strength did not lie in this direction. Drawings such as *Peterborough Cathedral*[5] and *Lichfield Cathedral*[6] are excellent in draughtsmanship, but they show the mere structure of buildings, the spirit of the architecture is not present. But after 1796 there is a profound change. Architecture is still, to a large extent, the chief theme, but now the antiquarian and topographical interest is absorbed in a more personal, spiritual approach. In *Rievaulx Abbey*[7] it is not the ruins that he paints: it is the sweep of the valley up to the encircling hills, the broad, still sky, the thin, slanting evening light, and all the centuries during which the rain and the sun have washed the Abbey stones. And it is not difficult to conclude that it must have been the influence of J. R. Cozens which caused this change. An anonymous writer[8] recognises this fact: 'It is no mean compliment to the talent of Cozens to know that Turner and Girtin have admitted that the contemplation, and the copying indeed, of some of his best works, opened to their minds that intelligence of effect in representing distant scenery which they adopted, and subsequently excelled in

[1] *Op. cit.*
[2] *Op. cit.*, Vol. III, 1832, p. 317.
[3] *Op. cit.*
[4] Coll. Mr. and Mrs. Tom Girtin.
[5] Coll. Mr. and Mrs. Tom Girtin.
[6] Coll. Mr. and Mrs. Tom Girtin.
[7] Coll. Mr. and Mrs. Tom Girtin.
[8] *Library of the Fine Arts*, III, 1832, pp. 307–319.

to so much greater a degree than their ingenious prototype.' It has not, I think, been sufficiently recognised that Girtin used much of the actual technique of Cozens, who differs from Sandby in that he was beginning to work with freedom, using colour dropped from a full brush, rather than in steady washes. If we look at some of Cozens' distances, at the broad treatment of trees on hill-sides, we shall find the beginning of the looser and wetter treatment which Girtin used with purpose and perfection. And not only in technique, but in outlook and vision, in sympathy for wide spaces, Girtin profited from what he absorbed in his study of Cozens at the house of Dr. Monro. Occasionally Girtin followed Gainsborough's method, though not with the full ease and enchanting grace of Gainsborough, as in *Lake in Harewood Park*[1] and *View on the Wharfe*.[2] Whether the treatment of the foliage, with its loops and a striation of black lines, was the result of the study of Gainsborough, or of the influence of Dr. Monro, who himself very successfully captured Gainsborough's characteristic manner, is open to question. The same influence appears in the small, but more charming, *Temple in Harewood Park*.[3] The truth is that Girtin was intensely receptive of the finest, when he saw it; and so we find him going so far afield for sources as to make water-colours from etchings of Piranesi and Marco Ricci (see the *Classical Composition*[4] and the Piranesi subjects[5]). In all this he was no more an imitator than was Brahms when he wrote variations and a fugue on a theme by Handel. Similarly, in the very last year of his life he was making drawings, which Randall Davies' brilliant discovery[6] shows to have been based on etchings by Swanevelt. One of these, the *Landscape with Hermit*,[7] is freely adapted from Swanevelt's *Repose in Egypt*. To the same group, perhaps, belongs *Garden Terrace*,[8] which has a hint of some old master, and recalls the grace and felicity of Gainsborough rather than Girtin's normal conception and handling. But though he absorbed, as every great artist must, something of the earlier masters, he cannot be considered in any sense as an imitator. He developed an outlook and a technique which were entirely his own. His vision and technique indicated a turning point in British water-colour. As Mr. Mayne wisely says: 'Not one characteristic English water-colour of the early nineteenth century could be imagined without pre-supposing Girtin.' Ruskin said of the *Cayne Waterfall*[9] (Pl. 4): 'There is perhaps no greater marvel of artistic practice and finely accurate intention existing.' Fine though the *Cayne Waterfall* is, it remains a drawing in which Girtin was using the best of the traditional methods and fell short of many other drawings which contain more of himself. It should not be put in the same class as the *Kirkstall Abbey*[10] at the British Museum, or that still nobler *Kirkstall Abbey*[11] (Pl. 6) in the Victoria and Albert Museum, in which Girtin depicts a brooding sense of twilight over an

[1] V.A.M. P.129–1920. [2] V.A.M. 380.
[3] Coll. Mr. and Mrs. Tom Girtin. [4] Manchester, Whitworth Art Gallery.
[5] Coll. Mr. and Mrs. Tom Girtin.
[6] 'Thomas Girtin in Paris', *Burlington Magazine*, LII, 1928, pp. 221–222.
[7] V.A.M. P.43– 1924 (other examples are in the collection of Mr. and Mrs. Paul Mellon).
[8] V.A.M. P.25–1928. [9] B.M. 1855. 2.14.2.
[10] B.M. 1855. 2.14.53. [11] V.A.M. 405–1885.

ancient building and solemn trees and quiet waters. With its low harmonies of colour broken only by a strip of primrose light in the sky with the shadows lengthening as the sun declines, its feeling of vast space, this is one of those simple but final works of art. It must have been some such drawing as this which made Ruskin say of Girtin: 'He is often as impressive to me as Nature herself.' In this drawing, as in many others by Girtin, the building is seen as a growth from the land, as a part of a wide prospect; and in common with Rembrandt's *Gold-Weigher's Field*, has conveyed in a small space so much suggestion of lateral width, so much feeling of undulating distance. De Wint alone among British painters can equal him in bringing the spectator, as Charles Johnson[1] says about *Kirkstall Abbey*, 'into an area vast in all directions'. Another masterly conception is *The White House at Chelsea*,[2] (Pl. 5) with its broad and simple design, its exquisite subtleties, its glowing sky, its flash of white—untrue, perhaps, in relation to surrounding tones, and yet so daring, so convincing. Here, again, Girtin has advanced beyond all his contemporaries. Turner rarely distributed praise, but one morning a dealer called upon him in a hackney-coach, and looking at his pictures, said, 'These are very fine, Mr. Turner, but I have brought something finer with me.' 'I don't know what that can be,' replied Turner, 'unless it's Tom Girtin's *White House at Chelsea*.'

Let us consider now what were those features of outlook and technique in which Girtin differed from all his predecessors, and what it was that he added to British art. We may well begin by quoting an almost contemporary account of his method and of his palette (a water-colour artist does not use a palette, but the convenient descriptive word may be used) written by W. H. Pyne:[3]

> Girtin was proceeding with the same observant eye to nature, and equally attentive to that captivating quality, local colour. These two aspiring geniuses [Girtin and Turner], emulous without envy, were developing new properties in the material with which they wrought their elegant limitations of nature, and raising the practice of water colours, which had hitherto procured no higher title for the best works of its professors, than tinted drawings, to the rank and character of painting in water colours. Thus these two distinguished artists, improving rapidly, as by inspiration, whilst young men, achieved the honour of founding that English school, as it now stands recorded, the admiration of all nations. . . . [Girtin] prepared his drawings on the same principle which had hitherto been confined to painting in oil, namely, laying in the object upon his paper, with the local colour, and shadowing the same with the individual tint of its own shadow. Previous to the practice of Turner and Girtin, drawings were shadowed first entirely through, whatever their component parts—houses, castles, trees, mountains, foregrounds, middle-grounds, and distances, all with black or grey, and these objects were afterwards stained, or tinted, enriched and finished, as is now the custom to colour prints. It was this new practice, introduced by these distinguished artists, that acquired for designs in water-colours upon paper, the title of paintings: a designation which many works of the existing school decidedly merit, as we lately beheld in the Exhibition of the Painters in Water Colours, where pictures of this class were displayed in gorgeous frames, bearing out in effect against the mass of glittering gold, as powerfully as pictures in oil. . . . Girtin's admirers tolerated a defect in his drawings, which

[1] C. Johnson, *English Painting*, 1932, p. 147.
[2] Two versions, Tate Gallery (4728) and coll. Sir Edmund Bacon, Bt.
[3] *Somerset House Gazette*, I, 1824, pp. 66, 67, 83, 84.

proves how much allowance the liberal connoisseur will make for the sake of genius. The paper which he most admired was only to be had of a stationer at Charing Cross; this was cartridge, with slight wire marks, and folded like foolscap or post. It commonly happened that the part which had been folded, when put on the stretching frame would sink into spots in a line, entirely across the centre of the sky; so that where the crease had been, the colour was so many degrees of a darker blue than the general tone of the sky. This unsightly accident was not only overlooked, but in some instances really admired, inasmuch, that it was taken for a sign of originality, and in the transfer of his drawings from one collector or to another, bore a premium, according to that indubitable mark. . . . The variety of light and shadow which he spread over his picturesque buildings, the manner in which he separated the masses, and the brilliancy of certain parts, which received a partial burst of sun-shine, diffused a splendour of effect to these scenes, which no artist before had conceived. His fine taste for colour, was most evidently conspicuous in these topographical scenes. Every tint of brick, stone, plaster, timber and tile, was combined, both in broad light, medium tint, and shadow, with such admirable feeling towards general harmony, that no one of the least taste could behold his best productions in this style, without admiration and delight.

His skies were generally composed either of large masses of clouds . . . with light red and indigo, Indian red and indigo, and an occasional addition of lake. The warm tone of the cartridge paper, frequently served for the lights, without tinting, acquiring additional warmth by being opposed to the cool colour of the azure, and shadow of the clouds. His skies in general were extremely luminous.

It was a great treat to see this artist at his studies, he was always accessible. When he had accomplished the laying in of his sky, he would proceed with great facility in the general arrangement of his tints, on the buildings, trees, water, and other objects. Every colour appeared to be placed with a most judicious perception to effecting a general union or harmony.

His light stone tints were put in with thin washes of Roman ochre, the same mixed with light red, and certain spaces, free from the warm tints, were touched with grey, composed of light red and indigo,—or brighter still, with ultramarine and light red. The brick buildings with Roman ochre, light red, and lake, and a mixture of Roman ochre, lake and indigo, Roman ochre, madder brown and indigo; also with burnt sienna and Roman ochre, madder brown and Roman ochre, and these colours in all their combinations. For finishing the buildings which came the nearest to the foreground, where the local colour and form were intended to be represented with particular force and effect, Vandyck brown, and Cologn-earth were combined with these tints, which gave depth and richness of tones, that raised the scale of effect without the least diminution of harmony,—on the contrary, the richness of effect was increased from their glowing warmth, by neutralizing the previous tones, and by throwing them into their respective distances or into proper keeping.

The trees, which he frequently introduced in his views, exhibiting all the varieties of autumnal hues, he coloured with corresponding harmony to the scale of richness exhibited on his buildings. The greens for these operations were composed of gambouge, indigo, and burnt sienna, occasionally heightened with yellow lake, brown pink, and gambouge, these mixed too sometimes with Prussian blue. The shadows for the trees, with indigo and burnt sienna, and with a most beautiful and harmonious shadow tint, composed of grey and madder brown; which, perhaps, is nearer to the general tone of the shadow of trees than any other combinations that can be formed with water-colours. Girtin made his greys sometimes with Venetian red and indigo. Indian red and indigo, and a useful and most harmonious series of warm and cool greys, of Roman ochre, indigo, and lake, which, used judiciously, will serve to represent the basis for every species of subject and effect, as viewed in the middle grounds, under the influence of that painter's atmosphere, so prevalent in the autumnal season in our humid climate: which constantly exhibits to the picturesque eye, the charms of rich effects, in a greater variety than any country in Europe.

14

With extended knowledge and fuller means of comparison it is possible to go a step further than Pyne in analysis of Girtin's technical methods. Girtin and his contemporaries were fortunate in having a slightly absorbent paper, made of linen rags, with a pleasant wire-marked surface. His colour settled without hard edges, and his second wash was absorbed without bringing the under colour away. There was not, and could not be, any rubbing or scrubbing, or anything but the slightest alteration in his work; the material demanded, and obtained, directness. In the use of a rather coarse cartridge paper, with slight flecks and blemishes which unobtrusively gave variety to the surface, Girtin antici- pated Cox. He found paper of a warmish tint which allowed him to leave it bare, or almost bare, in parts, and gave a key to the low harmonious tonality which characterises all his work; he was never driven to work up to a key of white. Early accounts exaggerate the extent to which Girtin worked on a folded paper, with the crease perforce showing in his drawing. There are very few instances of this in his extant work; the crease is more common in the case of De Wint, whose habit it was to use the double page of a sketch-book. The pleasant surface, the absorbent nature, and the warm tone of the paper which Girtin used for water-colour are part of his discovery. The progress of paper in later years to more thickness and solidity, with lavish application of size, and shininess of hot-pressed surface, enabled the artists to use extensive stippling and erasure, but contributed to a decline of water-colour from a pure simplicity to an over-wrought elaboration.

His subject was drawn in with pencil, and occasionally, to some extent, with pen. Turner, in his use of the pencil, was perhaps more brilliant, more observant of minute particulars then Girtin, but he never in his pencil work excelled Girtin's studies for his Paris etchings. Very characteristic of Girtin's pencil drawing is the way in which a line ends in a small hook, and the manner in which, all over the drawing, come tiny curls, usually in the shape of the letter S or the numeral 3, or the Greek E. In such a drawing as that of *Middleham*[1] in the 1800 sketch-book there are scores of these little hieroglyphs. It is sometimes difficult to distinguish the pencil drawings of Turner and Girtin. They worked together, each using a sharp-pointed pencil in much the same way, and each no doubt influenced the other. We find in Turner the same thinning and thickening of line, the same emphasis with the sharp point at the end of the line. We find hard dots, but we do not find these groups of 3's and S's. An important point, however, and one which has not been noticed, or has not been stated, by Binyon and other critics is that those little dots and touches, accents, eccentricities, which are usually the really personal element in an artist's work, are, in Girtin's case, pure imitation of Canaletto. The whole system of 3's and S's and similar curves derives from the Italian master's manner of drawing.[2]

In his pen-work—based on his study of Canaletto, and possibly, Guardi—Girtin is more fluent and descriptive than Turner. His methods with pen and pencil can be readily

[1] Coll. Mr. W. Shepherd.
[2] An exhibition *Canaletto and English Draughtsmen* was held in the B.M. in August 1953. Examples of drawings by Girtin, Samuel Scott, the Sandbys, W. H. Hunt, etc., in that Exhibition are listed in the Department of Prints and Drawings. Eds.

studied in the sketches at the British Museum for his London Panorama. Some are in pencil outline; others are mainly in brown or black ink, drawn with a loose, delicate line, ending in little spots and breaks, as in his pencil work. Where colour occurs, it is painted over the ink washes in the traditional way. There is not always pen-work in his water-colours. It does not, however, seem to have been recognised that Girtin constantly used reed pen and brown ink to reinforce a drawing after his colouring was finished. That seems to be the case with the *Richmond Bridge, Yorkshire*[1] and *Ouse Bridge, York*.[2] This method of using ink, to give accents and to emphasise form and structure in a completed drawing, is obvious in the fine *Bridgenorth*,[3] where pen-work, in the same brown ink which he uses for his signature, appears all over the drawing, almost certainly as a considered afterthought. The anchored boat on the left seems to be a final addition, made entirely with pen. In some places it is difficult to say definitely that something has been drawn with pen, and not with the point of a fine brush. His pen method and his pencil method—with their spots, blobs, thickening and thinning—approach closely to his brush method: and all are autographic. It may be added that reinforcement with the pen was a method used constantly by Turner. Even his latest, impressionist sketches are drawn in pencil and then freely worked over with black, brown or vermilion ink.

As to Girtin's colour, the account of his work in the *Somerset House Gazette*[4] shows that his palette was limited to fifteen colours, as follows:

Roman Ochre	Light Red
Yellow Lake	Indian Red
Gambouge	Venetian Red
Indigo	Burnt Sienna
Ultramarine	Madder Brown
Prussian Blue	Vandyke Brown
Cologne Earth	Brown pink
Crimson Lake	

In actual practice, probably not more than six or seven of these colours were ever used in any one drawing. The predominance of ochres, brown and reds is just what one would expect from a study of Girtin's work. No theory that he could not obtain more colours, or that he found himself in the wilds of Yorkshire with an insufficient supply, will hold, for it has already been shown that at this period a wide range of colours was at his disposal. His economy, then, such as we find in the *St. Mary's Abbey, York*,[5] so subtly wrought in cream and grey, was deliberately chosen, not enforced. One thing that he proved in water-colour is that there can be richness in low tones, in greys and sombre yellows, if they are fastidiously and harmoniously composed, even more than in vivid and positive hues which act as a more immediate, but less lasting, stimulus.

Girtin's muted colour enabled his lights and his shadows to harmonise. And, in his use of

[1] B.M. 1855. 2.14.7.
[3] B.M. 1849. 6.9.75.
[5] Birmingham, City Art Gallery.

[2] B.M. 1855. 2.14.31.
[4] *Somerset House Gazette*, I, 1824, pp. 83, 84.

colour he was one of the first to work not according to any arbitrary scheme, but finding and losing his lights and darks, mixing warm with cool. He was inventing and drawing with the brush, not merely filling outlined spaces, or tinting a drawing, like Sandby or Wheatley. He was ready to drop his colour in spots, strokes, patches, as well as in an evenly distributed wash; and this means that with him, perhaps for the first time in British water-colour, we get so-called 'broken colour', which later is a characteristic of De Wint, and still more, of David Cox. John Pye went so far as to describe the drawings of Sandby and the school before Cozens as 'unmeaning muddle', declaring that 'in them the eye always rested on objects individually'.[1] That may be an exaggerated criticism, but it remains true that with Cozens, and even more with Girtin, we get a largeness and unity of design and a sense of immeasurable space. All at once, Girtin makes Sandby and Dayes seem remote, almost obsolete.

Too much credit has been given to Girtin by Pyne and by later critics for being an innovator in the abandonment of monochrome under-painting over which the so-called 'local colour' was washed. Towne, Reveley and others, as has been seen, worked directly at times with pure colour, without any underlying basis of monochrome, long before Girtin. Girtin aimed to establish the fact that a painter could discard the preliminary under-paintings if he wished, or could substitute warm under-painting for a cold one; and, what is more important, he showed that the painter could obtain a depth and quality of colour, particularly in shadows, that was entirely unknown to his predecessors. In that respect he brought about a revolution, which makes the work of Varley and De Wint entirely different from that of Towne and Sandby. Between pre-Girtin and post-Girtin water-colour painting there is a wide gulf. All through Girtin's work we find him working, when he pleased, in the traditional manner (as in his *Carnarvon Castle*[2]—one of his later drawings) carrying thin washes of local colour over a lay-in of dead-colouring. But from 1795 we also find him constantly painting in local colour and modelling his first lights with later darks—that is to say, with an entire reversal of the traditional method. To take an instance, the distance in his *Durham Castle*[3] is nothing but local colour, but in much in the manner of Cotman. The delightfully simple *Landscape with a Church*[4] is painted in local colour, with dark touches over lighter colour washes. His *Landscape with a Hermit*[5] of 1801 is again all painted in local colour, with darker tones of green and blue added for the modelling and accenting of paler undertones. While Girtin to the end showed faith in traditional systems, he was also starting a revolution. Where he differs from his predecessors is that, in his later work, he established his masses of varying tone, light or dark, by means of warm sepia or burnt sienna, instead of a cold grey or an Indian ink.[6] It was the local colour which he was seeing. He was not regarding objects for their chiaroscuro first, not looking on them as mono-

[1] Roget, I, p. 123.
[2] V.A.M. P.30–1932.
[3] V.A.M. P.33–1928.
[4] V.A.M. 156–1890.
[5] V.A.M. P.43–1924.
[6] A. J. Finberg, *English Water Colour Painters*, 1906, p. 65. Finberg's intense concentration upon Turner tends to make him, as it made Ruskin, value Turner perhaps a little too highly, at Girtin's expense.

chrome tinged with colour, but as coloured things with their colour modified or subdued by shade. He drew brilliantly and expressively, but where outline, shade and colour can be distinguished as three separate parts in the work of his predecessors, with Girtin the separation is no longer distinct. He was content to obliterate his outlines, losing them in his broad fusion of colour, light and form. It was almost a natural consequence that his contemporaries should accuse him of slackness and inefficiency in drawing, and that later critics (forgetting the Paris pencil studies) should put the Turner of 1802 on a higher plane as a draughtsman than Girtin.

The skies, of strong and often coldish blue, which have been mentioned as a feature of Girtin's work, were regarded as an eccentricity by his contemporaries, who were used to a much more timid and pallid rendering of the sky. They failed to see that the blueness and brilliance of Girtin's skies, true enough in nature, were made obvious in his paintings by the contrast with landscape painted in much warmer and richer tones than had been prevalent. Dayes was once shown some drawings by a pupil of Girtin, and exclaimed, in his emphatic manner, 'Oh, ye Gods! The blue-bag—the blue-bag', adding: 'Because master *Tom* chuses to wash in dirty water, *ergo*, this puppy, this ass, this driveller, must wash in dirty water too.' What struck others was Girtin's power of representing light and air and sunshine by means of his warm tones of yellow and brown. The *Morpeth*,[1] stated on the back to be the last drawing which Girtin made, is all gold and russet and grey, superb in its breadth and its lighting; and we may note the skill of technique by which bare paper has been left for the two tiny figures, so perfectly placed as a patch of light on the bridge. Turner had a deep admiration for what he called Girtin's 'golden drawings' (*Durham Cathedral*[2] and *Carnarvon Castle*[3] are good examples of this type) and said of one of them, according to Thornbury,[4] 'I never in my whole life could make a drawing like that: I would at any time have given one of my little fingers to have made such a one.'

Nowhere is Girtin's originality more apparent than in his treatment of trees. His immediate predecessors, such as Gainsborough and Farington, had either indicated foliage by a conventional system of loops and scallops not without its fluid grace; or, like Dayes, had seen it in clusters rather resembling bunches of bananas; or, like Hearne and Rooker, had been bewildered by the difficulty of indicating masses of foliage, which are in fact composed of a number of tiny points of form and colour. Sandby, in one of his phases, sought out the irregular edges of trees, made by the sharp points of leaves, and worked in a more angular method with innumerable strokes and zig-zags. Cozens took a step towards simplification, but Girtin was the first to see the tree as a mass, to overcome his consciousness of its anatomy, to look at it with half-closed eyes as a dark rounded object in nature, with irregular broken contours, and to render its general tone, its lights and shadows, rather than its leaves. He was the forerunner of De Wint. As Hughes[5] sums up: 'His

---

[1] Coll. Mrs. N. D. Newall.
[2] Manchester University, Whitworth Art Gallery.
[3] V.A.M. P.30–1932.
[4] W. Thornbury, *Life of Turner*, 1862, p. 61.
[5] *Op. cit.*, p. 39.

masses of trees nestling against the hill-sides were painted with washes of colour, rounded and defined with other washes, and his nearer boughs stand out against the sky or the country beyond them in deftly shaped single sweeps of the brush which absolutely express his meaning without any meticulous explanation by way of afterthought.'

It has not been recognised by writers on British water-colour how much of an innovator Girtin also was with regard to skies. The topographers drew their skies, just as they drew their architecture, making an outline of form and tinting the circumscribed space. They left no room for experiment or accident. The sky, as it were, stood still for them. With colour washes, as polished and perfect as the classical epithets of Gray, they set out ' to greet the sun upon the upland lawn '. Girtin was one of the first to paint his skies, dashing in form and tone at fever heat, noting swiftly the haphazard movement, the rushing sweep of rolling clouds, the glint of light, the slant of the passing rain. A good example of his treatment of a stormy sky are the *Hawes, Yorkshire*[1] and the *Landscape*,[2] with its emotional rendering of a passing rain-storm. All the scud and scurry of clouds he registered with wet and broken colour, and so is one of the first to give a real feeling of atmosphere, of the suffusion of light and dark over fields and hills and water, of the true relation between earth and sky, of the brightness and gloom caused not by local colour but by the fact that the earth, though seeming dark and solid, is but a mirror over whose surface pass the reflections of the sparkle or the darkness of the sky. Who, before Girtin, ever began to approach such a realisation of the relentless *Sturm und Drang* of nature as is shown in the small *Tynemouth*,[3] so impressive in its rendering of the stark headland, the lonely dreary stretch of sands, the dark and swollen clouds pregnant with rain? Or who, before Girtin, ever tried to register in water-colour a passing effect of light and shadow, as in *Above Bolton; Stepping-Stones on the Wharfe*,[4] (Pl. 8) where the largeness of design is emphasised by the shadow cast across the river? And just as Girtin anticipates, here De Wint, and there Cotman, so also he anticipates Cox. *Near Beddgellert*[5] shows the kind of luminous atmospheric effect, over rain-bright and cloud-shadowed hills, rendered with vibrant touches of the brush, which was later to become Cox's theme.

Girtin knew the value of leaving bare paper, as is shown in an early drawing of *Gothic Ruins*[6] very freely drawn with pen and tinted with indigo and sepia; specks of white are deliberately left among the darks.[7] In his *Duff House*,[8] again an early drawing, his high lights are produced by scratching with a knife. This is a process rarely used by him, but the drawing shows that he knew its possibility. He never used touches of white in body-colour; many pseudo-Girtins have been given away by this.

Finally we come to the point—always interesting to painters—as to whether Girtin worked in colour out of doors or in the studio. There can be no doubt that many of his

[1] Birmingham, City Art Gallery.
[2] Cardiff, National Museum of Wales.
[3] Coll. Mr. and Mrs. Tom Girtin.
[4] Coll. Mr. and Mrs. Tom Girtin.
[5] B.M. 1855. 2.14.52
[6] Oxford, Ashmolean Museum.
[7] The author refers to the false idea that Girtin used a stopping-out mixture (Vol. 1, part 1, p. 36).
[8] Oxford, Ashmolean Museum.

water-colour sketches were made in the presence of nature; no painter can become proficient without study of this kind in the open air. Roget describes how, when sketching from nature, he showed a complete disregard for bad weather, sitting out in the rain to observe the effect of storms and clouds upon the atmosphere. But it is equally clear that a great deal of his output is studio work, based on a retentive memory of passing facets and changing colour. In the City Art Gallery, Birmingham, are his pencil sketch and the later water-colour of *Hawes, Yorkshire* showing how he worked out his studio subject from a pencil note. The sketch-book which he carried with him in Yorkshire in 1800[1] contains pencil sketches of which at least five supplied the material for later water-colours, among them the *White House at Chelsea*[2] and *Sandsend, Yorkshire*.[3] The oblong book, six by eight inches, contains one or two drawings almost certainly coloured at the time of their making. At some places where drawings have been cut out, are notes; 'Rippon Minster Col^d on the Spot sold £8. 8. o; Bolton Abbey. Colord on the spot. Sold to Mr. Rogers 8 G'; and 'Gravel Caves with a peep of the Sea. Colord on the Spot. Coast of Yorkshire. Sold to Miss Dinn, Hasted (?) Priory £4. 4. o.' For a larger, more finished drawing—of the type done in the studio—his price at this time was twenty guineas. These larger, more important, works, with their daring effects and their sober harmonies of colour, could not possibly have been made except in the studio. His painting-room in London, we are told, was always open to his brother artists, as well as his many pupils and dilettante friends. Surrounded by callers, he would go on with his work, chatting and telling anecdotes, discussing his work and his methods at the same time. One visitor referred afterwards to 'the "sword-play" of his brush'. Of his studio work we have the account of an eye-witness who says that 'his finely coloured compositions were wrought with much study and proportionate manual exertion, and that though he did not hesitate, nor undo what he had once done, for he worked on principle, yet he reiterated his tints to produce splendour and richness, and repeated his depths to secure transparency of tones, with surprising perseverance.'[4] Except from the technical aspect, it does not matter where his drawings were made, for as Corot wisely said, 'It is the interpretation, rather than the scene, that makes a picture.'

I have tried to show, from an examination of his technique, what new contribution Girtin made to water-colour. But most of all he imposed his own personality. Where his predecessors had been calm and dispassionate, Girtin was hot and impulsive. Where their brain had directed and controlled the hand, Girtin's brain, eye and hand were working in unison. Girtin knew that chance must play its part in a successful engagement with water-colour. One has the feeling that whereas the artists before him achieved their results by recognised principles and built up their work to a steady, foreseen finish, Girtin never quite knew what had happened, or how the result was achieved, till he saw his drawing as an

[1] M. Hardie, *A Sketch-book of Thomas Girtin*, Walpole Soc., XXVII, 1939, p. 89.
[2] Tate Gallery 4728, and Coll. Sir Edmund Bacon, Bt.
[3] Coll. Mr. and Mrs. Tom Girtin.   [4] *Library of the Fine Arts*, III, 1832, p. 318.

1 'The Thames from Westminster to Somerset House'
(drawn for the *Eidometropolis*)
B.M. 1855.2.14.27 $9\frac{5}{8} \times 21\frac{1}{4}$: 244 × 540   *Water-colour*
Thomas GIRTIN (1775–1802)

2 'Westminster and Lambeth' (drawn for the *Eidometropolis*)
B.M. 1855.2.14.23 $11\frac{5}{8} \times 20\frac{3}{4}$: 295 × 527   *Water-colour*
Thomas GIRTIN (1775–1802)

3 'Carnarvon Castle'

V.A.M. P.30–1932 $16\frac{3}{4} \times 22\frac{1}{4}$: 425 × 565   *Water-colour, signed*

Thomas GIRTIN (1775–1802)

4 'Cayne Waterfall, North Wales'
B.M. 1855.2.14.2 $19\frac{3}{4} \times 23\frac{7}{8}$: 501 × 605   *Water-colour and pen*
Thomas GIRTIN (1775–1802)

5 'White House, Chelsea'
Coll. Sir Edmund Bacon Bt. $12\frac{1}{4} \times 20$: 311×507 *Water-colour*
Thomas GIRTIN (1775–1802)

6 'Kirkstall Abbey—Evening'
V.A.M. 405–1885 $12 \times 20\frac{1}{8}$: 304×510 *Water-colour*
Thomas GIRTIN (1775–1802)

7 'Lake Scene with Two Herons'
Birmingham, City Museum and Art Gallery $10\frac{1}{4} \times 12\frac{1}{4}$: 261 × 311   *Water-colour*
Thomas GIRTIN (1775–1802)

8 'Above Bolton: Stepping Stones on the Wharfe'
Coll. Mr & Mrs Tom Girtin   12¾ × 20½ : 322 × 521   *Water-colour*
Thomas GIRTIN (1775–1802)

9 'Kirkstall on the Banks of the Aire'
Coll. Mr & Mrs Tom Girtin   12½ × 20½ : 316 × 520   *Water-colour*
Thomas GIRTIN (1775–1802)

10 'Paris, La Rue St Denis'

Coll. Sir Edmund Bacon Bt. $15\frac{1}{2} \times 18\frac{3}{4}$: 393 × 177   *Water-colour*

Thomas Girtin (1775–1802)

11 'Porte St Denis'

V.A.M. 37–1886 $18 \times 23\frac{3}{4}$: 456 × 601   *Water-colour*

Thomas Girtin (1775–1802)

12 'St. Vincent's Rocks, Clifton'
Coll. Mr & Mrs Tom Girtin   12½ × 20: 316 × 508   *Water-colour*
Thomas GIRTIN (1775–1802)

13 'From Boxley Hill near Maidstone'
Coll. Mr & Mrs Paul Mellon   9¼ × 14¼: 236 × 363   *Water-colour, signed and dated 1801*
William PEARSON (fl. 1798–1813)

accomplished thing. One great difference is that many of his drawings must have been wet all over, with running colour, and till they dried out the result remained, to some extent, unknown. Thus, with Girtin a new school begins—a school which allows for the widest scope of self-expression. From 1800 onwards water-colour had a new and larger horizon. Of the copyists and imitators, William Pearson, or Pierson (*fl.* 1789–1813), should be considered one of the closest. He exhibited at the Royal Academy from 1799 to 1804. The late C. E. Hughes owned a panoramic landscape by him (about 17 × 13 inches) which came convincingly close to Girtin in composition, drawing and colour. In 1943, Agnews exhibited *Haughmond Abbey*, an impressive drawing by Pearson in the Girtin manner even when shown in the same exhibition as Girtin's brilliant *Abbey Mill, Knaresborough*.[1] It is very probable that other similar drawings by Pearson have been absorbed as Girtin's *œuvre*. I have seen drawings signed by a very obscure artist, T. F. Dukes (working *c.* 1810) and his *Bridgnorth*, for example (exhibited at the Fine Art Society 1945), had kinship with Girtin and Francia in subject and manner.

[1] Coll. Lady Davies.

CHAPTER II
Joseph Mallord William Turner R.A.

John Martin   Francis Danby   Thomas Danby

In 1802, the year of Girtin's death, Joseph Mallord William Turner was elected a member of the Royal Academy. In its notice of that year's exhibition the *Morning Post* said that Turner was 'stepping forward with gigantic strides . . . he has the penetrating eye, exquisite taste, aided by powerful genius, that sublime faculty which could make him another Claude.' It might be thought from this that Turner had outstepped and outstripped Girtin in the field of water-colour, but the academic honour and the newspaper praise were given to the painter in oil who had exhibited the *Bridgewater Sea Piece* and the *Egremont Sea Piece*. Whatever contemporary critics may have thought, and however prominent Turner was in public esteem, it may be affirmed now that in 1802 he had not surpassed Girtin as a painter in water-colour. If we maintain our critical perspective and refuse to allow our awareness of the later Turner to overwhelm and distort our judgment, we can rightly and fairly say that in 1802 Girtin held the supremacy. There could be no better judge of this than Turner himself. 'If poor Tom had lived,' he said, 'I should have starved.' Once, after studying a drawing by Girtin of St. Paul's, he turned to him and exclaimed: 'Girtin, no man living could do this but you.' And, in later years, while looking at another of Girtin's drawings, he said: 'I never in my whole life could make a drawing like that: I would at any time have given one of my little fingers to make such a one.' Ruskin felt the same when he wrote: 'There were two men associated with Turner in early study, who showed high promise, Cozens and Girtin, and there is no saying what these men might have done had they lived; there might, perhaps, have been a struggle between one or other of them and Turner, as between Giorgione and Titian.'

If Turner by 1802 had not produced any water-colour so final in accomplishment as the *Kirkstall Abbey, Evening*,[1] that does not detract from his merit at the time or minimise his ultimate position as one of the greatest landscape painters of all time and of all countries. By 1802 he had not acquired Girtin's breadth and mastery of harmonious colour, but he was accumulating vast stores of knowledge about minute facts of Nature's appearance and

[1] V.A.M. 405–1885.

change; he was studying the movement of the sea; above all, he was embarking upon those experiments in recording light which were later to set him apart. He and Girtin were beginning to separate. Where Girtin accepted his subject and surrendered himself to it, searching out and interpreting the poetry of the facts, Turner was always eager to invent, to alter buildings and landscape to his own ends, to superimpose his own ideas upon his theme. Where Girtin was concentrated and restful, Turner was diffuse and restless. By 1802 he was on his way to surpass Girtin, and indeed all of his contemporaries, in expressing action and motion, whether in sky or sea, landscape or figures.[1] The *Sketch of a Pilot Boat*,[2] made rapidly with a few swift lines and blots from his ship or from a pier on his first journey abroad in 1802, is a masterly rendering of energetic action, and shows at this early stage in his career his power as a draughtsman, his keen perception, his quick seizure of essentials. Neither Girtin nor any water-colour painter before him could have conveyed so much animation in so few lines. Turner's figures may often be clumsy and mannered, at times even grotesque, but like the sailors in this drawing, they live and move, and are always well placed. The young artist who drew that pilot boat was clearly destined to paint the sea, as no one before him had ever done, whether in storm or in repose.

Joseph Mallord William Turner (1775–1851) was born on April 23, St. George's Day, the son of a barber in Maiden Lane, Covent Garden. The boy started making copies of prints and sketches from nature at an early age, and his drawings were hung round the entrance to his father's shop 'ticketed at prices varying from one shilling to three'. When in 1789 he was fourteen his father proudly announced, 'My son is going to be a painter', and entered him as a student in the Royal Academy. Young Turner worked there with fair regularity from 1790 to 1793. Some of his academic figure studies, painstaking rather than inspiring, are in the British and Victoria and Albert Museums. About this time he was a pupil of Thomas Malton, and acquired from him some useful knowledge of perspective and architectural drawing. He had his first exhibit, *Lambeth Palace*,[3] at the Royal Academy in 1790, two more in 1791, and thereafter was a regular exhibitor, being elected Associate in 1799 and Member in 1802. What Charles Lamb described as 'that emporium of our artists' grand Annual Exposure' was then at Somerset House.

In 1790 he made the first of his sketching tours, visiting Malmesbury, Bath, Clifton, Bristol; and in subsequent years there were few parts of England, Scotland and Wales through which he had not travelled. Even by 1796 he had visited Cambridge, Lincoln, Nottingham, Derby; he had been to Chester, Flint, Worcester, Gloucestershire, Shropshire, Hereford, Monmouth and Kent; he had made more than one sketching tour through North and South Wales; and he had been in the Isle of Wight, taking in Winchester and

---

[1] For movement of figures perfectly expressed—movement not only up and down but forward—see the water-colour of a *French Dance in Sabots*, B.M. CCLIX–197. Since the basement of the Tate Gallery was flooded some years ago, the drawings of the Turner Bequest have been placed in the Print Room of the British Museum.
[2] B.M. LXXXI–127.
[3] 'The Water-colours of Turner', *Studio*, Special no. Spring 1909, pl. I.

Salisbury on the way. He used to travel on foot, 'twenty to twenty-five miles a day, with his little modicum of baggage at the end of a stick'. These tours began to supply him with valuable material. An *Interior of Tintern Abbey*[1] and *Porch of Great Malvern Abbey*[2] were exhibited at the Royal Academy in 1794. Writing about these and other exhibits the critic of the *Morning Post* said: 'They are the productions of a very young artist, and give strong indications of first-rate ability; the character of Gothic architecture is most happily preserved, and its profusion of minute parts massed with judgment and tinctured with truth and fidelity. This young artist should beware of contemporary imitations. This present effort evinces an eye for nature, which should scorn to look to any other source.'

He was still working in the traditional manner, using faint washes of colour in cool blues over a grey monochrome drawing. His work, like that of Girtin at the same time, is almost indistinguishable from that of Dayes, whose influence is very clear. His skies with their clarity of white clouds follow those of Dayes, and his foliage in such early drawings as the *Windy Day, Lullingstone Park, 1792*,[3] and the *Dent-de Lion, near Margate, 1792*,[4] though not quite so crisp and angular as that of Dayes, is not unlike it in mass and movement. In the latter drawing the whole subject is drawn with the pen, brown ink being used for the middle distance, black ink for the foliage and tree-trunks in the foreground. His *Christ Church from the River, 1792*,[5] is a remarkable work for a boy of seventeen. Not only is it fine in drawing and silvery colour, but the figures are put in with a skill which seems to have forsaken the artist later; or were they added for him by Dayes or Malton? He was in demand now for the popular topographical views, and by 1798 over thirty of his drawings had been engraved for *The Copper-Plate Magazine*, *The Pocket Magazine* and similar illustrated albums.

Up to 1795, when eight more of his drawings were hung at the Academy, Turner was still the industrious apprentice, working with indomitable energy, fostering dexterity of hand and eye, struggling with technique, but as yet without individual vision or the power to transmute facts into ideas. But he had painted landscape scenery of every kind, architecture, figure subjects, a cottage interior, a scene in Oxford Street after a fire, a storm on a rocky coast. Then, and all through his life, Turner accumulated notes in his sketchbooks, which germinated years afterwards.

Turner is said to have first met Girtin when they were employed as boys in colouring prints for John Raphael Smith, and in the preceding chapter much has been said about their association and methods of technique which were common to them both. About 1795 they were working together in the evenings, as has been related, at Dr. Monro's house. A sketch which is supposed to have been made by Dr. Munro in 1796 shows Turner making a drawing by candle light at a sort of double desk, and absorbed intently in his work.[6] Dr.

[1] V.A.M. 1683–1871.
[2] Manchester University, Whitworth Art Gallery.
[3] Northampton, Mass., Smith College of Art.
[4] A. J. Finberg, *Life of J. M. W. Turner*, 1939, pl. 3.
[5] Oxford, Ashmolean Museum.
[6] Coll. Mr. Kurt F. Pantzer, Indianapolis (previously owned by Dr. Foxley Norris, Dr. Monro's grandson); Illus. Finberg, *Life*, pl. 2.

Foxley Norris told me that his Aunt Isabel—rather refined, and a beauty in her day, as shown in a drawing by Henry Edridge—used to have her dinner sent up to her room when Turner was in the house; she found him 'so rough'. Miss Ann Dart, who met him about 1798 in her uncle's house at Bristol, gave Ruskin her recollections of Turner as being careless and slovenly in his dress, anything but a nice-looking man, talking of nothing but his drawings, impolite and lounging about at table.

Lest it be thought that the sordidness of Turner's surroundings has been exaggerated, we have an unprejudiced account by an independent eyewitness. In 1837, at the height of Turner's prosperity, William Callow, who had been living in Paris for several years, came over to London and obtained an introduction to Turner from Charles Heath, the engraver. Here is Callow's own account:

> On presenting myself at his residence in Queen Anne Street, the door was opened by his old housekeeper, who requested me to wait in the hall whilst she delivered the letter to Mr. Turner. To my surprise, Turner himself came out to me and upon my asking permission to see his gallery, he abruptly though kindly said, 'Go up.' So upstairs I went, delighted not only at getting an opportunity of seeing his wonderful paintings, but at meeting the painter himself. It was a painful surprise, however, to find Turner's gallery in a most dilapidated condition. Many of the pictures, some on the ground and others leaning against the wall, were cracked and damaged. The walls were in a deplorable state of damp, with the paper hanging down in strips.[1]

And when Ruskin took his wife to call upon Turner in 1848 they had to knock for some time before the great man opened the door himself and took them into a 'room without a fire and bare and miserly'.

To return to Turner's association with Girtin in his early days, it is clear that in both cases the maturing of a new vision began to appear about 1796. Turner's two sketch-books of that year show his advancing skill with pencil and with colour, and contain many themes which he expanded then or later. It is evident that he was finding a new and wide demand for his work. A leaf in each book[2] is headed *Order'd Drawings*, and contains a list of commissions from useful patrons such as the Earl of Essex and Sir Richard Colt Hoare among others. For the latter, from 1796 to 1802, he made a set of eight drawings of Salisbury Cathedral. Two of them, *South View of Salisbury Cathedral from the Cloister*[3] and *Entrance to the Chapter House, Salisbury Cathedral*[4] are in the Victoria and Albert Museum. Ten of his water-colours were in the Academy of 1796, notably some that, like the Salisbury drawings, were amazingly skilful renderings of architecture, but still what Ruskin called 'head work rather than heart work'.

Of his first forty subjects exhibited at the Royal Academy, thirty-one are architectural. Among his four exhibits in 1797 was the *Transept of Ewenny Priory*,[5] singled out by Finberg as the first work to manifest Turner's genius as opposed to his talent. Comparing it with the earlier *Marford Mill, near Wrexham*[6] we might borrow Wordsworth's phrase, written a year

---

[1] H. M. Cundall, *William Callow*, 1908, p. 66.
[3] V.A.M. 502–1883.
[5] Cardiff, National Museum of Wales.
[2] B.M. Turner Bequest XXIV and XXVI.
[4] V.A.M. 503–1883.
[6] Cardiff, National Museum of Wales.

later in the preface to the *Lyrical Ballads*, the subject was no longer 'standing upon external testimony, but carried alive into the heart of passion'. When painting *Ewenny Priory* the artist was not so much concerned with the definition of form as with the emotional effect conveyed by the gloom and mystery of the vast neglected Norman interior. He was no longer searching, except in his unnecessary and disturbing foreground detail, for rational shapes but for wandering tones and atmosphere produced by the shafts of light that strike through windows and the open door. A contemporary critic declared *Transept of Ewenny Priory* to be 'one of the grandest drawings he had ever seen, and equal to the best pictures of Rembrandt. There is mind and taste in everything the man does.'[1]

Of his work of 1798 the *Norham Castle*[2] and the *Kirkstall Crypt*[3] show again that he was advancing towards the fusion of details in a largeness of emotional conception. According to Farington,[4] Hoppner said that, 'Mr. Lascelles as well as Lady Sutherland are disposed to set up Girtin against Turner, who they say effects his purpose by industry—the former more genius—Turner finishes too much'. The truth of this is borne out by a comparison of Girtin's *Kirkstall Abbey* with Turner's *Kirkstall Abbey* of 1798. Turner's is a grandiose composition full of detail, and with a waterfall in the foreground, where no waterfall ever was. Their versions of *Harewood House*[5] in 1798 show the same contrast between elemental simplicity and exuberance of detail.

We learn from Farington[6] that Turner had 'sixty drawings now bespoke. . . . He has no systematic process for making drawings—He avoids any particular mode that He may not fall into manner. By washing and occasionally rubbing out, He at last expresses in some degree the idea in his mind.' And in November comes the note that 'Turner has no settled process but drives the colours about'. Those last two comments show that with Turner, as with Girtin, a new and broader use of water-colour had begun, and—the most important thing—a realisation that, by driving colour about, tone could be worked into tone, local colour being submerged in broad masses of light and shade. The topographers never washed and scrubbed; they never drove their colour about. Once again it may be repeated that the change which took place at the turn of the century, the 'step in advance' which Samuel Redgrave misunderstood, was not merely in the direct rendering of local colour without a monochrome underpainting (Skelton, Towne and others had rendered local colour directly in a high key), and not in the substitution of a variety of colour for the simpler tints used by the earlier artists, but in the study of reflected light, of atmospheric changes, of wind and weather; above all, in the massing and merging of tones.

Turner's work of 1799 can be seen at the Victoria and Albert Museum, which owns his *Bridge over the Usk*[7] and *Warkworth Castle—thunder storm approaching at sun-set*,[8] both exhibited at the Royal Academy, if we may take the former to be the picture originally

---

[1] Whitley, 1700–1799, II, p. 215.
[2] London, Soane Museum.
[3] London, Soane Museum.
[4] *Diary*, February 9, 1799.
[5] Girtin—Coll. Earl of Harewood; Turner—B.M. Turner Bequest XXXIV–76.
[6] *Diary*, July 6, 1799.
[7] V.A.M. 978–1900.
[8] V.A.M. 547.

entitled *Abergavenny Bridge, Monmouthshire clearing up after a showery day*. The title of an oil-painting of that year was *Kilgarran Castle on the Twyvey, hazy sunrise, previous to a sultry day*. Those titles show that the artist was giving his attention to conditions of light and weather; topography was becoming subordinated to atmosphere. In both of the water-colours he is abandoning the clear, sharp, decisive handling of his earlier work. There is a new perception of sunlight, of varied gradations, of the value of massed tones. Both of them resemble Girtin in subject matter and outlook, but where breadth and simplicity were natural to Girtin, they had to be painfully acquired by Turner. Not till a year or two later, when he produced his *Easby Abbey, Yorkshire*[1] did he begin to match Girtin's bold simplification, and avoidance of irrelevant detail, and massive opposition of light and shade.

More and more at this period Turner was becoming occupied by painting in oil, and the work in his sketch-books was slighter and more flimsy. In 1800, besides his oil landscapes, he showed six water-colours, five of them being large views, painted for Beckford, of his capricious and pretentious Fonthill Abbey. In the course of this year Farington drank tea with Turner at 64 Harley Street, where he had J. T. Serres as his fellow-lodger, and Turner told him that he 'thinks of charging Mr. Beckford 40 guineas each for the drawings of Fonthill. They are seven in number'. In 1801 he 'did' Scotland in under three weeks. Of his two hundred drawings on this tour many are little more than unintelligible memoranda, and the sixty 'Scottish Pencils', as they are described in the Turner Bequest, are extremely dull. He told Farington that he 'thinks Scotland a more picturesque country to study in than Wales. The lines of the mountains are finer, and the rocks of larger masses'.

In 1802 he was elected a full member of the Royal Academy, and celebrated his promotion by setting out on the first of his foreign tours. The Peace of Amiens had unbarred the gate into France for English visitors, and the road to the Alps was open. To Turner at that time Switzerland must have meant Cozens, and Cozens' Switzerland. He had copied scores of Alpine scenes by his great predecessor; and who can doubt that in the first place his journey was a pilgrimage to the shrine of Cozens? He had imitated Wilson; he was eager to rival Cozens, as he was eager to rival Claude. His contemporary critics were quite justified in saying that his works were compounded of art. Turner was not satisfied with what he had already done. With a mind full of Cozens, he would see whether he could find inspiration where Cozens found it. So on July 14, 1802, Farington notes that 'Turner sets off for Paris to-morrow on his way to Switzerland'.

On this tour through Switzerland between July and October he made four hundred sketches, only about a score being coloured. For these he abandoned his delicate washes on white paper and used body-colour on a paper which he had first covered with a grey wash. Body-colour, drying very quickly, enabled him to do rapid outdoor work, and he could scrape and wash his priming of grey so as to obtain the more subtle modulations of

---

[1] Whitworth Art Gallery. Manchester owns a superb collection of drawings by Turner. Sixty-one in the Whitworth Institute include twenty-five which were presented in 1892 by the famous collector Edward Taylor. Others belong to the City Art Gallery.

tone. In the Turner Bequest the drawings made on this tour include what Ruskin rightly described as the 'quite stupendous' studies for the *Devil's Bridge*, *The Source of the Arveiron*, and the *Mer-de-Glace* subjects,[1] all of which were to figure in the *Liber Studiorum* or in later paintings. His *Upper Falls of the Reichenbach*,[2] with its daring rainbow in front of the cascade, shows very clearly the inspiration of Cozens. Turner's more personal and emotional response to Alpine scenery, and his growing search for stability in a marshalled and unified design, are shown in his *Great Fall of the Reichenbach*, which he completed later for exhibition in 1804. In this large drawing, over forty inches high, the varying structure of crag rising above crag, to the remote summit whence the water descends, is built up into a solid and satisfying whole. All the multitudinous delicacies and complexities are merged into a magnificent unity. The painter is using water-colour for the expression of a vast and solemn and romantic theme. For the first time, it should be noted, he is adopting rococo forms, using large ogee curves, as in his *Passage of Mont Cenis*,[3] *The Longships Lighthouse*[4] and many later works, to act as the structural basis of a swinging rhythm in his design. There were no trees there in nature. The trees were planted there, twisted and destroyed there, by Turner, to add to the grandeur and desolation of his theme.

No artist, it may be said, ever drew a tree, its knots and twists, its grace and thrusting energy, its foliage and branches swinging from weight to feathery lightness, with the same skill and searching knowledge of its inner life as Turner. He thought that Swiss trees, mainly pines, were 'bad for a painter', and he imported trees of English origin, or blasted and broke his Swiss pines as in the *Reichenbach*. The *Chamounix*, another of these earlier Swiss subjects, once in the Farnley Hall collection, is equally brilliant in design, and full of atmosphere and movement. The trees, superbly drawn, are seen against a dramatic sky, where mountains, clouds and mist are all struggling together in front of an infinite distance of clearest blue.

In poetry and nobility of conception Turner had now equalled his earlier rival. In technique, as shown in the drawings just mentioned and in others of the same period, he passed far beyond the domain of Girtin. The *Reichenbach* and the *Chamounix* show developments to which Girtin was only just feeling his way. Fresh colour has been floated over portions that have been washed down; lights are taken out by the use of a wet brush and the application of blotting-paper or rag, and by free scraping with a knife. From now onwards he is increasingly prone to work in stipple or to break up tones into innumerable spots, by the infinite labour in removing colour with the fine point of a wet brush.

Actual witness to Turner's method in 1802 is given by Andrew Robertson, the miniature painter. Newly arrived in London, he sent a drawing to his brother who was estab-

---

[1] B.M. Turner Bequest LXXV.
[2] Coll. Sir Stephen Courtauld. Six years before his own Swiss tour Turner had copied a drawing by Cozens of the Reichenbach. Original and copy are reproduced in C. Monkhouse, *Earlier English Water-Colour Painters*, 1897. In W. Armstrong's *Turner*, 1902, pl. 10, *Between Chamouni and Martigny* by Cozens, and Turner's copy of it, are reproduced side by side. Both of these drawings were sold from the Asa Lingard collection at Sotheby's in March 1944.
[3] Birmingham, City Art Gallery.   [4] Coll. Lady Agnew.

lished as an artist and drawing master in New York. With it he wrote a letter, dated September 18, 1802, explaining his work as an example of 'Lights washed off. Turner uses it much . . . very narrow minded. His style is to rub, sponge and wash off lights, draws on thick vellum . . . Colman [Cotman] ditto. Girton [Girtin] upon firm cartridge.' A. P. Oppé, who quotes this letter,[1] points out that the passage is interesting as showing how calmly immediate contemporaries regarded the practices of Turner which the next and succeeding generations came to magnify as epoch-making discoveries. Still, the sponging and washing out of lights was very definitely a new development at this period.

The new methods made an impression upon William Daniell, who showed Farington in 1804 some of his drawings, which were 'executed in Turner's manner very well'. He told Farington[2] that:

> The lights are made out by drawing a pencil [i.e. brush] with water in it over the parts intended to be light (a general ground of dark colour having been laid where required) and raising the colour so damped by means of *blotting-paper*; after which with crumbs of bread the parts are cleared. Such colour as may afterwards be necessary may be passed over the different parts. A white chalk pencil (Gibraltar rock pencil) to sketch the forms that are to be light. A rich draggy appearance may be obtained by passing a camel Hair pencil *nearly dry* over them, which only *flirts* the damp on the part so touched and by blotting paper the lights are shown partially.

This dragging of dryish colour from the side of a brush was part of Turner's practice from about 1800. This method, with its crisp granulation of dry colour and its pleasant suggestion of broken texture, was freely used later by Bonington, Cotman, Boys and others. More particularly, Turner was of the vanguard in the keying of colour to a higher and higher pitch of brightness. His opponents, as we shall see, found this innovation unforgivable in his oils. Perhaps it was at the oils that the veteran Sandby was tilting when he spoke of the 'invasion of the Yellow Fever'.

In 1804 Turner decided to furnish a large gallery (it was seventy feet long) in his own house for the exhibition of his pictures, and from this time he sent few water-colours to public exhibitions. The two large drawings, *The Great Fall of the Reichenbach*[3] and *The Passage of St. Gothard*,[4] both dated 1804, were probably among the first pictures on view in the private gallery. Though his oil-paintings roused fierce criticism and contention, his water-colours were apparently considered innocuous and acceptable. In oil he was the 'over-Turner', and Farington records many adverse and abusive comments upon his work. In 1803 Sir George Beaumont, who for many years was to wage a sort of holy war against Turner, found the foregrounds in his oils 'comparatively *blots*', and was followed by Constable, who in his early days looked at Turner's landscapes and 'cannot reconcile them as being true to nature'. Constable revised his opinion later, when he wrote about the Turners in the Academy of 1828 as 'golden visions, glorious and beautiful; they are only visions, but still they are art, and one could live or die with such paintings'. In 1806

---

[1] A. P. Oppé, 'The Water-Colour Drawings of J. S. Cotman', *The Studio*, 1923.
[2] *Diary* March 28, 1804.   [3] Bedford, Cecil Higgins Museum.
[4] Coll. Mr. and Mrs. Esmond Morse.

Benjamin West said that Turner 'had become intoxicated and produced extravagancies'. One evening in June of that year, Beaumont, Edridge, Thomas Daniell and William Alexander were regaled at Farington's house on cold roast beef and pigeon pie: 'We passed a very social evening. We had a strong conversation on the merits of Wilson as a Landscape Painter, and the vicious practise of Turner and his followers was warmly exposed.' For years to come his work in oil stirred people to extremes of admiration or disgust. On the other hand his water-colours excited no unfavourable comment. Water-colour painters, as well they might, regarded him as their leader, and but for the disqualification caused by his membership of the Royal Academy he would no doubt have taken a prominent part in the foundation of the Society of Painters in Water-Colours in 1804. He was a close friend of W. F. Wells, its founder.

Turner from the beginning of his career was a water-colour painter, and his attempt to introduce into oil-painting the lightness and clarity of water-colour was what chiefly roused the antagonism of Beaumont and others. The older men, brought up in the classical tradition, did not realise that landscape, the youngest branch of painting, was perhaps the only one from which new truths and new achievements might emerge as the result of an enhanced and enlarged artistic vision. Beaumont in 1806, as Farington records, said that Turner was 'perpetually aiming to be extraordinary, but rather produces works that are capricious and singular than great: his Colouring has become jaundiced'. Turner and his followers were dubbed the 'White Painters'. The older school, in search always of the heroic and sublime (and as an oil-painter Turner began as an adherent of this school), had obtained atmosphere and recession by making their foregrounds very dark and by alternating planes of light and dark till they melted into a clear distance. In his oils Turner, the water-colour painter, abandoned the brown tree; his foregrounds and his shadows were not black or neutral, but full of reflected light and colour. He brought air and what he called 'flittering light' into the whole of his picture. All this rose from his practice as a water-colour painter, and his water-colour work, constantly and progressively pursued, exercised a deep influence upon his work in oil.[1] It was because he was a water-colour painter that he liberated landscape painting in oil from its conventions and rejuvenated its spirit. The gist of the whole matter is in Beaumont's statement to Farington[2] that 'much harm has been done by endeavouring to make paintings in oil appear like water colours, by which in attempting to give lightness and clearness the force of oil painting has been lost'.

When a writer in the *Literary Gazette* of 1823 thought that Turner was leading all the other artists astray and that 'the powerful attraction of colours . . . is the vice of our modern school', he was ignoring the intensification and heightening of colour which Turner had developed for many years in his water-colours. Oil-paintings such as the *Bay of Baiae* struck his contemporaries as far too light in key and too resplendent in colour; but

[1] We see the opposite process with Sargent, who began entirely as an oil-painter and whose work in oil profoundly affected his water-colour method.
[2] *Diary*, October 21, 1812.

Turner by that time was well aware that, while his water-colours would retain all of their first brilliance, time and varnish would mellow his oils and lower their tones. One feels that Turner got more real satisfaction and sheer enjoyment out of water-colour and that, however brilliantly he worked in oil, he preferred the qualities of the lighter medium to the more sticky and rebellious material of the oil-painter.

It was his friend, W. F. Wells, who conceived a further project for extending Turner's reputation, and urged him to embark on the publication of the series of engravings known as the *Liber Studiorum*. Turner saw in engraving a means of avoiding an idle hour, of satisfying his own passion for work, of securing his reputation in the eyes of a much larger public, which might include posterity, and of putting money in his purse. In October 1806, in Wells' house at Knockholt, he made his first five studies for the *Liber Studiorum*. They were not 'studies' in our modern sense. They embodied all his profound knowledge of nature, and it was his intention to issue engravings of a hundred landscapes, with (as an early prospectus stated) 'a classification of the various styles of landscape, viz. the historic, mountainous, pastoral, marine and architectural'. Turner himself etched the plates, which were then rocked with a mezzotint ground and were engraved, either by Turner himself, or by Thomas Lupton, Charles Turner, William Say and others. Every plate which was not engraved by Turner himself received his constant care and supervision. Verbally, or by notes on the proof, he conveyed to his engraver full directions and instructions as to all the changes and refinements which he considered essential for the perfect rendering of his own ideas. He was often in conflict with his engravers, sometimes about the work, more often about the price. The patient Thomas Lupton sometimes spent seven to eight weeks in working on a plate for which he was paid five guineas. Charles Turner, whom Finberg unfairly describes as a 'rapacious gentleman', required an advance from eight to ten guineas for engraving a plate, and this Turner declined to grant. When F. C. Lewis asked for eight guineas instead of five, Turner refused to give him a second plate, and George Clint also gave up the work because of the inadequate pay. The plates actually published, between 1807 and 1819, number seventy and a frontispiece, form a monumental work recording the highest expressions of the artist's genius.

Turner kept on his gallery in Queen Ann Street, but early in 1807, when the first part of the *Liber Studiorum* was published, he was living at Upper Mall, Hammersmith, in a house with a garden running down to the river. Here he painted some of his finest pictures, besides enjoying some fishing, his only sport. Oil-painting occupied most of his time, but in the following years he painted many notable water-colours such as the glowing and luminous *Scarborough Castle: Boys Crab-Fishing*[1] of 1809, and the more developed variant, *Scarborough Town and Castle*, bought by Mr. Fawkes in 1811. In the summer of 1811 he made a tour through Dorset, Devon, Cornwall and Somerset in search of material for his illustrations to Cooke's *Picturesque Views of the Southern Coast of England*, which was published

[1] London Wallace Collection.

31

in parts from 1814 to 1826. He was back in Devonshire in 1813, in search of further subjects for the *Southern Coast*, among them *Plymouth Dock from Mount Edgecumbe*,[1] *Plymouth with Mount Batten*[2] and, for Cook's *Rivers of Devon* he made his lovely drawing of *Ivy Bridge*[3] (Pl. 17). The drawing of the *Ivy Bridge* was in the engraver's hands in 1816, and with its fine colour, its inimitable perfection of technique, its studied interplay of flickering light and shadow, may be taken as showing the ripe fullness of Turner's art at this middle period of his career.

By 1816 Turner was the greatest force in English painting, and in one of his papers Hazlitt[4] published his views about Turner:

> We here allude particularly to Turner, the ablest landscape-painter now living, whose pictures are however too much abstractions of aerial perspective, and representations not properly of the objects of nature as of the medium through which they are seen. . . . They are pictures of the elements of air, earth and water. . . .
>
> It was a common cant a short time ago to pretend of him, as it formerly was of Wilson, that he had other things which Claude had not, and that what Claude had besides, only impaired the grandeur of his pictures. The public have seen to the contrary. They see the quackery of painting trees blue and yellow to produce the effect of green at a distance.

From 1815, for many years to come, Turner's water-colours were destined to provide material for line-engravings. Cooke's *Picturesque Views of the Southern Coast of England*, with forty prints after his drawings, appeared in parts from 1814 to 1826; the *Views in Sussex*, with nine plates, 1816 to 1820; *The Rivers of Devon*, four plates, 1815 to 1823; Hakewill's *Picturesque Tour in Italy*, eighteen plates, 1818 to 1820; Whitaker's *History of Richmondshire*, twenty plates, 1818 to 1823; *Provincial Antiquities of Scotland*, twelve plates, 1819 to 1826; and *Picturesque Views in England and Wales*, for which Turner supplied no less than ninety-six drawings, from 1827 to 1838. To these must be added his illustrations to *Roger's Poems*, 1834, and to *Byron's Life and Works*, 1832 to 1834; his *Rivers of France*, embracing over sixty drawings made on his annual tours of the Loire and the Seine, 1833 to 1835; his illustrations to Scott's *Poetical and Prose Works* 1834 to 1837; and much besides. W. G. Rawlinson, in his *Engraved Work of Turner*, catalogues over 800 engravings which appeared in Turner's lifetime, all of them based upon water-colour originals.

It was not in Turner's nature to hand over his drawing and to accept whatever interpretation an engraver might make of it. He trained a whole school of engravers and personally superintended their work. When the engraver had made his plate correspond with the drawing, Turner worked on the proof, drawing upon it, touching it with white, praising the good parts, criticising the weak, making endless refinements and alterations. Line-engraving indeed was transformed as a technique under his inspiration. So harmonious was the result that few of us, if any, could separate or distinguish the unsigned work of Cooke, Miller, Brandard or Willmore; but each engraving is always the unmistakable rendition and reflection of a Turner drawing. In the first part of the *England and Wales*,

---

[1] Coll. Mr. R. W. Reford, Montreal.
[3] B.M. Turner Bequest CXXV.47.
[2] V.A.M. 3053–1876.
[4] W. Hazlitt 'Round Table' essay, *The Examiner*, 1816.

published in 1827, Turner's demands for subtlety of tone, lightness of key, and precision of detail, were carried out perfectly by Richard Wallis in his renderings of *Bolton Abbey* and *Colchester*, by Edward Goodall in *Rievaulx Abbey* and *Fall of the Tees*, by William Miller in *Rouen from St. Catherine's Hill*, noble water-colours all of them, nobly interpreted.

These reproductions, whether executed upon copper or steel, are always described as 'line engravings', but actually nine-tenths of the work was etched, and only a small portion executed with the burin. The comparative ease with which etched lines could be burnished out, rebitten or altered allowed Turner to treat the work almost like washes of colour and to make up for the elimination of actual colour by a fuller definition of form and by stronger contrasts of tone. There is a vast gulf between the dull heaviness of prints by Woollett after Claude or Wilson, and the sparkling clarity and fluidity of an engraving by W. B. Cooke or W. Miller after a Turner water-colour. As John Pye said in his evidence before the Select Committee on Arts and Manufactures in 1835, English engravings were 'free translations from pictures, instead of being rigid copies' and partook 'more of the character of a fine art than in any country'. How much all this development was due to Turner is emphasised by Dr. G. F. Waagen, Director of the National Gallery at Berlin, who visited London in 1835 and referred to 'the landscapes of the favourite painter Turner, who is known throughout Europe by his numerous, often very clever, compositions for annuals and other works, where they appear in beautiful steel engravings'.

There was a danger in making these hundreds of drawings with an eye to their being engraved. Turner became more prone to consider his drawings as a means to an end and to sacrifice some of his own ideals in order to meet the limitations of a process or to simplify the engraver's task. It is true, however, that when he had once educated his engravers in the difficult art of interpreting his colour in line and tone, he could ignore their requirements and paint as he pleased. At the same time he had always been troubled by an inclination, which he found difficulty in overcoming, to sacrifice breadth for a distracting variety of detail and incident. In producing the engravings he was apt to consider the preferences of the large public and not just the sophisticated taste of a small group of cultured patrons. He was driven to remember that the great public required the avoidance of generalisation, of what contemporary critics described as 'blotches' in his painting, and asked for clean-cut descriptive details which they could understand and enjoy. For these reasons, though most of his water-colours engraved in the *Southern Coast*, the *Richmondshire*, the *England and Wales*, are magical renderings of colour and atmosphere, in many other instances they tend to be overcrowded and to display too much insistence upon isolated particularities and secondary motives, which only his immense skill and knowledge have woven into a semblance of harmony. The crowded figures of *The Hoe, Plymouth*,[1] and *Old London Bridge*,[2] and the intricacies and complexities of *Hornby Castle, Lancashire*,[3] to take three drawings in the Victoria and Albert Museum, are examples of

[1] V.A.M. 521–1882.   [2] V.A.M. 522–1882.
[3] V.A.M. 88.

33

this lavish profusion, this wish to satisfy his public. In drawings such as *Upnor Castle*,[1] his art became at times pyrotechnic in colour and display.

All these engravings required constant journeys in search of new material. In 1817 Turner explored the banks of the Rhine from Cologne to Mayence, coming home with some two hundred pencil sketches. From these he made a series of about fifty water-colours, swift and suggestive, beautiful in their handling, which were bought by Walter Ramsden Fawkes. With few exceptions these Rhine drawings are in body-colour on a white paper, which he prepared with a dark grey priming, as he had done for the St. Gothard drawings of 1802. Some of the finest of these drawings are in a delicate scheme of blue and gold, such as *Marxbourg*[2] (Pl. 24), *Abbey near Coblenz*[3] (Pl. 16), and *Brübrich Palace*[4] in the British Museum. In these Rhine subjects he used body-colour with the same mastery with which he had long handled the transparent medium, and used it rightly for the recording of rapid impressions which required no wrought-out elaboration. The *Mainz and Castel*[5] may be noted as showing Turner in experimental mood. The dark cloud in the sky was obviously produced by letting colour drop and splutter on a very wet paper, in contrast with the dry work of the sky on the left and the crisp touches which give notes and accents on the boats. Later, in 1826, when he explored the Meuse and the Moselle, he worked in a similar way on sheets of actual blue paper, not a paper primed with blue. Body-colour was used with a pleasantly pastel-like effect. Details of architecture and landscape were indicated by touches of brown ink added with a pen. Possibly by this time he had commenced his practice of mixing Chinese white in his water vessel, bringing the water to the consistency of thin milk. The slight opacity which this gave to his pigments would account for their somewhat dry appearance, as of pastel.

Perfection of finish in transparent water-colour will be found in the drawings which he made at the same period while staying at Farnley Hall.[6] For the expenses of this sketching tour he took £110 in his pocket. His sketch-book records this, and also details of the expenses incurred on the journey from London to Leeds: 'Porterage, 2s. 8d., Fare to Leeds £2. 2s. Coachman 1s., Dinner at Eaton 5s. 6d., Coachman-Scrooby, 1s. 6d., Ditto 7s., Breakfast at Doncaster, 2s. 3d., Brandy & Water, Grantham, 1s. 6d., Coachman & Guard, 4s. 6d., Total £3. 2s. 11d.' There is a pleasant tale of Squire Fawkes sitting beside Turner in his workroom and watching the paper being 'soaked, blistered, daubed, rubbed, and scratched with the thumbnail, until at length beauty and order broke from chaos'. Turner was frequently a guest at Farnley Hall between 1802 and 1825, and Walter Fawkes had 200 of his friend's water-colours and seven oil-paintings to display proudly to his guests.

---

[1] Manchester University, Whitworth Art Gallery. In a letter to *The Times*, January 20, 1876, Ruskin referred to this drawing, with the *Frank Encampment* of J. F. Lewis, as 'unsurpassable standards' of pure water-colour and pure body-colour respectively.

[2] B.M. 1958. 7.12.422.

[3] B.M. 1958. 7.12.412.

[4] B.M. 1958. 7.12.420.

[5] Private collection U.S.A.

[6] For an account of Farnley Hall and of Turner's work for the Fawkes family, see 'With Turner in Wharfedale,' by G. B. Wood, in *Country Life*, September 20, 1946.

From Farnley Hall in 1816 Turner travelled all over Yorkshire on horseback, on one occasion in Teesdale being 'bogged most completely Horse and its Rider, and nine hours making 11 miles'. 'Of all his drawings', wrote Ruskin, 'those of the Yorkshire series have the most heart in them, the most affectionate, simple, unwearied, serious finishing of truth. . . . I am in the habit of looking to the Yorkshire drawings as indicating one of the culminating points in Turner's career. In these he attained the highest degree of what he had up to that time attempted, namely, finish and quality of form united with expression of atmosphere and light without colour. . . . No complicated or brilliant colour is ever thought of in them; they are little more than exquisite studies in light and shade, very green blues being used for the shadows, and golden browns for the lights.'[1] Belonging to that period, or retaining much of its charm, are *Entrance to Gardens at Farnley Hall*,[2] *Wharfedale from the Chevin*,[3] *Fountains Abbey*,[4] *Bolton Abbey*,[5] *Lonely Dell near Wharfedale*,[6] the subject of one of the finest of Sir Frank Short's mezzotints, and the masterly *Crook of the Lune*.[7]

Let it be said here that when Turner painted a place, he was not exact in his topography. He painted not merely what he saw, but the universe. Many of his water-colours were built up from the most rudimentary notes made many years before. *Ely Cathedral*[8] and *Laugharne*,[9] for instance, were painted about 1830 from pencil sketches made nearly thirty years earlier. He painted not only when he was at his work. He painted while he was thinking, while he was for ever storing his impressions. His memory was prodigious. Ruskin doubts 'whether Turner's composition was not universally an arrangement of remembrances, summoned just as they were wanted, and each set in its fittest place'. Turner never hesitated to alter the actual scene to suit his own imagination. A critic in 1825 described his oil-painting, *Dieppe*, as a 'most splendid piece of falsehood'. In his water-colours he rebuilds Kilchurn Castle, and from memories of Loch Fyne makes Loch Awe lively with fishing smacks, on an inland water where no fishing smack was ever seen. Small boats may approach Laugharne Castle by a winding creek, but the sea is two miles away. His pencil sketch gives an outline of the actual scene, but in his water-colour of *Laugharne Castle*, made thirty years later, the stormy sea breaks at the foot of the castle, a dismasted vessel lies at anchor, the foreground is strewn with wreckage, rocks are crowded with figures busily salving the flotsam and jetsam. Ruskin devotes eloquent paragraphs to a description and analysis of the rolling breakers; but they were brought there by Turner, who was concerned not with place so much as with dramatic possibilities of sea and air. Ordinary low cliffs in other places are made into vast, beetling crags; *Launceston*[10] becomes a towering city in a scene of Alpine grandeur. Look at familiar places in the engravings of the *Southern Coast* or *England and Wales*—at Dunwich, Aldeburgh, Dover, Dartmouth, Boscastle, for instance—and everywhere we find untruths mingled with the larger truth.

[1] *Modern Painters*, Pt. II, Sec. I, Chapter VII.
[3] Coll. Mr. A. Dawson.
[5] B.M. 1902. 2.12.282.
[7] Coll. Sir Stephen Courtauld.
[9] Once Coll. James Gresham.
[2] Coll. Major LeG. G. W. Horton-Fawkes.
[4] Coll. Rev. Canon Ronald Allen.
[6] Leeds, City Art Gallery.
[8] Coll. Miss Jonas.
[10] Once Coll. J. F. Schwann.

Another thing should be said here with reference to the drawings of 1820 onwards, of which so many were engraved in the *England and Wales*. In this middle period he excels in the rendering of light and shadow sweeping over hill and dale, of sunshine entangled in delicate intricacies of foliage, of splendour in his skies, but the quiet and silvery tones of his early period are giving place to positive colour. He is obtaining animation by intensified colour and not merely by form. The flash and flare of hot sunshine pervades his *Windsor Castle*[1] (Pl. 25) and his *Knaresborough*,[2] and the effect is gained by prismatic and scintillating colour. It was this type of drawing, with hot reds and yellows contrasting with blue, which clearly went to Cotman's head and drove him to an unsteady and inebriated imitation. On the other hand, no colour could be more restrained than the grey, grey-blue, white, and silver of his *Longships Lighthouse*, painted about 1834, to my mind perhaps the finest of Turner's water-colours, marking the beginning of his last great period, and a fore-runner of *Rain, Steam and Speed*. There are no bold or bright or varied colours in this rendering of wild weather on the Cornish coast. The picture is all air and space, with the whole vivid drama of the scene—raging storm, screaming gulls, spectral lighthouse, silver foam, tossing spindrift, leaping spray, wreaths of vapour, wild cliffs half-hidden in the mist—made impressive by subdued tones, and by a design of those interlocking curves and circles which express the writhing fury of the elements and by their own form bring a subconscious suggestion of infinity.

Since his election as an Academician in 1802, he had only exhibited water-colours at the Academy on rare occasions. They were so generally known and esteemed because he exhibited them instead in his own gallery, which was open to the public, also in 1819 his patron, Walter Fawkes, admitted the public to his town house at 45 Grosvenor Place, to view his large collection of water-colours by contemporary artists. Apart from nearly a hundred drawings by Turner he showed twenty-five examples of Varley, Glover, Prout, Havell, De Wint, Fielding, Atkinson, Ibbetson and others. A newspaper cutting of April 1819, in the Victoria and Albert Museum, provides a first-hand account:

On Tuesday Mr. Fawkes opened his house in Grosvenor-place for visitors, who were admitted by tickets, to see his collection of water-colour drawings by English Artists. We must first mention the house, as a very stately and noble mansion, furnished with great elegance, not with French elegance, but something that we like much better, the solid and pure taste of England. Without having previously known the owner's habits, we should have pronounced it to be the house of an opulent and manly-minded English landholder. . . . The visitors gave their tickets in the hall, and were ushered up a handsome flight of stairs, with marble statues in niches, into the suite of rooms in which the pictures were. Catalogues were lying on the tables, and thus every advantage was given for indulging in those fine works of art. The front drawing-room contained several landscapes and figure pieces by celebrated Artists, Prout, Atkinson, &c. and one by Robson, a *Mountain View*, of extraordinary size and beauty. From this the visitors passed through a suite of three handsome rooms. The last with a southern aspect, and exhibiting the finest landscapes that we have ever seen in water-colour. They are, we believe, all by Turner, the Royal Academician, and almost all from the noblest scenery in the world—the Swiss Alps; views of *Mont Blanc, The*

---

[1] B.M. 1958. 7.12.432.   [2] Manchester, City Art Gallery.

Devil's Bridge, Chamouny, The Great St. Bernard, The Mer de Glace, mountains mingling with the clouds and rich with all the effects of storm and sunshine, cataracts plunging into an invisible depth, lakes shining like blue steel under the Alpine sun, or clouded by forests hanging over them from the hills, uplands covered with vines and olives, and solitary sweeps of splendid snow. Turner is perhaps the first artist in the world in this powerful and brilliant style, no man has ever thrown such masses of colour upon paper, and his finest works have been collected in this house. The art itself is *par excellence* English, no continental pencil can come near the force, freedom, and nature of our professor's, and as such, independently of the general promotion of fine taste, there is a patriotic spirit displayed in its patronage. The intermediate apartments were filled with finished drawings, by leading names and sketches by Turner, of Yorkshire scenery, and chiefly, we believe, of the striking points of view on Mr. Fawkes's estate.

Later on, W. B. Cooke, and Messrs. Moon, Boys and Graves, in 1831, were to hold public exhibitions of water-colours by Turner before they were distributed to the engravers.

At the beginning of August, 1819, Turner set forth on his first visit to Italy, spent a fortnight or more in Venice[1] and then travelled by the usual post-route to Rome. A letter written to Sir John Soane by his son describes Turner with amiable gossip:

> Turner is in the neighbourhood of Naples making rough pencil sketches to the astonishment of the Fashionables, who wonder of what use these draughts can be—simple souls! At Rome a sucking blade of the brush made the request of going out with pig Turner to colour—he grunted for answer that it would take up too much time to colour in the open air—he could make 15 or 16 pencil sketches to one coloured, and then grunted his way home.

In his monograph A. J. Finberg[2] showed that Turner—for the reason given to the sucking blade of the brush—relied mainly upon pencil work during this first Italian tour. Only a few of the Venice drawings are coloured, and about twenty or thirty among those made in Rome, Naples and Tivoli; and probably a very small proportion, if indeed any, were coloured at the time in the open air. His production for the six months' tour was nearly 1500 sketches in pencil.

On his way home from Italy in January 1820 he found on reaching Turin that the ordinary coach service to Savoy was in abeyance owing to a fall of snow. Though told that it was madness to proceed, he joined with some other determined travellers and secured a coach. At the top of the pass the coach capsized, and the carriage door was so completely frozen that the passengers had to climb out through the window and flounder through the deep snow to Lanslebourg. On his return he made a record of the episode for Mr. Fawkes in a water-colour inscribed *The Passage of Mt. Cenis, 15th Jany, 1820.*[3] The dramatic qualities of the scene are rendered with a power as overwhelming as that of nature itself. The circling fury of the storm-clouds is echoed in the curve of the plunging horses which threaten to overturn the coach. Neither rain nor snow, nor cold, nor adverse circumstances, ever daunted Turner or made him miss an opportunity; he must have had not only an exceptional power of mobilising instantly all his resources of eye, brain and hand, but a

---

[1] This visit in 1819, not known to any of Turner's biographers, was proved by A. J. Finberg from his study of Turner's sketch-books.
[2] A. J. Finberg, *In Venice with Turner,* 1930.   [3] Birmingham, City Art Gallery.

constitution of iron. His oil painting of a *Frosty Morning*[1] was the result of a brief halt upon a journey by stage-coach, when other passengers must have stamped their feet or wrapped themselves closer in their rugs. And it seems to me that the water-colour of *Lancaster Sands*, 1820,[2] is another piece of Turner's autobiography, typical of his many journeys by coach or on horseback in the wildest of weathers.

Of Turner as a traveller there is a delightful description, quoted in the *Memoir* of Thomas Uwins.[3] It was written to Uwins by a young Englishman, knowing nothing about art or artistic reputations, who was Turner's fellow-traveller in 1829 on a journey by diligence from Rome to Bologna:

> I have fortunately met with a good-tempered, funny, little, elderly gentleman, who will probably be my travelling companion throughout the journey. He is continually popping his head out of window to sketch whatever strikes his fancy, and became quite angry because the conductor would not wait for him whilst he took a sunrise view of Macerata. 'Damn the fellow,' says he. 'He has no feeling.' He speaks but a few words of Italian, about as much of French, which two languages he jumbles together most amusingly. His good temper, however, carries him through all his troubles. I am sure you would love him for his indefatigability in his favourite pursuits. From his conversation he is evidently *near kin to*, if not *absolutely*, an artist. Probably you may know something of him. The name on his trunk is, J. W. or J. M. W. Turner.

Turner in his vagrant life travelled thousands of miles, at home and abroad, on foot, on horseback, in cart, gig or coach. Elsewhere I have spoken of the kit carried by Samuel Palmer on similar journeys. About Turner's usual luggage we get a hint from a list of the contents of his valise which he lost during a Rhine tour in 1817: a sketch-book, a guide book, one night shirt, three day shirts, a pair of stockings, a waistcoat, a razor, six ordinary cravats, one large cravat, a box of colours, a ferrule for an umbrella, and half a dozen lead pencils.

With reference to the few water-colours made by Turner during his first visit to Italy or soon after his return, A. J. Finberg[4] gives a valuable note about technique:

> As it has often been stated that Turner's first visit to Italy revolutionised his way of painting, it is well to scrutinize the technique of these first drawings with some care. So far as I can see they differ hardly at all from the drawings which he had been producing during the five or six years before he went to Italy. They are in practically the same key as the first half of the *Southern Coast* drawings, the *Views in Sussex* and Hakewill's *Picturesque Tour in Italy*. As with these drawings, their dominant colours are blue and yellow—yellow ochre and real ultramarine, I believe— with faint underpaintings in the shaded parts of some neutral tint, like Payne's grey. The accents on the buildings and figures are put in with sepia or Indian red, and there are some touches of Prussian blue and indigo.

It was fifteen years before Turner returned to Venice. In the meantime Prout was there in 1824, Wilkie and Bonington in 1826, and paintings of Venice were constantly in the exhibitions of the Old Water-Colour Society. In 1830 Rogers' *Italy* appeared with vignette

---

[1] London, National Gallery.
[3] Mrs. Uwins, *A Memoir of Thomas Uwins*, 1858 II, p. 240.

[2] B.M. 1910. 2.12.279.
[4] *Venice, op. cit.*, p. 77.

illustrations after Turner and Stothard. It was this volume which produced Lady Blessington's caustic comment: 'It would have been dished, were it not for the plates.' In that same year, Turner was engaged upon a series of illustrations of Byron's works, and perhaps a close study of *Childe Harold's Pilgrimage* renewed his recollections of the historical and romantic glamour of Venice. It was in 1835 that he made his second visit. His drawings of fifteen years before had been almost entirely pencil notes for the purpose of collecting architectural and topographical information, for the surroundings were new to him. He had not then succumbed to the real spirit of Venice, nor did he know all the changes of its atmosphere. In *The Rialto*,[1] the *Salute from the Academy Quay*,[2] and other water-colours made after the first visit, he relied too much upon memory and over-stressed the glittering detail of bridges, multicoloured façades and painted sails. He was recording the impression made in Venice upon a tourist absorbed in its outward shapes and colours. He was painting for other tourists, like Fawkes, who remembered Venice as a sort of fairyland, with baroque palaces fringing a labyrinth of waters beneath azure skies. In 1835 he was painting for himself, and was much more concerned now with light and atmosphere, with the true *genius loci* rather than the form and vivid colouring of individual buildings. Venice, with its freedom of space, its brilliancy of light, its variety of tone, its massive simplicity of general form, its low sky-line, was a new source of inspiration. The mirage-like effect of long low buildings floating upon water and melting ethereally into the sky was after his own heart. He was painting light; buildings and water seem to melt and glow, and change from rose to gold in the palpitating radiance of dawn and sunset. A great deal of his work was done rapidly in body-colour on grey or brown paper for the seizure of passing effects. What he made of these notes can be seen in the magnificent *Storm at Sunset*,[3] *Calm at Sunrise*,[4] and *Calm at Sunset*[5] or *A Storm in the Piazzetta*.[6] He was in Venice for a final visit in 1840. In his late Venetian and Swiss drawings he is absolute master of his subject and workmanship, and seems just to breathe upon paper the delicate films of sensitive and vaporous colour.

From 1835 to 1845, when his health began to fail, Turner spent increasing time on the Continent, adding sometimes several sketches a day to the extraordinary total of over nineteen thousand drawings, which were his bequest to the nation in 1851. During the period from 1830 onwards his work in water-colour passed into its latest and highest phase. It is spiritual and creative rather than interpretative. The colour is light and delicate as the sparkling tints seen in the rainbow spray of a fountain, or the down on a butterfly's wing. To this period, of visionary dreams of light and colour in the slightest sketches, belong highly-finished drawings such as the *Ehrenbreitstein*,[7] the *Lake of Constance*,[8] the *Splügen Pass*,[9] the *Windermere*,[10] the *Lake of Lucerne*,[11] with its atmosphere all rose and silver, and

[1] Coll. Mr. Kurt Pantzer, Indianapolis.
[2] Coll. Mr. R. W. Reford, Montreal.
[3] Cambridge, Fitzwilliam Museum.
[4] Cambridge, Fitzwilliam Museum.
[5] Cambridge, Fitzwilliam Museum.
[6] Edinburgh, National Gallery of Scotland.
[7] Possibly the version in Bury, City Art Gallery.
[8] Coll. Gwen, Lady Coleman.
[9] Coll. Messrs. Thomas Agnew & Sons.
[10] Coll. Mrs. Radcliffe-Platt.
[11] Coll. Mr. H. A. Haworth.

those two masterpieces *The Rigi at Sunset*[1] and *The Rigi at Sunrise*,[2] known as the *Red Rigi* and the *Blue Rigi*. In making drawings of this kind other painters may bore us with their mechanism and dexterity, but Turner never lost impulse and pictorial harmony. In the Rigi drawings he was the insuperable master of technique. He used every possible manipulation of brush, colour and paper, every device, every weapon in his armoury, sponging, rubbing, washing, stippling, hatching, touching and retouching, to express the vibration and radiation of light. Like Shelley, he saw in Switzerland mountains 'mingling their flames with twilight'. Light was his theme. Sometimes it may seem the light that never was on sea or land, but, like the poet's dream, it may make a picture more living than life. Someone who knew Turner's ways said that 'he had seen the sun rise oftener than all the rest of the Academy put together'. While Constable painted mid-day and afternoon, Turner studied the miracle of sunset, when all nature is hushed and gilded in transient gleams quivering through a film of russet or smoky gold, and the more rarely seen miracle of dawn, when life that has been passive and suspended begins to glow with a new faint flush like a child waking from sleep. That tender opalescence of sun-filled haze is what makes his Venetian, his Lucerne and other Swiss drawings so poetic and so memorable. A verse of Tennyson seems to epitomise the quality of the later Alpine subjects:

> *How faintly-flush'd, how phantom-fair,*
> *Was Monte Rosa, hanging there,*
> *A thousand shadowy-pencill'd villages*
> *And snowy dells in a golden air.*

In his *Notes on the Drawings exhibited at the Fine Art Society, 1878*, Ruskin tells how the *Splügen Pass* and the *Rigi* drawings came into existence. In the winter of 1841 Turner brought back fifteen studies from Switzerland. He expected to sell ten finished watercolours, and in anticipation of this he completed four, among them the three just mentioned. Early in 1842 he brought the four drawings and the fifteen sketches to his agent Griffiths. Ruskin quotes the conversation. Says Mr. Turner to Mr. Griffiths: 'What do you think you can get for such things as these?' Says Mr. Griffiths: 'Well, perhaps, commission included, eighty guineas each.' Says Mr. Turner: 'Ain't they worth more?' Says Mr. Griffiths: 'They're a little different from your usual style—but—yes, they are worth more, but I could not get more.' Griffiths placed the drawings before his clients, but nine commissions only were obtained with difficulty. 'The *Splügen Pass*', says Ruskin, 'I saw in an instant to be the noblest Alpine drawing Turner had ever till then made, and the *Red Rigi* such a piece of colour as had never come my way before.' But Ruskin's father, who might have bought the drawing for him, was away, and on his return the coveted works were gone. Ruskin had to be content with *Lucerne Town*,[3] but many years later he acquired the *Red Rigi*. Long afterwards, Vokins tried to persuade Ruskin to sell a Turner drawing.

---

[1] Melbourne, National Gallery of Victoria.   [2] Coll. Mrs. Andrew.
[3] *Notes by Mr. Ruskin on his collection of drawings by the late J. M. W. Turner* 1875, pp. 75, 76.

'Well,' said Ruskin, 'I have none to spare, yet I have a reason for letting one first-rate one go, if you give me a price.' 'What will you take?' 'A thousand pounds.' 'I wished', adds Ruskin, 'to get *dead* Turner for one drawing, his own original price for the whole ten, and thus did.' Ruskin would have rejoiced to know that his thousand pounds was far below the normal value of one of those drawings today.[1] The two Rigi drawings, and several others of the same period, from the collection of the late Walter Jones, were sold at Christie's in 1942. With them were eight Scottish drawings which were once the property of Sir Walter Scott, engraved as illustrations to *Provincial Antiquities and Picturesque Scenery of Scotland*, 1819. The frame containing the drawings was made by Tom Purdie from the wood of an oak felled while Turner was at Abbotsford in 1818.

Something more remains to be said about Turner's technique during the last fifteen years of his life. After using body-colour for his Petworth drawings in 1830 and for the *Rivers of France* series, engraved in 1833, he employed the opaque medium much less consistently. Some of his finest Venetian drawings of 1835 are in body-colour, but by 1840 he had abandoned the use of tinted paper and body-colour except sparingly and on special occasions. During his last visits to Venice in 1835 and 1840 his pencil sketches were much more swift and careless than those of 1819, perhaps because he was no longer concerned with definition of detail, perhaps because by this time he could almost draw the Salute or the Dogana with his eyes shut. The lyrical qualities of sky and water interested him more than any close-up of buildings. Up to 1835, in Venice and elsewhere, he had made many accurate studies in pencil, and had chosen later from these—for the making of completely fused and finished water-colours, like the Rigi drawings—the subjects which specially stirred his imagination. But the finished water-colours were separate, elaborated productions. In his actual work done during his tours he was putting colour over the pencil drawings, sometimes with small touches which left the paper partly uncovered, as in *Venice from the Lagoon*,[2] sometimes with washes of very diluted and fluid tint. My own belief is that he found that a wash of water was helpful in fixing his pencil work and that the thinnest wash of colour would fix it even better. When he sat down in the evening he found intense pleasure in adding colour to preserve his day's work of perhaps a dozen sketches. He discovered, I believe, the beauty of a pale flush of red or blue or ochre, which held but never impaired the pencil accents and at the same time communicated a sense of glowing atmosphere, visionary rather than real. And then, in Switzerland or Italy or in his studio at home, he added to his drawing, skilfully placing notes of colour, or reinforcing it with pen work, frequently with touches of a glowing vermilion ink. No one has ever produced an effect so impressive by the use of a little coloured water floated over a piece of white paper. A typical drawing of this style is the *Calm at Sunrise*.[3] The colour scheme, is severely limited to the faintest of reds, yellows and blues, but there is the most subtle

[1] The *Red Rigi* at Christie's in 1928 realised £8295, the auction record for a Turner drawing. In 1942 at a time of general unsettlement, there was a revaluation. The *Red Rigi* was sold for 1100 guineas, and the *Rigi at Sunrise* for 1500 guineas.
[2] Cambridge, Fitzwilliam Museum.   [3] Cambridge, Fitzwilliam Museum.

variation even where the tints are most diaphanous, and an exquisite rising scale from the white of the paper to touches of grey and brilliant vermilion. In these apparently slight drawings he is more the creative artist than when he painted the *Ivy Bridge*. He had discovered that form could be lost or even distorted[1]; that colour could in itself be musical. Thackeray, when very young and inexperienced as an art critic, showed his wisdom by saying with reference to Turner that 'the great artist makes you see and think of a great deal more than the objects before you; he knows how to soothe or to intoxicate, to fire or to depress, by a few notes, or forms, or colours, of which we cannot trace the effects to the source, but acknowledge the power'.[2]

All through his fruitful middle years Turner had been absorbed by craftsmanship, intoxicated a little by his own exuberant felicity of technique, trammelled by his love of descriptive detail. But at no point in his career was he satisfied with past success. He swerved off all the tracks he had established, dazzling and irritating his contemporaries. All through his long life he was experimenting, adjusting, altering, probing new possibilities for water-colour, without any consciousness of his ultimate objective. His latest drawings, slight to the point of fragility, embody a life-time of accumulated knowledge, experience and craftsmanship. A fine example, described by A. P. Oppé as 'a distillation of form through a mind steeped in thoughts of colour' is *Venice, the mouth of the Grand Canal*.[3] These final works are based on vision—with all that the word implies of inner guidance and emotion—rather than on visual observation. In his hands matter is becoming miracle. He had shown all that could be done in the way of chiaroscuro and realistic representation. He had used light to separate, sharpen, set into relief, all the shapes and complexities of the objects in his landscape. He is now showing what he can do with the intangible and impalpable. Light now penetrates every object, breaking up the solids till they become semi-transparent, and flooding them with mystery. He is no longer concentrating upon foreground dimensions, but is gazing through space into deep, airy distances. His visions of Swiss valleys and Venetian lagoons flutter into a radiant existence like the may-fly emerging into sunlight from its enshrouding husk.

Turner's latest phase, roughly from 1830 onwards, has always been controversial. It may be said to begin with studies, both in oil and water-colours, of interiors at Petworth, with groups of inmates and guests casually occupied. In Turner's impressions, facts are forgotten or lost, and colour leaps up in a flash of light. Room and figures and furniture become, as it were, just a casket of jewels, coruscating with vivid green and gold and crimson in a cataract of sunshine poured through tall windows and striking back from lofty walls. To anyone who wants firm construction, solid and architectural, Turner's later output may seem flimsy and irritating. There are many who still regard this later work as superficial and unreal; seeing in it the loose improvisation of an old and tired man. But as

---

[1] The *Spectator* in 1844 said that 'when he comes to represent a railway-train, as in *Rain, Steam and Speed*, the laxity of form and licence of effect are greater than people will allow'. We accept now that he was painting exactly what his title said, and not making blue-prints for engineers.

[2] *Fraser's Magazine*, 1839, p. 42.   [3] Huntington Library, San Marino, California.

far back as 1806, when Turner was thirty-one, Sir George Beaumont said that Turner's pictures 'appeared to him to be like the works of an *old man* who had ideas but had lost his powers of execution': the italics are those of Farington.[1]

If some people see Turner's latest drawings as a senile epilogue, for others of us they embody the music of the spheres. In many estimates of Turner there is one point which, I think, has been overlooked. In the course of his long life, he produced a far larger corpus of work than any artist in history. While other artists have struggled with failure of energy, paucity of subjects, and poverty of ideas, his labour lay in making a choice among infinite riches. Other painters—almost every painter mentioned in these volumes—have had their lapses, their empty days, their disappointments and frustrations. What puts Turner in a class by himself is that he never seems to have experienced failure and always to have lived and worked in a spirit of inspiration, often ecstatic inspiration.

Turner died in 1851, the year of the Great Exhibition, fourteen years after Queen Victoria came to the throne. It is difficult now to realise that the man who was Girtin's friend and rival might be considered as Victorian. 'He was a child of the Romantic Revival, a creature of emotion and of memory, a dreamer whose secret spirit dwelt apart in delectable mountains, an artist whose subtle senses caught, like a shower in the sunshine, the impalpable rainbow of the immaterial world'. Although this was written by Lytton Strachey in *Eminent Victorians* about Cardinal Manning, so different from Turner in spirit and mode of life, it could be an appropriate epitaph for the painter.

John Ruskin (1819–1900) is so closely associated with Turner that, besides reference to his work as a water-colour painter, something should be said here about his importance as a writer. The son of a prosperous wine-merchant in London,[2] he made Turner's acquaintance in 1840, and in 1842, when he had just taken his degree at Oxford, he read a review in which Turner's pictures were ridiculed. He set to work at once on the first volume of his *Modern Painters, by a graduate of Oxford*,[3] with the idea of defending Turner from ignorant abuse and of demonstrating his genius. The book, of which the first volume appeared in 1843, developed into a treatise on the general principles of art criticism, and included a survey, however limited and however unjust in some cases, of contemporary art in water-colour. He has—for instance—little or nothing to say of J. R. Cozens, Hearne, Dayes, Girtin, Bonington, Müller or Cotman. He has a great deal to say about lesser men such as Copley Fielding, William Hunt, Harding, Nesfield and others. All whom he mentions, even with praise, are subservient at all points to Turner, 'the only great man whom the school [of modern landscape] has produced'. At the same time it must be admitted that, however invidious and often unreasonable his prejudices were, his close study and advocacy of water-colours, and the opinions which he uttered so pontifically and so brilliantly,

[1] *Diary*, April 5, 1806.
[2] In his *Diary*, January 4, 1861, G. P. Boyce notes: 'Old Ruskin gave us some sherry out of the same cask that Nelson drew his from before the battle of Trafalgar. It was very strong.'
[3] When the second volume appeared in 1846, the authorship was an open secret, but his name did not appear on the title-page till the edition of 1851.

43

did help to give not only encouragement but a definite status to water-colour art. No critic has ever had such influence upon public taste. As early as 1854 Ruskin wrote as one claiming authority: 'I don't say that I wouldn't care for reputation if I had it, but until people are ready to receive all I say about Art as "unquestionable", just as they receive what Faraday tells them about Chemistry, I don't consider myself to have any reputation at all worth caring about.'[1] Within a few years after that his reputation was won, his word was final.

Ruskin tells us that his admiration of Turner, though 'wild in enthusiasm' gave Turner 'no ray of pleasure'[2]; and that 'he always discouraged me scornfully . . . and he died before even the superficial effect of my work was visible'.[3] But in the later volumes of *Modern Painters* which appeared just before or after Turner's death (the third and fourth in 1856, the fifth in 1860), Ruskin had attained a much deeper insight into the animating principles of Turner's art. He lived in order to justify Turner. He examined every available painting and drawing by Turner. He studied searchingly the phenomena of Nature; he investigated scientifically the formation and aspect of rocks, trees, clouds, waves; he used the results of his research, together with all his wealth of poetic diction and imagery, to prove that all of Nature was reflected, as in a mirror, in Turner's art. Of Constable, as we shall see, he wrote that his 'reputation was most mischievous in giving countenance to the blotting and blundering of Modernism'. Neither to Constable nor to any other painter did he devote the loving care with which he sought out Turner's motives in his slightest and most evanescent efforts. With Turner he was thorough, and his thoroughness is shown by the fact that he sought for evidence of Turner's unity and infinity and fidelity in every place where his pictures had been painted, in England, Scotland and throughout France, Switzerland and Italy.

Ruskin was typical of the age in his compound of wild prejudice and generous enthusiasm and in the firm belief, which he shared with Gladstone, in his own straightforwardness and honesty of opinion. Like Gladstone he showed 'equal readiness to fight for the shadow or the substance, a comma or a creed'. He was censorious and fastidious like Matthew Arnold. In all the great Victorians, Carlyle and Tennyson among the writers, Landseer and Leighton among the painters, there was the same mixture of high intellect, religious faith, self-assurance, intractability, partisanship, dignified presence, sometimes a suspicion of hypocrisy. And yet they had character and a common heroic quality.

If Ruskin's references to the work of water-colour painters other than Turner are grudging and perfunctory; if, for his own purposes, he exalts the humble and degrades the mighty, *Modern Painters* remains a great and inspiring work. Though painters like Cox and De Wint are not comparable in his eyes with Turner, he is prepared to divert the limelight for a moment and to cast a flash of illumination upon some aspect of their art. Not enough attention has been drawn to Ruskin's own work as a skilful and conscientious

---

[1] *Letters from Ruskin to F. J. Furnivall*, 1897, p. 31.
[2] *Works*, VII, p. 453.
[3] *Ibid.*, XVIII, p. 148.

14 'Tintern Abbey'
B.M. 1958.7.12.400   13½ × 10 : 342 × 253   *Water-colour*
Joseph Mallord William Turner, R.A. (1775–1851)

15 'Kew Bridge'
B.M. XCV–42   10⅛ × 14⅜: 258 × 375   *Water-colour*
Joseph Mallord William TURNER, R.A. (1775–1851)

16 'Abbey near Coblenz'
B.M. 1958.7.12.412   7⅝ × 12¼: 193 × 309   *Water-colour*
Joseph Mallord William TURNER, R.A. (1775–1851)

17 'Ivy Bridge, Devon'

B.M. CCVIII–X   11 × 16 : 280 × 406   *Water-colour*

Joseph Mallord William TURNER, R.A. (1775–1851)

18 'The Mer de Glace, Chamonix'

Coll. Mr & Mrs Paul Mellon   27 × 40 : 485 × 1014   *Water-colour*

Joseph Mallord William TURNER, R.A. (1775–1851)

19 'Patterdale'

Coll. Mr & Mrs Paul Mellon $10\frac{3}{4} \times 15\frac{1}{4}$: 273 × 387   *Water-colour*

Joseph Mallord William TURNER, R.A. (1775–1851)

20 'Weathercote Cave'

B.M. 1910.2.12.281 $11\frac{3}{8} \times 18$: 290 × 457   *Water-colour*

Joseph Mallord William TURNER, R.A. (1775–1851)

21 'Venice, S. Giorgio from the Dogana'
B.M. CLXXXI-4 $8\frac{7}{8} \times 11\frac{1}{4}$: 226 × 286   *Water-colour*
Joseph Mallord William TURNER, R.A. (1775–1851)

22 'Burning of the Houses of Parliament'
B.M. CCLXXXIII–6 $9\frac{1}{4} \times 12\frac{3}{4}$: 235 × 323   *Water-colour*
Joseph Mallord William TURNER, R.A. (1775–1851)

23 'Lancaster Sands'

B.M. 1910.2.12.279 $10\frac{7}{8} \times 15\frac{7}{8}: 276 \times 403$ *Water-colour*

Joseph Mallord William TURNER, R.A. (1775–1851)

24 'Marxbourg'
B.M. 1958.7.12.422   11½ × 18: 292 × 457   *Water-colour*
Joseph Mallord William TURNER, R.A. (1775–1851)

25 'Windsor Castle'
B.M. 1958.7.12.432   11¼ × 17⅛: 286 × 434   *Water-colour*
Joseph Mallord William TURNER, R.A. (1775–1851)

26 'Florence from near San Miniato'
B.M. 1958.7.12.426 $11\frac{1}{8} \times 16\frac{3}{8}: 283 \times 315$ *Water-colour*
Joseph Mallord William TURNER, R.A. (1775–1851)

27 'The Arsenal'
B.M. CCCXVI–28 $9\frac{5}{8} \times 12\frac{1}{8}$: 244 × 308   *Water-colour*
Joseph Mallord William TURNER, R.A. (1775–1851)

28 'A Gurnard'
V.A.M. P.18–1938 $7\frac{1}{2} \times 10\frac{7}{8}$: 191 × 276   *Water-colour*
Joseph Mallord William TURNER, R. A. (1775–1851)

29 '"Chamounix" 1850'

B.M. 1944.10.14.168 $20\frac{1}{2} \times 15: 521 \times 381$ *Pen and brown wash*

John Ruskin (1819–1900)

30 'Fribourg, 1859'
B.M. 1901.5.16.4 $8\frac{7}{8} \times 11\frac{3}{8}$: 226 × 290
Water-colour and body-colour on blue paper, inscribed Fribourg *etc. 1859, but signed in 1879*
John Ruskin (1819–1900)

31 'Coast Scene and Thunderstorm'
B.M. 1891.5.11.48 $6\frac{1}{4} \times 9\frac{1}{2}$: 160 × 242   *Water-colour, initialed*
John Martin (1789–1854)

32 'Landscape with Figures'
B.M. 1887.7.22.1 $7\frac{5}{8} \times 10\frac{3}{8}$: 194 × 263   *Monochrome*
John MARTIN (1789–1854)

33 'Cambyses on his Way to Desecrate the Temple of Jupiter'
V.A.M. Dyce 966 $6 \times 9\frac{5}{8}$: 152 × 244   *Monochrome*
John MARTIN (1789–1854)

34 'Conway Castle'
B.M. 1890.5.12.42   12 × 18: 304 × 456   *Water-colour*
Francis DANBY, A.R.A. (1793–1861)

35 'River leading to a Cavern'
B.M. 1912.5.13.8 $10\frac{5}{8} \times 16\frac{3}{4}$: 270 × 425   *Brown monochrome*
Francis DANBY, A.R.A. (1793–1861)

36 'Welsh Mountains—Morning'

V.A.M. 385–1891 $16\frac{7}{8} \times 25\frac{7}{8}$: 428×656 *Water-colour, signed*

Thomas Danby, R.H.A. (1818–1886)

37 'The Passing of 1880'

Coll. Mr & Mrs Paul Mellon $12 \times 18\frac{1}{2}$: 304×470 *Water-colour, signed*

Thomas Danby, R.H.A. (1818–1886)

II 'Lyons'

V.A.M. 97–1900   9½ × 12: 241 × 305   *Water-colour*

Joseph Mallord William TURNER, R.A. (1775–1851)

draughtsman and colourist, whose actual practice was bound to support and strengthen his critical power. He studied drawing under two excellent teachers, Copley Fielding and J. D. Harding, whose work he was to analyse later with the utmost detail. In his Epilogue, added in 1883 to the second volume of *Modern Painters*, he describes how in 1840 and 1841, before he took his degree at Oxford, he was making pencil sketches in imitation of Prout and David Roberts, and was attempting water-colour drawings and vignettes, 'which were extremely absurd and weak', in imitation of Turner. He had advanced much further when he made a tour of Switzerland and Italy with Harding in 1845. He gives an enlightening description of how they worked side by side:

> Harding had vivid, healthy, and unerring artistic faculty, but no depth of science, and scarcely any of sentiment. . . . In general, if the forms of the subject were picturesque, it was all he cared for, nor would he with any patience analyse even those. So far as his art and aim went, I was able entirely to sympathize with him; and we both liked, in one way or another, exactly the same sorts of things; so that he didn't want to go and draw the marshes at Mantua when I wanted to draw Monte Monterone—but we could always sit down to work within a dozen yards of each other, both pleased. I did not mind his laughing at me for poring into the foreground weeds, which he thought sufficiently expressed by a zigzag, and heartily admired in him the brilliancy of easy skill, which secured, and with emphasis, in an hour or two, the effect of scenes I could never have attempted.

There is enough in that passage to show that Ruskin had no use for what he described as 'blottesque'. The fidelity to Nature, the painstaking truth, which he always advocated in others, comes out in his own work. It was analytic rather than sensitive. His nature led him to investigate and codify rather than to seek for what lies beyond and behind the visible realities. He had a keen interest in geology, as a basis of his study of Turner, and drew rocks and the structure of mountains with exquisite skill. Details of architecture were another favourite subject, and this enabled him to illustrate his own works, such as *The Seven Lamps of Architecture*, 1849, and *The Stones of Venice*, 1851–1853. He could not have been so indefatigable a student of Turner's art without absorbing a love of colour; and he used colour well and delicately to enforce his own work in pen or pencil. Good examples are *Zermatt*[1] and the *Fribourg*[2] (Pl. 30), which, in its fine pen-work and gentle tints, has what Laurence Binyon describes as 'something of the quality of a drawing by Dürer'.[3] Ruskin was elected an Honorary Member of the Old Water Colour Society—a rare honour —in 1873, and his work was shown in its annual exhibitions. He said at the time of his election: 'Nothing ever pleased me more. I have always been abusing the artists and now they have complimented me. It's very nice to think they give me credit for knowing something about art.'[4] He was elected Slade Professor of Art at Oxford in 1869, and lectured there until 1884. We shall return to him in a later chapter as the champion of the Pre-Raphaelites.

---

[1] V.A.M. P.15–1921.   [2] B.M. 1901. 5.16.4.
[3] L. Binyon, *English Water-Colours*, 1933, p. 175.
[4] Quoted by W. G. Collingwood, in prefatory note to catalogue of the Ruskin Exhibition at the R.W.S. Gallery, 1901.

One of the most remarkable romantics was John Martin (1789–1854). Born at Eastland Ends, Haydon Bridge, near Hexham, he spent a poverty-stricken childhood in the Tyne Valley. He was apprenticed to a coachpainter in Newcastle, from whom he ran away and was given painting lessons by an Italian artist, Boniface Musso, at Newcastle. Coming to London in 1806, he exhibited at the Royal Academy from 1811 to 1852, the British Institution, the New Water Colour Society and elsewhere. Farington[1] records: 'British Institution I went to and saw the modern pictures exhibited for sale this year. "Balshazzar's Feast" by John Martin, engaged most attention. Price 800 guineas, Directors of the Institution have complimented him with 200 gs. as a testimony of their approbation.' The *Balshazzar's Feast* was one of the first in a series of grandiose 'historical landscapes' in oil, which included the *Fall of Babylon* and the *Fall of Nineveh*. Dramatic, filled with immensities of dream architecture and hundreds of figures, they mingled the material elements of nature with the exotic inventions of a wild imagination. They were sensational, but undoubtedly cast a spell upon many minds, for engravings of his scenes from the Bible and Paradise Lost were in thousands of nineteenth-century homes. Bernard Barton, the Woodbridge poet, friend of Fitzgerald, Southey and Lamb, wrote some flattering lines in praise of Martin's work:

> *The awful visions haunt me still.*
> *In thoughts by day, in dreams by night*
> *So well has art's creative skill*
> *There shown his fearful might,*
> *Light and shadow, death and doom,*
> *Glory's brightness, horror's gloom,*
> *Grandeur of the bursting storm.*

And Ruskin, fully conscious that Turner at times was guilty of exaggeration in his passionate presentment of cosmic energy, said that 'reckless accumulation of *false* magnitude as by John Martin is merely a vulgar weakness of brain, allied to nightmare'. But Martin's nightmare visions, especially to his contemporaries, for whom hell fire was a reality, were terrifying and titanic emblems of destruction and doom.

Besides painting his vast visionary themes in oil Martin used water-colour, commonly in sepia monochrome, for the treatment of similar subjects on a smaller scale. He also employed the medium for a more realistic treatment of landscape taken from actual places and from nature and less controlled by melodramatic emphasis, for example in his *Richmond Park*[2] and *An English Landscape*.[3] He not only won fame as a painter, but conducted a long campaign for a purer water supply in London, for the proper disposal of its sewage, and for its architectural improvement. In the British Museum are his designs, made in 1820, for a *Proposed Triumphal Arch across the new Road from Portland Place to Regent's Park*.[4]

---

[1] *Diary*, February 9, 1821.
[3] B.M. 1891. 5.11.49.

[2] V.A.M. 535.
[4] B.M. 1867. 3.9.1706, 1707.

46

Francis Danby (1793–1861) was born near Wexford and studied with J. A. O'Connor, a landscape painter nicknamed the 'Irish Claude'. He came to England in 1813, settling eventually in Bristol where he made a living as a drawing master and where he painted those direct and simple landscapes like *Clifton Rocks from Rowanham Fields*[1] which are typical of his earlier style. In 1825 he was elected an Associate of the Royal Academy and, until 1829, when a private scandal apparently disrupted his career, he enjoyed an outstanding success and the support of Sir Thomas Lawrence. From that time began to appear those spectacular historical landscapes like *The Opening of the Sixth Seal*[2] which may be compared with the work of John Martin and which were also no doubt a product of Danby's experience of Turner's art. Between 1830 and 1840 he lived abroad spending his time mainly in Switzerland and France as well as visiting Norway and Italy. A few years after his return to England he settled in Exmouth where he worked as a boat-builder as well as an artist. His later reputation—and the Athenaeum obituary called him 'England's most distinguished painter of the Romantic school'—was based mainly upon his landscapes without historical attributes but presenting strong effects of light and weather—sunsets and storms—elaborately worked out with an intense, suggestive colour, as in *The Evening Gun*.

His work in water-colour follows the same range of subject as the oil-painting I have mentioned. Although it is most diverse in technique his art is unmistakable in its naturally romantic feeling and strongly personal expression. Danby's reputation quite failed to survive his death, but in recent years he has been carefully revalued and now stands, if not at the point where his most enthusiastic contemporaries placed him, as one, at least, of the most interesting and gifted artists of the romantic period.

Thomas Danby (1818–1886), Francis's son, travelled abroad with his father, working in oil, and finding congenial subjects in Switzerland and the Italian Lakes. After his return in 1841 he transferred his attention almost wholly to North Wales with occasional visits to Scotland, and began to exhibit his oils at the British Institution and the Royal Academy. It was not till 1866 that he concentrated upon water-colours and used the medium to such advantage that in 1867 he was elected an associate of the Old Society, becoming a full member in 1870. He painted in rich and harmonious colour, and his compositions were effectively arranged. Roget tells us that he was devoted to real ultramarine, yellow ochre, and earth colours of the quietest and most permanent character, and wisely never used indigo. Thackeray spoke very highly of his pictures, saying that 'you stand before them alone, and with a hushed admiration, as before a great landscape when it breaks on your view. He describes a scene of natural grandeur and beauty—of darkling forests tinged with the brightening dawn, of woods and calm waters gilded with sunset or fading into twilight'.

[1] Bristol, City Art Gallery.
[3] Coll. Lord O'Neill.

[2] Dublin, National Gallery of Ireland.

CHAPTER III

John Constable R.A.

Thomas Churchyard

Constable's water-colours, like the etchings of Crome, were done 'for pleasure and remembrance'. He won the interest of others for the water-colours of Cozens and Girtin; he bought De Wint, but he rarely exhibited his own work,[1] and certainly never showed to the public those free sketches which are a distillation of his art. Probably he looked upon his water-colours as mere notes and memoranda, made because he could not help making them.

Constable's work in water-colour was little known in his life-time and his influence on the British water-colour school of his day was not profound. It was not until forty-one years after his death that his importance as a water-colour painter began to be fully appreciated. In 1888, Miss Isabel Constable gave to the Victoria and Albert Museum over three hundred sketches and drawings by her father. With those and many others as our source of knowledge it is now plain that he broke away from all his predecessors and contemporaries and brought into water-colour as into oil landscape a new grasp of nature and her moods, a new knowledge of wind and weather, of light and atmosphere. His water-colours are intensely alive, they scintillate with flecks of light and flashes of colour, as do his oils.

Constable, like Rembrandt, was the son of a miller. Both of them were brought up among country sights and country sounds. Each of them must have watched great sails rising and falling against a background of white or stormy clouds. For Rembrandt, landscape became only a part of his life as a painter. Constable, on the other hand, devoted his whole life to landscape; he became a master of skies. Later on in his life he himself wrote about landscape, 'the sky is the keynote, the standard of scale, and the chief organ of sentiment . . . the sky is the source of light in nature, and governs everything'.[2] To this may be added the authentic tale of Fuseli saying to Callcott at the Academy of 1823, 'I like de landscapes of Constable; he is always picturesque, of a fine colour, and de lights in

---

[1] Less than twenty of his hundred and four exhibits at the Royal Academy from 1802 to 1837 were in water-colour or pencil.
[2] C. R. Leslie, *Life and Letters of John Constable, R.A.*, 1896, p. 104.

48

III 'Clouds'

V.A.M. 240–1888   7½×9: 191×228   *Water-colour*

John CONSTABLE, R.A. (1776–1837)

de right places; but he makes me call for my great coat and umbrella.'[1] Another anecdote relates that Fuseli, when Keeper of the Royal Academy, leaving his room to ascend to the exhibition, called down the geometrical staircase at Somerset House (the staircase of Rowlandson's drawing) to one of the servants: 'John. Pring me my omprella; I'm going to see Mr. Constable's picture.'[2]

John Constable (1776–1837) was born at East Bergholt, which overlooks the fertile valley of the Stour. In later life he said: 'I associate "my careless boyhood" with all that lies on the banks of the Stour. Those scenes made me a painter, and I am grateful.'[3] His best work was always done in that country-side of his birth and boyhood. With all his knowledge of other places and of other men's pictures, he never allowed that knowledge to obscure the indigenous imprint upon his mind. Salisbury, Brighton, Hampstead, may have held his heart for a time, but he always returned to his first love, the Essex of his youth. He found there clouds that were more impressive than any range of mountains; he found mill-ponds that were as gay with sparkling light as the lake of Lucerne or the Giudecca at Venice which Turner travelled so far to see. Constable, painting quietly in Suffolk and in Essex, showed how the familiar and modest scene can be unforgettable when recorded by a genius.

His father, Golding Constable, inherited considerable property from a rich uncle, including the water-mill at Flatford, and afterwards purchased a water-mill at Dedham, and two windmills at East Bergholt. In the grammar school at Dedham, at the age of sixteen or seventeen, Constable was already drawing instead of attending to his French lessons. At that time also he formed an alliance with John Dunthorne, a neighbouring plumber and glazier, who when he was not plumbing and glazing gave all his spare time to painting landscapes from nature. Subsequently Constable worked for about a year in his father's mills (not all of them water-mills) and by a wind-miller every change of sky is watched with the keenest interest. This is what Constable himself wrote, about 1830[4]:

It may perhaps give some idea of one of those bright and silvery days in the spring, when at noon large garish clouds, surcharged with hail or sleet, sweep with their broad shadows the fields, woods, and hills; and by their depths enhance the value of the vivid greens and yellows so peculiar to the season. The *natural history*, if the expression may be used, of the skies, which are so particularly marked in the hail squalls at this time of the year, is this:—The clouds accumulate in very large masses, and from their loftiness seem to move but slowly: immediately upon these large clouds appear numerous opaque patches, which are only small clouds passing rapidly before them, and consisting of isolated portions detached probably from the larger cloud. These floating much nearer the earth may perhaps fall in with a stronger current of wind, which as well as their comparative lightness causes them to move with greater rapidity; hence they are called by wind-millers and sailors, *messengers*, and always portend bad weather. They

---

[1] Leslie, *op. cit.*, p. 123.
[2] The Hon. A. Shirley, *The Published Mezzotints of D. Lucas after J. Constable*, 1930, p. 82.
[3] Leslie, *op. cit.*, p. 105.
[4] Leslie, *op. cit.*, p. 5. This is quoted for two reasons: first, to show that early environment had its effect upon all of Constable's work; second, to show that Ruskin misunderstood, or minimised, Constable's seriousness as a painter and his consummate knowledge of natural effects. See later, P. 56.

float midway in what may be termed the lanes of the clouds; and from being so situated, are almost uniformly in shadow, receiving a reflected light only, from the clear blue sky immediately above them. In passing over the bright parts of the large clouds they appear as darks; but in passing the shadowed parts, they assume a grey, a pale, or a lurid hue.

To the two influences caused by his natural surroundings and his kinship of interests with John Dunthorne, the intervention of his mother added a third. She obtained an introduction for her son to Sir George Beaumont, whose mother resided at Dedham. Perhaps Beaumont is most memorable for his worship of the 'brown tree', his insistence that 'a good picture, like a good fiddle, shall be brown'. It was Constable himself who, on a visit to his patron, when he had come to know him well, laid Beaumont's brown fiddle on the grass, to make the grass seem greener still. Constable owed much to Beaumont, who was one of the first to discover and foster his genius, as he had already done in the case of Wilson and Girtin. Though the first sight of Beaumont's Claude marked an epoch in Constable's life, his taste was most affected by the work of his contemporaries. The opinion has already been expressed that he made a close study of Beaumont's own drawings, and he was fortunate in that Beaumont possessed about thirty water-colour drawings by Girtin, only a year senior to Constable, which Sir George advised his young friend to study as examples of breadth and truth. Constable said that 'no great painters are self-taught', and those words recall his own debt to Girtin and Beaumont, to Rubens, Ruisdale and Gainsborough. Despite that debt, however, he was essentially an innovator, upholding freedom of self-expression and a personal technique.

In 1796, at the age of twenty, Constable was still making immature drawings of Suffolk cottages.[1] They were careful work, done in pen outline, by a youth whose knowledge depended largely on etchings and engravings, probably of the Dutch School. Constable must have had far less knowledge of art than Turner and Girtin in London, when in 1797 he was working in his father's counting-house. Though he was making experiments in etching, his mother still hoped that 'John will attend to business, by which he will please his father and ensure his own respectability and comfort'.[2] In 1798 Constable's father sent him,[3] with an introduction, to obtain the advice of Joseph Farington, R.A., who said at an early period of their acquaintance that Constable's style of landscape would one day 'form a distinct feature in the art'. In 1798 Farington wrote[4]: 'Mr. J. Constable of Ipswich called with letter from Mrs. W.—devoted to art though not necessary to profess it.— Knows Sir G. B.', and on the next day there follows the entry: 'Constable called & brot. his sketches of landscapes in neighbourhood of Dedham—Father a merct., who has now consented that C—shall devote his time to the study of art.—Wishes to be in Academy. I told him He must prepare a figure.' Later we find[5]: 'At 9 o'clock we entered Dovedale. I made a sketch of the first appearance of the entrance, and while I was so employed Mr. Constable came up to me, He having come a 2d time to make studies here.'

[1] V.A.M. 358–358J–1888. [2] Leslie, *op. cit.*, p. 7.
[3] Farington's Diary proves that the date was 1798, not 1795 as stated by Leslie and repeated by Holmes.
[4] *Diary*, February 25, 1798. [5] *Diary*, August 19, 1801.

In 1800[1] Constable had followed Farington's advice, and was admitted a student at the Royal Academy Schools. In August 1799 he had written from Ipswich to his friend, John Thomas Smith,[2] that he fancied he 'saw Gainsborough in every hedge and hollow tree'. In 1800 he was sketching at Helmingham Park; in 1801 he was in Derbyshire. In 1802 his first exhibit appeared at the Royal Academy. It was in this year that he submitted a rejected picture of Flatford Mill to Benjamin West, who took a piece of chalk and showed Constable how he might improve the chiaroscuro by some additional touches of light between the stems and branches of the trees, saying, 'Always remember, sir, that light and shadow *never stand still.*' Constable said it was the best lecture on chiaroscuro he had ever heard, and when West added that he should always aim at brightness in his skies, and that even in solemn or lowering skies there should be brightness in the darks which 'should look like the darks of silver, not of lead or slate', his advice was addressed to an attentive ear, for the dark of silver is in all Constable's clouds.

In the Derbyshire drawings of 1801, done in pencil and sepia, there is an enormous advance in knowledge from the work of 1796, and two drawings of *Windsor Castle*[3] show a further step in their use of colour. All his numerous sketches in black and white during the period of 1800–1807 are based, as Sir Charles Holmes has pointed out,[4] 'upon the style of Gainsborough, sometimes aping it so nearly as to make immediate discrimination between the two far from easy'. That was mainly in the case of his studies of trees, typical Gainsborough subjects drawn in chalk. Constable, like his great predecessor, rarely tinted this type of drawing, though he has added colour to one of *Cows and Trees*,[5] dated 1803, and to *Skirts of a Wood, with Cattle*,[6] one of the finest of his early drawings, which we may attribute to 1805. It is a curious phenomenon that while he followed Gainsborough so closely when working with chalk or pencil in this kind of woodland subject, his work in larger and more open landscape is almost invariably based upon reminiscences of the style of Girtin. That he knew the work of Willem Van de Velde, probably from prints or drawings in the possession of Sir George Beaumont, is shown by some drawings of 1803, in pencil and wash, of shipping on the Medway and in sketches of the *Victory* at Chatham, But when these studies culminated in the large drawing, of *The 'Victory' in the Battle of Trafalgar*,[7] exhibited in 1806, the more immediate influence of Girtin's colour and methods is distinctly seen.

In 1806 Constable made a sketching tour of about two months in Westmorland and Cumberland, and in the large number of drawings which he brought back the authority of Girtin's breadth, richness and solemnity can be clearly seen. None the less Constable was beginning to express his individual talent. He was already noting the effects of natural lighting, and grasping the value of design, both aims being apparent in his *A Bridge,*

[1] The date, 1799, given by Leslie and others, is corrected in Whitley, *1800–1820*, p. 13.
[2] Leslie, *op. cit.*, p. 10.   [3] V.A.M. 803 and 804–1888.
[4] Sir C. Holmes, *Constable, Gainsborough and Lucas*, 1921.
[5] V.A.M. 627–1888.   [6] V.A.M. 595–1888.
[7] V.A.M. 169–1888.

Borrowdale[1] (Pl. 39), inscribed on the back *Borrowdale Oct. 2, 1806—twylight after a very fine day*. Another admirable drawing of this year, belonging to a group which includes many compositions of singular dignity and majesty, is the *Sketch at Borrowdale*[2] inscribed '*Borrowdale 13 Oct. 1806—afternoon*'.[3]

For the next ten years or more, Constable made copious pencil notes, or washes of Indian ink, for hasty memoranda, but he employed water-colour more sparingly, and preferred oils for the studies on which he expected to base his larger works. To this period, in which the foundation of his reputation as a landscape painter in oil was well and truly laid, belongs his patient courtship of his future wife. As his first biographer pointed out, 'the affections of his heart were so inseparably blended with all that related to painting that it does not seem possible to give a true impression of his character as an artist without making the reader intimately acquainted with him in the private relations of life'. In 1811 he formed an attachment to Miss Maria Bicknell, but her father made an objection 'on the score of that necessary evil—money', and Maria wrote to her wooer, saying that she had been told to 'leave off a correspondence that is not calculated to make us think less of each other'. The father was not without right, for although Constable painted portraits rising to a top price of fifteen guineas in 1813, it was not till the next year, when he was thirty-eight, that he sold a single landscape to any but his friends. 'We have many painful trials required of us in this life', Maria wrote to Constable, 'and we must learn to bear them with resignation. You will still be my friend, and I will be yours.' He, however, surprised her by 'continuing sanguine on a subject altogether hopeless', although his own father advised him to defer all thoughts of marriage for the present. Correspondence, however, was followed by some stolen meetings, and in February 1815, Maria 'received from papa the sweet permission to see you again under this roof (to use his own words, 'as an occasional visitor'). 'From being perfectly wretched I am now comparatively happy'. So things went on till the summer of 1816, for Miss Bicknell's father and her grandfather Dr. Rhudde, the Rector of Bergholt, were still bitterly opposed to the marriage. Constable, whose parents were now dead, and who was making progress in his profession, wrote that she should cease to listen to any arguments; and, after all, Maria was twenty-nine, and entitled to determine for herself. In August 1816, Constable received a letter from his friend, John Fisher, afterwards Archdeacon Fisher, and at the time chaplain to his uncle, the Bishop of Salisbury. Fisher wrote, 'I intend to be in London on Tuesday evening, the 24th; and on Wednesday shall hold myself ready and happy to marry you. . . . So, do you follow my example and get you to your lady, &, instead of blundering out long sentences about "the hymeneal altar" etc, say that on Wednesday, September 25th, you are ready to marry her.' The lady, vowing that she would never consent without her father's approval, consented, and on October 2, 1816, the marriage took place. Mr. Bicknell did not long with-

---

[1] V.A.M. 188–1888.   [2] V.A.M. 193–1888.
[3] A fine Borrowdale drawing, of the same series, belonged to Randall Davies, and yet another to Sir Edward Marsh.

hold his forgiveness, and though Dr. Rhudde was not so soon reconciled, at least he left his grand-daughter, when he died in 1819, a legacy of £4000.

Constable's biography may be completed by saying that he was elected an Associate of the Royal Academy, in 1819, and by 1820 was settled at Hampstead with wife and children. His pencil drawing of *Fir Trees at Hampstead*[1] is inscribed *Wedding Day, Hampstead, Oct. 2, 1820.* Eight years later, however, just before his election as a full member of the Academy, his wife died, a blow from which he never quite recovered. 'Too late,' he sadly said. He died, nine years later in 1837.

During the time of his happy marriage Constable seems to have concentrated on oils, both for small and large subjects, except that about 1824–1825 he produced a group of beach subjects at Brighton, carefully drawn with pen, and slightly washed with colour. The *Old Houses, Harnham Bridge, Salisbury*[2] (Pl. 41) has always been ascribed to the year 1821 and has been regarded as marking a new achievement in Constable's career.[3] Actually it was not finished until ten years later. The catalogue entry gives 'Dated at back 1821' but I felt this date must be wrong and, on having the drawing re-mounted, the inscription was found to be *Houses on Harnham Bridge Salisbury Novr 1821 Retouch* [retouched] *at Hamp^d the day aftger the Coronation of W^m 4th, at which I was present—being eleven hours in the Abbey.* So this drawing, probably only a pencil sketch in 1821, was actually completed in colour on September 9, 1831. It shows how his use of the medium had developed since the days in which he was a follower of Girtin. He had now become himself, in subject, in movement of sky and in the contrast of gloom and silvery light. As Sir Charles Holmes said about this drawing,[4] 'he still retained much of Girtin's breadth of mass and richness of tone, but enlivens it with much more broken forms and glittering lights than his predecessor would have admitted'. All over the drawing—and this is a mark of his later practice —specks of light have been flicked out with the point of a sharp pen-knife.

Constable's full accomplishment in water-colour belongs to the years 1828 to 1834. It was at this later time that he wrote about the qualities which he chiefly aimed at in his pictures: 'light—dews—breezes—bloom—and freshness; not one of which has yet been perfected on the canvas of any painter in the world'.[5] He may have been thinking about his oils when he wrote those words, but they apply equally to his water-colours. One of the most perfect and most typical of these is the *Old Sarum in Storm*.[6] Dated June 1828, and six by seven inches in size, it seems to me more beautiful than the larger *Stonehenge, Wilts*[7] (Pl. 43), of 1835, which Constable himself described as a beautiful drawing. The *Old Sarum in Storm* is a vibrant, breezy sketch, all moist with rain under swollen clouds, full of the weather that comes 'between the thunder and the sun'. Almost more than any other water-colour by Constable, it has the solidity, massiveness and sparkling life of his work in

[1] V.A.M. 251–1888.　　　　　　　　　　　　　　　[2] V.A.M. 218–1888.
[3] See, for instance, Sir C. Holmes, *Constable and his Influence on Landscape Painting*, 1902, p. 163.
[4] *op. cit.*, p. 220.　　　　　　　　　　　　　　　　[5] Leslie, *op. cit.*, p. 270.
[6] Coll. Mr. and Mrs. Paul Mellon.　　　　　　　　[7] V.A.M. 1629–1888.

oil. He seems to have used this sketch when he painted, with more finish but much less freedom, his larger *Old Sarum*,[1] exhibited at the Royal Academy in 1834.

Though the Victoria and Albert Museum is particularly rich in work of this 1828–1834 period, there are several important drawings in the British Museum; one that is more completely finished as a picture than most being the *Stoke by Nayland*[2] (Pl. 42). In these later drawings he has developed further the looseness of style and the broken forms of his *Harnham Bridge*. He may have learned something from the work of David Cox, without following him as he had followed Girtin; at any rate, he works more often with separate, vibrant touches, rather than with an even wash. He has, as it were, stepped back across his drawings of the Brighton type and, after years of close study with pen and pencil, has returned to the much looser colour method of his early days. But the looseness is more controlled and intentional and, as might be expected, the structural content is more apparent. Constable was now drawing with brush as well as pencil, less consciously, but more effectively than in the early days. His work, therefore, seems to fall into three stages.

To 1833 belongs his *View at Hampstead, looking towards London*,[3] beautifully worked on a wet paper, a drawing clearly made from the house in Well Walk, Hampstead, which he occupied from 1826 onwards. 'This house is to my wife's content', he wrote, 'it is situated on an eminence, and our little drawing-room commands a view unsurpassed in Europe—from Westminster Abbey to Gravesend, the dome of St. Paul's in the air seems to realise Michael Angelo's words on seeing the Pantheon: "I will build such a thing in the sky."' Four similar sketches, with distant views of St. Paul's, are in the British Museum. As a point of technique, it is of note that, in the *View at Hampstead* and in his *Well Walk, Hampstead*,[4] 1834, he used the knife freely for his high lights, and in the latter case he clearly knew the trick of taking out lights with the wooden end of his brush while the colour is just beginning to dry. To this last period must belong the very advanced *Landscape Study*[5] (Pl. 44) which anticipates Wilson Steer, an artist who comes nearer to Constable than any other successor. Other drawings of this period include *Landscape*[6] in beautiful warm greys with a liquid touch of yellow in the sky, and *Fittleworth Bridge and Mill, Sussex*[7] (Pl. 45) of 1834, sketched in pencil and chalk which has been allowed to run into the wet colour. In a scheme of grey and silver, with touches of madder on the buildings, this is one of the most perfect and most spontaneous of Constable's water-colours.

During this period he found material for numerous drawings as well as oil-paintings in and around Salisbury. *Stonehenge, Wilts*[8] in the Victoria and Albert Museum was probably the most 'important' drawing, in size and finish, which Constable made, and was exhibited at the Royal Academy in 1836. Constable himself was pleased with it, for he wrote with pleasure to Leslie, on September 14, 1835,[9] 'I have made a beautiful drg. of Stone

[1] V.A.M. 1628–1888.
[2] B.M. 1888. 2.15.29.
[3] V.A.M. 220–1888.
[4] V.A.M. 175–1888.
[5] V.A.M. 203–1888.
[6] B.M. 1875. 8.14.1438.
[7] V.A.M. 273–1888.
[8] V.A.M. 1629–1888.
[9] Leslie, *op. cit.*, p. 306.

Henge; I venture to use such an expression to you.' That he regarded it very seriously is shown by the fact that he made many sketches of the subject before working out his theme. There are studies for it both in the British Museum and in the Victoria and Albert Museum. In the finished drawing Constable used what is a favourite device in his water-colours—that of making all the foreground very light against a sky of deep blue. With Constable the sky was never a painted cloth hung behind his trees and buildings, nor the 'white sheet behind a landscape', of which Reynolds spoke. It was always a deepening and extension in space of the enveloping atmosphere.

Constable's earlier work of 1801 to 1806 was done *en plein air*: this is shown not only by its character but also by notes indicating colour effects varying with the time of day. Knowing how much he made pencil notes out of doors, I am inclined to think that, though he made constant outdoor studies, particularly of sky effects, in oil, all his later water-colours were made indoors, chalk and ink and colour being added to the pencil note while the effect was fresh in his memory. This was certainly Turner's method, and, with regard to Constable, it is surmise based on a study of his later drawings. There is only one definite piece of evidence in support of it, that Fisher[1] wrote in 1825, to Constable, about an expected visit: 'We will wander home from the shore about dusk to the remnants of dinner, as heretofore, and spend the evening in filling up sketches.' Colour work added in this way is usually simple, and in his water-colours Constable's palette was certainly limited to very few colours. Then there is the fact of his water-colours frequently showing a join, as in a remarkable *Ruins of Cowdray*,[2] 1824, where a page of a sketch-book has been extended by a portion added at home. Finally, in a sketch-book at the Victoria and Albert Museum some of the drawings have been coloured, and an artist does not usually employ for out-door work in colour—with the paper blowing about and cockling when wet—a small book like this, about $4\frac{1}{2}$ in. × 7 in. in size. These three pieces of actual evidence derived from a study of his drawings all support the inference that his colour was applied later, often while the memory of the scene was still fresh.[3]

His drawings, whether in fact finished outdoors or at home, whether in black-and-white or in colour, remind us of Rembrandt's outdoor sketches. Constable's great predecessor in Holland was not thinking of picture-making, but just satisfying his own heart as he wandered about, noting such things as a barn and its uneven thatch, the light falling on a crumbling wall or a broken fence. In the same way Constable's sketches are delightfully fresh and intimate. Even more than the paintings they reveal the art of being careless of artistry. He never designed, like Cotman, in a definite pattern. His swift method did not allow for deliberation. But that is not to say that he was not a great composer, using cloud forms to weld earth and sky in happy union, and letting light and shade play with perfect pictorial contrast over balanced masses formed by windswept trees or mill or houses or

[1] Leslie, *op. cit.*, chapter IX.　　　　　　　　　　[2] B.M. 1888. 2.15.31.
[3] Holmes, *op. cit.*, p. 163, says that Constable worked from ten until six o'clock each day and it is difficult to find more than a few sketches which could not have been made after an early breakfast or within a quarter of an hour of sunset.

cathedral spire. Whatever is solid is enveloped in atmosphere; whatever is static is used to enhance an element of motion. Looking at a Constable gives the experience as of looking up into the sky, that the earth is really spinning and moving.

Constable had something to express, and he felt that if the result pleased others, so much the better; if not, he had satisfied his own soul—and that is how great art is made. Asked once by Vernon whether he had painted *The Valley Farm*[1] for anyone in particular: 'Yes', he said, 'for myself.' Again he wrote in 1832[2]: 'My limited and abstracted art is to be found under every hedge and in every lane, and therefore nobody thinks it worth picking up', and, later, on a scrap of paper, found among his memoranda: 'My art flatters nobody by *imitation*, it courts nobody by *smoothness*, it tickles nobody by *petiteness*, it is without either *fal-de-lal* or *fiddle-de-dee*; how then can I hope to be popular?'[3]

Ruskin, certainly, did not appreciate Constable. He wrote that 'Constable's reputation was most mischievous in giving countenance to the blotting and blundering of Modernism'. He also said that he had never seen any work of his 'in which there were any signs of his being able to draw'.[4] This, of the man who drew in pencil the *Fir Trees at Hampstead*,[5] 1820, and the *Cart and Horses*.[6] Ruskin was more unkind still when he wrote: 'Unteachableness seems to have been a main feature of his character, and there is a corresponding want of veneration in the way he approaches Nature herself. His early education and associations were also against him; they induced in him a marked preference for subjects of a low order.' Against these last remarks one may place a paragraph written by a contemporary of Constable in *The Athenaeum*[7] with reference to the publication of a set of mezzotints by David Lucas after Constable, with the title *English Landscape*:

> Constable has been unjustly accused of being a mannerist: Alas! how many a man of genius be condemned outright, or 'damned with faint praise,' by critics who never saw an honest 'bit of nature' in their lives. The mannerism lies at the door of nature, if mannerism there be. Living by, or within sight of, or in the mill (what matters where Genius condescends first to alight), Constable has watched and felt all the intricacies—all the sense, the solitude, the simplicity, the beauty of mill scenery;—and, heart in hand, he has dedicated himself to his native field, tree and water—knowing and feeling that in nature's plainest mood. there is a soul of beauty.

An even better reply to Ruskin was given by Constable himself in one of his lectures: 'The landscape painter must walk in the fields with a humble mind. No arrogant man was ever permitted to see nature in all her beauty; and, if I may be allowed to use a very solemn quotation, I would say most emphatically to the student, Remember now thy Creator in the days of thy youth.'

---

[1] Tate Gallery, 327.
[2] Leslie, *op. cit.*, p. 251.
[3] Leslie, *op. cit.*, p. 257.
[4] J. Ruskin, *Modern Painters*, I, Pt. II, Section I, 18; and III, Appendix I.
[5] V.A.M. 251–1888. William Blake once looked at a drawing of fir-trees—perhaps this very drawing—in one of Constable's note-books, and said, 'Why, this is not drawing, this is inspiration!' 'I never knew that before,' said Constable drily, 'I meant it for drawing.'
[6] V.A.M. 353–1888.
[7] June 26, 1830.

38 'Trees in a Meadow'

Coll. Mr & Mrs Paul Mellon $11\frac{1}{2} \times 9\frac{1}{2}$: 292 × 242   *Water-colour*

John CONSTABLE, R.A. (1776–1837)

39 'A Bridge, Borrowdale'

V.A.M. 188–1889 $7\frac{3}{8} \times 10\frac{5}{8}$: 187 × 270   *Water-colour*

John CONSTABLE, R.A. (1776–1837)

40 'Trees, Sky and Red House'

V.A.M. 594–1888 $6\frac{3}{4} \times 10 : 172 \times 254$ *Water-colour*

John Constable, R.A. (1776–1837)

41 'Old Houses, Harnham Bridge, Salisbury'
V.A.M. 218–1888 $6\frac{3}{4} \times 10\frac{1}{4}$: 172 × 260   *Water-colour*
John CONSTABLE, R.A. (1776–1837)

42 'Stoke-by-Nayland'

B.M. 1888.2.15.29 $5\frac{5}{8} \times 7\frac{3}{4}$: 143 × 197   *Water-colour*

John CONSTABLE, R.A. (1776–1837)

43 'Stonehenge, Wiltshire'
V.A.M. 1629–1888   11½ × 19: 292 × 482   *Water-colour*
John CONSTABLE, R.A. (1776–1837)

44 'Landscape Study'

V.A.M. 203–1888 $8\frac{3}{8} \times 7\frac{1}{8} : 212 \times 181$ *Water-colour*

John Constable, R.A. (1776–1837)

45 'Fittleworth Bridge and Mill'
V.A.M. 273–1888   8 × 10¼: 209 × 260   *Pencil and water-colour*
John CONSTABLE, R.A. (1776–1837)

46 'An Estuary'
Oxford, Ashmolean Museum   7¾ × 11¾: 198 × 298   *Water-colour*
Thomas CHURCHYARD (1798–1865)

The result of the exhibition of his *Hay Wain* and two other pictures in 1824 at the Paris Salon is well known. It was in Paris that Hazlitt, the conservative critic of his day, saw a Constable, and like the most advanced French painters of his time was pleased with its 'green, fresh and healthy look of living Nature'.

His fame rests, perhaps too much, on the infinite variety of his masterly work in oils. With regard to his water-colours, he could never be described, as he was by Delacroix, as '*le père de notre école de paysage*'. Water-colour, a lighter, more gentle, and more tender medium, did not allow him to present Nature with all the force and flexibility and solidity that he could obtain with oils. In water-colour he was more restrained, but here too he brought novelty and freshness into British art. His water-colours, in his own phrase applied to his *Lock*, are 'silvery, windy and delicious, all health, and the absence of anything stagnant'. Infinite peace and greenness are in them, sunshine and heat, rain and cloud. None before him obtained such movement, such broken jagged edges, such fret and scurry, in his clouds—and such movement, not only in the clouds, but in the flying shadows that sweep over the landscape beneath.

In the Library of the Victoria and Albert Museum is a copy of *Songs Divine and Moral; for the use of Children* by the Rev. Isaac Watts, D.D., published in 1832, which was decorated in water-colour by Constable as a birthday gift to his little daughter Emily, and bears the inscription on a flyleaf: *Emily Constable a birthday present from her dear Papa By whom the pictures were painted on purpose for her 1833*. The half-title has a little extra picture, of a hovering dove, and against the line 'Let dogs delight to bark and bite,' Constable has written, *For Landseer!* With the book is a letter dated March 25, 1833:

> Dearest Emily I send you my most affectionate good wishes on your birthday—hoping always [you will] be as happy and as good as you now are—and still to go on improving in all good things as you have done. You asked for your hymn book I therefore send it to you and Liza has made you a cake

I remain
My dear child
Your most affectionate father John Constable.

Preserved with the same volume is a letter from Constable, dated March 27, 1833, written to his son Charles. The beginning of this is of general interest, where it says:

> I well remember your birth day—I was about the large picture of the Waggon crossing the River which went to Paris—and for the painting of which I received the largest of my gold medals inscribed with my name *John Constable Peintre du Paysage London* . . . I have coloured all the little pictures in Dr. Watts' hymn book for dear Emily to be sent to her on her birthday—it looks very pretty.

Those letters show his kindly and benevolent spirit, and his last mission on the evening of March 31, 1837 was on a charitable errand connected with the Artists' General Benevolent Institution.[1] Within an hour or two after his return he was dead.

---

[1] Leslie wrongly says that Constable's errand was in connection with the 'Artists' Benevolent Fund'. Constable was a member of the Council of the Artists' General Benevolent Institution from May 1818 until his death. The Minutes show that he attended his last Council Meeting on March 30, 1837.

For reasons which have been stated Constable had little influence upon the water-colour work of his contemporaries. But the art of the later nineteenth century was profoundly affected by knowledge of his work, particularly in the case of Wilson Steer.

This chapter may appropriately close with brief reference to an amateur artist, Thomas Churchyard (1798–1865). He was a Suffolk lawyer and a bosom friend of Edward Fitzgerald, the translator of Omar Khayyám, and of Bernard Barton, the Quaker poet and friend of Charles Lamb. The trio were known locally as 'the three Wits of Woodbridge'. Churchyard was one of the earliest admirers and collectors of the work of the Norwich School, in particular of John Crome, whom, according to an obituary notice in 1865, 'he studied and copied with such exactitude as . . . to deceive the most eminent connoisseurs'. Making sketches in the heart of the Constable country, at Woodbridge, Manningtree, and other places on the Stour, and at Harwich, Churchyard produced many drawings which are more than a 'colourable imitation' of Constable. Here and there, during recent years, since Churchyard has become better known, some well-known collector has had to re-attribute a 'Constable' drawing. Fortunately these pious deceptions were not the only result of his artistic ability. He had always been a keen nature lover and student of botany; and the power of accurate and sensitive observation thus developed was beautifully manifested in his personal water-colour sketches of Suffolk scenery, which have all the virtues of the best amateur work.

CHAPTER IV

The Norwich School

John Crome   John Thirtle   James Stark
Henry Ninham   Joseph Stannard   E. T. Daniell
Thomas Lound   Henry Bright   John Middleton

From his death in 1821 till about the end of the nineteenth century John Crome was an inconspicuous figure, and his work was insufficiently appreciated. It is true that in 1823, two years after Crome's decease, a London newspaper stated that: 'Mr. Crome may be regarded as the founder of a school of landscape which promises to do credit to its ingenious preceptor and to identify the county of Norfolk with the arts. Future connoisseurs will talk of Constable and Gainsborough, of Crome and Vincent and Stark, as the old English masters. . . . The city of Norwich of late years has merited the approbation and applause of the metropolitan artists, from the number of landscape painters and draftsmen who have successfully studied the arts within its ancient walls.' But Crome's position as one of the great painters of the British School was far from being established. He had never become even an Associate of the Royal Academy; he was not deemed worthy of a place in Cunningham's *British Painters* in 1833. His *Mousehold Heath, Norwich*, painted 'for air and space', was sold by him for £25 to William Yetts of Great Yarmouth, and in 1862 the nation bought it from Mr. Yetts for £420, a respectable but not a memorable sum, especially if it be recalled that in the following year a water-colour by Copley Fielding realised 760 guineas in the sale-room. The reassessment of Crome really began in 1897 with Laurence Binyon's *John Crome and John Sell Cotman* and was finally secured by Collins Baker's *Crome* of 1921. But, even so, he remains underrated as a water-colour painter.

'Old Crome', as he became known in distinction from his son, John Berney Crome, lived quietly and obscurely in Norwich. The narrative of his life would occupy a small space if he had not been the founder of the Norwich School, and if James Reeve, tenth Curator of the Norwich Museum (housed since 1894 in the square Norman keep that dominates the city) had not assembled much documentary material which passed in 1902, along with his splendid collection of drawings by Crome, Cotman and others, into the possession of the British Museum. Reeve's long life was spent in amassing and annotating virtually every scrap of information relating to the Norwich School. His memory of

Crome's pictures went back almost to 1850, a period before, as Sir Charles Holmes[1] said, 'The Old Crome (sometimes spelt with an "h") of sale-room catalogues, a many-headed monster, had engulfed in his fraudulent carcase a whole host of forgotten—and deservedly forgotten—relatives, pupils and forgers of the real man.'

John Crome (1768–1821) was born at Norwich where his father, the inn-keeper at 'The Griffin', was said by some to have been a journeyman-weaver as well. John was born eight years before Constable, seven before Turner, fourteen before Cotman. The Royal Academy, with Reynolds as its president, was founded in the year of Crome's birth. After an education of the slightest, he became errand-boy in a doctor's surgery at the age of twelve. In 1783, then fifteen, the little boy at 'The Griffin' sought a man's work, and was apprenticed to Francis Whisler, painter of houses, coaches, carriage panels and inn-signs. As an apprentice he learned sufficient of the trade and mystery of mixing and mani-pulating colours to enable him later to produce *The Poringland Oak*. There, too, he had as fellow-apprentice, Robert Ladbrooke. They were to marry sisters, and both of them were inspired by the same artistic ambition which was to culminate in the foundation of the Norwich School. It was a help to Crome in the freeing of himself from the journeyman painter's trade that he had access to the collection, at Catton House, of Thomas Harvey, a typical dilettante amateur painter, etcher and collector of the day. Crome copied some of his landscapes by Hobbema and Richard Wilson, and at the same time met Sir William Beechey, R.A., who said: 'Crome, when I first knew him, was an awkward, un-formed country lad, but shrewd in all his remarks on art, though he wanted words to express his meaning.' And, before 1800, his portrait was painted by Opie, who had successfully courted the beautiful Amelia Alderson of Norwich, afterwards well-known as Mrs. Opie the novelist. Among such people, and at the home of the Gurneys, the great Quaker bankers of Norwich, Crome's character developed and his ambition took shape.

In 1792, two years after his indentures with Whisler ran out, he married and was making some money by the sale of occasional pictures and as a drawing-master. Mottram[2] gives in full his account for supplying paper, pencils and other material to Master Sparshall, son of a Quaker wine-merchant, his tuition fee for the half-year being one guinea. In 1798 he was appointed drawing-master to the charming young daughters of John Gurney. One of those daughters was to win fame and national gratitude as Elizabeth Fry. There is an entry, for January 17, 1798, in the diary of Richenda, aged fifteen: 'I had a good drawing morning, but in the course of it gave way to passion with both Crome and Betsy [Elizabeth, then aged seventeen]—Crome because he would attend to Betsy and not to me, and Betsy because she was so provoking.' A few years later, Elizabeth, who had become a 'strict Friend', protested against the vanity of portraiture, and refused to look at the portrait which Opie was painting of her father.

[1] C. H. Collins-Baker, *Crome*, 1921 (intro. by Sir Charles Holmes, p. xxi).
[2] R. H. Mottram, *John Crome of Norwich*, 1931, p. 71.

Crome thus became the good-natured 'Young Ladies' Drawing Master', teaching the rudiments of sketching in Earlham Park to five or six pupils, and accompanying the Gurney family, as their drawing-master in 1802 and later, on one or more trips to the Lakes, where 'Mr. Gurney showed Crome a mountain for the first time.' It is of special interest that he was at Ambleside with the Gurneys in the summer of 1806, for during September and October of that year Constable was busy making his Cumberland sketches. Both were men of the plains, and while Crome once used his mountain knowledge, Constable, after all the wonderful studies of that tour and the finished works that resulted from them, never painted a mountain again. Crome probably never had time. As holiday companion and drawing-master during all these years he worked seven days a week, Sunday being his only day for painting his own pictures.

In 1801 he is entered in the Norwich Directory as 'John Crome, Drawing-Master'. His pupils in various country-houses were probably as many as he could manage, and, like a country doctor, he had to keep two horses to do his rounds. On February 19, 1803 was founded the Norwich Society. Its avowed purpose was characteristic of those wonderful years, and beggars any other description of its aims: 'An enquiry into the Rise, Progress and Present State of Painting, Architecture, and Sculpture with a view to point out the Best Methods of Study to attain to Greater Perfection in these Arts.'[1] Crome and his brother-in-law, Robert Ladbrooke, were members from the start. The Society's first exhibition of pictures was held in 1805 at Wrench's Court, the unoccupied mansion of Sir Benjamin Wrench, a physician. Seven out of the score of exhibitors bear names that have come to be included in what is now called the Norwich School; and the list of thirty-seven names of artists whose works composed the Norwich School Exhibition of 1927 can now be accepted as a complete record of the members of the school. Crome contributed twenty-two exhibits to the Society's first exhibition, many of which have been identified by Dickes[2] as sketches or water-colours, nearly half of them made during his northern or Welsh holidays, whether with the Gurneys or alone.

In 1806 he exhibited two landscapes at the Royal Academy, and it was in this year that Cotman joined the Society and made the superb pencil and wash drawing of Crome's close-cropped bullet head, which is now in the British Museum.[3] In 1807 Crome was Vice-President and became President of the Society in 1808, when Robert Ladbrooke was Vice-President, and Cotman became a full member. Young John Berney Crome exhibited, at the age of thirteen, three oil paintings and two drawings, while in 1810 appeared two pencil drawings by Master James Stark (then aged fifteen) possibly the best pupil Crome ever had. In that year Cotman became Vice-President. In 1811 George Vincent made his first contribution to the Society's exhibition, and a little later, Joseph Stannard, a pupil of Ladbrooke, joined the ranks. Thus, with contemporaries and pupils and children, there

[1] Mottram, *op. cit.*, p. 107.
[2] W. F. Dickes, *The Norwich School of Painting*, 1905.
[3] B.M. 1885. 5.9.1399.

was gathering around Crome the circle of painters whom we now call the Norwich School. 'Norwich was the only place', says Binyon,[1] 'which possessed artists of sufficient strength to create a rival centre to London, and the Norwich School would not have been possible had Crome left his native city for London, like every other genius of the provinces.'

In 1811 Crome was not only still teaching members of the Gurney family, but was drawing-master at Miss Heazel's Seminary in Tolls' Court, Briggs Lane, and in 1813 became the Grammar School drawing-master. Among his pupils were George Borrow, and James Brooke, afterwards Rajah of Sarawak. A year or two later, in 1816, there was a rift in his friendship with Robert Ladbrooke, who formally withdrew from the Norwich Society and started one of his own, the Norfolk and Norwich Society of Artists. He took with him Thirtle, who as a water-colour painter stands not far below Crome and Cotman in modern estimation, and his own pupil, Joseph Stannard. The Norwich Society flourished, however, and under the presidency of Mr. Coppin (Crome's companion during an excursion to Paris in 1814), opened an exhibition containing 269 works. After holding three annual exhibitions the rival Society, with dwindling members, gave up the contest, and most of the original adherents drifted back into Crome's fold. After Crome's death, John Berney Crome followed in his father's footsteps as President. Thomas Lound was a notable recruit, Cotman far and away its greatest mainstay, if not its most prolific contributor, and Robert Ladbrooke, as the result of probably 'inspired' correspondence in the Press, exhibited with the Society. Crome's untimely decease was due to a chill; he died in his fifty-third year. In his delirium he fancied himself at the easel in his Blue Room completing a masterpiece. On the day of his death he addressed to his son the words so often quoted: 'John, my boy, paint, but paint only for fame; and if your subject is only a pigsty, dignify it.'

Crome's subjects tended northward and eastward to Cromer and Yarmouth beach, southward to the Suffolk border, and west to the villages of mid-Norfolk, but Norwich (particularly Mousehold Heath) was his spiritual home. Living and working within the microcosm of a small part of Norfolk, Crome to that extent was parochial in his art, as Constable was, as Turner never was. Crome and Constable, each within the limits of a circumscribed corner of England, found a universal sky and beneath it an epitome of all English landscape. Like Constable, Crome painted just what he found about him: the open heath, the country lane, the rich brown of the earth, the yellow of a sand-pit, the red of a cottage roof, the particular character of English trees.

Crome's water-colours are rare, but far from negligible, and they show the same colour as his oils, the same muted employment of cream and umber and pale grey, the same unity and spaciousness. He used water-colour in simple washes to enhance his work in chalk or pencil; he made no technical experiments. His water-colours, like his etchings, were done 'for pleasure or remembrance', or possibly as preparatory notes for his oil-

[1] Laurence Binyon, *John Crome and John Sell Cotman*, 1897, p. 6.

paintings. Like Gainsborough, he was content with economy of colour, so long as the forms and tones were justly recorded. The accents were lights sketched with pen, and the colour applied in notes rather than in complete washes. There is a certain sameness, a certain timidity, about his tree subjects in water-colour, yet their knowledge and their peaceful colour lends them special charm. A typical *River Scene*[1] is in a quiet scheme of grey, grey-green and yellow. Several good examples of his water-colour work are in the British Museum, among them *The Hollow Road*[2] with its great white cloud adding to its grandeur of conception, and a *Study of Trees*,[3] a perfectly balanced design in contrast of light and shade. This drawing, dating between 1800 and 1807, was originally given by Crome to Madame de Rouillon, who with her two sisters, the Misses Silke, established a ladies' school at the Chantry, Norwich, in 1795. Crome taught at the school and was their personal friend. Most would agree with Binyon that the finest of Crome's water-colours is the *Landscape with Cottages*[4] (Pl. 47) (actually a view up a lane, with cottages under trees on the right and called *The Shadowed Road* by Collins Baker[5]). The colour, and the flicker of light and shadow, have peculiar charm; and it is a drawing in which the actual laying of the colour, in carefully superimposed washes, shows an affinity with the work of Cotman in his early period. Outstanding also in the Victoria and Albert Museum collection are *Old Houses at Norwich*,[6] and the *Wood Scene*[7] (the Castle Museum, Norwich has another version). Collins Baker reproduces two good examples, a *Blacksmith's Shop*[8] and *Houses and Wherries on the Wensom*.[9] Two drawings which show how spacious and dignified Crome's work could be are the *River through Trees*[10] and *The Blasted Oak*.[11] (Pl. 50)

In many of Crome's drawings their golden tint is due to the fading, through exposure, of the stronger green and blue of the original colours. *River Scene* and *Study of Trees*, already mentioned, are typical of this slightly decolourised harmony. Crome did not, like Girtin, make deliberately what Turner describes as 'Girtin's golden drawings'. The autumnal tints, of which I have spoken, are in fact autumnal; time and sunlight and the passing of the seasons have had their mellowing effect. Dickes calls them 'sallow', a good and descriptive word. Or one might say 'sere', a word still used in Norfolk and Suffolk meaning dry or parched. Perhaps Crome used the cheap, possibly fugitive colours, especially an indifferent indigo, which were supplied by some Norwich stationer to Master Sparshall and his other pupils. Perhaps he made them himself, with little knowledge of the chemical property of powdered pigments, and with the use of an indifferent or insufficient binding material. In London colours of a wide range were obtainable and water-colour painters whenever they congregated would discuss the merits and quality of particular pigments. But Norwich was remote and was only in its beginnings as an artistic centre. I suggest that

[1] Coll. Sir Stephen Courtauld.
[2] B.M. 1902. 5.14.374.
[3] B.M. 1902. 5.14.373.
[4] V.A.M. 620–1877.
[5] C. H. Collins Baker, *Crome*, 1921, p. 45.
[6] V.A.M. S. Ex. 8–1885.
[7] V.A.M. 1749–1871.
[8] Coll. Miss Ethel Colman.
[9] Manchester University, Whitworth Art Gallery.
[10] Coll. Sir Edmund Bacon, Bt.
[11] Coll. Sir Edmund Bacon, Bt.

from about 1800 to 1810 Crome, and Cotman in his early work, used a limited supply of indifferent colours, and that a part cause of Cotman's change from the lovely muted schemes of his early drawings to an urge for florid brilliance was due to his discovery in London of more reliable colours in a much wider range. The unaccustomed stimulant went to Cotman's head.

The fact that Norwich was a great school of etching as well as of painting seems never to have received adequate recognition. In his chapter in *Etching and Etchers* on the revival of etching in England, P. G. Hamerton ignores the men of Norwich as though they had never existed. Sir Frederick Wedmore in his *Etching in England* does scant justice to Crome and Cotman, but never mentions Vincent, Daniell, Ninham, Stannard and the rest. Later books have given due credit to Crome, Cotman and Daniell, but it still remains for Stannard's brilliant etched line to win general esteem. Yet it is in this Norwich School that the modern revival of etching really began, and in their hands etching became in this country a living art, instead of a mechanical adjunct to engraving, useful merely for producing topographical views or for multiplying designs. Crome was the first Englishman of any note—except Gainsborough—to take up etching for its own sake. How Crome and Cotman learnt to work in the rare method of 'soft-ground', which each of them used so perfectly between 1800 and 1815 is for me a mystery.[1]

Crome's etchings were for him the idle amusement of an empty day, bits of personal observation, records of rambles through East Anglian lanes or tangled woods or by winding stream. They were done as a relaxation from drawing lessons or after his larger work on canvas. Some ill-bitten, careless proofs were given to his friends, Dawson Turner among them, but Crome himself set no great store by them, and though in 1812 he issued a prospectus for their publication and gathered the names of a number of subscribers, he seems finally to have shrunk from the responsibility of issuing them to the world. The Print Room at the British Museum possesses a fine collection of Crome's work, made complete and indeed unique from the series of seven hundred etchings of the Norwich School acquired from the collection of James Reeve whose manuscript catalogue and notes furnish reliable information as to the history of the etchings both before and after publication. It was not till 1834, thirteen years after Crome's death, that a set of thirty-one of his plates was published at Norwich by his widow and son in a folio volume bearing the title *Norfolk Picturesque Scenery*. Four years later at Norwich there were two issues, one consisting of seventeen of the hard-ground plates, the other of the complete set of thirty-one. The volume was entitled *Etchings of Views in Norfolk, by the late John Crome . . . with a Biographical Memoir by Dawson Turner*. In the Reeve collection is a set of the earlier proofs, which have been retouched by Crome's son, and the following note: 'The etchings which form this set

---

[1] Mr. Alec Cotman's information is that Cotman learnt the method in London and probably taught Crome. Dickes suggests that Crome owed some of his knowledge of etching to Thomas Harvey, who possibly owned a copper-plate printing-press. (See Dickes, *op. cit.*, pp. 85, 126.) Several soft-ground etchings and pencil studies by Harvey are in the B.M. Print Room.

with the exception of two, show the alterations made by John Berney Crome with the brush and pencil and the names of the subjects written in ink for Henry Ninham's guidance for the rebiting, etc. of the plates. . . . The original sky of the *Mousehold Heath* was removed by Ninham, and afterwards sent by Dawson Turner to W. C. Edwards, Engraver, Bungay, who added the ruled sky and made other objectionable alterations as seen in the later impressions.' This note treats the matter with extreme mildness, for it was unpardonable to use machine-ruled lines to replace a sky by Crome, and to issue these plates, botched and bungled by some hack, re-working Crome's delicate, free lines, as etchings by Crome. Even in 1850 the series was republished by Charles Muskett, and the plates remained in the possession of Ninham till 1860, when they were purchased by John Hutton of Norwich. Hutton added a soft-ground etching which had not been published before, and issued a hundred sets in a portfolio with the title, *Thirty-two Original Etchings of Norfolk, by Old Crome*. Crome should not be judged as an etcher without seeing his early impressions in the Print Room at the British Museum.

Crome was not a draughtsman like Cotman. He was a fine colourist, seeing the large masses and contrasts, painting air and space; but his figures are often ill-drawn and entirely out of scale (as instanced by the figure in his fine oil-painting of *Mousehold Heath* in the Victoria and Albert Museum); and drawing, in the sense of precise, expressive line, was a trouble to him. On this point Kaines Smith[1] has advanced an interesting theory as to the relationship between Crome's paintings and his etchings. The etchings were not the kind of thing to take the public eye, there was no market for them, they were tentative, and hesitant in technique. Kaines Smith suggests that they were the work of a man conscious of his own disability, who felt that he must force himself to face the intricacy and detail of the forms that challenged him. That is one reason. The other was—and this is still Kaines Smith's theory—that these etchings were not made as etchings, but as studies of composition and tone (the wonderful little etching of cattle under trees with a spacious distance on the right is a case in point) which he meant to use and develop. They gave him his structure and his masses; and the fact that so many counterproofs exist shows that Crome really intended to view his subject pictorially as he had first seen it, and not with the change given by reversal in the printing of the plates. It is important also to note that many proofs exist with washes and blots of monochrome, suggesting that Crome was working out his pictorial scheme, yet was always holding tight to his structural scaffolding.

I cannot better end these notes upon Crome than by quoting Borrow's famous panegyric.[2] The writer's brother was about to study art in Rome, full of youthful enthusiasm, hastening to bow before Raphael's *Transfiguration*, to him the greatest work of the greatest painter the world had known.

Seekest thou inspiration? Thou needest it not, thou hast it already; and it was never yet found by crossing the sea. What hast thou to do with old Rome, and thou an Englishman? . . . Seek'st

[1] S. C. Kaines Smith, *Crome*, 1923.

[2] *Lavengro*, chapter XXI.

models? To Gainsborough and Hogarth turn, not names of the world, may be, but English names—and England against the world! A living master? why, there he comes! thou hast had him long, he has long guided thy young hand towards the excellence which is yet far from thee, but which thou canst attain if thou shouldst persist and wrestle, even as he has done, midst gloom and despondency—ay, and even content; he who now comes up the creaking stair to thy little studio in the second floor to inspect thy last effort before thou departest, the little stout man whose face is very dark, and whose eye is vivacious; that man has attained excellence, destined some day to be acknowledged, though not till he is cold, and his mortal part returned to its kindred clay. He has painted, not pictures of the world, but English pictures, such as Gainsborough himself might have done; beautiful rural pieces, with trees which might well tempt the little birds to perch upon them: thou needest not run to Rome, brother, where lives the old Mariolater, after pictures of the world, whilst at home there are pictures of England; nor needest thou even go to London, the big city, in search of a master, for thou hast one at home in the old East Anglian town who can instruct thee whilst thou needest instruction: better stay at home, brother, at least for a season, and toil and strive midst groanings and despondency till thou hast attained excellence as he has done—the little dark man with the brown coat and the top-boots, whose name will one day be considered the chief ornament of the old town, and whose works will at no distant period rank among the proudest pictures of England—and England against the world!—thy master, my brother, thy, at present, all too little considered master—Crome.

George Borrow was an East Anglian who had lived among Crome's subjects and he understood his art. 'The wind on the heath': 'trees which might well tempt the little birds to perch upon them'—that was what Crome painted. 'The wind on the heath' connotes the sky; Crome, like Constable, or like Boudin was a master of skies. In a letter to his old pupil, James Stark,[1] comes the passage: 'Do not distress us with accidental trifles in Nature, but keep the masses large and in good and beautiful lines, and give the sky, which plays so important a part in all landscape, and so supreme a one in our low-level lines of distance, the prominence it deserves, and in the coming years the posterity you paint for shall admire your work.'

Although Cotman is the subject of the following chapter it seems appropriate here to refer to other members of the Norwich School, some of whom have been briefly mentioned as belonging to the Norwich Society. After Crome and Cotman the outstanding member of the School, so far as water-colour is concerned, is John Thirtle. He has been overshadowed by Crome and Cotman, but he falls not far short of them at times, and is a much better artist than Vincent, Stark and others who have become better known by their landscapes in oil. In the field of water-colour alone, Thirtle may well be considered a greater artist than Crome; the rarity of his known work is the reason for his relative neglect.

John Thirtle (1777–1839), the son of a shoemaker, was born at Norwich. He tried his hand at miniature painting, and after a period in London, learning the trade of a frame-maker, carver and gilder, returned in 1800 and set up a business in his native town. He was a foundation member of the Norwich Society, and exhibited at the Royal Academy in 1808. He married in 1812 Elizabeth Miles, whose sister Ann had become Cotman's wife in

---

[1] Quoted by W. G. Rawlinson, *Turner's Liber Studiorum*, 1906, p. lii.

1809. He died at Norwich and was buried in the Rosary Cemetery, Thorpe Hamlet. The late Sydney Kitson owned three drawings which had been copied by Thirtle from Joshua Cristall, and he suggested to me that in the 'frame-making' period of Thirtle's life he was wont to sell frames containing a copy of his own miniature work as wall furniture. Thirtle contributed five drawings to the Norwich Society's exhibition in 1805, before his brother-in-law, Cotman, became a member. He was five years senior to Cotman, and it seems possible that the example of his work, quite different from that of Crome, helped to form Cotman's style; but, unless one could find dated drawings by each, of 1800 to 1805, it would be difficult to say how much, and to what extent, one influenced the other. As with any two artists working in close touch there was probably give and take. At any rate, Thirtle and Cotman in the opening years of the century were bringing something new into water-colour, something based perhaps on the methods and teaching of Varley, but different from the art of J. R. Cozens, Sandby, Dayes, Turner and Girtin. They were definitely painting in a decorative manner, seeking out a simplification of shapes, working flatly and somewhat disregarding shadow except for its value as part of their design. It is work which allows no room for frills or excrescences; it is constructed upon a well-planned armature. Like Cotman in his early period, Thirtle loved the subtleties of form, rendered in colour which is refined and subdued, and rich in quality not because of its strength but because of its perfect relationship between tone and tone, delicately matched and interwoven to form a harmonious whole. There can be no better example of this than *The River, King Street, Norwich*.[1] This is a drawing which shows all the careful selection, the flat spaced-out patterning, the 'left' spaces, which characterise an early Cotman. It is superb in its dark accents, its rightness of tone and beauty, its soft russets and greys like cloud shadows over a summer sea. The same beauty of colour, in half-tones of grey, yellow and brown is shown in *Old Waterside Cottages*,[2] in *Fye Bridge*[3] (Pl. 51), and the even finer *Whitefriars Bridge*,[4] very subtle in its tones of white and grey. A *Sion House*[5] is fresh in colour, with the foreground boat and figures excellently put in. A good example of his lighter, more delicate manner, is his drawing, in the Ashmolean Museum, *A Waterfall* of two figures under a cascade. But there are two sides to Thirtle's art, and his London drawings are often inferior, because they were more ambitious and more forced.

The British Museum contains over a dozen fine examples of Thirtle's art; and one of the many volumes of Reeve's collectanea[6] contains manuscript notes, newspaper cuttings and other matter relating to Thirtle. Fine examples of his earlier and simpler manner, on an absorbent toned paper, before he discovered Whatman paper and a fuller range of colours, are the *Tan Yard, Norwich*,[7] *Old Foundry Bridge, Norwich*[8] (Pl. 52), and *The Devil's Tower*.[9]

[1] V.A.M. P.26–1926.
[2] Manchester, City Art Gallery.
[3] Norwich, Castle Museum.
[4] Norwich, Castle Museum.
[5] Coll. Mr. and Mrs. Tom Girtin.
[6] B.M. 167. c.9.
[7] B.M. 1902. 5.14.382.
[8] B.M. 1902. 5.14.482.
[9] Norwich, Castle Museum.

What has been said about the fading of Crome's drawings applies to much of Thirtle's work. Like Crome, he seems to have used a fugitive blue, probably of an indigo type. One meets what must once have been fine drawings by him, now faded to almost uniform tints of brown and Indian red; the Norwich Museum has works of this nature, from which the blue has almost entirely disappeared.

James Stark (1794–1859), born at Norwich, was the third son of a Scottish dyer who had settled in Norfolk. From 1811 to 1814 he was a pupil of John Crome, and in 1812 became a member of the Norwich Society. In 1814 he went to London, where he was influenced by his friendship with W. Collins, R.A., the father of Wilkie Collins, and in 1817 became a student in the Royal Academy Schools. He and George Vincent were at one time next-door neighbours at 85 and 86, Newman Street. From about 1818 to 1830 he lived at Norwich and Yarmouth, but for the remainder of his life from 1830 to 1859, he was resident at Windsor or in London. Stark painted landscapes, chiefly in oils, but produced a large number of cleanly worked, thoroughly competent, water-colours of rural subjects and of scenes on the Norfolk coast.

Henry Ninham (1793–1874), a good but inconspicuous member of the Norwich School, was born at 11, Chapel Field, Norwich, the son of John Ninham, heraldic painter and engraver. He was for many years employed in painting armorial bearings on coaches, produced many etchings and lithographs, and contributed oil- and water-colour paintings to the Norwich Society's exhibitions from 1816 to 1831. The British Museum contains a water-colour *Interior of St. James's Church, Norwich*,[1] showing the influence of Cotman in its precise drawing and simple colour scheme; and *Lakenham Mills*,[2] which is an admirably direct drawing in the manner of Thirtle, with white spaces of the paper left untouched for a horse and figures; like Thirtle too in its clever dispositions of darks. In the Victoria and Albert Museum is a *Quay Side, Norwich*,[3] by Thirtle, which after his death was finished by Ninham. Like Crome and Cotman, Ninham clung to Norwich, and died in the house where he was born.

Joseph Stannard (1797–1830) studied for seven years under Robert Ladbrooke, and worked in Holland during 1821–1822. At Norwich from 1816 to 1830 he exhibited marine and river subjects, and practised etching, as noted above. But for his early death he might have become a more prominent member of the School.

One of the most interesting figures of the Norwich School is the Rev. E. T. Daniell (1804–1842), a prosperous amateur—but not really an amateur, because art was the core of his existence and the Church a side-issue. Edward Thomas Daniell was born in Charlotte Street, Fitzroy Square, London. On the death of his father, a retired Attorney-General of the Island of Dominica, at his residence, Snettisham Lodge, Norfolk, the widow and son removed to 68, St. Giles' Street, Norwich, and a few years later Edward was sent to the Grammar School, where he was taught drawing by John Crome. With a view to taking

---

[1] B.M. 1902.5.14.448.   [2] B.M. 1902.5.14.447.   [3] V.A.M. 23–1874.

47 'Landscape with Cottages'

V.A.M. 620–1877 $20\frac{1}{2} \times 16\frac{3}{4}$: 522 × 425   *Water-colour*

John CROME (1768–1821)

48 'Palings and Tree by a Pond'
B.M. 1902.5.14.381 $4\frac{3}{4} \times 10\frac{3}{4}$: 121 × 274   *Water-colour*
John CROME (1768–1821)

49 'A Boat Load'
Coll. Mr & Mrs Paul Mellon $4\frac{7}{8} \times 9\frac{1}{8}$: 124 × 232   *Water-colour*
John CROME (1768–1821)

50 'The Blasted Oak'
Coll. Sir Edmund Bacon Bt. $23 \times 17\frac{1}{4}: 584 \times 438$ *Water-colour*
John Crome (1768–1821)

51 'Fye Bridge, Norwich'
Norwich, Castle Museum $7\frac{1}{8} \times 10\frac{7}{8}$: 181 × 276   *Water-colour*
John THIRTLE (1777–1839)

52 'The Old Foundry Bridge, Norwich'
B.M. 1902.5.14.382 $5\frac{3}{4} \times 8\frac{5}{8}$: 147 × 220   *Water-colour*
John THIRTLE (1777–1839)

53 'The River, King Street, Norwich'
V.A.M. P.26–1926   15 × 17¾ : 379 × 451   *Water-colour*
John Thirtle (1777–1839)

54 'Church Interior'

Oxford, Ashmolean Museum   10¾ × 14⅜ : 274 × 364   *Water-colour*

John Thirtle (1777–1839)

55 'Rochester'

Oxford, Ashmolean Museum $7\frac{1}{2} \times 13\frac{3}{4}$: 190×348 *Water-colour*

James STARK (1794–1859)

56 'Pull's Ferry, Norwich'

Norwich, Castle Museum $9 \times 10\frac{1}{2}$: 229×267 *Water-colour*

James STARK (1794–1859)

58 'Smiling Girl in a Bonnet'
Coll. Mr Alec Cotman
$2\frac{7}{8} \times 2\frac{1}{2}$: 73×63
Water-colour
Joseph STANNARD (1797–1830)

57 'Meadow near a Village'
V.A.M. A.L. 9183 $8\frac{3}{4} \times 11\frac{1}{4}$: 222×286 *Water-colour*
Joseph STANNARD (1797–1830)

59 'Fishing Party'
V.A.M. D.500–1889 $8\frac{1}{8} \times 7\frac{1}{2}$: 206×190 *Water-colour*
Joseph STANNARD (1797–1830)

60 'Lakenham Mills'

B.M. 1902.5.14.447   4½ × 6: 115 × 150   *Water-colour*

Henry NINHAM (1793–1874)

61 'Ely Cathedral'

Norwich, Castle Museum   12⅞ × 25⅜: 327 × 643   *Water-colour*

Thomas LOUND (1802–1861)

62 'Burgh Bridge, Aylsham, Norfolk'
Norwich, Castle Museum $9\frac{1}{4} \times 16\frac{1}{8}$: 235×409 *Water-colour*
Rev. Edward Thomas DANIELL (1804–1842)

63 'On the Ramparts, Constance'
Norwich, Castle Museum $9\frac{3}{8} \times 16\frac{3}{4}$: 238×425 *Water-colour*
Rev. Edward Thomas DANIELL (1804–1842)

64 'On the Road at Thorpe'

Norwich, Castle Museum $10\frac{7}{8} \times 17\frac{1}{4}$: 277×437 *Water-colour*

Henry BRIGHT (1814–1873)

65 Sunset on the Coast

B.M. 1880.2.14.242 $8\frac{1}{4} \times 13\frac{1}{2}$: 210×342 *Water-colour*

Henry BRIGHT (1814–1873)

66 'Trees and Rocks'
Norwich, Castle Museum   17½ × 26: 444 × 659   *Water-colour*
John MIDDLETON (1827–1856)

67 'Dock Leaves'
Norwich, Castle Museum   9 × 13¾: 228 × 349   *Water-colour*
John MIDDLETON (1827–1856)

Orders he entered Balliol College, Oxford, in 1823. During his vacation all his leisure time was spent in the studio of Joseph Stannard.[1] There he practised etching and produced a series of remarkable landscapes in dry-point, free and instinctive work in the manner of Rembrandt. He surpasses the other Norwich etchers in his use of the burr of dry-point to convey richness of texture and a sense of colour. If only more proofs from his fine plates were available for collectors and museums he would be more readily placed among the great etchers of the world.

The years 1829 and 1830 were spent by Daniell in France, Italy and Switzerland, sketching mainly in water-colour. He was ordained Deacon in 1831 and Priest in 1833, obtaining a curacy at St. Mark's, North Audley Street; but he always remained in touch with his Norwich friends. His independent means and genial nature enabled him to entertain at his London house all the art celebrities of the time. Round his hospitable table used to sit Turner, Stanfield, Mulready, Roberts, Dyce, Linnell and others. In 1840 he gave a dinner to several important guests at 13, Green Street, and showed them David Roberts' drawings of Egypt and Palestine. These drawings so impressed Daniell that he determined to set out himself for the East. He resigned his curacy in 1841 and joined the Survey Party sent out in the *Beacon* to fetch the Lycian antiquities, now in the British Museum, which Sir Charles Fellowes had discovered at Zanthus. At Adalia he was struck down with fever, and died at the early age of thirty-eight.

A large collection of Daniell's water-colours, made in 1840–1842 in Greece, Egypt, Nubia, Syria, Palestine and Asia Minor, is in the Colman Collection[2]; and sixty-four of his water-colour sketches made in Asia Minor are in the British Museum. His water-colours are somewhat akin both as to subjects and treatment with those of Edward Lear. In both cases the main purpose was to give a general idea of interesting localities and antiquarian remains. In the words of Dickes[3]: 'these sketches, drawn on half-sheets of buff-toned paper, loosely outlined with a hardish pencil; the local colours indicated with somewhat sloppy washes of sepia, ultramarine, brown pink and gamboge; the details enforced with a reed pen, in bistre and burnt sienna, and sometimes heightened with white, are always satisfactory and sometimes very charming indeed'. . . . Daniell's water-colour art may be described as the perfection of free sketching. The speed and hurry of it, telling of short time and fleeting opportunity, endow it with many accidental charms, maybe of colour, maybe of form, or even—through the imperfect drying of a wash—of texture. The use of ink is very evident in his work, as in that of Lear. Influenced perhaps by his work as an etcher, he uses the strong line given by a reed pen, not as a basis of his design, but afterwards to reinforce his somewhat slight work in pencil and colour. The Norwich Art Circle held an exhibition of Daniell's works in 1891, and the catalogue comprised 31 etchings and 67 water-colours.

---

[1] E. T. Daniell was in close touch with Henry Ninham. Several letters to Ninham are in the Reeve collection in the B.M. Print Room.
[2] Norwich, Castle Museum.   [3] *Op. cit.*, p. 553.

Thomas Lound (1802–1861), more truly an amateur than Daniell, was engaged in the brewing trade at Norwich. After studying under Cotman he became known as a successful painter of landscape, both in oil and water-colour. He was never a member of the Norwich Society, but exhibited at Norwich from his eighteenth year until 1833, exhibiting oils and water-colours at the Royal Academy from 1846 to 1855. At his death in 1861 he was the owner of seventy-five pictures by Thirtle. His *Framlingham Castle*[1] is a broad sketch reminiscent of some of De Wint's drawings, but his *View looking up the Wensum at Norwich*,[2] dated 1832, is much more typical of the Norwich School. In his use of water-colour Lound shows a more impulsive style than his Norwich contemporaries; he is more akin to Cox, whose work he admired and owned, in his use of juxtaposed brush-marks instead of broad washes. From the Reeve Collection came his *Richmond Castle*[3] and *Ely Cathedral, with a Marsh Mill in the Foreground*.[4] Another distant view of *Ely Cathedral* (Pl. 61) is in the Norwich Museum.

Henry Bright (1814–1873), though he was associated with Norwich in his early years, was actually a Suffolk man, born at Saxmundham the son of a jeweller. He was apprenticed to a chemist at Woodbridge, and afterwards obtained employment with the firm of Paul Squire at Norwich, adding to this the duties of a dispenser at Norwich Hospital. Bright, as a boy, had shown talent in drawing, and his employer, Paul Squire, put him in touch with Cotman and John Berney Crome; Lound and John Middleton were among his companions. In 1836 he cut adrift from business, went to London, and in the following year exhibited the first of his twenty-six pictures sent to the British Institution. His slick and rather showy method of drawing made him a popular teacher. He took over a class from J. D. Harding, augmented it with scores of aristocratic pupils, and is said to have made as much as £2000 per annum from this source at one period of his career, possibly helped by such publications as *Bright's Drawing Book* and *Bright's Graduated Tint Studies*. It was by his water-colours that he won most credit, and he was welcomed in 1839 by Stanfield and Prout as a member of the New Society of Painters in Water-Colours (now the Royal Institute). In 1849 he went to live at Grove Cottage, East Ealing, where he practised and taught drawing for many years. Bright's work is characterised by breadth and freedom; the passing effects of sky and cloud, light and shadow were his favourite subjects. In his rapid and vigorous work he made frequent use of chalk and pastel, sometimes combining them with water-colour. Many drawings made by him in this way on grey paper, notably a set of Cornish subjects, are lurid and theatrical. Some large works by him in the Maidstone Museum show the depths to which he could descend. Throughout his career he displayed dexterity rather than poetic feeling, and bravura rather than serious search for form in his drawing. Queen Victoria and Grand Duchesses bought his work; and in Haldane Macfall's *History of Painting* he is styled 'the brilliant genius, Bright'. Typical

[1] V.A.M. P.192–1874.
[3] B.M. 1902. 5.14.432.

[2] V.A.M. P.14–1926.
[4] B.M. 1902. 5.14.431.

examples of his work will be found at the Victoria and Albert Museum and the British Museum.

John Middleton (1827–1856), who has been mentioned for his association with Henry Bright and Thomas Lound, was educated at Norwich and had instruction from J. B. Ladbrooke. He went to London for the years 1847 and 1848, returned to Norwich, and died of consumption at the early age of twenty-nine. During his short life he produced some unusually fresh and vigorous water-colours.

CHAPTER V

John Sell Cotman

Miles Edmund Cotman   John Joseph Cotman
Pryce Carter Edwards

So far as is known, only three letters written by Crome remain in existence. One of them, addressed to Stark in 1816, speaks of 'our Norwich School' (the first use surely of this title) and goes on: 'Breath must be attended to, if you paint but a muscle, give it breath [breadth].[1] Your doing the same by the sky, making parts broad and of good shape, that they may come in with your composition, forming one grand plan of light and shade, this must always please a good eye, and keep the attention of the spectator and give delight to everyone. Trifles in Nature must be overlooked that we may have our feelings raised by seeing the whole picture at a glance, not knowing how or why we are charmed. I have written you a long rigmarole story about giving dignity to whatever you paint.' A letter that is artless in its phraseology, but makes one wish that Crome had struggled still further in giving expression to his ideas.

Cotman, on the other hand, was a prolific letter-writer (at least one hundred and fifty of his letters are preserved), and on that account alone his surroundings and the atmosphere in which he worked can be much more clearly recaptured than in the case of Crome. Then, about Cotman there is a considerable amount of biographical and critical literature.

Biographers of John Sell Cotman (1782–1842) have stated that he was the son of a silk mercer, whose business was so prosperous that he was enabled to 'reside in a villa, with garden sloping down to the river at Thorpe, the Richmond of Norwich'. That is an imaginary tale, except that in his old age Cotman's father did retire into a small semi-detached cottage at Thorpe. In reality his father Edmund Cotman and his uncle John Cotman were hairdressers at Norwich. Edmund, who took up the freedom of the city as a barber in 1785, was probably working as assistant to his older brother when, on May 16 1782, John Sell Cotman was born, seven years after Turner, another barber's son. Three weeks later the boy was christened in the church of St. Mary Coslany, close by his uncle's shop; it

---

[1] R. H. Mottram, *John Crome of Norwich*, 1931, pp. 163–167. Mottram suggests that 'breath' may not be an illiterate, or Norwich, mis-spelling of 'breadth' and thinks Crome may have wanted to express that every picture must be alive and breathe. This is contradicted by Crome's statement, within ten words of 'breath', about making the sky 'broad'.

was the church in which John Crome and Robert Ladbrooke were married, and in which the Rev. E. T. Daniell at times ministered and signed the registers.

At the age of eleven Cotman obtained a free place at the Norwich Grammar School. There was no record of a drawing-master being on the staff in 1793; and it was stated many years after by one of Cotman's sons that his father never received any tuition in drawing. Crome was not appointed as drawing-master at the Grammar School until twenty years later, in 1813. It may be assumed that somewhere about 1796 John Sell was working in his father's shop, but before 1800 his father gave up the dwindling barber's business and became a draper instead (hence the story of the prosperous 'silk mercer'); and somewhere about the autumn of 1798 Cotman went to London 'to learn to be a painter'. His father had consulted John Opie, who, as has been said, had descended upon Norwich in that year as a celebrity from the metropolis, married the daughter of a Norwich doctor, and painted Crome's portrait. Opie's verdict was straight from the shoulder: 'Let him rather black boots than follow the profession of an artist.' Some years later Opie became Professor of Painting at the Royal Academy, and in one of his lectures he elaborated this advice: 'Should any student happen to be present who has taken up the art on the supposition of finding it an easy and amusing employment—anyone who hopes by it to get rid of what he thinks a more vulgar and disagreeable situation, to escape confinement at the counter or the desk . . . let him drop it at once and avoid the walls of this Academy and everything connected with them as he would the pestilence; for he may pine in indigence, or skulk through life as a drawing master or pattern drawer to young ladies.' The truth of the statement was proved to some extent in the case of Cotman, who was impelled by the 'real and unconquerable passion for excellence', of which Opie had spoken in the same lecture, yet was doomed to 'pine in indigence' and 'to skulk through life as a drawing master and pattern drawer to young ladies'.

Perhaps young Cotman was present when someone asked Opie how he mixed his colours and heard the famous reply, 'With brains, Sir.' Perhaps Cotman felt that he possessed the brains, for in spite of Opie's adverse opinion, he went off to London, a youth of sixteen, and later was to write to Mrs. Dawson Turner: 'London, with all its fog and smoke, is the only air for an artist to breath in.' He found employment colouring aquatints for Rudolph Ackermann, whose Repository of Arts was at 101, Strand. There Ackermann had revived the drawing-school established by William Shipley, was running a prosperous business as printseller and dealer in fancy articles and artists' materials and was embarking on his enterprising career as a publisher.[1] Cotman was not satisfied with his conditions of service and left Ackermann's in the following year, but was fortunate in receiving the help and patronage of Dr. Monro. There is evidence that he stayed with this kindly helper of young artists at his country house at Fetcham, Surrey, during the summer of 1799. After this summer holiday he went to work at Dr. Monro's house in Adelphi Terrace. In the

[1] For a full account of Ackermann and his publications, see M. Hardie, *English Coloured Books*, 1906.

Monro Sale of 1833 one of the lots was 'A Bundle of very early Sketches by J. S. Cotman'. Cotman's earliest drawings, notably one of *Ashtead Churchyard, Surrey*,[1] show how powerfully the young artist was influenced by Girtin, not only in composition and lighting, but in the actual touch. And what gives special interest to this early drawing is that, some two or three years later, Cotman developed it into a drawing-copy, now in the Ashmolean Museum, eliminating and condensing, making it all beautifully simple and direct, turning the crumbling Girtin touch into something solid and compact.

In 1800 Cotman exhibited at the Royal Academy for the first time, sending six drawings from his address at 28, Gerrard Street, Soho; and in the same year was awarded 'the larger Silver Palette', for his drawing of a mill, by the Society for the Encouragement of Arts, Manufacture and Commerce. For the next two years Cotman supported himself by making drawings for sale in the print-shops of the Soho district where he lived. Peter Norton, a print-seller of Soho Square, specially befriended him and sent him off to Bristol with an introduction to his brother James, a Bristol bookseller. After making portrait drawings of all the Bristol family in return for his keep, Cotman set forth at the end of June 1800 on his first painting tour, travelling through Wales from south to north. Sydney Kitson[2] brings circumstantial evidence to show that in July Cotman was one of a group of young artists gathered by Sir George Beaumont at Conway, and that he worked side by side with Girtin. This actual association with Girtin, then at the full maturity of his power, must have been of enormous help to Cotman, and indeed is reflected in his early drawings of *Bridgnorth*[3] (1800) and *St. Mary Redcliffe, Bristol*[4] (c. 1801). The beginnings of Cotman are well summarised in two drawings, both made in 1801, *Harlech Castle*[5] and *Llanthony Abbey*.[6] Both are a little gloomy and undeveloped. From Wales he went to Norwich, and returned in the late autumn to his lodgings in London. The sketches from his portfolio containing work done in Wales and Norfolk were converted into water-colours of the kind which were sold in large quantities as drawing-copies; he had begun his career as 'pattern drawer to young ladies'. The summer of 1801 was spent at Norwich, and in the autumn he made a tour of South Devon and Somerset, ending up with his friends, the Nortons, at Bristol. It was probably during this visit that he produced the *St. Mary Redcliffe*, nobly composed and finely handled; but its heavy masses and subdued tones show that he was still leaning upon Girtin.

In 1799 a group of young artists, with Girtin at their head, had formed a society—they were known as The Brothers—for the study of romantic landscape. They met in one another's rooms, and made drawings from a set subject, conveyed by a verse from the poets.[7] The Society was languishing at the time when Girtin left for Paris in 1801, but

[1] S. D. Kitson, *The Life of John Sell Cotman*, 1937, pl. 2.
[2] Kitson, *op. cit.*, p. 21.
[3] B.M. 1849. 6.9.75.
[4] B.M. 1859. 5.28.117.
[5] Coll. Herbert Powell (N.A.C.F.).
[6] Coll. Herbert Powell (N.A.C.F.).
[7] See Kitson, *op. cit.*, chapter III, and Roget, chapter II; and, specially for Cotman's work, A. P. Oppé, 'Cotman and the Sketching Society', *The Connoisseur*, LXVIII, December 1923, where seven drawings by Cotman are reproduced; see above, chapter I.

Cotman then became a member, and appears as President in 1802, John Varley and P. S. Munn being among the members, W. Alexander and T. R. Underwood were visitors. Another member was the future Sir Robert Ker Porter, brother of Jane Porter, the novelist, whose book *Thaddeus of Warsaw* relates some of Cotman's early adventures as a struggling artist, in the guise of Thaddeus when an exile in London. Varley was four years senior to Cotman, but Kitson is inclined to think that he was influenced and dominated by his more brilliant young colleague. This however seems to be special pleading. Up to this time Cotman was still inclined to use grey under-painting; his colour was muddy; he had not learned the value of letting white paper shine through transparent pigment. If we are to account for the change and advance in Cotman's method about this date, it seems fairer to accept that from Varley he learned to abandon the monochrome under-painting of the eighteenth century and to go much further than Girtin in suggesting local colour by superimposing clean washes of pure colour, one upon another. It must be remembered also that whereas Cotman was a boy of twenty from the provinces, Varley had been brought up in London in close contact with Turner, Girtin and other painters. At the date of the Drawing Society meetings, where he worked with Cotman from 1802 to 1804, Varley was not only older, but a painter of repute, and not only that but a man of strong convictions and a born teacher. His early style was broad and simple, deriving freshness from pure tints and facile washes. Cotman was no imitator of Varley, but it seems reasonable to accept that from Varley he absorbed that use of pure colour, laid in clean flat washes—a complete alteration from his previous technique—which he was to adapt so individually to his own purpose. His *Ouse Bridge, York*,[1] 1803, shows strong traces of the Varley influence, particularly in the foreground. John Varley's *Kirkstall Abbey, Yorkshire*,[2] 1803, is in the style and method that Cotman was to adopt and bring to perfection a year or two later.

In 1802 Cotman accompanied Paul Sandby Munn on a sketching tour in North Wales. They travelled light, unencumbered by water-colour materials, but filled their sketch-books with outline pencil drawings. These pencil notes were to serve Cotman, who never visited Wales or saw a mountain again, both for water-colours and for etchings during many later years. And here it may be noted that throughout his life Cotman's water-colour drawings were nearly always indoor work founded upon pencil notes and outdoor observation. His technique demanded the leisure, the deliberation, and the slow construction, for which a flat table in the studio was an essential requisite. *Dolgelly, North Wales*,[3] painted in 1803 from one of these pencil sketches, still shows his stylistic alliance with Girtin and with Munn, and his *Plas y Nant, near Snowdon*,[4] 1802 is closely related to Constable's Lake District drawings of 1806. Girtin was their common ancestor. But in his

---

[1] V.A.M. E.3795–1934.
[2] Stoke-on-Trent, City Art Gallery.
[3] Cambridge, Fitzwilliam Museum.
[4] Once belonging to the late Sir Thomas Bodkin.

Chirk Aqueduct,[1] (Pl. 68) painted about 1804 from his pencil note, Cotman shows definitely the beginning of his new and individual method. The subject is the Aqueduct then recently completed by Telford and in a distinguished composition, so modern in its outlook and its grasp of the stark simplicity of the theme, so different in subject and manner from the work of his predecessors, Cotman produced something essentially his own and a landmark in his career. No wonder that, on his annual visit to Norwich, in the summer of 1802 after his return from Wales, he published an advertisement with the confident statement that he proposes, for three weeks or a month, 'giving lessons in drawing to those Ladies and Gentleman who may think his sketching from Nature or Style of Colouring beneficial to their improvement'.

In 1802, when Cotman was making hack drawing-copies for P. S. Munn's brothers at their printsellers' establishment at 107, New Bond Street, and eking out his existence by occasional lessons at half-a-guinea an hour, fortune tipped the scale. He found a patron in Francis Cholmeley of Brandsby Hall, some fifteen miles north of York, and at his house spent the summers of what Kitson describes as the three most impressionable years of his life. In Yorkshire Turner was to be the friend and guest of Walter Fawkes of Farnley Hall; and Lord Harewood had kept a bedroom ready for Girtin at Harewood House; now Cotman had like advantages. In describing the development of Turner under the influence of Yorkshire, Ruskin wrote: 'Of all his drawings I think those of the Yorkshire series have the most heart in them, the most affectionate, simple, unwearied finishings of truth.' Word for word, that applies to Cotman too. On July 7, 1803, when Cotman and Munn were on a sketching tour at York, they were taken by Mrs. Cholmeley in the family coach to Brandsby Hall. They went sketching at Richmond and Durham, passing over Greta Bridge and by the park at Rokeby; they were at Airedale; they made drawings of the Abbeys of Kirkstall and Fountains, and of Bolton Priory. From time to time they returned to Brandsby Hall, and the commonplace-book of the Hall which records such items as 'Grunty pigged fourteen pigs' and 'First Laylac gathered,' reports on August 3: 'Mr. Munn went away.' Cotman stayed on for another six weeks, giving lessons to Mrs. Cholmeley and her four daughters, and exploring the surrounding country, sketch-book in hand. Above all, in a well-timbered land he was studying the form and anatomy of trees, and mastering their growth. Trees and quiet waters were now to become his theme, developed and expanded in a whole series of drawings totally original in vision, totally individual in technique.

In the summer of 1804 he found another patron, Dawson Turner, who was a successful Yarmouth banker devoted to antiquity and archaeology. After staying at Covehithe on the Suffolk coast with the Dawson Turners, Cotman returned with them to Yarmouth, and immediately after this visit went to Castle Acre and Croyland on his way back to Norwich. While at Croyland he drew a draining mill, with a procession of other mills

---

[1] V.A.M. 115–1892.

receding into the distance. Cotman made use of this sketch again and again. The large contemporary version in the Victoria and Albert Museum, with the title *Windmill, Lincolnshire*,[1] though much faded, is one of the noblest of his drawings.

In 1804 and again in 1805 he was staying with the Cholmeleys at Brandsby, and the year 1805 marks a peak in his development. He was using, rather than imitating, the work of his elders. Cotman would allow that he had been much influenced by Girtin, Varley and Munn. In the light of his own wisdom, with added emotional power and a new technique, he was now to produce a series of what can be deliberately described as master-pieces in the art of water-colour.

Staying with the Cholmeleys he made those superb drawings *Duncombe Park, Yorkshire*[2] and *The Drop Gate in Duncombe Park*[3] (Pl. 69), which are now in the British Museum. These and other drawings, contrary to his usual practice, were 'coloured from Nature and close copies of that ficle [*sic*] Dame', as he wrote to Dawson Turner. It is possible that he did not mean to imply that the colouring was done out-of-doors. A facsimile of the whole letter appears in the catalogue of the Cotman Exhibition held by the Norwich Art Circle in 1888. *The Drop Gate* is a drawing of nothing but some broken rails hanging over a stream—a drop-gate, a water pool and some weeds—but the design is such as no other painter of the time would have conceived; a design of straight lines, horizontal or diagonal, and sharp angles contrasted with the soft contours of foliage and the curves of burdock, lyrical in its rhythm and colour.

Following on an introduction from the Cholmeleys, he stayed shortly afterwards for six weeks with John Morrit at Rokeby Park, where the Greta runs on the eastern side of the demesne to join the Tees. For an hour or two every day he gave instruction to Mrs. Morrit, and then was free to dream and work amid surroundings of ideal beauty. Eight years later Sir Walter Scott, an intimate friend of Mr. Morrit, with whom he frequently stayed, was to publish his *Rokeby*, with its word pictures of the enchantment of Greta woods and Brignall Banks:

> *O Brignall Banks are wild and fair,*
> *And Greta woods are green,*
> *And you may gather garlands there*
> *Would grace a summer-queen.*[4]

Cotman had already found the full poetry of every scene in this wonderland of narrow wooded dales which run greenly to the rivers down the sides of wine-dark moors.

Though some of the Greta drawings may have been literally coloured from nature, most of them are too formal, with patterns too subtly woven, for *plein air* painting. The *Greta Woods from Brignal Bank*,[5] for instance, is based upon a careful study in pencil. The *Distant View of Barnard Castle*[6] is a lovely drawing, with full greens and blues, painted on a thick absorbent paper, such as would allow of no tentative outdoor treatment. And so with

[1] V.A.M. F.A.–662.
[2] B.M. 1902. 5.14.13.
[3] B.M. 1902. 5.14.14.
[4] Canto III xvi.
[5] Leeds, City Art Gallery.
[6] Leeds, City Art Gallery.

The Devil's Elbow, Rokeby,[1] *A Shady Pool,*[2] *Greta Woods,*[3] *Greta Bridge*[4] (Pl. 70) and *Near Greta Bridge.*[5] In all these drawings the design, the subtle gradation of the various washes have been studied, balanced and arranged in the studio; chance elements have been controlled and brought into a unity of repose and a static perfection produced with an ease and mastery under which all the formal mechanism is concealed.

In nearly all these drawings there is the same harmony of colour, hovering between green and blue and grey, with subtle contrasts of lights and darks. In the deep stillness of the woods the trees, though highly stylised, seem perfectly natural, falling in cascades of green foliage. At this period Cotman did without the use of some red tiles or a scarlet cap or cloak as a note of contrast. No other painter had approached more daringly the salad freshness of English meadows, the prolific greenery of woods. It was an 'abstract' art.

The *Greta Bridge,* the most famous drawing of this period, has stronger yellows and browns. The bridge, the stone-roofed house, are still there, and it is clear that this drawing is no mere replica of Nature. The river has been much widened; the foreground rocks have been reshaped and redisposed; but with sure instinct those dark rocks have been made to repeat the dark circle under the bridge, and curves have been used to contrast with straight lines. Pattern is the basis of this superb drawing, a pattern of colour as well as line and mass, perfectly rhythmical and balanced in the interrelation of every form and space. In all these Greta drawings, natural form and preconceived design are completely controlled and combined.

Laurence Binyon[6] is right in his deliberate description of these Greta drawings as 'the most perfect examples of pure water-colour ever made in Europe'. And they were made under ideal conditions for a young artist. Kind hosts looked after his physical well-being, cultured people, who felt no disdain for a man of genius who was the son of a barber. He was for them their 'dear Cottey'; and deeply graven in the trunk of an old hornbeam in the grounds of Brandsby Hall may still be seen the inscription COTTEY, cut there by his young pupils as a memento of his three visits to Yorkshire. During those visits he was free to plant his camp-stool where he willed on the banks of the Greta and the Tees, happy in filling his sketch-book. In these Greta drawings Cotman knew his most inspired moments when every touch seemed inevitable and infallibly right.

Not often in later life did Cotman recapture the ease and exaltation of these works. In this Greta period, when 'shades of the prison-house' were not yet closing about him, there seems to have come to Cotman a quickened consciousness, which was not merely mental, but mechanical also. That leads us to study his technical method at this time of his highest achievement. His draughtsmanship and the basis of his colour, are not merely uniformly picturesque—every point is intentional. His pencil line is much more sympathetic,

---

[1] Norwich, Castle Museum.
[2] Edinburgh, National Gallery of Scotland.
[3] Coll. Dr. L. S. Fry.
[4] B.M. 1902. 5.14.17.
[5] Coll. Sir Edmund Bacon, Bt.
[6] L. Binyon, *Landscape in English Art and Poetry,* 1931, p. 132.

perceptive and expressive than that of Prout. He does not rely on tricks of personal short-hand. He makes a searching study of individual characteristics—it may be the mass or ramification of a tree, the joints and interstices of stones or crumbling bricks, the way that ivy clings to a wall or works its way round a square corner. Where he excels is in his definition of detail combined with largeness of pattern. In architecture especially he never overweights his drawing with elaborate detail, but gives just enough to suggest material, whether bricks, stones or plaster, leading the eye round angles and contours of every crannied wall. Here and there he uses detail as a kind of symbol, inducing us by a sort of imaginative repetition to enlarge and extend his symbols with fuller definition till mentally we see much more of surface and of texture than he actually records.

Cotman realised, as Crome never did, what a varied entity a line can be, what an individual part of a picture it may become. Though Crome and Cotman are united as the leading members of the Norwich School, they are quite different. With Crome a line was only part of a framework to suggest where light and dark and colour should be placed. With Cotman lines were the very bones on which the life of the work was supported. Even in his water-colours they are essential to the whole design, used like the leading in a glass window, though not so obtrusively, to enclose the coloured shapes. His line, too, is not merely a boundary to a patch of colour but a boundary to the space left between the masses or patches of dark and light. Nature actually provides no outline. Cotman was always percipient of the left spaces, whether he was drawing architecture or pure land-scape.

His trees are drawn with a series of sheer conventions for the nearer foliage; not the large loops of Gainsborough, but a set of smaller loops, like a bunch of bananas, repeated over and over again. In spite of the falsity and lack of scale, the treatment serves its purpose with triumphant success. The air is stirring in the trees, life and growth is in their branches and coolness in the gloom of their shadows. The eye is not thwarted by angular detail, but passes over the shapely though conventional mass and is led to some superb and more detailed pattern beyond.

The British Museum and Victoria and Albert Museum are rich in pencil sketches which show Cotman's method of approach, and in the Norwich Museum is a collection of over 300 pencil drawings, important for understanding his technique. For a full knowledge of his draughtsmanship it is essential also to study his set of etchings, mainly in soft-ground,[1]

[1] Sydney Kitson makes many errors with regard to the technique of Cotman's etchings. It is a mistake to say that for a soft-ground etching the paper was placed 'over a copper-plate covered with tallow'. The ground used on the plate for a soft-ground etching has to be impervious to acid. It is an ordinary etching ground, composed of bees-wax, asphaltum and Burgundy pitch, with an admixture of tallow to soften it. Kitson adds that the plates became worn owing to 'the richness of the burr'. Burr is a term used for the slight edges of copper thrown up by the cut of a dry-point needle or a graver; there is no burr in soft-ground. Then we are told that Cotman 'took up seriously the method of etching by means of the graver'. A graver is only used in line-drawing. What Kitson meant is that Cotman took up the ordinary method of etching, i.e. working with a needle on the usual hard ground, and not with pencil and paper on a ground made soft by the addition of tallow. These and other errors are merely mistakes due to ignorance of practical technique. The fullest thanks are due to Sydney Kitson for his very learned account, from the historical aspect, of all Cotman's etchings and their relation to his drawings.

collected and published in 1838 with the title of *Liber Studiorum*, and his various publications containing etchings of the antiquities of Norfolk, Normandy and elsewhere.[1] Many of the etchings in these publications are cold and formal statements of precise facts. Not so, the soft-ground etchings of the *Liber Studiorum*, where he worked to please himself and not the antiquarian. These soft-ground etchings, which from the nature of the method are almost facsimiles of pencil drawings—the print is like the drawing seen reversed as in a mirror— are little masterpieces of composition and design, whether they deal with landscape or architecture, and are remarkable for their cunning suggestion of texture and surface. To his son, John Joseph, Cotman wrote: 'Draw sternly and true, *Leave out, but add nothing.*' And, in the use of soft-ground, no other etcher has ever surpassed Cotman.

Cotman's superb draughtsmanship can be seen in such examples as his *Ruins of Thetford Abbey*[2] and especially two other drawings in black-and-white, *Breaking the Clod*[3] and *Domfront*[4] (Pl. 77). *Breaking the Clod*, a chalk drawing made about 1810, is an example of perfect rhythm and design. The white and dark edges of clouds repeat in reverse the curved backs of the white and black horses; the straight lines of shadow, and the field's edge and the tree trunks, radiate from the central straining group, counteracting and stabilising the curves. This contrapuntal system, the deliberate contrast of curves and stark, rectilinear shapes, is a basic part of Cotman's style. In matter and in sentiment *Breaking the Clod* is a little masterpiece. *Domfront*[5] has less of sentiment but shows even more concentration on design. It was drawn in August 1820, when he made several 'views of the town and rocks—extremely grand', rendered with pencil and sepia washes of infinite variety and the most subtle gradation. The drawing has all of those qualities which have since been epitomised as advanced art. There is the balance, without mechanised symmetry, of the large triangular masses of rock in the foreground, the contrast of the dark triangle on the right, the light triangle on the left, repeated in the small triangle formed by the gendarme and the hound: and then the lines all radiate from a central point below to the encircling arc of the cliffs. Besides the bold framework of the structure, there is the wealth of detail. A drawing by Cotman, or by De Wint, is an invitation to take a country walk; *Domfront* alone gives the essence of Cotman's art.

In his early days as a student and at the Sketching Club, Cotman made many copies of original compositions in monochrome. These were worked strongly in sepia, and by this means he learned to see large masses in silhouette, finding for each the lowest common denominator of tone. When he came to colour he used it on a restricted scale with a minimum of selective washes as in his sepia drawings. In his coloured drawings Cotman built up his design with lines and washes very much in the manner of a Japanese artist who,

[1] A list of these is given by Kitson in *O.W.S. Club*, VII, 1930, pp. 22, 23.
[2] V.A.M. E.1061–1926.
[3] B.M. 1902. 5.14.44.
[4] Coll. Mr. and Mrs. Paul Mellon.
[5] A companion drawing of *Domfront from the Town, looking N.W.*, was in the collection of Sydney Kitson. In both these are faint indications that they have been squared, probably with a view to making water-colour versions.

80

in making a colour wood-cut, first fashions a key-block in monochrome to give his outline, and then prints flat colours, one after the other, from superimposed blocks. Cotman's lines are like those of the Japanese key-block, giving the structural foundation. His colour, certainly in the Greta period, was applied with certainty and directness of tint laid over or against tint, as though from flat printing of one block after another, always registering with the key lines. He never used a blurred edge, or the blotting of one colour into another. The analogy with block-printing is only possible because Cotman did not, like De Wint, run more colour into a wet, or at any rate moist, first painting. His second washes were put over a first painting which was dry or almost dry. Each touch, therefore, was not merged in the under-painting, but had a definitely drawn, individual, shape.

Cotman always ordered and controlled his washes. While painters like Cox enjoyed a certain orderly disorder in nature and in art, Cotman shows the exercise of civilised consciousness, a planning and ordering as of spaces and squares in a stately city. Painting as he did, Cotman could stop, think, and paint again. It is strange that in the work of a man whose head was so often in the clouds there should be a method in work as austere as that of Flaubert in his choice of words. Before putting colour on paper Cotman seems to have planned out and anticipated the final result. A Cotman drawing was never held up to let the colour run, or put under running water. But although ordered and controlled, his work was inspired by genius and was a compound of logic and poetry.

Cotman's colour method can be seen perfectly in an unfinished *Study of Trees*[1] and in a similar drawing of *Trees at Harrow*,[2] both belonging to 1805. As in a Japanese print, a second green goes over the first green, plane over plane, wash over wash, with cunningly left spaces of white paper or of the undercolour, all of it with an accuracy which appears mechanical in its rightness. His paper was of the ideal texture; in Binyon's[3] words, 'its acceptance of the stain of colour is a beauty in itself'. The *Study of Trees* illustrates two main features in Cotman's art:—first, his method of obtaining depth and slight contrast by the superimposing of a second wash of the same tint. This was in the manner not only of the Japanese but of early makers of stained-glass windows who used, not a darker colour, but two or three thicknesses of the same blue, red or green glass, to gain a greater depth of translucent colour; second, his use of 'left spaces' or 'reserved spaces'—to use the term applied by writers on Greek vases to a somewhat similar method. This is an outstanding aspect of his art. A tree branch by this means stands out light against its dark background; a fence is white under trees; a rock sparkles in a stream, the ripples flash; all of them are bare paper. *The Drop Gate* is another drawing which illustrates this principle in its most simplified form.

Incidentally it may be noted that Cotman's deliberate use of left spaces finds little parallel in his time unless in the admirable work of Tobias Young (d. 1824), born

[1] V.A.M. P.34–1921.
[2] Manchester University, Whitworth Art Gallery.
[3] L. Binyon, *English Water-Colours*, 1933, p. 144.

probably at Mildenhall, near Marlborough.[1] His *Netley Abbey*[2] in the Victoria and Albert Museum, is closely akin to Cotman in its method. But looking at the Greta drawings, we realise that it is Francis Towne with whom Cotman is connected in his search for structure and his instinct for pictorial pattern. Towne, who in 1805, the year when Cotman's art was at its peak held an exhibition of nearly 200 of his drawings in Lower Brook Street.[3] Cotman was in London at the time and may well have been impressed by Towne's use of spatial harmonies. Both have the same sense of flat-patterned planes, but in sensitivity and the management of colour Cotman passed far beyond his predecessor. Here also it may be noted that in quality of paint, in the use of simple flat patterns, in the avoidance of too much chiaroscuro, Cotman anticipates some of the work of Corot. We have but to look at Corot's *Palais des Papes à Avignon*, of 1836, to realise how close the comparison is.

Cotman does not, like the Japanese, eliminate shadow, but he uses it in flat simple areas to supply a definite proportioning of light and dark. He realised that shadows are not black or neutral, that they contain in a deeper degree the same colour as their surroundings. By the simplest of methods, by doubling or trebling his washes of the same colour, and to that extent excluding the white light of his paper, he gives depth to his darks. Even in the laying of these shadows the likeness to the colour-print method is apparent. There is no doubt that our modern understanding and appreciation of the Japanese colour-print has led to a new conception of the value of Cotman's art. He himself, we may be sure, had never seen a Japanese print. The finest work of Utamaro and Hiroshige was contemporary with his own. The Manzi and Bing collections were not being formed in Paris till the latter part of last century; and in our own country it was not until after 1860, that, through Whistler and Rossetti, Japanese prints were appreciated.

It is always a matter of technical interest to decide how much of an artist's work in colour was done before Nature and how much in the studio. Kitson had pencil studies by Cotman (and there are many others) squared out and afterwards enlarged and developed in colour. Cotman made most deliberate and searching pencil drawings out-of-doors, but it must be repeated here that his abstract method of colouring is an indoor one. In his finished drawings there are none of the wet blobs, the accidents, the unsteadiness, which mark outdoor notations of natural effects. The very fact that there are two distinct versions of *Greta Bridge, Dieppe*, and other drawings, and at least four of the *Windmill, Lincolnshire*, shows that he made deliberate studio variations or paraphrases of his original theme. Even where we find storm-tossed clouds or thunder skies and the fluent animation of buoyant waves in his sea-pieces, it must be realised that the colour scheme is planned out by the aid of memory, just as it is in most of Turner's work. This kind of indoor work allows for the lapse of time implicit in Wordsworth's phrase, 'emotion recollected in tranquillity' and provides an element of aesthetic distance. Moreover, the painter is not

---

[1] Possibly a relation of J. T. Young who is also represented in the V.A.M.
[2] V.A.M. P.73-1920.
[3] The catalogue is reprinted in Adrian Bury, *Francis Towne*, 1962, pp. 118-122.

distracted by the multitudinous detail of nature. And when Cotman wrote to Dawson Turner about some of his Greta drawings being 'coloured from Nature and close copies of that ficle Dame' he was not conscious of his own mental and artistic processes and had not realised how abstract, how personal to himself, that colour was. He was not painting material objects, but colour itself; an emanation, or exhalation of colour.

Such were the ingredients which made up Cotman's style at the time of his Greta drawings and for several years later. Before 1810 he was sometimes painting in strong colour, and as time went on it became still higher in key and more varied, but it was applied in a similar way. The main difference after 1807 was that his earlier method was applied to a much wider range of subjects, more calculated to win approval. In 1806 he abandoned his struggle for fame and fortune in London and settled down as an artist in his native city, with the intention of opening a 'School for Drawing and Design'. He became Secretary of the newly-founded Norwich Society of Artists, in 1810 its Vice-President, and in 1811 its President. About this time he may have painted the superb *Landscape with River and Cattle*[1] which has been identified as representing the Tees between Hawesworth and Rawcliffe Scar with Rockcliffe Park in the background. It has more colour than the earlier Greta drawings. Those woodland and landscape drawings on the Greta and the Tees had been too personal, subjective, and subtle to attract buyers; and so Cotman now returns to architectural subjects. His noble Durham drawings of 1805 had perhaps won greater approval. The *Walsingham Priory*[2] is one of the most lovely of a series of drawings, made among the Priory ruins about 1807. The building itself is set among trees, with dominant notes of grey-green and umber as an echo of the Greta drawings and with Cotman's favourite device of a brilliant blue sky, flecked with white summer clouds. Another of the finest drawings in this series, in which the ruins, with perfectly balanced masses of shadow, stand light against a dark background of trees is the *Refectory of Walsingham Priory*.[3]

Cotman was exploring still further possibilities of subject when in 1807 he exhibited at the Norwich Society what he described as 'A coloured sketch of the *Market Place, Norwich*, taken from Mr. Cooper's (at the N.E. corner of the Square)'. The pencil work is closely studied; the colour is slight, golden in tone, and kept to a simple scheme of yellow, grey and brown, with touches of russet-red on the tiled roofs. It is crowded with human activity: the almost shadowless spotting-in of all the figures is Japanese-like, and in many light spaces the paper has never been touched. The tessellated spots of colour, set irregularly side by side and often with only slight differentiation, occur frequently in his work. It is of interest to note that the whole sheet was washed once with gum, probably with the idea of fixing the pencil drawing, much of which is not covered by colour. The drawing was once owned by Bernard Barton, the Quaker poet, friend of Charles Lamb and Edward

---

[1] V.A.M. 93–1894.
[2] Coll. Dr. L. S. Fry.
[3] Leeds, City Art Gallery.

Fitzgerald, and was aptly described by him as a 'jewel of a drawing'. He never tired of looking at it, and in 1845 wrote a poem, the last verse of which reads:

> *Thirty-eight years gone by*
> *Thus did this motley moving medley look;*
> *And still unto mine eye*
> *It utters more than any printed book.*

Another even more architectural drawing of 1807 is *Exterior of St. Luke's Chapel, Norwich Cathedral*, appropriately housed in the Norwich Castle Museum. The buildings, the curved chapel with its Norman arcading, and the south transept of the Cathedral beyond, are entirely dominant, grand in their austere severity, majestically composed, with brilliant contrasts of light and dark masses. To the making of the picture, which is as grave and ascetic as a Dutch interior by Bosboom, went all the fine draughtsmanship and the systematic placing and shaping of colour which distinguishes Cotman's purely landscape work. A complete contrast is offered by another outstanding work of this 1807–1810 period, *Cheyne Walk*[1] (Pl. 74), formerly known as *Twickenham, Mid-day*, because an exhibit with this title appears in the Norwich Society catalogue for 1808. A related pencil study, discovered a few years ago, is inscribed *Chany Walk, London*. It depicts an animated scene of noon-day sunshine, with the white sails of boats, and the bright dresses of figures going aboard, sparkling against the foliage which ranges from silver to a deep brown-green. The superb *Draining Mill, Lincolnshire*,[2] of 1810, is again a contrast, showing Cotman returning to Girtin's mood and method, but adding his own fuller colour and in particular his own squareness and stability of design.

A few years later, about 1812, he painted *The Ploughed Field*[3] (Pl. 73), which excels in its simple, flat colouring, its beautiful placing of line and mass, of light and dark, its subtle use of curves in the trees and in the central path which connects and counteracts the broad horizontal strips in landscape and sky. It is perhaps greater than *Breaking the Clod*[4] because with all its beauty and sentiment that is an echo of an old traditional, romantic spirit, while here Cotman may be treating a familiar subject, but he has created a new rhythm as the expression of a new mood.

Cotman's marriage in 1809 and the arrival of children during the following years, imposed a strain on his meagre resources and gave stimulus to his output. He became busy with oil-painting, and began to experiment with water-colours which might vie with oil. But in his case, as in that of other painters, a gain of strength and intensity might impress the public but involved the loss or suppression of the delicacy and transparency of water-colour. It was about this time that Francis Cholmeley wrote, warning him that 'every artist must, to a certain degree, obey his master the public. . . . Two-thirds of mankind, you know, mind more *what* is represented than *how* it is done.' Cotman was doomed to be the slave of the public, and so we find the more solid and intense handling of *The Marl Pit*[5]

[1] Norwich, Castle Museum.
[3] Leeds, City Art Gallery.
[5] Norwich, Castle Museum.

[2] B.M. 1902. 5.14.19.
[4] See above, p. 80.

and, in addition, the popular appeal of *The Harvest Field, a Pastoral*,[1] in 1810. This year he began his series of archaeological etchings, and was driven to fall back upon his work as a teacher. 'Saving but for the best scholars it's but a sorry drudgery and only calculated for money-making when a man fags from door to door merely for the pound sterling', he wrote in 1811. Within six months of his wedding he issued in *The Norfolk Chronicle* an advertisement which shows the forced nature of his livelihood:

A Circulating Collection of Drawings

J. S. COTMAN

Has opened to the Public on the plan of a Circulating Library a *Collection of Six Hundred Drawings*, consisting of Landscapes, Compositions on Design, and Figures. Coloured Sketches from Nature, Sketches in Claro obscuro, and his original Pencil Sketches from the Saxon, Norman and Gothic Architecture, chiefly from the counties of Yorkshire, Lincolnshire, Essex and Norfolk.

Quarterly subscription Ticket, One Guinea. J. S. Cotman will attend the delivering of the drawings to the subscribers, that he may facilitate their copying them by his instructions.

Days of delivery Mondays and Thursdays, between the hours of twelve and two.

The drawings done as models for pupils were carefully numbered, and this means of livelihood was continued to the end of his life.

In 1812 he left Norwich and at the instigation of Dawson Turner moved to Yarmouth. It was a tacit acknowledgement of defeat, even though he had steady employment in teaching Mrs. Turner and her daughters, and as purveyor of archaeological drawings to Dawson Turner. His patron encouraged him to make hundreds of etchings of Norman and Gothic architecture in the county of Norfolk and of sepulchral brasses in Norfolk and Suffolk, demanding accuracy more than artistic quality (though the artistry is apparent). Those plates must have meant unremitting toil by day and night. In 1817 Dawson Turner sent Cotman off to Normandy in order to make accurate drawings of Romanesque architecture for comparison with buildings of the same character at home.[2] He made three journeys in all to Normandy, in 1817, 1818 and 1820 (the Normandy sketches of Prout and Edridge also belong to these years), taking no painting material, but filling sketch-books and small sheets of paper with studies and memoranda. On his return more finished drawings in pencil and sepia were submitted to Dawson Turner, who selected those which were to be reproduced as etchings in the proposed *Architectural Antiquities of Normandy*. From Dieppe in 1817, at the outset of his first tour, Cotman wrote: 'Good Heavens, what a lovely country! Everything is picturesque. Of the peasants coming to market I want words to express my delight. Women, men, horses, mules and carriages, with such attire, harness, etc. The harbour is like a lake filled with vessels—and such colouring. Oh! had I the fortune and time beyond the limits of mortal man, what might be done!!! Nothing

---

[1] Once Coll. The Misses Bulwer. Kitson thinks the figures were perhaps derived from Joshua Cristall. I suggest that they are based on some engraving after Raphael.

[2] H. Isherwood Kay, *John Sell Cotman's Letters from Normandy*, Walpole Soc., XIV, 1925/26, p. 81; and XV, 1926/27, p. 105.

even as to colour can be seen in England like it.' He found what he calls 'an artist's day,' a day of 'fine clouds, the shadows of which give life and spirit to everything, and change upon change takes place like magic, from light tones to the darkest purples'. Fortunately for us, Cotman was prone to forget the main object of his journey and to travel, like Dr. Syntax, in search of the picturesque, looking not just at the bare bones of architecture to satisfy Dawson Turner, but at larger aspects of nature, to satisfy himself. Thus, at the start, he drew Dieppe and its harbour from the heights above it; making, some years later, two versions of the subject, which are now united in the Victoria and Albert Museum.[1] The one which entered the Museum from the Lady Powell Bequest is probably the original. It is drawn freely with reed pen and brown ink, and better preserved, quieter and more intimate; the replica, executed after an interval of perhaps two or three years, tends towards the hot colour associated with his later work. His *Gateway to the Castle of Arques*,[2] dated June 21, 1817, was the very first of hundreds of pencil and sepia drawings which fulfilled the stipulated purposes of his journey. His pencil was never out of his hand, and though on his second journey he was very much the cicerone and drawing-master-in-attendance to the whole Dawson Turner family, who this time accompanied him, he brought back at least a hundred and fifty drawings.

Towards the end of his first journey Cotman visited Mont St. Michel, which he described as towering over him 'like a gigantic vision', and it became one of his stock Normandy subjects in later days, when his colour had become florid and opulent. He was more fortunate when the packet-boat on his return journey to England, anchored off the Isle of Wight and supplied him with the origin of one of his most lovely drawings, *The Needles*[3] (Pl. 76). The water-colour, I imagine, must have been made soon after his return home, while the impression was still vivid and not conjured up artificially as in the *Mont St. Michel* drawings. *The Needles* is executed in two or three colours only, but they unite sky and headland, ships and sea, in a gentle rhythmical harmony. Just for once, in this later work the spirit of the Greta drawings appears, though in a different guise, blue silvery drawing, and seemingly effortless. Of the same type in simplicity and lucidity is the *Dismasted Brig*,[4] with clean-cut rectilinear shapes in sky and water, always a feature of Cotman's work but particularly apparent here. In May 1836 the *Dismasted Brig* was included in a sale at Christie's of the collection of the Rev. James Bulwer, and was bought by Cotman himself for seventeen shillings. It was in the same sale that he saw his *Greta Bridge* knocked down for eight shillings. No wonder that mental brain-storms and chronic depressions blackened his life.

On his return to Yarmouth between and after his visits to Normandy, Cotman devoted all his energies to the completion of the hundred etchings for two large volumes of *The Architectural Antiquities of Normandy*, but any dream of making a competency was far from

[1] V.A.M. 3013–1876 (William Smith Bequest) and P.26–1934 (Powell Bequest).
[2] B.M. 1902. 5.14.51.
[3] Norwich, Castle Museum (repro. *O.W.S.* VII, 1929–1930, pl. X).
[4] B.M. 1902. 5.14.32.

coming true. The visits to Normandy, with their constant strain of travelling and intensive work, coupled with poor living for economy's sake, and followed by the immense labour of making a hundred etchings, resulted in a complete break-down of his health. His large etching of the *West Front of Rouen Cathedral* alone was 'a work of more than twenty weeks' hard labour'.

The original drawings for *Norfolk Architectural Antiquities* were left in Cotman's hands and on the brown paper wrapper of the published etchings was a notice offering the drawings for sale at One Hundred Guineas. They were bought by the Rev. James Bulwer, a member of an old Norfolk family; and it was a bold move for a young man, fresh from taking his degree at Cambridge, and just ordained. The drawings, dating from 1806 to 1818, give a clear picture of Cotman's development during this period. This portion of the Bulwer collection was bought from his descendants by Augustus Walker, of Bond Street and was sold in 1926.[1] In 1818 the drawings were probably regarded by most people— Bulwer was more wise—as dull studies for a county history. In 1926 the drawings, whose original cost was less than seven shillings apiece, were bought solely for their artistic quality at prices which would have freed Cotman from anxiety for the rest of his life. James Bulwer, it may be added, took up his residence in London, as curate of St. James's, Piccadilly, in 1833 and enjoyed close friendship with Cotman. A few years later he moved to Aylsham in Norfolk, and it was in his company that Cotman made, in the last autumn of his life, several of those happy drawings which will receive later comment.

From Normandy in 1820 Cotman had written of his suffering from intense depression, of 'a mind now diseased'. From now onwards he was a prey to profound melancholy, increased by the fact that his work found few purchasers. He fell victim to what was known as Accidie, one of the seven deadly sins, a collapse into mental misery, black despair, and hopeless unbelief. A devoted husband and father, he toiled day after day in the precarious drudgery of private drawing-lessons, and watched the straitened circumstances of his wife and family with anxiety and something of bitterness. Thrown back upon his teaching for a livelihood, he decided in 1823 to return once again to Norwich. His red brick Georgian house still stands in St. Martin's-at-Palace Plain. With slender resources, often harassed about his rent, he conducted there his 'School for Drawing. . . . Terms, One guinea and a Half the Quarter.' To pay for removal and furnishing he took the step, unusual for an artist, of sending some two hundred of his Normandy and other drawings to Christie's for sale on May 1, 1824; and after deduction of commission and expenses they realised only £165. In 1825 he confessed to Dawson Turner that his position in Norwich was a painful one, owing to the pressure of his creditors, and that his entire income from teaching was about £150 a year, while his paintings were at most a shadowy asset. In penury and despair, suffering from the nagging nerves, the clogging uncertainties, which made his life such a burden he sought to find some means of producing work which would ensure more popularity.

---

[1] C. F. Bell, 'John Sell Cotman (The Bulwer Collection)', *Walker's Quarterly*, XIX/XX, 1926.

He was like Samuel Palmer, who wrote in 1846: 'I must, D.V., strike at once a NEW STYLE.' It may be that Cotman strayed from his, but had he persisted in the same standpoint and the same theme, his work would have become fatally standardised. Cotman was justified in varying his view-point and seeking new ways of bringing hand and mind into productive contact. If it is the Greta drawings which please our modern taste, they won no great favour at the time. It was the same with Samuel Palmer. His early Shoreham drawings, which we now value most, evoked no response from others and were hidden away by him all through his life. Palmer's Shoreham drawings and Cotman's Greta drawings were probably treasured by each as a secret part of the innermost self.

Cotman was mistaken in thinking that his progress should be from quiet harmony of colour to brilliant contrasts, richer hues and a fiercer sun. Cotman's inner nature was never attuned to the carnival spirit. It was not his forte to 'wrench the sun'. In his earlier work, with its unconscious sense of style, its limpid transparent washes so aptly joined and superimposed, he stands as a supreme master. In his later work the felicity of his earlier drawings coarsened into an extravagant exuberance of colour. They became florid and flamboyant. His saffron and mustard yellows, as gold as he could make them, his touches of vicious emerald and crimson lake became hot as coals in a furnace, their heat intensified by contrast with the cold blue and white of his skies. He made lavish use of smalt or cobalt instead of the warmer indigo. Bluer tones in the shadows of architecture and landscape or greyer notes in his clouds might have mellowed and fused the effect, but the brilliant raucous contrast was an impossibility, neither true to nature nor sound as decoration. He projected a series of architectural compositions, which were to win him fame by their 'splendour and imagination', and their impressiveness of colour. *The Town on the Continent*[1] and various versions of *Mont St. Michel* and of the *Maison Abbatiale, Rouen* are typical of the false and flashy colouring. It is not without interest to see that a contemporary critic shared our condemnation. Here is what was said about the *Hotel de Ville, Ulm*, exhibited at the Old Water-Colour Society in 1830:

> The latter works of this original-minded artist are compounded of qualities, which though incongruous, are yet rendered so compatible by that modern skill which combines extravagance with simplicity, that at the same time that it invites inquiry as to its pretensions to rank with fine art, almost bids defiance to criticism. Vocal musicians complain of screwing up the instruments above concert pitch. Such a custom produces terrible wear and tear of the voice. Fashion or caprice may demand these novelties, and at length they are endured. It is vain to preach against them whilst the paroxysm rages. So it is with the graphic art; every year screws colouring up to a higher scale according to Exhibition pitch, until the very shadow of a cloud is rendered more intensely blue than Byron's classic sea, and the sober gray granite column of a temple blazes prominently brighter than Corinthian brass. Yet as the ear of Fashion accommodates itself to notes sharper and sharper still, so does the prejudiced eye see harmony in this graphic hyperbole—for all is compatible with the Exhibition key.[2]

[1] The Huntington Library, San Marino, California.
[2] *Library of Fine Arts*, I, 1831, p. 515.

And in 1825, Robert Hunt,[1] in the *Examiner*, had denounced Cotman's *Mont St. Michel* and *Dieppe* in the Water-Colour Society's exhibition for their 'sudden opposition of reds, blues and yellows', and adjured artists in general 'to guard against an intemperance of bright colour, and to look at the *nature-taught* practice of Messers. Barret and De Wint'.

Cotman himself gives a clue to his own feelings about colour at this period in a letter of January 6, 1834.[2] He describes how he had seen a number of Lewis's drawings of Spain and orders his sons to discontinue landscape and to turn to figure, piling on the colour. 'My poor Reds, Blues and Yellows for which I have in Norwich been so much abused and broken-hearted about are *faded fades* to what I saw there. Yes and Aye, FADED FADES and trash, nonsense and stuff.'

As A. P. Oppé points out,[3] Cotman's early restrained style, to which he is so largely indebted for his recent revival of popularity, had become completely out of date; such drawing could not have stood out against the heavy gold frames required by the Water-Colour Society. There can be little doubt that Cotman's later drawings of the florid type were made, to some extent, in emulation of Turner, and we can find prototypes in Turner's *Malvern Abbey*[4] and *Dunstanborough*.[5] But though Turner was at one time unduly florid, too prone to emphasise passages of hot colour, he never lost the value of contrast, the contrast of hot colour with cool notes of evanescent grey. In such a drawing, for instance, as *Zurich*[6] there is hot colour, but the whole drawing has a shimmering iridescence which Cotman's flatter washes and more emphatic colouring could never attain.

As early as 1823 Cotman's *Mount St. Catherine, Rouen*[7] shows clearly a conscious effort to rival Turner's brilliance of colour. It is something of a showpiece, more scattered in design than is usual for him but saved by the dark masses of the central trees and boats. It is an unusual Cotman in another way, because he abandoned his direct methods and scraped freely with a sharp knife or razor. He not only flicked out lights here and there, but scraped sky and distance and part of the foreground as well. There can be few drawings by any artist in which the knife was so freely used. Even when in 1824 he took up a sketch made in 1802 and painted a large water-colour of *Snowdon with the Lake of Llanberris, from Dolbaddern Castle*,[8] he deserted his earlier method of leaving clear spaces, scratched out streaks on the water, and used the knife for broken texture on the mountain-sides. An equally remarkable change at this period was his abandonment of 'reserved spaces' in his trees. Where he wanted some solitary branch, some wreath of two or three motionless large leaves, to stand light against dark, he traced the forms with a wet brush and wiped them out with a rag—the method in which Turner excelled. A perfect example uniting

[1] Brother of Leigh Hunt.
[2] Kitson, *op. cit.*, p. 306.
[3] A. P. Oppé, 'Cotman and his Public', *Burlington Magazine*, LXXXI, 1942.
[4] Manchester, City Art Gallery.
[5] Manchester, City Art Gallery.
[6] B.M. 1958, 7.12.445.
[7] Coll. Constance, Viscountess Mackintosh of Halifax.
[8] Coll. Constance, Viscountess Mackintosh of Halifax.

Cotman's middle and last periods is the *Anglers*, lovely in colour and interesting in technique, once in the collection of Mr. Victor Rienaecker, and exhibited at the Fine Art Society in 1942. Another difference, apart from his heightened colour, is that he used the device of dragging colour almost dry (the 'scumbling' of the oil-painter) across his work, to obtain a pleasing crumbly texture. We feel that where Turner became the master, Cotman became the victim of technical ingenuity. At least it may be said of Cotman that, like Turner, he wanted his artistic life to be replete with experience and not with mere repetition. In search of a new style, he would vie with Turner, plagiarise Turner—though I do not believe he was deliberately an imitator—rather than plagiarise his own past.

In 1825 it must have cheered Cotman for a time, in his constant depression and despondency, that he was elected an Associate of the Old Water-Colour Society, the more so because he was admitted without the formality of submitting work for approval. During the remaining seventeen years of his life he exhibited there only forty-six drawings, an average of less than three a year, whereas Copley Fielding sometimes sent as many as seventy works to a single exhibition. Cotman's contributions were rarely bought, and, probably owing to his casual appearances, he never won election to full membership. He found himself still 'but a mere drawing master—the very thing I dreaded most on setting out in life'. In 1827 he wrote to Dawson Turner that he was about to begin a series of drawings 'for Reputation—and, I hope, for Profit'. In this letter and in many others there are passages, however sincere in Cotman's case, which are pure Micawber: 'I have obtruded myself upon your notice whilst I was wretched, heart-broken and in despair—when I found that all my efforts were unavailing to raise myself into notice or even above the prospects of a debtor's prison. A tide has I hope at last set in my favour. Reputation, and consequently a fair standing among my friends is what I have worked hard for and desired above all temporal things; and had I not felt I deserved it for my industry, if not for my talent, I should perhaps, ere this, have ceased to struggle, even for my family. For many weeks one overwhelming flood of despairing thoughts made every atom of my composition a separate torture' (Cotman to Dawson Turner, 1827). Then, in 1829, to the Rev. W. Gunn[1]: 'My views in life are so completely blasted that I sink under the repeated and constant exertion of body and mind. Every effort has been tried, even without the hope of success. Hence that loss of spirits amounting almost to despair. My eldest son, who is following the same miserable profession as myself, feels the same hopelessness with myself; and his powers, once so promising, are evidently paralysed, and his health and spirits gone. My amiable and deserving wife bears her part with fortitude—but the worm is there. My children cannot but feel the contagion.'

Cotman was lying ill, with the Normandy etchings still waiting publication, when Varley on a visit to Norwich called to see his old friend. The servant who opened the door

---

[1] The original letter, printed in full in the catalogue of the Cotman Exhibition at Norwich, 1888, is in the Library of Edinburgh University.

informed the cheerful visitor that her master was very ill and going to die. 'Die!' said Varley. 'Impossible! Won't die these twenty years. Let me see your mistress.' On Mrs. Cotman's appearance and her announcement that, 'Poor Cotman is given over by the doctors', Varley replied with confidence, 'Pooh! Nonsense! They know nothing about it. His time is a long way off. Let me see him.' Introduced to the sick chamber, he rallied his friend: 'Why, Cotman, you're not such a fool as to think you're going to die! Impossible! No such thing! I tell you there are twenty years for you yet to come.' Varley, known as 'Vates', who predicted the death of Paul Mulready at sixty and of William Collins to the day, used his astrological gifts with almost equal exactness on this occasion. Cotman lived for nineteen years and three months longer.

Cotman, whose self-tormenting melancholia was anything but fictional, was always hoping that something would turn up. But his drawings done 'for reputation' were of the nature described above, gaudy and theatrical, heightened by vermilion and emerald green in contrast with hot yellows and brilliant blues. He made an annual visit to London, his journey in the summer of 1830 resulting in his large water-colour *Crosby Hall*.[1] In this his colour is strong, but not unduly forced. It is a romantic treatment of the subject at a time when the building was in use as a warehouse; hence the two traders seated at a table covered with vivid green cloth, and the bales of richly coloured fabrics on the floor. *The Green Lamp*[2] (Pl. 78), painted in 1839, is in a way a companion, and is even finer. Figures on the left—Cotman, his wife and his daughter Ann—are poring over a book in their drawing-room at Bloomsbury, glorified into a palatial reception room with baroque decoration. The green lamp in front of them is rendered by a piece of paper from the green shade of Cotman's own colza lamp, stuck on by himself.

About the year 1830 there begins what may be called Cotman's third, or final, period. His first period is that which embraces the Greta drawings, almost oriental in the simplicity of their flat washes. They have what Coleridge described as one of the essential characteristics of poetry, 'the power of reducing multitude into unity of effect'. Then comes a middle period, in which he was more exuberant and diffuse, making experiments with strong and then still stronger colours, which ended in an attempt to rival oil in brilliance and richness, with raw vehemence of vermilion, ochre and azure, crude and gay like the decoration of a canal barge. In his last period, beginning about 1830, he used a new medium for a large portion of his work; and the invention seems to have been his own. He experimented with a material described as the albuminous liquid which rises to the top of rotting flour paste, and Kitson suggests that there may have been other ingredients such as the white of egg. It may—I believe from experiment—have been just a simple method of using ordinary flour or rice paste, not necessarily sour or rotten, with perhaps an admixture of some Chinese white, as a medium to mix with pure colour. At any rate, this paste method is semi-opaque, but still does not destroy completely the luminosity of white

---

[1] V.A.M. P.19–1927.   [2] Norwich, Castle Museum.

paper. It allows, indeed, of a singular intensity of colour, particularly in blues. The advantage is that colour with a mixture of paste remains moist on the surface of the paper for an appreciably longer time than pure water-colour, and while still tacky can be dragged about and lifted or manipulated, like oil paint, with a hog's hair brush, which Cotman employed for this purpose instead of the usual sable. The method and its results have clearly been an inspiration, though not necessarily closely followed, to later artists such as C. J. Collins, Cecil Hunt, Bertram Nicholls, Gordon Forsyth, H. Tittensor and others.

Cotman used his discovery for imaginative landscape, and it allowed him to recapture some of the emotional sensitivity of his earlier days. His spirit seems to refute the artificial pose of his middle years and to regain some of the innocence of youth. The first drawings which show the new method fully exploited belong to 1830. It was used brilliantly and effectively in *Storm on Yarmouth Beach*[1] of that year, with its group of fishermen beneath a lowering sky. It was misused in *The Shepherd on a Hill*,[2] which shows Cotman recapturing his earlier style in the scarlet and emerald green of the central figure set against a blue and white sky. The paste medium appears at its best in the imaginative landscapes which he painted on small sheets of paper, about seven inches by ten, during his last years in Norwich and London. Some of these drawings were bought by J. H. Maw and descended to his grandson, Derwent Wood, the sculptor. Two of the finest, *Rocky Landscape, Sunset*[3] and *The Lake*[4] (Pl. 79) being now in the Victoria and Albert Museum. The use of a hog's hair brush for manipulating the colour is clearly apparent in the glowing blues of the *Rocky Landscape*. *The Lake* is well described by Oppé as 'a rhapsody of line and form, with inter-playing depths of receding plane, which is just such an effusion of pure imagination in landscape as old Alexander Cozens might have wished to issue from the inspired working of his Blotting brush'. Another superb example, *Cader Idris*, is in the Castle Museum, Norwich, and three more belong to the National Museum of Wales, Cardiff. Of these, *Blue Afternoon*, with its lovely group of trees and slanting shadows, is a variant of the *Chateau in Normandy*[5] at the British Museum: and *The Fisherman*[6] shows clearly the use made by Cotman of the end of his wooden brush in lifting pigment and giving form to the reeds. This method of taking out lights can be employed in the darker portions of any water-colour in the few seconds when the colour is approaching dryness. In the paste method it can be used even more effectively and with more leisurely action owing to the sticky softness of the medium. The same devices are apparent in that very poetic monochrome drawing, *The Shadowed Stream*.[7]

In 1834 an unexpected change took place in Cotman's fortunes. Through his old pupil Lady Palgrave, Dawson Turner's daughter, who resided in London with her husband, Sir Francis Palgrave, came a suggestion that Cotman should apply for the post of drawing-master in the recently established King's College in London. Tradition states that J. M. W. Turner, R.A., was his strongest champion and when asked whom he would

[1] Norwich, Castle Museum.
[2] Liverpool, Walker Art Gallery.
[3] V.A.M. P.21–1926.
[4] V.A.M. P.20–1926.
[5] B.M. 1902. 5.14.36.
[6] Norwich, Castle Museum.
[7] B.M. 1902. 5.14.57.

recommend said: 'Why, of course, Cotman. I am tired of saying what I say again—Cotman! Cotman!!!' Doubt has been thrown upon this story, especially as the Turner in question might have been Dawson Turner, or William Turner of Oxford, and because Cotman himself spoke diffidently of approaching J. M. W. Turner through Thomas Phillips, R.A. But Turner knew Cotman well; he must have met him more than thirty years before, when Cotman was working at Dr. Monro's; and at a later period Cotman inscribed a drawing as a gift to *my old and esteemed friend, J. M. W. Turner*. Turner's advocacy is probably true and to his credit. And so, three years before Queen Victoria's accession, Cotman went to the School which lay on the eastern side of Somerset House, and took up his duties, at a salary of £100 a year. He earned a guinea a head for each pupil beyond the first hundred; and his work occupied only two days each week. How little did the students at King's College ever imagine that their diffident, melancholy drawing-master was one of the country's greatest artists. Did Rossetti, who was one of his pupils, ever feel that he was learning from a genius, or did he just regard him as a tiresome pedagogue? Ruskin, too, at the age of seventeen, was attending lectures on English literature at King's College. He must have known of Cotman, though there is no record of his having attended a drawing-class. In the thirty-seven volumes of the Library edition of Ruskin and in the vastness of its index, Cotman's name never once appears.

Cotman, of course, had not realised that London was a more expensive place in which to live than Norwich. His family for a time were still in lodgings at Norwich; Cotman and his son, Miles Edmund, in lodgings in Soho. He writes to Dawson Turner: 'I was sanguine enough in my folly to suppose I could live in London with my family. *The income is not sufficient.*' To avoid this trouble a sale of his collection of prints, drawings, copper-plates and a few pictures was held at Norwich in September, 1834, and brought in about £500, meeting his outstanding liabilities so far as Norwich was concerned. By the end of 1834 his family had joined him and settled in at 42, Hunter Street, Brunswick Square, quite close to the Foundling Hospital. Miles Edmund acted as his unpaid assistant at King's College, while John Joseph took his place as a teacher in Norwich. The whole family, father, two sons and a daughter, were 'drawing-mad, working for the College pupils', and the family drawing-copies grew in number. James Reeve has placed it on record that Cotman would sometimes, 'by way of complimenting a pupil whose drawing pleased him, add to it the name of "Cotman" with a number, and place it in a folio for teaching purposes'. The Dawson Turner family were adept at covering Cotman drawings with a blank sheet of paper and tracing them against a window pane, as a preliminary to producing an imitation of deceptive fidelity. C. F. Bell[1] writes that: 'Seldom, at least, in dealing with a period so late as the nineteenth century is the "Science of a Connoisseur" called upon to tackle questions so delicate and baffling as the separation of authentic works by Cotman from those of his scholars and copyists.' At first sight, it may be said, for Cotman was one of those rare masters who was never second rate as an executant. The quality, using the word in its

[1] *Op. cit.*, pp. 11, 12.

technical sense, of his pencil lines and his water-colour washes; the refined intuition with which he recognised the points needing accent and, even more infallibly, upon the features requiring to be omitted, are beyond imitation. It is, none the less, only after close scrutiny that the true and the false can be discerned, so specious is much of the latter. There were more than 2000 of Cotman's drawing-copies in existence when he left Norwich. Many of the later London ones were inscribed, with a rubber stamp, *Cotman, King's College, London*: No. 2300 is in the Norwich Museum, as well as an unstamped No. 2631. Kitson gives the highest known as 4139. It was a strange and inadequate system of teaching drawing to set his pupils, according to their taste, to copy a Welsh landscape, fragments of Norman architecture, *Strong Symptoms of the Gout, The Dragon of Wartley*, or *Robinson Crusoe finding Friday's footmarks on the Sand*, No. 4134. Attendance at the College, the constant output of these copies; some work of his own in holiday times; such was Cotman's life.

In the autumn of 1841, the last autumn of his life, Cotman determined to take advantage of a remainder of his summer holidays and, leaving his son to act as his deputy in London, spent nearly two months in his home town, where he was now not without honour. Homage was paid to him as a distinguished London artist, a Professor of Drawing in a London College. This was some reparation for his years of deprivation, frustration, mental ill health and harsh criticism. As if in response to this recognition he made a large series of drawings in black and white chalk on grey paper, notably *The Wold Afloat*,[1] dated October 19, 1841, now in the British Museum. He was warned by his old friend and patron, Dawson Turner, who he visited at Yarmouth, not to get over-strained and excited by making too many sketches, of which surely he had sufficient abundance, but he replied: 'tis as impossible to pass a fine subject and not to book it as it is for a miser to pass a guinea and not pick it up'. Perhaps for the first time, when he became the drawing-master at King's College, did Cotman seem to fit into the mechanism of life. But even after that there were always subjects to be booked, always something beckoning round the corner of life, which could never be picked up. He returned to London on November 20, and six months later he was seriously ill. He died on July 24, 1842, and was buried on July 30 in the churchyard of St. John's Wood Chapel, Marylebone.

On May 18–19, 1843, a sale of his drawings and paintings at Christie's brought in the melancholy total of £219 17s. 6d. There was another large dispersal of his drawings by Messrs. Spelman at Norwich in 1861. James Reeve, the young curator of the Norwich Museum, bought some of the finest examples of Cotman's work, and these are now at the British Museum. He gave three guineas for *Rocks on the Greta*. The *Drop Gate at Duncombe Park* realised three guineas, and the superb *Meeting of the Greta and the Tees*, now in the Scottish National Gallery, fetched only fifty shillings. For another sale in 1862, John Joseph Cotman put together every remaining scrap of his father's work which could be found, including the brilliant chalk drawings made in the autumn of 1841. These were secured by James Reeve, and many of the finest are now national property.

[1] B.M. 1902. 5.14.146.

Throughout his career Cotman's talent was confined by the harsh necessity of work as drawing-master, made still more arduous by his incessant production of small drawings as copies for his pupils. His life was nothing but humdrum plodding, disappointed hope and unrewarded labour; to reclaim waste ground, and through years of disillusion and poverty he toiled unceasingly. His duty towards his family, his slavery to mechanical reproductive work for Dawson Turner, and his employment as a teacher, hindered the concentration and freedom required for the high and steady flight of genius. It is to be wondered that he produced so many masterpieces. He was feckless. He suffered from an appalling sense of failure. He was an artist whose talents led him nowhere, fighting a daily battle to support a home and family; rich in ideas of form and colour for which he could find no market. Every time that he failed to make his occupation more practical and more profitable, the more ineffectual his whole life seemed, the more secretly woebegone he became; but he continued to tackle each daily task with missionary zeal. His letters reflect his spirit of hollowness and neglect, his ill health, restlessness and discontent. He was never quite down and out, but—what was worse—he thought he was. He has no self-assertiveness, like Turner and De Wint and he was too inclined to accept lack of appreciation as a pathetic but natural misfortune.

With regard to Cotman's fight against poverty and neglect, it is only fair to say that there is a somewhat divergent view, and that A. P. Oppé[1] disputes the general idea of 'Cotman as an artist whose life and work was largely frustrated by drudgery and distress'. Oppé produces evidence that Cotman was neither crushed by the demands of Dawson Turner nor repressed by the hostility of critics and the indifference of the public. Certainly the reading of Kitson's biography leaves one in sympathy with Dawson Turner for his long-sufferance in dealing with Cotman's curious temper and his tangled finances. The truth perhaps lies between the two views. Against Oppé's evidence, Cotman did meet with fiercely adverse criticism as well as high praise, and nothing can alter the fact that in 1836 he had to watch his finest water-colours being sold at Christie's for a few shillings apiece. If, as Binyon puts it, Cotman was 'half-submerged in drudgery', he was also half-submerged in poverty, but both drudgery and poverty were to a large extent the figments of his unstable and abnormal temperament. He may have been reduced to his last shilling, but that shilling was always in his pocket.

Samuel Butler[2] said wisely: 'Composition is the one word common to painting, sculpture, architecture, music and literature. This shows that the main merit in each case depends upon the arrangement in relation to one another of the objects and incidents that are dealt with.' Cotman in this sense was a composer. His art does not offer the excitement and surprise of Turner, but it is so rooted in basic laws of design that it should survive all temporary dogmas of fashion. In his orderly arrangement of rectilinear shapes, Cotman somewhat anticipates an aspect of Post-Impressionist and Cubist art; but he never allows

[1] A. P. Oppé, 'Cotman and his public', *Burlington Magazine* LXXXI, 1942, p. 163.
[2] *Further Extracts from the Notebooks of Samuel Butler* (1934) p. 228.

95

his discovery of geometrical form to lead him into any mannerist extravagance or excess. Again to quote Oppé, 'He always retains his sense of the actual drawing or painting as a thing of artistic and emotional value in its colour, line and massing, over and above, or at best through and through, the significance of the objects represented.'

At the Exhibition of British Art, organised by the Royal Academy in January, 1934, Cotman was represented by nine oil-paintings, fifteen water-colours and five monochrome drawings. Looking at them with Roger Fry, that acute, enthusiastic and inspiring critic, I was astounded to find that he regarded Cotman as 'the perfect drawing-master', and not as one of the greatest of British painters. I had thought that Fry would recognise in Cotman those qualities of 'significant form' and 'plastic content', which in Cézanne and others he lauded with such apostolic fervour. But Fry could perceive only technical skill and inevitable correctness in Cotman's work. For myself, a Cotman drawing here and there shows the exquisite and final flawlessness of a Sung vase or a Yuan painting, yielding an instant of emotion before its dissolution into purest thought. I would accept the opinion of Laurence Binyon when he says that 'Cotman made the most perfect examples of pure water-colour ever made in Europe'.

Something more should be said about two of Cotman's sons. Redgrave, in his *Dictionary of Artists*, gives a few patronising lines to Miles and does not trouble to mention John Joseph. Both were clearly dominated by their father during a great part of their lives and compelled to follow, as best they could, a code of painting as rigid as the domestic Victorian code of morals and manner. Miles Edmund (1810–1858), the elder, became his father's pupil, companion and assistant, as has already been related. His art career began at the early age of thirteen, when he first contributed to the Norwich Exhibition, to which he sent paintings or drawings regularly from 1823 to 1833. He became his father's assistant at King's College in 1835 and was officially styled Assistant Drawing Master in December 1836. He assumed the entire responsibility of the classes towards the end of his father's life. John Sell saw a certain dullness in his son's work and wished his drawing 'to be dashing and sketch-like, to get him out of his hard, dry manner'. His work, when it represents purely his own thought and execution, though good in drawing and design, does lack freedom and is too prim and precise. But there is genuine merit in *Unloading Timber Ships*,[1] in *Greenwich Reach*,[2] and particularly in *Early Morning on the Medway*[3] (Pl. 81), all of them in the British Museum. The last of these shows more than a hint of his father's manner, but the younger man was also clearly influenced by Müller and Bonington. Nearly a hundred drawings by him from the Bulwer Collection were exhibited at Walker's Galleries in 1926, and gave strong proof of these influences. The drawings were mainly of architectural subjects in Norfolk, and such as were dated belonged to the years 1838–1841. It would not have been unreasonable, but for the signatures and the known provenance, to attribute *Hellesdon* and *West Dereham* to Müller, or *Old Roman Catholic Chapel, Norwich* to Bonington. *Thorpe Valley on the Yare* and *On the Yare, Coldham Hall* showed his more native instinct. For

[1] B.M. 1902. 5.14.338.　　　　[2] B.M. 1902. 5.14.337.　　　　[3] B.M. 1902. 5.14.339.

68 'Chirk Aqueduct'
V.A.M. 115-1892 $12\frac{1}{2} \times 9\frac{1}{8}$: 318 × 231   *Water-colour*
John Sell COTMAN (1782-1842)

69 'The Drop Gate in Duncombe Park'

B.M. 1902.5.14.14   13 × 9$\frac{1}{8}$: 330 × 230   *Water-colour*

John Sell COTMAN (1782–1842)

70 'Greta Bridge'

B.M. 1902.5.14.17   9 × 13 : 242 × 330   *Water-colour*

John Sell COTMAN (1782–1842)

71 'Greta Woods'

Coll. Dr L. S. Fry   13 × 9: 330 × 228   *Water-colour*

John Sell COTMAN (1782–1842)

72 'The Shady Pool, where the Greta joins the Tees'
Edinburgh, The National Gallery of Scotland $17\frac{7}{8} \times 14 : 455 \times 355$ *Water-colour*
John Sell Cotman (1782–1842)

73 'The Ploughed Field'
Leeds, City Art Gallery   9½ × 14: 241 × 355   *Water-colour*
John Sell COTMAN (1782–1842)

74 'Cheyne Walk'
Norwich, Castle Museum   9¼ × 11¾: 236 × 299   *Water-colour, signed*
John Sell COTMAN (1782–1842)

75 'Binham Priory'

Coll. Dr L. S. Fry   16 × 12 : 407 × 304   *Water-colour*

John Sell COTMAN (1782–1842)

76 'The Needles'
Norwich, Castle Museum $8\frac{1}{4} \times 12\frac{3}{4}$: 210×323 *Water-colour*
John Sell COTMAN (1782–1842)

77 'Domfront'
Coll. Mr & Mrs Paul Mellon $11\frac{1}{8} \times 16\frac{5}{8}$: 282×412 *Sepia, signed*
John Sell COTMAN (1782–1842)

78 'The Green Lamp'

Norwich, Castle Museum $13\frac{1}{8} \times 18\frac{7}{8}: 333 \times 478$ *Water-colour, signed and dated 1839*

John Sell COTMAN (1782–1842)

79 'The Lake'

V.A.M. P.20–1926 $7\frac{1}{8} \times 10\frac{1}{2}: 181 \times 267$ *Water-colour*

John Sell COTMAN (1782–1842)

80 'Irmingland Hall'
Coll. Mr & Mrs Paul Mellon   6 × 9½ : 152 × 241   *Water-colour*
Miles Edmund COTMAN (1810–1858)

81 'Early Morning on the Medway'
B.M. 1902.5.14.339   3⅞ × 5¾ : 98 × 146   *Water-colour*
Miles Edmund COTMAN (1810–1858)

82 'Thorpe'

Norwich, Castle Museum   14 × 10¾: 355 × 274   *Water-colour*

John Joseph COTMAN (1814–1878)

83 Gravel Pit, Sprowston, Norwich

Norwich, Castle Museum   9 × 13 : 229 × 330   *Water-colour*

John Joseph COTMAN (1814–1878)

some years after resigning his London appointment he painted and taught at North Walsham.

Cotman's second son, John Joseph (1814–1878), was born at Southtown, Great Yarmouth. Of much stronger character than his brother, he worked for a time with his uncle Edmund Cotman, the haberdasher, but soon rebelled against the duties of the shop and spent all his time in qualifying for the family profession of drawing-master. He moved to London with his father in 1834, but returned to Norwich and took over the teaching connection there from his brother Miles. Morbid by temperament, handicapped by what Dickes calls 'the buzzing bee of cerebral irritability', suffering from constant fits of brooding and depression, conscious in his own words of 'indecision and want of perseverance', he was, like his father, ill equipped for the contests of life. He exhibited from 1852 to 1856 at the British Institution and in 1853 at the Royal Academy. In his water-colours he worked with much more freedom, much more drive and surge than his brother. In his later years, when freed from his father's influence, he showed an independent spirit. His *Norwich from the Yare*,[1] painted in 1873, was executed in a crisp, luminist style of broken colour, in as high a key as the later Impressionists sought. Very noticeable in his work is his love of intense contrasts of brilliant cobalt and the yellow and russet hues of autumn foliage.

As a determined follower, almost an imitator, of Cotman, may be mentioned a Welsh artist, Pryce Carter Edwards, who flourished in the 1830's. Six water-colours by him, and thirty-seven sepia drawings, are in the National Museum of Wales. In a period of naturalism he is interesting for his dramatic simplification and sense of pattern.

---

[1] Present whereabouts unknown.

CHAPTER VI

The Varleys

John, Cornelius, William Fleetwood and other members of the Varley family

Of the sixteen original members of the Old Water-Colour Society John Varley (1778–1842) probably bears the most familiar name. In his lifetime he exercised greater influence than any of the others and always, I think, for good. He was a consummate craftsman, and many of his drawings have outstanding qualities both of design and colour. It must be admitted, on the other side, that A. J. Finberg[1] dismisses him cynically in four lines as 'a facile systematiser who attracted a large number of pupils by his astrological pretensions and feats of strength. A number of his paintings at South Kensington bear witness to his deficiencies as a teacher.' That cursory statement cannot be accepted as applying with any degree of truth to a painter whose example and precept influenced strongly such men as William Hunt, John Linnell, Mulready, Copley Fielding, Cotman, Cox, Turner of Oxford, De Wint, F. O. Finch and Samuel Palmer. Nor is it fair to suggest that his influence was entirely due to any personal charm or attraction, though he was undoubtedly a character. To use a distinction which Goethe was accustomed to make, he was 'a nature', and no creature of the passing convention. We may think of him as a confident, commanding, picturesque, humorous and combative figure, full of the zest of life, loving each day's work, making technique into science, passing on to others his gusto and experience.

Varley came of intelligent middle-class parentage. He was born in a house, formerly an inn called The Blue Posts, abutting on Hackney churchyard, to which his father had moved from his home town of Epworth in Lincolnshire. John Varley was the eldest of five children by his father's second wife. His father, like so many other fathers of artists, declaring that limning was a bad trade and that none of his children should be artists. His three sons, however, John, Cornelius and William Fleetwood, all took to the brush, and one of their sisters, Elizabeth, married William Mulready, R.A. John, at the age of thirteen, was placed by his father with a silversmith, but in 1791 before he entered on a definite apprenticeship, his father died and the family were left in straitened circumstances. From a humble dwelling in a court off Old Street, near St. Luke's Hospital, John started off daily

---

[1] A. J. Finberg, *English Water Colour Painters*, 1905, p. 158.

to various menial posts in London offices. On one occasion, having expended his slender stock of money in paper and pencils, he played truant and set off on his first sketching excursion. His mother saw nothing of him for some days, when he returned, driven home by hunger, with sketches of Hampstead and Highgate. His demands on his mother's meagre purse for drawing paper were such that she used to say: 'When Johnny marries, it will be a paper wife.'

At the age of fifteen he managed to obtain admission to the evening drawing-school kept by Joseph Charles Barrow at his house, 12, Furnival's Inn Court, Holborn. Francia was an assistant teacher at the school, and young Varley had to pay for the advantage of drawing beside the other pupils by acting as a lower sort of assistant and errand-boy. In 1796 he met John Preston Neale, seven years his senior, and would accompany Neale on a day's sketching, a crust of bread his sole provender, at Hoxton, Tottenham and Stoke Newington, rural districts in those days. His teacher, Barrow, evidently thought well of Varley's progress, for he took him to Peterborough on a sketching excursion. From studies then made, Varley exhibited a careful pencil drawing, *View of Peterborough Cathedral*,[1] at the Royal Academy in 1798. In this year, or in 1799, he accompanied George Arnald, afterwards A.R.A., on a tour in North Wales. He visited Wales again in 1800 and 1802. To judge by the long list of his Welsh subjects in later years, these visits to Wales had a most decisive influence upon his career. About the year 1800 he became one of the select few who enjoyed the hospitality of Dr. Monro at his home in Adelphi Terrace and his country house at Fetcham. In a drawing inscribed *View from Polsden near Bookham in Surrey, made in company with Dr. Monro by John Varley, October 1800*,[2] the trees show the influence of Sandby, but the flat panoramic distance with its striped fields and dotted trees is pure Girtin and suggests that Monro had held up Girtin as the best exemplar for his young protégé. Through Monro's kindness Varley came into touch with discriminating patrons, and began to take pupils. One of his first patrons was Edward, Viscount Lascelles, a discerning collector and amateur water-colourist. As has been told, Girtin and Turner were also his guests and made drawings of Harewood House. Adrian Bury[3] quotes an entry dated March 16, 1801 in Viscount Lascelles' account books. 'To paid Mr. Varley for a drawing £15 15s. od.' This is probably *Harewood House from the South-East*, and it was followed in 1803 by *View of Harewood House from the South*.

From 1802 to 1804 Varley was a member of the Sketching Club, which was founded by Girtin and continued by Cotman. By 1804, when he helped in the foundation of the Old Water-Colour Society, he was counted as one of the leading water-colour artists in London. When, for instance, Francis Nicholson embarked about 1803 upon his exposure of drawing-masters who took a share in 'faking' the works of their pupils for exhibition at the Society of Fine Arts, he called in Varley, who was twenty-five years his junior, as a witness.

[1] Newcastle-upon-Tyne, Laing Art Gallery.
[2] Newcastle-upon-Tyne, Laing Art Gallery. Reproduced *O.W.S. Club*, II, 1924–1925 pl. IV.
[3] A. Bury, *John Varley*, 1946.

'It is useless', said Nicholson, when asked to substantiate his charge, 'to consider this as a matter of opinion. My friend Mr. Varley can prove the truth of what I stated to the Society and accompanied me here for that purpose.'

From 1798 to 1804 Varley exhibited at the Royal Academy, but after the formation of the Water-Colour Society he abandoned the Academy for twenty years and became one of the Society's most prolific contributors, showing on its walls over 730 works in all. To the first exhibition in 1805 he sent forty-one drawings; in 1808, fifty-two; and in 1809 as many as sixty. In 1842 he forgot all about the coming exhibition till six weeks before it opened. On being reminded he set to work, and completed within the six weeks forty-one drawings, ranging in value from £10 to £150.[1] It is said that on the eve of an exhibition he would go home at night and appear in the morning with a batch of fresh drawings under his arm. His fellow-members called them Varley's Hot Rolls.

His brother artists and his pupils were infected by his whole-hearted enthusiasm. He despised secrets, and gave help to all and was one of those rare teachers who devote themselves to their disciples, being determined to encourage whatever talent they might possess. He insisted upon hard work and detested idling. If a noise came from the room where his pupils were carrying out his instructions, he would burst in, wearing his yellow dressing gown and castigate them indiscriminately, with a brass-edged ruler. If the lads had a visitor, then the visitor came in for his share of blows.[2] At houses which he visited as drawing-master, even the servants were inspired to take up brush and paper; and once, before mounting the stairs to give a lesson to the mistress of the house, he was found at the hall table instructing the footman how to wash in a sky. When John Dobson, a well-known northern architect, who built the Central Railway Station at Newcastle, came to London as a youth in 1810 to obtain instruction in water-colour before entering his profession, he went to Varley. Fully occupied all day, Varley had not even half an hour to spare for any novice, but on seeing the young man's intense disappointment, consented to give him lessons at five in the morning, and to make this possible invited young Dobson to stay in his house. In the Laing Art Gallery at Newcastle is a river scene with cattle inscribed: 'This drawing was executed by John Dobson when studying under John Varley.'

By 1812 Varley's terms for teaching amateurs had risen to a guinea an hour, and his services were in wide request. A lady with her three daughters once visited Nollekens, the well-known sculptor, to show him the drawings of her youngest, who was considered a natural genius. Upon looking at them, Nollekens advised her to have a regular drawing-master; 'And I can recommend you one. He only lives over the way, and his name is John Varley.'[3] On December 12, 1823, Archdeacon Fisher writes from Salisbury to his friend Constable: 'Varley is here, teaching drawing to the young ladies. "Principles", he says, "are the thing. *The warm grey, the cold grey, and the round touch.*"' He used to tell his

[1] C. Monkhouse, *Earlier English Water-Colour Painters*, 1897, p. 167.
[2] Eliza Finch, *Memorials of F. O. Finch*, 1865.
[3] J. T. Smith, *Nollekens and his Times*, 1949, chapter XIII, p. 191.

pupils that flat washes of colour in a good lay-in are like silences, for as every whisper can be distinctly heard in a silence, so every lighter or darker touch on a simple and masterly lay-in told at once, and was seen to be good or bad. There are many other tales of the blunt, characteristic remarks which he fired at his pupils: 'Did you ever notice a barber sharpen a razor? That's what your work wants, the decision and the smacks.' 'Nature wants cooking,' he would say; or, 'Every picture ought to have a *look-there*.' Constable, it is true, found him a little dogmatic, and self-confident. In 1831, at the height of his career, when he had been a member of the Royal Academy for two years, Constable wrote to Leslie: 'Varley, the astrologer, has just called on me, and I have bought a little drawing of him. He told me how to "do landscape", and was so kind as to point out all my defects. The price of the drawing was "a guinea and a half *to a gentleman*, and a guinea to an *artist*".'[1]

For the benefit of beginners Varley published his *Treatise on the Principles of Landscape Design*, issued in eight parts, from 1816 to 1821, with sixteen aquatint plates from his own drawings. His subject is classified under the headings of (1) Principles of Light and Shade, (2) Principles of Objects reflected in Water, (3) Epic (Pastoral) and Pastoral, (4) River Scene, (5) Sunshine, (6) Principles of Skies in Fine or Stormy Weather, (7) Marine, (8) General Landscape; Mountainous Landscape. He was clearly basing his classification in part upon that of Turner's *Liber Studiorum*. In this book he writes systematically on the theory of "effect", gives general rules of composition, and explains the objects of each device, to conduct the eye from point to point, to arrest the gaze, or to heighten an impression by the sense of contrast—in short, to ensure his 'look-there'. The general shape and arrangement of the masses, and the various dispositions of light and shade, are shown to be susceptible of the most businesslike manipulation; while the attitude no less than the position of a figure, or the colour of a cow (we shall note, later the value of a white cow in a drawing by De Wint), may play an important part in impressing the effect of the whole scene upon the spectator. He also issued, in parts between 1815 and 1820, a *Practical Treatise on the Art of Drawing in Perspective*, and *Precepts of Landscape Drawing*. Apart from the evidence of his contemporaries, these books show him as an original and inspiring teacher. Roger Fry's description of Cotman as 'the perfect drawing-master' applies with much more fitness to Varley.

Varley was known to his friends as 'Vates' or 'The astrologer', as we have seen in Constable's letter. He was 'a believer and student of the vain science of astrology', and was rarely introduced to anyone without asking within a short time for the date and hour of his birth. From about the year 1818, when Linnell introduced him to Blake, he was a constant companion of Blake, and the latter's voyages into the visionary world had strong attractions for the younger man. At Varley's house in 1819 and 1820 were drawn the visionary heads or spiritual portraits which Blake summoned before him at will. Usually,

---

[1] C. R. Leslie, *Life of Constable*, 1912, chapter XII, p. 169.

the portraits were of historical personages; and the apparition of a flea, received by both with absolute seriousness, made an extraordinary variation. On the back of the drawing of *The Ghost of a Flea*[1] is written: 'The Vision of the Spirit which inhabits the body of a Flea, and which appeared to the late Mr. Blake, the designer of the vignettes for Blair's "Grave", and the Book of Job. The Vision first appeared to him in my presence, and afterwards till he had finished the picture. The Flea drew blood in this. . . . J. Varley.'

Gilchrist and Redgrave tell many tales of Varley's uncanny powers in casting nativities and making prophecies, frequently with accuracy, or with a near approach to accuracy, as in the case of Cotman.[2] His prowess in these matters brought him into touch with the famous Lady Blessington. In the spring of 1836 Lady Blessington, whose portrait by Lawrence in the Wallace Collection shows that her charm and beauty are not exaggerated by those who have written her biography, moved from Seymore Place to Kensington Gore. Her mansion, known as Gore House, had once been the residence of William Wilberforce, and had large gardens and wide lawns at the back. Here she entertained her friends, the great 'dandy' Count d'Orsay, Disraeli, Bulwer Lytton, Landor, Dickens, Captain Marryat and many others.

'It was at this time a striking and singular figure might be seen in her drawing-room. This was none other than John Varley, one of the founders of the Society of Painters in Water-Colours, an artist, a mystic, an astrologer. A man of great stature, his face was rugged and earnest, his eyes had the sadness of the seers. Lady Blessington was sufficiently broad-minded to feel interested in all theories, philosophies, and sciences, and rather than deny the possibility of facts that were outside her own experience, or repudiate statements that seemed incredible and erroneous, she preferred to hear them discussed and explained: deferring her judgment until knowledge had been obtained.

'Seated beside her chair of state at the end of the long library where she nightly received her friends, John Varley, the wise man of her court, discoursed to the eager circle around, on the ancient science by which man's fate was read by the stars, according to the constellations occupied by the planets, and their position to each other at the moment of his birth. . . .

'He would bring witnesses to prove he had foretold many important facts, amongst them the date on which William Collins died. James Ward his friend and brother artist, for whose children Varley had cast their horoscopes, burned these hieroglyphics, because their predictions falling out so truly, he was convinced that Varley held commerce with the devil. Nay he would occasionally single some stranger out of the circle around him, the day and hour of whose birth he would demand, and there and then with a pencil on the fly-leaf of a letter, would draw a horoscope from which he stated facts concerning the individual's past, and make predictions regarding the future.

'None listened to him more attentively than Bulwer, to whose mind all things mystic presented a vivid fascination, and it was from Varley the novelist took lessons in astrology, as did at a later date young Fred Burton whose strange career and Oriental travels were foreshadowed by the artist.[3]

Then Varley would tell of his friend the mystical artist, William Blake, who died in 1827. The

---

[1] L. Binyon, *Followers of William Blake*, 1925, pl. 49: Coll. Miss A. G. E. Carthew.
[2] See above chapter V, p. 91.
[3] Presumably this refers to Sir Richard Burton, who, at the age of nineteen when a student at Oxford in 1840, sought out John Varley to have his horoscope cast.

Philistine had regarded as mad this man whose amazing genius had produced poems that held the key to spiritual knowledge, and drawn pictures that are amongst the most wonderful the world has seen. Varley would gravely narrate how, at his suggestion, Blake would summon to his presence such persons as David, Moses, Mark Anthony, or Julius Caesar, whose portraits he would proceed to draw, looking up from his paper from time to time with straining eyes towards presences invisible to all but himself, waiting now and then whilst they moved or frowned, and leaving off abruptly when they suddenly retired. Blake in this way executed some fifty such pencil drawings for Varley, the most curious of which was *The Ghost of a Flea*, as he called the strange human figure he depicted.'[1]

Another excellent portrait of Varley, teacher this time as well as astrologer, is drawn in a letter written by Miss Elizabeth Turner, when Varley was staying with the Dawson Turner family at Yarmouth in 1822[2]:

'All this week we have been much and most delightfully employed in listening to and observing Mr. Varley, the water-colour artist. It is not enough to tell you that we have been delighted with this most singular man: I must try to describe his character a little, it is so rare and extraordinary. Far from feeling any jealousy for himself in his art, Mr. Varley possesses so high an opinion of its excellence and so true a desire for its extensions, that, as *Moses*—solely earnest for the honour of his God—wished all the people might be prophets, so he would make everyone an artist, and as good a one as himself. Not only has he, with most unwearied diligence, sought to show us every way of copying his drawings, he has also tried to make us compose, and explained to us all those principles of composition, which after many years of hard fagging he discovered himself. But alas! All his endeavours are vain! We can copy, and that is all. . . . It is not Mr. Varley's fault if we are not now all Michael Angelos.

'I have not however yet mentioned the strangest part of Mr. Varley's character, and that which makes mere casual observers esteem him mad. With all his nobility of mind he unites a more than childish simplicity and credulity, and he entirely believes in astrology, palmistry, raising of ghosts and seeing of visions. . . . And this part of his character lies open at first sight, for he dashes at once into astrology and was not happy till he had cast all our nativities. Yet he is quite sane in mind, even in this insane topic. . . . Mr. Varley loves and excels in conversation, which he illustrates by practical and beautiful similes. Though very rapid he is always intelligible; and, however harassed, always unruffled in temper and unbroken in spirits. In his judgement of character he is extremely acute and discerning, as all his remarks, especially on other artists with whom we are mutually acquainted, oblige me to perceive. In short I never before saw a man so entirely devoid of selfishness, jealousy and all that train of low and petty feelings which are too truly esteemed an ingredient of our fallen nature.'

Varley's work as a painter may be divided broadly into three periods. His early drawings, which show the powerful influence of Girtin, are marked by careful draughtsmanship and closely wrought detail. Their thin colour washes are low in tone and reminiscent of the tinted drawings of his predecessors. To this period belong riverside views of the Thames and the earliest of his Welsh subjects. His *Sunrise from the top of Snowdon*[3] is dated 1804 and still retains the Girtin spirit. In his rendering of the long chain of hills below a golden sky, with peak rising beyond peak towards the dim distant horizon, there is a sense of

---

[1] J. Fitzgerald Molloy, *The Most Gorgeous Lady Blessington*, Vol. II, 1896, pp. 181, 186.
[2] S. D. Kitson, *Notes on a Collection of Portrait Drawings formed by Dawson Turner*, Walpole Soc., XXI, 1932–33, p. 74.
[3] Coll. Mr. D. L. T. Oppé.

beauty and poetry of feeling which, in his more sophisticated phase, he lost or was unable to recapture. There is no sign of the facile systematiser in this noble drawing. Of about the same date, though possibly a year later, is a superb drawing, *Distant View of Bamborough Castle and Holy Island*[1] (Pl. 84), very close to Girtin in its tones of grey and blue, and unusually fine in its spacious and windy sky of rolling clouds. No drawing could show better the extent to which Varley connects Girtin to Cox and De Wint. This drawing, which had been kept in a portfolio is perfectly preserved in colour.

In his second period Varley begins to apply the principles of constructive composition which he found in Claude, Poussin, in old engravings of landscape and, no doubt, in Turner's *Liber Studiorum*. He was following his own precept that 'Nature required cooking'. In 1805 sixteen of his exhibits were described as 'Views' and one as a 'Composition'. In the following year eight of his exhibits were 'views' and twenty-one 'compositions'; and right up to 1843, the last year in which he exhibited, we find an occasional drawing with 'Composition' as its only title. This indicates his general approach throughout life to his subjects, which sometimes had an exact origin, and sometimes were invented landscape compositions. His leaning towards definite and formal rules of design shows its early beginning in *Mountainous landscape: Afterglow*[2] (Pl. 88), which, I think, may be assigned to a date about 1805. Looking carefully at this drawing, one notes how subtly, but intentionally, the foreground rock, figures, and prow of a boat, duplicate and repeat the shape and outline of the castle and mountain top on the sky-line. His *Scene in a Village Street*,[3] 1808, is a fine example of his early period, with light and shade studied carefully and perfectly distributed. The sky and foliage are very close to Cotman in their handling. Cotman's *Yarmouth River*[4] has 'much in it which resembles Varley's handiwork' says Stanley Kitson, 'and were it not for its unimpeachable pedigree it might be mistaken for the work of that artist.'[5] For some time their methods of the first lay-in and the second wash were closely related. As will be argued later, it was Cotman, I think, who profited by Varley's example. The change in Varley's work is well shown by comparing his *Cader Idris*[6] (of about 1810) and his later *Snowdon from Harlech*.[7] 'The former is based very closely on his personal experience in front of this view; the latter is equally clearly a composition that may have been put together from a dim recollection of a view actually seen, but, for all the drawing itself has to tell us, might equally well have been based on an engraving by some anonymous topographer.'[8] After about 1812 he settled down to a still more classical and conventional method of picture-making. The years 1812 to 1830 may be taken as roughly covering the middle period of his art. More and more he gave weight to abstract principles; opposed warm to cool colours; contrasted round with square, regular with irregular forms, and upright or

---

[1] Coll. Miss Helen Barlow (once incorrectly called *Oban*).
[2] V.A.M. P.27–1930.
[3] Once in the A. N. Gilbey coll.
[4] B.M. 1859. 5.28.116. (once called *The Mumbles, Swansea*).
[5] S. J. Kitson, *Life of J. S. Cotman*, 1937, p. 68.
[6] Cardiff, National Museum of Wales.
[7] Cardiff, National Museum of Wales.
[8] D. K. Baxandall, National Museum of Wales handbook, *The British Water-Colour School*, 1939, p. 23.

pyramidal lines with horizontal. C. E. Hughes[1] well defines this new aspect of his art: 'In Varley's typical landscapes an English castle, such as Conway or Flint, took the place of the Grecian temple, and clusters of bushes and undergrowth of a somewhat stereotyped cast of foliage were substituted for the architectural fragments of the classical foreground. Trees, singly or in groups, with leafy heads and bare trunks curiously serpentine, usually occupied one side of the picture.' His foliage in his more formal works was definitely that of the older school and was based, I feel, on the conventions of the engraver. His unfinished *Snowdon*[2] (Pl. 85) gives a good clue not only to his methods of laying washes but to his compositional approach. Typical of Varley at his best in this middle period is the *Moel Hebog near Beddgellert*.[3] Two Welsh landscapes of 1815[4] still show the lingering influence of Girtin, but are clearly studio compositions, bringing lake, castle and mountains into an ordered and unemotional design. These and many similar drawings of Welsh mountain scenery show felicity in their formal arrangement and in their massive simplification and large serenity. Though his style swings uncertainly between great brilliance and hasty makeshift, in all its inequalities it displays breadth and personality. Varley's work, as was the case with his pupil William Turner (of Oxford), was at its best very near the beginning of his career, about 1805–1810.

In his third period Varley was courageous but ineffective; his lack of the dynamic force which only clear convictions can supply is shown in the debâcle of this final phase. If he had possessed stable standards, he would have realised that his final output was flagrantly artificial, and that his fine talent was more and more, as the years went on, wasted. He had become an arm-chair painter, recollected aspects of nature satisfying his wants. He was less interested in the facts of nature than in his curious surmises and speculations. His drawings now have no precise topographical connection, though Wales seems to float in his mind, sometimes actually as in his *Tal-y-Llyn and Cader Idris*,[5] more often vaguely in an *olla podrida* of mountains, trees and water. His simplicity and directness seem to have gone, his restraint was abandoned. Perhaps the old man wanted to outdo his pupils. If John Linnell and Samuel Palmer revelled in the flame and flare of sunsets, if Cotman sometimes exaggerated the picturesqueness of medieval buildings, then Varley would paint classical landscapes flooded with purple, violet and gold. It could, however, be argued that all of them were influenced by the view that water-colour could emulate oil painting and that the times demanded an art which was more spectacular and richly orchestrated in colour, texture and detail.

For outdoor work Varley recommended a thick paper, such as cartridge, of rough texture. He added that 'if the thin wove papers be used, they should be mounted; that is pasted on two thicknesses of cartridge paper, previously pasted together and strained on a board, in the manner of pasteboard'.

[1] C. E. Hughes, *Early English Water-Colour*, 1950, p. 53. [2] V.A.M. P.52–1924.
[3] Coll. Miss A. Scott-Elliot. Ill. *R.A. Exhibition 1934*, pl. CLXXV.
[4] Coll. Mr. and Mrs. Paul Mellon.
[5] Bethnal Green Museum–1107–1886.

In 1824 Varley had been making experiments in heightening his water-colours with white and varnishing them with gum or copal. The *Somerset House Gazette*,[1] makes an explicit statement about this:

> Mr. John Varley we have lately seen busily engaged in his study, on his new process of landscape in water-colours, heightened with white and varnished with copal. How this process would succeed for larger works is yet to be proved; but on some of his designs in small, the style is so effective, that they approximate to the richness and depth of paintings in oil.

During his final years it was his custom to sit down of an evening and run off a number of sketches from which he would select next day those he liked best, for completion in colour. The sketches were roughed in with sticks of cedar charcoal which he made by burning them in a candle as he used them. He then worked out the broad masses of light and shade with Cologne earth, and upon this preparation the colours were laid. One evening he took up some whitey-brown paper (perhaps the wrapping of a druggist's bottle) which chanced to lie on his table, and began to sketch on that. It was the kind of paper which had appealed to Alexander Cozens, and Varley liked its texture and tint. But the thin paper was difficult to manipulate, so he conceived the idea of laying it down upon a white card, as is done with etchings printed on India paper. The white under the thin transparent paper gave brilliance to the colour, and he sometimes exposed it by scratching away the superimposed layer in parts of the sky. His darks were often enriched by a varnish of gum-arabic. Some of his drawings executed in this manner, the hot-house products of studio forcing, were made more falsely pretty and undignified by being cut to an oval. The Victoria and Albert Museum, which shows amply this worst aspect of Varley's work, shows him also at his earlier best.

John Varley's *List of Colours*, published in 1816, from 44 Conduit Street, Hanover Square, is as follows:

1. Cobalt Blue	11. Warm Grey
2. Prussian Blue	12. Purple Grey
3. Indigo	13. Neutral Tint
4. New Carmine, Madder Lake	14. Dark Warm Green
5. Gamboge	15. Warm Green
6. Burnt Sienna	16. Olive Green
7. Yellow Ochre	17. Orange
8. Venetian Red	18. Roman Ochre
9. Vermilion	19. Sepia
10. Burnt Umber	

This list was apparently re-issued throughout his lifetime and after his death, for in a list dated 1850 from 3 Elkins Row, Bayswater, the only change is No. 19, where in place of Sepia we have Cologne Earth.

[1] September 25, 1824, p. 381.

During all his three periods Varley broke away from his formal and definite rules of composition, and painted quite simple and direct rural landscapes. Many of his slighter sketches have great charm. In them, as in his more finished and atmospheric *Cheyne Walk, Chelsea*,[1] 1811, we find a direct and naturalistic treatment of trees, very different from the formal foliage which he was wont to adapt from engravings after French and Italian classicists. In his sketches the trees are handled with a blotty treatment from a round brush instead of rigid outlining and separation of branches and leaves. *Houses by the Thames*,[2] 1816, and *Windmill at Battersea*,[3] are delightful examples of his fresh out-door work.

Though Varley made several water-colours of Spanish subjects in 1813, it must not be supposed that he ever crossed the channel or that he visited Spain. His Spanish drawings were worked up from sketches made by Captain Dumaresq. Nine of them appeared for sale at Sotheby's on October 22, 1947. His charming *Vanbrugh House, Greenwich Park* (Walker's Gallery, 1943) dated 1823 shows that, even as late as this, he could successfully adapt the mantle of Girtin.

Varley was no genius, but he was a fine craftsman, and always a master of the broad wash. Even in his early days, when he was the obvious disciple of Girtin, there is a boldness in his washes. Whereas the latter tended to complicate his areas of colour with smaller strokes and details. Varley's clean regulated washes were laid in such a way as to retain all that luminous, vaporous, effect which is one of the qualities of water-colour. He excelled not merely in the flat wash but in the gradated wash which he used so skilfully for recording the receding planes of skies and mountains. Clouds recede behind cloud, like mountain behind mountain, till they are lost to sight on the vaporous horizon. In that Varley never fails, even if he works a little mechanically and systematically, as Finberg suggests. Wherever his washes were laid, whether on skies, mountains, trees or buildings, they were laid with the confidence and sure knowledge that they would dry out in clean brilliant colour. Varley never achieved the inspiration of Girtin and De Wint; only rarely does his art show imaginative intuition, but at its best it reveals quality.

Perhaps his fault lay in his conscientious assiduity. His prolific output was due largely to his own improvidence and his inability to handle money. At one time he made £3000 a year, a large income for those days, but he was always in financial difficulties, unable to realise a competence for himself and his family. From the age of fifty he was familiar with tipstaffs and the debtors' prison. He gave away cash prodigally: he backed bills which were dishonoured: he resorted to money-lenders. On Linnell's asking him one day how he was getting on, he answered: 'Much better, much better; there are only four men, I think, now, who can put in executions.' In the last year of his life several writs were out against him, and he was rescued from the sheriff's officers by William Vokins, the well-known picture dealer. At Vokins' house in Margaret Street, Cavendish Square, where he continued to paint bravely to the last, Varley died in 1842.

[1] V.A.M. 176–1894. [2] Coll. Mr. and Mrs. Tom Girtin. Reproduced in *O.W.S. Club*, II, 1924–25, pl. iii.
[3] Coll. Mr. and Mrs. Tom Girtin. Reproduced in *O.W.S. Club*, II, 1924–25, pl. vi.

Cornelius Varley (1781–1873) was the second son of Richard Varley. About 1800 he decided to follow his brother's profession and joined him in frequenting Dr. Monro's house. In 1802 he visited North Wales with his brother John, and went again in 1803 in company with Joshua Cristall. By 1804 he was sufficiently advanced as an artist to join his brother among the founders of the Old Water-Colour Society. His works include various classes of subject—landscape, marine, architecture, with groups of figures. According to Graves[1] his exhibits at the Royal Academy, Suffolk Street and elsewhere amount, throughout his long life, to only 62 in all. This may be because his early instruction, till he was nineteen, under his uncle Samuel, a watch-maker and manufacturer of scientific apparatus, had bred in him a taste for science. In 1811 he took out a patent for a Graphic Telescope, apparently an adaptation of the camera lucida. The specification states: 'My invention consists in combining one or two reflecting surfaces with a simple kind of telescope that inverts the object, and thereby gaining an erect image without any additional length to the telescope—placing the telescope out of the way of the image—and apparently projecting the said image flat on a table, so that it may be easily traced on paper; the image being seen by one eye, and the pencil or tracer by the other or by both eyes.' Examples of drawings made by John Varley with the aid of this instrument will be found in a collection of portrait drawings (1812–1825) formed by the Dawson Turner family at Yarmouth,[2] among them many portrait studies by Cotman. Among Varley's portraits made with his brother's graphic telescope is one of Dr. Thomas Monro, inscribed in pencil: 'Dr. Monro, the first Collector of Turner and Girtin's Drawings. Done with the Graphic Telescope April 12th, 1812.' Cotman carried one of Varley's graphic telescopes with him to Normandy, but found it was more trouble than it was worth, particularly as it had to be set up on a stand or table. Cornelius used it himself, notably for a drawing of Newstead Abbey in 1824. His *View from Ferry Bridge, Yorkshire*[3] has his signature followed by P.G.T., which may signify 'Per Graphic Telescope,' or possibly 'Proprietor (or Patentee) of the Graphic Telescope'.

In the year 1814 Cornelius Varley became an active and useful member of the Society of Arts, receiving from that body its Isis gold medal for improvements in the construction of microscopes, and two silver medals for machinery used in grinding and polishing specula and for observations and illustrations of the circulation of sap in water-plants. In this kind of work and in the making of illustrated records of natural and mechanical science he was fully occupied; and I suspect that his rare water-colour exhibits from 1814 onwards were either dug out of old portfolios or based on earlier drawings. His *Ruins of Kerry Castle*,[4] 1830, for instance, is painted from a sketch made in 1808.

The scarcity of his work has hindered general knowledge of its fine quality, but the acquisition by the Victoria and Albert Museum of nine drawings by him in 1924, in

[1] A. Graves, *A Dictionary of Artists 1763–1893*, 1901.
[2] V.A.M. 2 vols. Those mounted ref. 94.D.2.
[3] B.M. 1886. 10.12.564.   [4] V.A.M. P.65–1924.

84 'Distant View of Bamborough Castle and Holy Island'
Coll. Miss Helen Barlow $18\frac{5}{8} \times 9\frac{5}{8}$: 473×245 *Water-colour*
John VARLEY (1778–1842)

85 'Snowdon'
V.A.M. P.52–1924 $14\frac{7}{8} \times 18\frac{3}{4}$: 377×476 *Water-colour*
John VARLEY (1778–1842)

86 'Dolbadarn Castle'

Coll. Mr & Mrs Paul Mellon   19¼ × 26 : 489 × 655   *Water-colour*

John VARLEY (1778–1842)

87 'Mountainous Landscape'

Coll. Mr & Mrs Paul Mellon   8¾ × 13½ : 222 × 342   *Water-colour, signed and dated 1840*

John VARLEY (1778–1842)

88 'Mountainous Landscape: Afterglow'
V.A.M. 827–1930 $10\frac{1}{8} \times 17\frac{1}{4}$: 257 × 437   *Water-colour*
John VARLEY (1778–1842)

89 'Snowdon from Moel Hebog'
V.A.M. 699 $17\frac{3}{8} \times 23\frac{3}{4}$: 441 × 602   *Water-colour*
William Fleetwood VARLEY (c. 1785–1856)

90 'The Market Place, Ross'

V.A.M. 108–1895 $11\frac{5}{8} \times 18: 295 \times 456$ *Water-colour, signed and dated 1803*

Cornelius VARLEY (1781–1873)

91 'View from Tallyllin'

Coll. Mr & Mrs Paul Mellon $19\frac{1}{2} \times 25: 495 \times 634$ *Water-colour, signed*

Cornelius VARLEY (1781–1873)

addition to five already in the collection, gave fuller opportunity of studying his art. His *Sunset over a Wide Plain*,[1] a distant view of Conway, is a poetic drawing, thoroughly personal in design and feeling. Cornelius was at once more sensitive, and less ambitious, than his brother. He never uses a full range of colour, like John, but works in quiet tones, preferably of dove-like greys. There is lovely quality of grey (perhaps it was his brother's teaching: 'The warm grey, the cool grey, and the round touch') in such a drawing as his *Market Place, Ross*[2] (Pl. 90), 1803. Indeed, all of his work that I know is peculiarly satisfying. Another drawing of the same type, very like Thirtle in quality, is his *Cottage, with well and woman in foreground*.[3] About the drawing of the market-place at Ross, Roget tells an amusing tale.[4] Cristall and Varley fell in with William Havell at Ross, and while making his drawing of the market-place Varley excited Havell's envy by using a sheet of ass's skin for a palette (his experimental science was clearly beginning). Havell, burdened with the weight of an earthenware palette, was charmed with the lightness of his friend's contrivance. Varley thereupon pulled out another sheet and gave it to him. This so delighted Havell that he stuck his earthen palette up in the market-place and pelted it with stones until he had broken it to pieces, much to the amusement of a crowd of spectators. In 1808 Varley was in Ireland, at Killarney and elsewhere, and during this trip a hunted fox took refuge under his campstool over which he had thrown his overcoat. Noticing an unusual odour, Varley got up and the fox ran off. Soon after, the hounds arrived, and finding the scent very warm, upset the artist and his traps. He took refuge in a tree, greatly to the amusement of the huntsmen when they came up to the spot and found that the hounds had treed not the fox but a painter, who had dropped his 'brush'.[5]

Cornelius Varley's work as an artist may be described as belonging to the opening years of the nineteenth century. After 1808 his exhibits at the Old Water-Colour Society averaged less than three a year and ceased with his resignation in 1820. Absorbed in his scientific pursuits he reached the great age of ninety-one. In 1875 his remaining works, in 230 lots, were sold by Christie's. One hundred drawings by Cornelius, all but three in the former ownership of Alfred H. Varley, a grandson of the artist, were exhibited at the Squire Gallery, in 1937. They belonged mainly (several of them were dated) to the period 1801 to 1811; and only three bore later dates, 1817, 1820 and 1824. Some imaginary subjects in monochrome were no doubt executed at meetings of the Chalon Sketching Society of which Cornelius was a foundation member in 1808, and others were evidently done for the series of lithographs of boats and river scenes which he published about 1810.

Miss E. M. Spiller, who knew Cornelius Varley when he was living in his last years at The Quadrant, Kentish Town, described him to Basil Long[6] as an undersized, pink, cherubic-faced little man, but withal, impetuous; outrageously careless in his dress,

[1] Birmingham, City Art Gallery.
[2] V.A.M. 108–1895.
[3] V.A.M. E.1395–1924.
[4] Roget, I, p. 172.
[5] A. T. Story, *James Holmes and John Varley*, 1894, p. 217.
[6] B. Long, 'Cornelius Varley', *O.W.S. Club*, XIV, 1936/1937, p. 4.

generally to be found in his shirt-sleeves, even at meals; eccentric in his feeding—salt, sugar or vinegar, for instance, being alternative condiments to most things, whether meat or sweets. His girls were in ill-cut dresses, which he insisted on being always green. This eccentric but brilliant family had all sorts of scientific toys, electric batteries, microscopes, megaphones, telegraphs and telephones, camerae obscurae, a telescope, etc. Music, both on orthodox and eccentric instruments, played its part in the entertainment of their guests. The whole family belonged to the Sandemanian sect.

The third brother was William Fleetwood Varley (c. 1785–1856). From 1804 to 1818 he exhibited at the Royal Academy. He taught drawing in Cornwall in 1810, and afterwards at Bath and Oxford. At Oxford he was nearly burned to death by the thoughtless frolic of a party of students, and never recovered from the shock; he died at Ramsgate. Albert Fleetwood Varley (1804–1876), John Varley's eldest son, who was a teacher of drawing, died at Brompton. Edgar John Varley (d. 1888), son of Charles S. Varley, and grandson of John Varley, exhibited from 1861 to 1887 at Suffolk Street, the Royal Academy, the Royal Institute, and elsewhere. He was curator of the Architectural Museum at Westminster.

CHAPTER VII

The Foundation of Water-Colour Societies

Girtin died in 1802, and some food for thought is supplied by a brief survey of other painters and writers who were living in that year. De Wint was then eighteen, Cox and Prout nineteen, Cotman twenty, Varley twenty-four, Constable twenty-six, Turner twenty-seven. Of the older men, Dayes was thirty-nine, Blake forty-five, Rowlandson forty-six, Farington fifty-five, Towne sixty-two, while Paul Sandby was a veteran of seventy-two.

In the year which witnessed Girtin's death and the reception of Turner into higher rank at the Royal Academy there was little in the way of an open market for water-colours. The Society of Artists of Great Britain had held exhibitions of oil paintings and water-colours from 1760 to 1791, and The Free Society of Artists from 1760 to 1783, but both Societies had closed their doors owing to lack of public support and possibly because they were unable to compete with the attractions of the Royal Academy, which was founded in 1768. Painters depended upon commissions from publishers of topographical engravings, upon private patrons, and upon their teaching practice. After 1791 the Academy exhibition, held from 1780 at Somerset House, was the only place where a water-colour artist could display his work publicly. At the Academy, however, water-colours were still regarded merely as tinted or stained drawings, and were neither hung well nor shown in prominent places. They were often surrounded by garish and staring pictures in oil which had been ousted from the 'great room',[1] or by miniatures and oddments such as medals, reproductive engravings, and architectural designs. Water-colours were often crowded, up to a height of over six feet, and the lighting from windows at the side of the room was inadequate. Some of them were relegated to a gloomy room containing the sculpture; Redgrave describes it as 'a species of condemned cell'.

Water-colour painters had another and serious ground of complaint in the wording of the Instrument of Foundation of the Royal Academy. When the Academy was founded in 1768, it was provided that the members were to be 'Painters, Sculptors or Architects'.

[1] W. H. Pyne, *Somerset House Gazette*, I, 1823, p. 130.

No water-colour drawing in 1768 was ever described as a painting. Painters at that time meant painters in oil; and the distinction was made clearer by the law that 'There shall be an Annual Exhibition of Paintings, Sculpture, and Designs'. By 1804, however, when the Old Water-Colour Society was founded, the tinted drawing and the stained drawing were relics of the past. The immediate success of the Society's first exhibitions must have shown members of the Academy that their Instrument of Foundation was too openly and too obviously exclusive, and in 1810 the law apparently excluding water-colour painters was repealed as 'no longer necessary to the welfare, but repugnant to the honour and interests of the Royal Academy'.[1] At the same time it must be remembered that the Instrument of Foundation of the Royal Academy provided in its first Law that the members: 'Shall all be artists . . . resident in Great Britain . . . and not members of any other society of artists established in London.' That law continued in force till 1863, when a Royal Commission appointed to enquire into the present position of the Royal Academy passed a recommendation: 'That it is not desirable that artists should cease to belong to other Art Societies before they can be admitted to the honours of the Royal Academy, and that in exhibiting their works they should not be restricted to the Royal Academy Exhibition.' In consequence the law was shortly afterwards repealed. Its existence accounts for the fact that up to 1843, or a little later, several members of the Old Water-Colour Society (among them J. D. Harding, James Holland and George Cattermole) resigned their membership in order to seek Academic honours. Possibly the fact that J. F. Lewis retired from his Presidency of the Old Society in 1858, to become A.R.A. in 1859, was a strong factor in the abolition of a law which was clearly unreasonable. At the same time, it was not until 1943, one hundred and seventy-five years from the foundation of the Academy, that a water-colour painter, *as such*, was deemed worthy of election to Academy associateship. It should be added that the Academy has always given great encouragement to water-colour art, and during the last fifty years has devoted increasing space to water-colours in its annual exhibition which within limits is open to all painters.

From the attitude of the Academy up till 1810 it is apparent that the time was ripe for water-colour painters to establish an independent exhibition of their own. They felt that the Academy was giving them rather a raw deal and that their work, no longer to be described as a 'tinted drawing' but as a 'water-colour painting', was a serious rival to oil-painting. This rivalry was noted by Thomas Uwins. His own first exhibit at the Academy was in 1799, and in 1833 he says[2]: 'The writer is old enough to recollect the time when the council-room of the Royal Academy was devoted to the exhibition of paintings in water-colours. Here were to be seen the rich and masterly sketches of Hamilton, the fascinating compositions of Westall, the beautiful landscapes of Girtin, Callcott, and Reinagle, and the splendid creations of Turner—the mightiest enchanter who has ever wielded the magic power of art in any age or country. At this time the council-room,

[1] Whitley, 1800 to 1820, p. 177.
[2] Mrs. Uwins, *Memoirs of Thomas Uwins, R.A.*, I, 1858, pp. 30, 31.

instead of being what the present arrangement makes it, a place of retirement from the bustle of the other departments, was itself the great point of attraction. Here crowds first collected, and here they lingered longest, because it was here the imagination was addressed through the means of an art which added the charm of novelty to excellence. It was the fascination of this room that first led to the idea of forming an exhibition entirely of pictures in water-colours.'

So, on the evening of November 30, 1804, ten artists assembled at the Stratford Coffee House in Oxford Street and founded the Society of Painters in Water-Colours. The originators of the scheme, William Frederick Wells, Samuel Shelley, Robert Hills and William Henry Pyne, were present; and Nicholas Pocock, Francis Nicholson, John and Cornelius Varley, John Claude Nattes and William Sawrey Gilpin were invited to join them in council. Pyne, who was 'known to go out to a breakfast party and by entertaining to detain all the company till one o'clock the following morning', probably did most of the talking. All of the ten who joined in the creation of the Society dwelt almost within a stone's throw of each other, and four of them had the then fashionable quarter, George Street, Hanover Square, as their address. The *Decemviri* drew up a set of rules, and after some discussion as to whether the novel term *painters* in water-colours 'might not be considered by the world of taste to savour of assumption', they formally assumed the title of the Society of Painters in Water-Colours. The Society was to consist of no more than twenty-four members. They must be 'of moral character'. (The Royal Academy by its instrument of institution required its members to be 'men of fair moral character'.)[1] There was the usual provision for a President and Officers to be elected annually. The profits of the exhibition, after carrying forward a sum for the expenses of the following year, were to be divided among the members 'in sums proportioned to the drawings sent in and retained for exhibition'.[2] William Sawrey Gilpin was elected as the first President and very soon the original promoters were strengthened by the addition of six principal draughtsmen in the profession: George Barret, Joshua Cristall, John Glover, William Havell, James Holworthy and Stephen Francis Rigaud.

These sixteen members held their first exhibition on April 22, 1805, at 20 (now 54) Lower Brook Street.[3] The house had been built for show-rooms or sale-rooms by Gerard Vandergucht, belonging to a family which had flourished for more than a hundred years in England, as engravers, painters, and dealers in pictures and objects of art. Gerard died in 1776, aged eighty. Benjamin Vandergucht, his thirty-second child by one mother, who survived her husband, succeeded to the business. When Benjamin was drowned in the

---

[1] It should be said that when the Academy was founded in 1768 'fair' was used in the sense of 'unblemished'.
[2] This rule was obviously destined to be a cause of trouble. The division was made in accordance with the artists' own estimates of the value of their work. At the first exhibition for instance, Shelley set himself down as contributing a share of attraction worth £743, whereas the modest total of Cornelius Varley was £44 12s. 6d. The average prices of exhibits ranged from £26 10s. 6d. for Shelley, and £22 1s. 0d. for Glover to £4 14s. 0d. for John Varley, £4 9s. 6d. for Barret, and £3 14s. 0d. for Cornelius Varley.
[3] It is of interest that this first exhibition followed Francis Towne's exhibition in the same gallery.

Thames in 1794, the rooms were occupied by Thomas Barker (Barker of Bath) as a show-room for his own paintings. Then they were taken over by Henry Tresham, who opened the premises as a gallery in association with 'several other gentlemen picture dealers' for the sale of 'Raphaels, Correggios, and *stuff*'. This commercial undertaking was perhaps inconsistent with the dignity of Tresham on becoming a Royal Academician in 1799, and he was ready to let the great room, with its appurtenances, to the newly formed Society.

The opening exhibition proved a great success. Connoisseurs, *dilettanti*, artists and critics vied with each other in loud commendations of the collected works. 'The noble in rank and the leaders of fashion graced it with their presence. An eager curiosity seized upon those who claimed to live in the exclusive region of taste.'[1] During six weeks nearly 12,000 persons paid their shilling for admission. The members were good business men, for they made the novel move of facilitating sales on the premises, instead of the would-be purchaser having, as was the case at the Royal Academy, to seek out the artist. A catalogue gave the prices, and the purchaser entered his name and address in a book, depositing ten per cent. of the price, with a guarantee to pay the remainder on delivery of the picture.

The Society's claim to exist was set out in the following note at the beginning of the catalogue:

> The utility of an Exhibition in forwarding the Fine Arts arises, not only from the advantage of public criticisms, but also from the opportunity it gives to the artist of comparing his own works with those of his contemporaries in the same walk. To embrace both these points in their fullest extent is the object of the present Exhibition, which, consisting of Water-Colour Pictures only, must, from that circumstance, give to them a better arrangement, and a fairer ground of appreciation, than when mixed with pictures in oil. Should the lovers of the art, viewing it in this light, favour it with their patronage, it will become an Annual Exhibition of Pictures in Water Colours.

The nature and extent of the exhibition are admirably analysed thus[2]:

> John Varley sent no less than 42 works, Pyne and Shelley 28 each, Glover and Hills 23 each, Wells 21, Gilpin 20, Pocock 17, Nicholson 14, Havell and Cornelius Varley 12 each, Barret 11, Cristall 8, Rigaud 6, and Holworthy and Nattes 5 each. As was to be expected, the main strength of the collection lay in its landscapes. But the figure element was present also, and it gave a variety to this first gathering, the absence of which was complained of a few years after, when landscape seems to have acquired an all but absolute dominion. . . . Including eight portraits by Shelley, the figure subjects formed less than 20 per cent of the whole collection. . . .
>
> The great majority of the drawings . . . were landscapes, of one kind or another. And it was in this department that the change was chiefly manifest which had come over water-colour drawing. Here there was visible just enough both of the old motives and of the old processes in painting, to indicate the states of art and practice out of which the present developments had sprung. The early tinted manner survived in the works of Pocock, old architectural topography in those of Nattes; and in one or two examples by Gilpin there was just a reminder of the old craze for 'gentlemen's seats'. The 'classic' or ideal element derived from Claude and Poussin, which had been paramount in our landscape art until the time of Gainsborough, was also present, and probably reigned over a group of 'compositions', so named, among the drawings sent by Glover, Havell, and John Varley, and in nearly all cases, over the works of Barret.

[1] Roget, I, p. 203.   [2] Roget, I, pp. 203–206.

Under the generic names 'landscape', 'view from nature', 'a lake scene', etc., may also have been included representations more or less characteristic of particular kinds of scenery, without the aim of giving importance to an actual locality. But by far the larger number of the landscapes belonged to the class which might still be called topographic, though in that wider acceptation of the term which does not exclude from its scope mere natural scenery, provided that the features peculiar to a given spot are duly recorded. It was the form of landscape in which the classic school on the one hand, and the 'dry-as-dust' topography of the olden time on the other, had finally met and merged. Except eight views in Norway by Wells, and a few others of small importance, the whole of the remaining landscapes were scenes in the British Isles, forty-three per cent. being from Wales. Of these Welsh views more than two-fifths are by John Varley, besides from three to seven drawings each by Cristall, Havell, Nicholson, Pocock, and Cornelius Varley, all belonging to the Celtic contingent. The North of England, chiefly Yorkshire with her abbeys, supplied the subjects of twenty-four drawings by various artists; and ten, mostly by Nicholson, were from Scotland. Gilpin brought six Irish views from the Lakes of Killarney.

There were two further ingredients which varied the interest of the exhibition as a whole, namely: Hill's studies of cattle, sheep, and deer; and a series of spirited drawings by Pocock, of British sea-fights, some of the great engagements that had taken place within the memory of all visitors to the gallery.

The second exhibition, with W. F. Wells as President in place of William Sawrey Gilpin, who had resigned owing to his appointment as Drawing Master to the Royal Military College at Great Marlow, was held in Brook Street; but in 1807 the Society shifted its headquarters to the rooms at 118 Pall Mall, which had once been occupied by the Royal Academy. The structure proved to be unsafe, especially for large crowds, and for the exhibition of 1808 the Society made another move, renting two large rooms at 16, Old Bond Street. A coloured aquatint by Stadler, from a drawing with figures by Rowlandson and architectural features by Pugin, appeared in the *Microcosm of London* (1808) and shows the entire aspect of this exhibition, with a second room opening from the larger one. In this detailed illustration it is at once noticeable that more than half the exhibits were on a very large scale, that all of them were framed close up in the gilt frames which were in vogue for oil paintings, and that the walls were hung to a height of over twelve feet, with the topmost pictures tilted well forward. Farington records that 'Lawrence called in the even'g in raptures with the Water Colour drawing Exhibition in Bond Street',[1] and, two months later he writes: 'Sir George Beaumont reprobated the rage for Water Colour drawings but it was sd. that the passion is subsiding. Haydon said, That a gentleman had laid a wager of 20 guineas that in *three years* there will be no Water Colour Exhibition.'[2] As will be seen, the gentleman was very nearly right. As to Sir George Beaumont, he had his knife into the Society almost from its start. In May 1807 he remarked to Farington 'on West so strongly speaking of the merit of the water-colour drawings now exhibiting by that Society, & sd. He wondered at it. For His own part when He went into the room there was such a want of harmony, such a *chattering display*, that it afforded him little pleasure.'[3]

The year 1809 saw yet another move, this time to Wigley's Rooms in Spring Gardens.

[1] *Diary*, April 18, 1808.　　　　[2] *Diary*, June 1, 1808.　　　　[3] *Diary*, May 8, 1807.

But Wigley's Rooms were used for all manner of entertainments, and were not always available when the Society required them. There was a crisis in 1816 when the Committee met to arrange the exhibition, and 'instead of finding the place cleared for their entrance, the orchestra was standing, with the glasses, the lamps, and partitions of the ball-room. Scattered about the room were broken combs and locks of ladies' hair; and on the harpsichord stood a quart porter-pot. To complete the picture, the learned pig, and his not less sapient masters, were parading at their ease and taking the air on the Society's premises.'[1] For many years the Society had to endure similar difficulties and indignities, until in 1820 there was a migration to the Egyptian Hall in Piccadilly, associated in later years with the names not of great painters, but of Maskelyne and Cooke, illusionists.

The frequent changes of habitation suggest that the Society led not only a vagrant but a chequered existence. Some of its vicissitudes must now be recorded. The first was caused by competition in the Society's own field. In its early days the Society reserved its walls entirely for its limited number of members and associates (twenty-four in 1808), and many proficient painters of high standing were left outside the charmed circle. To meet the demands for an open exhibition, a rival institution, the 'New Society of Painters in Miniature and Water-Colours', after two preliminary meetings had been held at the Thatched House Tavern, Great St. James's Street, came into being in 1807, and changed its title for its opening exhibition in 1808 to 'The Associated Artists in Water-Colours'.[2] The new group included William Westall, J. Laporte, Samuel Owen and H. W. Williams. Though not members, Louis Francia, Peter De Wint, Frederick Nash and others were invited to contribute; and later catalogues include the names of John Sell Cotman, Luke Clennell and Samuel Prout. David Cox was President in 1810. One of the first resolutions of the Society was that: 'Although works of imagination should be considered as the basis of the intended Exhibition, the Society are of opinion that Portraits will increase its attractions and are therefore proper to be admitted.' Members were required 'to furnish five original subjects *at least*, of which or any greater number, two-thirds may consist of Portraits, but the remainder must be works of imagination'.

The Society became a formidable rival to the older Society, though it was stated in their first catalogue that 'they were not influenced by any sentiment of hostility or opposition to the society which originated a few years ago under a similar appellation'. But though the twin exhibitions were regarded as concurrent annual sights of the London season, each was bound to detract interest from the other. One trouble was that the exhibits had too much in common; and it is interesting to amplify Roget's account of the landscape work at the Water-Colour Society's first exhibition by a contemporary note on the Associated Artists' opening show:

[1] Roget, I, p. 402.
[2] Minutes of the meetings of the Society, and other documents relating to it, are in the Library of the Victoria and Albert Museum.

The first thing that strikes an observer, both at Spring Gardens and Bond Street,[1] is the overwhelming proportion of landscapes, a proportion almost as unreasonable as that of the portraits at Somerset House. In pacing round the rooms the spectator experiences sensations somewhat similar to those of an outside passenger on a mail-coach making a picturesque and picturizing journey to the North. Mountains and cataracts, rivers, lakes, and woods, deep romantic glens and sublime sweeps of country, engage his eye in endless and ever-varying succession. For a while he is delighted, but as he proceeds the pleasure generally fades; he feels that even in variety there may be sameness, and would freely exchange a dozen leagues of charming landscape for a scene among 'the busy haunts of men'.[2]

In 1810, when Cox was President, the new Society changed its title to 'Associated *Painters* in Water-Colours', but its fifth exhibition in 1812 proved a financial failure in spite of an effort to revive its drooping prospects by admitting oil-paintings and by electing William Blake as a member. There was no surplus of profit, and finally the landlord seized the contents of the gallery in distraint of rent. The chief sufferer was David Cox, the whole of his year's work being taken from him and sold without compensation.

Thus closed the short career of the 'Associated Artists'. The older Society was in little better plight. In 1809 its prosperity had reached a climax. Admissions numbered nearly 23,000, and every member, apart from his sales, received a share of about twelve per cent. of the profits. Thomas Heaphy carried off £130, John Glover £104, and the rest in due proportion. No wise reserve was made for an emergency which was to come only too soon. The renewed contest with France had strained the resources of the wealthy, and public attention was now absorbed in the events of the Peninsular War; in these circumstances patronage began to diminish. In 1812 the Society's profits were trifling, and caused reasonable apprehension of a future loss. It was obvious that something must be done to save the ship from foundering like that of the 'Associated Artists'. The proposal of Glover, who was then President, to add interest to the exhibitions by an admixture of oil-paintings, led to dissension and resignations. It was plain to many members that such a policy had merely hastened the end of the rival Society. Accordingly, at a meeting held at the house of Robert Hills, with William Havell in the chair, a resolution was passed: 'That the Society, having found it impracticable to form another Exhibition of Water-Colour Paintings only, do consider itself dissolved this night.'

In strictness it may be insisted that by the end of the year 1812 the original Society of Painters in Water-Colours had ceased to exist. But there was not a complete disintegration. The reforming party, even before the fatal resolution was passed, had already met at John Varley's house, in order to found 'a society for the purpose of establishing an exhibition consisting of pictures in oil and water colours'. Nicholson took the chair, and was supported by Barret, Cristall, Havell, Holworthy, John and Cornelius Varley, 'Warwick' Smith, Thomas Uwins, Copley Fielding and two 'outsiders', James Holmes and John Linnell. At a second meeting, at Glover's house, a list of members was drawn up, which included David Cox, John Glover and William Turner, in addition to those mentioned.

[1] The exhibition was at 20 Lower Brook Street, off Bond Street, the first headquarters of the original Society.
[2] Ackermann's *Repository* III, 1809–1828, pp. 423.

Though the original Society had in reality been dissolved, this new group decided to ignore the breach of continuity, and their exhibition of 1813 was boldly numbered as 'The Ninth'. In 1819 they determined to efface the memory of the break in 1812, and solemnly resolved that the Anniversary meeting of the society should be held on November 30, the day of the original foundation. From 1813 to 1820 their exhibitions, which included some oil-paintings, were held, as has been said, in Wigley's 'great room' at Spring Gardens.

In 1817 the Society showed wisdom in deciding to fund its profits instead of dividing them among members, but considered itself sufficiently solvent to hold an annual dinner, at the cost of the fund, and to institute three premiums of £30 each, to be awarded by lot, 'for the benefit of the exhibition and the improvement of the Society'. It is significant that works eligible for these awards were required to be at least thirty inches long, if figure subjects; and thirty-nine inches, if landscapes. But, with the exhibition of 1820, admissions were below the average, there was an increasing deficit in the exchequer, and the admixture of oil paintings was condemned as a contributory cause. On June 14, 1820, it was accordingly resolved: 'That the Society shall henceforth be a Society of Painters in Water-Colours only, and that no Oil Paintings shall be exhibited with their Works.' There was no break this time. Those who had been members of the 'Oil and Water Colour Society' remained as members for the 'seventeenth' exhibition of the 'Society of Painters in Water Colours'. From that day to this, save for the addition of 'Royal', decreed by Queen Victoria in 1881, the Society has prospered under its original title of 1804. 'This little self-constituted Academy in *aqua*' ranks in London as the professional art society next in seniority to the Royal Academy. With the reconstruction of the Society in 1820 it had become obvious that larger and more attractive exhibitions must be contrived, and that a permanent home must be secured. This was found in a building which at that time was in course of erection on Crown property in Pall Mall East.[1] For two more years the exhibitions were held in the Egyptian Hall and then from 1822, for one hundred and sixteen years, the Society flourished in its own spacious gallery. That gallery is part of the history of Water-Colour.[2] Thackeray describes how:

> Titmarsh with a valuable gingham umbrella, with a yellow horn head representing Lord Brougham or Dr. Syntax, is seen with his hat very much on one side swaggering down Pall Mall East to the Water-Colour Gallery. He flings down 1s 6d in the easiest way and goes upstairs. . . .
> Issuing then from the National Gallery—you may step over to Farrance's by the way, if you like, and sip an ice, or bolt a couple of dozen forced-meat balls in a basin of mock-turtle soup—issuing, I say, from the National Gallery, and after refreshing yourself, or not, as your purse or appetite permits, you arrive speedily at the Water Colour Exhibition, and cannot do better

[1] In 1823 it was No. 6; from 1824 to 1874, No. 5; and from 1875, when some alterations were carried out, and a new entrance hall and staircase were erected, it became 5A. The Society owns two interesting pencil drawings by J. F. Lewis showing the gallery before the opening of the 1830 exhibition, its walls crowded with identifiable pictures, with heavy looped drapery hanging above them. (Reproduced in *O.W.S.*, I, 1923–1924.)
[2] And part of the history of Etching. The Gallery was shared by the Royal Society of Painter-Etchers and Engravers as sub-tenants from 1888 to 1938 and the association between the two Societies has continued at 26 Conduit Street.

than enter. I know nothing more cheerful or sparkling than the first *coup d'œil* of this gallery. In the first place, you never can enter it without finding four or five pretty women, that's a fact; pretty women with pretty bonnets peeping at pretty pictures, and with sweet whispers vowing that Mrs. Seyffarth is a dear delicious painter, and that her style is so 'soft'.

In giving his memories of the private views at 5A Pall Mall East, Ruskin,[1] as we might expect, is more serious than Thackeray but indulges in a pleasant flippancy:

I cannot but recollect with feelings of considerable refreshment, in these days of the deep, the lofty, and the mysterious, what a simple company of connoisseurs we were, who crowded into happy meeting, on the first Mondays in Mays of long ago, in the bright large room of the old Water-Colour Society; and discussed with holiday gaiety, the unimposing merits of the favourites, from whose pencils we knew precisely what to expect, and by whom we were never either disappointed or surprised. Copley Fielding used to paint fishing-boats for us, in a fresh breeze, 'Off Dover', 'Off Ramsgate', 'Off the Needles', off everywhere on the south coast where anybody had been last autumn. . . . Mr. Robson would occasionally paint a Bard on a heathery crag in Wales; or—it might be—a Lady of the Lake on a similar piece of Scottish foreground, 'Benvenue in the Distance'. A little fighting in the time of Charles the First was permitted to Mr. Cattermole; and Mr. Cristall would sometimes invite virtuous sympathy to attend the meeting of two lovers at a Wishing-gate or a Holy well. But the highest flights even of these poetical members of the Society were seldom beyond the confines of the British Isles; the vague dominions of the air, and vasty ones of the deep, were held to be practically unvoyageable by our un-Dædal pinions, and on the safe level of our native soil, the sturdy statistics of Mr. De Wint, and blunt pastorals of Mr. Cox, restrained within the limits of probability and sobriety alike the fancy of the idle, and the ambition of the vain.

When, in 1938, there were threats that the gallery, which had been visited so often by Thackeray and Ruskin, might be demolished by the owners of the property, the Society moved to its present quarters at 26 Conduit Street.

Two further points may be mentioned in connection with the early history of the Royal Water-Colour Society. In 1821 the Society issued a manifesto, setting forth the claims of water-colour to extended public recognition:

Painting in Water colours may justly be regarded as a new art, and in its present application, the invention of British Artists; considerations which ought to have some influence on its public estimation and encouragement. Within a few years the materials employed in this species of painting, and the manner of using them, have been equally improved by new chemical discoveries and successful innovations on the old methods of practice. The feeble tinted drawings, formerly supposed to be the utmost efforts of this art, have been succeeded by pictures not inferior in power to oil paintings, and equal in delicacy of tint and purity and airiness of tone. Those who are acquainted with the splendid collection of Walter Fawkes, Esq.,[2] that liberal and judicious patron of the Fine Arts and of this art in particular, must be sensible of these modern improvements; which must also be well known to all who have compared the neat but inefficient drawings of Sandby, Hearne, and others of their day, with the works which have been introduced to public notice in the exhibitions of the Royal Academy and of this Society. But when

---

[1] J. Ruskin, *Notes on Prout and Hunt*, 1880, pp. 25, 26.
[2] The collection of Mr. Fawkes, of Farnley Hall, famous for its rich array of drawings by Turner, had been exhibited in 1819 at the owner's town house, 45 Grosvenor Place. 'Mr. Walter Fawkes's fine collection of drawings', said Ackermann's *Repository*, 'did more to stamp the character of water-colour art upon general attention than any other effort within our recollection.'

this art first began to develop new and extensive powers, the prejudices which probably originated in a contempt of its ancient feebleness, degenerated into a species of hostility, not very consistent with philosophy, or a genuine attachment to the Fine Arts. As the beauty and power of water colours were incontrovertible, an opinion was industriously spread abroad, that these qualities were evanescent, and the material on which these works were executed, so frail and perishable, that the talents of the artist were rendered useless by the ephemeral nature of his productions. Some failures which occurred in the infancy, or experimental age of the art, might appear to a superficial observer, to justify those objections; but no philosophical reasons ever were, or could be adduced against the possibility of producing, by means of water-colours, pictures equal in beauty and permanency of colour, as well as durability, to those executed in oil. . . . Whatever imperfection may still exist in water-colour paintings, they must be allowed their advantages, as they are not, like those in oil, liable to the change in the oil itself, of the lead which enters into so many pigments, of the varnish, the dirt and smoke which it acquires, and, above all, of the destructive practices of picture cleaners, which, however reprehensible, originate in the imperfection of the materials of oil pictures.

The manifesto, in spite of a good deal of mild untruth and special pleading, is useful and illuminating as giving the considered opinion of a society of water-colour painters in 1821.

Another event, worthy of special record, is the organisation by the Society, in 1823, of an important Loan Exhibition of water-colours, one of the first of its kind. It included 212 drawings, which had been executed prior to January 1 1822, by any British artists, living or dead. There were nineteen drawings by Girtin, but only one by Turner, the *Tivoli*, belonging to J. Allnutt, who was the largest contributor of loans. Cristall, then President of the Society, was represented by thirty-three works. There were twenty by Havell, thirteen by Varley, ten each by Clennell and Copley Fielding, with examples of Rooker, Hearne, Edridge and Cotman, who did not become an associate till 1825. A much less ambitious choice, consisting of twenty-four works by deceased members of the Society (I had the honour of assisting Sir Charles Holmes in the selection), was organised in 1943 as part of the Society's 200th Exhibition.

Apart from the brief period when the Associated Artists were a rival team, the Society of Painters in Water-Colours remained for many years the sole body holding annual exhibitions in water-colour exclusively. The Norwich Society of Artists, which was founded in 1803 and held its first exhibition in 1805, admitted works in oil as well as water-colour, though exhibits in the latter method predominated. In London the Society of British Artists was founded in 1823, mainly as an exhibition centre for oil-paintings. Heaphy and Glover were among its founders, and Heaphy its first President, an office held soon after by James Holmes. Its galleries in Suffolk Street were designed and built by John Nash. The first exhibition was opened on April 14 1824, and on the preceding night a banquet was held, with Heaphy in the chair and the Duke of Sussex as the chief guest. The Duke counselled the members to avoid all unworthy jealousies of other institutions; 'The Society and the Royal Academy should go hand in hand.' A Charter of Incorporation was granted in 1846 and, forty-one years later, in the Jubilee year of 1887, Whistler (during his brief, erratic and stirring period of Presidency)[1] won from Queen Victoria the right for the Society to call itself 'Royal'. The Society, though concerned chiefly with paintings in oil, has always admitted water-colours. In its first twenty years its exhibitions were supported by Cotman and other members of the Norwich School, by T. Shotter Boys (who showed his first work at Suffolk Street when a mere boy), by Turner, Constable, Samuel Palmer, the brothers Varley, Thomas and Benjamin Barker of Bath, Glover, James Ward, and William Turner of Oxford.[2] In later times the encouragement given to water-colour art has been continued by the Society, which for a long time has set aside two rooms for water-colours in its annual exhibitions.

The exclusiveness of the 'Old' Society again led to the foundation of a rival society in 1831. In 1829 the 'Old' Society elected none of the candidates for admission to its ranks, and in 1830 only two out of seventeen applicants were chosen, in spite of the fact that the class of Associates had never been raised to its allowed complement. Though there was grave discontent, it was admitted that the walls of a gallery are inelastic and that an increased membership could only hamper the action and curtail unduly the privileges of the members. The Society was undoubtedly a close corporation, and considered that it was preserving its own interests and doing best service to water-colour art by maintaining the standard at a level which would be impossible with the exercise of a less severe discretion.

A contemporary critique of the 1831 Exhibition[3] made a virulent attack:

> The monopoly of this Institution, by the paltry, mercenary workings of its members, has contributed mainly to this corruption and degradation. It is a farce, a notorious farce and falsehood, to suppose that Academies and Institutions, professedly 'for the promotion of the best interests of the Fine Arts', are anything, in fact, but monopolies for the promotion of the selfish interests of the few that constitute them. This Institution, for instance, is exclusive in the narrowest degree as if measured by the minds of the Directors, and proceeds entirely on the profitable principle of 'the fewer, the better cheer'. No one out of the pale of the Society, however much his works may eclipse their own (and perhaps, for that prudent reason alone) is permitted to exhibit here, and the consequence is that many draftsmen of the finest talent, but disdainful of the mere slip-slop character of water-colour painters, are refused the entrée; while those within, lining the walls, as it has been known, with fifty pieces by a single artist, spoil the Exhibition by a dull, tedious monotony; and if they can be said to reign in this confused region, it is because they are one-eyed monarchs of the blind. . . . This illiberal policy, the offspring of sordid ignorance, has over-reached itself, and set afoot another Gallery, on a more enlightened and encouraging principle, which may easily, and we hope will soon, as Launcelot Gobbo says, 'raise the waters' to a fairer level.

This prejudiced writer apparently had inside information that a group of water-colour painters, who were outside the pale, were joining in the promotion of a rival institution.

[1] When this was over, he said that 'the Artists left, and the Royal British remained'.
[2] These and other names of deceased artists who were either members or exhibitors appear in the catalogue of a commemorative exhibition, the 200th of the Society, held amid all the difficulties of war-time in 1943.
[3] Inserted in a copy of the catalogue, in the V.A.M. Library. The detailed criticisms, which recall the days of Anthony Pasquin, are amusing, particularly that on No. 60, in these words: 'Asses, Hills and Robson—This is a puzzler. We examined their faces well, but we give it up. We cannot tell which is which.'

Under the title of the 'New Society of Painters in Water-Colours', it held its first exhibition, open to all artists, in 1832 at 16 Old Bond Street. Probably from that year dates the common appellation of the 'Old Water-Colour Society', which is established by Roget in the title of his book and still survives in the 'Old Water-Colour Society's Club'. The leading spirit in the foundation of the New Society was Joseph Powell, and with him were associated W. Cohen, J. Fuge, T. Maisey, G. F. Phillips, G. S. Shepherd, W. B. S. Taylor and T. Wageman. None of them was distinguished by special artistic power, but as indicated by their own words prefixed to the 1833 catalogue there was apparently a need for an institution where 'men of talent may have a fair opportunity of exhibiting their Works to advantage. . . . The unfriended man of merit who is unknown to the public will receive equal attention, and will have a fair opportunity of publicly displaying his Works without any restraint, except such as good reason, good feeling and impartial justice require.'

Like the Royal Society of British Artists, the New Society had an elected membership, but both Societies gave every artist a chance of exhibiting and of winning his spurs. Edward Duncan, James Holland, T. S. Boys, C. Bentley and James Stark were among the early exhibitors at the New Society. In 1834 the Society was remodelled 'upon the understanding that none but responsible members shall be exhibitors, and that they agree to share equally the labour and expenses necessary for the same'. In the same year a circular was issued referring to 'another evil which, if not provided against, must prove fatal to the Society is the fact that . . . artists whose views are directed towards the Senior Society . . . are no further interested on the prosperity of the Association than as affording a means of present advantage'. Each member was bound to forfeit the sum of twenty guineas on leaving the Society without the consent of its members but it proved very difficult to enforce any legal payment of the forfeit.

The New Society contained the germ of what is now the Royal Institute of Painters in Water-Colours.[1] The title of 'Institute' was first adopted in 1863. From 1835 to 1838 the New Society's exhibition was held in Exeter Hall; then from 1838 to 1883, during which period it became the Royal Institute, at 53 Pall Mall East. The present spacious galleries, called the Prince's Hall, at 195 Piccadilly, were specially built for the Institute, and completed in 1882. They form the largest range of galleries occupied by any London art society apart from the Royal Academy.

The Institute has numbered among its members many outstanding landscape painters such as Tom Collier, E. M. Wimperis, H. G. Hine, C. E. Holloway, Sir George Clausen, Mark Fisher, Arthur Severn and Claude Hayes, some of whom, it is true, seceded to the Old Society. But it has always given particular encouragement to subject-painting and illustration, especially under such Presidents as Louis Haghe and Sir James Linton; one has only to mention Charles Green, William Simpson, Caton Woodville, Edwin Abbey,

[1] For a full account of the history of the R.I., see *One Hundred Years*, by C. Reginald Grundy, in the catalogue of the Centenary Exhibition, 1931; and Norman Wilkinson, P.R.I., 'The Royal Institute', *The Studio*, July 1944.

Randolph Caldecott, Kate Greenaway, Walter Crane, Hugh Thomson and Phil May. Under the presidencies of Sir David Murray, Terrick Williams and Norman Wilkinson the Institute's catholic policy has been extended and its prestige enhanced.

In 1881 the Institute made a proposal for amalgamation with the Royal Society of Painters in Water-Colours,[1] but the latter Society decided that there were difficulties of various kinds which they found insurmountable. In the following year, synchronising with its move to larger premises, the Institute absorbed some of the leading exhibitors at the Dudley Gallery. This Gallery originated from a movement started by a committee of twenty-six artists and amateurs, with the security of 102 guarantors. One of its founders was William Stephen Coleman, a rather dull but proficient painter, whose younger sister, afterwards Mrs. Angell, won great distinction as a painter of flowers. The first exhibition was held at the Egyptian Hall in 1865. The title of the show was the *General Exhibition of Water-Colour Drawings*, but it soon became popularly known as the 'Dudley Gallery' or 'The Dudley', the name having become attached to the room in which the Earl of Dudley had exhibited his collection of paintings by old masters in 1852. The success of the venture was assured from the first, for no less than 1700 drawings were sent in, and over 500 were hung. The Dudley, during its existence from 1865 to 1882, became a natural feeder both of the Institute and the Old Society. Forty-four of its members, some by way of the Institute as a stepping-stone, found a place in the Old Society.

Meanwhile, in 1878, a Scottish Water-Colour Society (now Royal, like its compeers), came into being. An account of its aims and work are deferred to a later chapter dealing with the Scottish School. The year 1886 saw the foundation in London of the New English Art Club. Its influence is again the subject of later discussion.

---

[1] The documents and correspondence are quoted in full by Roget in an Appendix to Vol. II.

CHAPTER VIII

The Old Water-Colour Society

*John Glover   George Barret II   William Havell
William Sawrey Gilpin   William Frederick Wells
Sir Robert Ker Porter   John Claude Nattes   James Holworthy
Joshua Cristall   Thomas Heaphy   Paul Sandby Munn
Francis Stevens   Robert Hills   James Ward*

Something has already been said about several artists, such as Nicholson, Pyne and Shelley, who took an active part in the establishment of the Old Water-Colour Society. But many well-known painters, who were among the founders and original members, have been mentioned by name only. And so, before dealing fully with outstanding individuals who were famous members of the Society, Varley, Prout, Cox, De Wint and others—some attention must be given to a few of their elders and immediate predecessors, especially those whose work has points of technical interest. This is particularly the case with John Glover.

John Glover (1767–1849) was born of poor parents in the same year as Barret and Cristall, at Houghton-on-the-Hill, about six miles east of Leicester. His father gave him a 'good plain and Christian education', and encouraged him from childhood in his bent for drawing. From boyhood he had a love of agricultural work and a natural fondness for the rural scenery which surrounded him at Houghton and Ingersby. He developed an extraordinary power of taming birds, which would fly back from the woods at his call. He was a keen musician, and perhaps could whistle their songs. At one time he had a young skylark, a white water wagtail, a yellow wagtail and a titmouse, which all came to him for food, and slept in the same basket. While helping his father to till the midland acres he became so proficient in calligraphy that he was appointed, at the age of nineteen, as writing-master in the Free School at Appleby. During this employment he found time to pursue his drawing practice, and—following many artists who found this their first pathway to profit—he painted views of gentlemen's seats in the neighbourhood. Very wisely he made four visits to London, to see picture exhibitions and to take a course of eight lessons from William Payne, and one from 'Warwick' Smith.[1]

---

[1] Farington, *Diary*, December 30, 1794.

During 1794 Glover moved to Lichfield, where he set up as a drawing-master, 'teaching pupils both public and private'. He now began to practise etching and to paint in oil as well as water-colour, and in 1795 exhibited three drawings at the Royal Academy. From 1799 his work in both media won rapid appreciation; indeed, there were some who considered him a serious rival to Turner.[1] He resided at Lichfield for about eleven years, but painted also in Wales, Scotland, Derbyshire and Yorkshire. His pupil, Edward Price, who was with him for six weeks in Wales, said that Glover was always up before five and kept on at work every day till dark. His sketch-book was always in his hand, and into its pages went studies of scenery, donkeys in a rain-storm, cattle or a goat.

While residing at Lichfield, he made frequent visits to London, where he used to stay with his pupil, James Holworthy. Farington records calling upon Glover at Holworthy's house, 4 Mount Street, on May 30, 1804, and in his usual way he gathered information about Glover and his work. 'He lodged with a young man who was instructed by Him. His name Holworthy, he came from Bosworth in Leicestershire, and teaches drawing. Glover teaches drawing also.' Farington[2] tells us that:

> Miss Moserby (of Stow, near Lichfield) has taken lessons from *Glover* in the Country. He resides at Sutton near Lichfield during most part of the winter, & has a wife and 10 children.[3] His two eldest sons instruct in drawing. In the country He goes from family to family, & has 2 guineas a day at each House. He begins a drawing His pupil standing by and having proceeded as far as He considers it to be a lesson leaves it with his pupil to copy. The next visit He advances the drawing, & so goes on till He has finished the drawing, the pupil also gradually advancing the copy to completion. When He begins a drawing He first *finishes* the Sky which He does with proper colours, but all the other parts of the drawing He first washes with bluish and grey tints made of Indigo & India Red & towards the foregrounds of a warmer tint. In this manner He produces almost a finished effect before He lays on any colours; which is His last act. The drawing He makes for His pupil to copy remains His own property which he disposes of at a large price.—He gives lessons in London in the same manner, but has *two guineas* for a lesson of *three Hours*. Havil [William Havell] came to Glover's the other day while Miss Moserby was there. She sd. He is a well looking young man, but appears to be conceited.

Glover's success with work which he sent to London exhibitions led him to settle with his family in town. That was in 1805, and with his pupil Holworthy he became a member of the Society of Painters in Water-Colours, and contributed twenty-three works to its opening exhibition in that year. He won instant success, Farington[4] recalling that 'Glover is said to have sold drawings since he came to town to the amount of 700 guineas'. Glover's participation in the ups and downs of the Old Society has already been mentioned. He was its President in 1807–1808 and 1814–1815. Between 1805 and 1817, the year in which he resigned, he contributed 290 works to its galleries. But he always aspired to be a painter in oils, and perhaps left the Old Society in order to become a candidate for membership of the Royal Academy, though his ambition was never attained. 'Glover has

[1] *Gentleman's Magazine*, XXIV, 1850, p. 96.
[2] *Diary*, April 20, 1808.
[3] Farington was exaggerating. Glover appears to have had four sons and two daughters.
[4] *Diary*, June 20, 1805.

tumbled into oil', said Shee to Constable at the Academy, where there was no very friendly feeling towards the draughtsman-painter. Glover's devotion to oil-painting and his wish to be considered as the 'English Claude' are shown by the fact that about 1817 he sold a house which he owned near Patterdale for £1100 in order to buy a Claude.

For the sale of his oils and water-colours, after he had ceased to belong to any Society, Glover opened an exhibition of his own in April 1820, and continued it for several years in the galleries at 16 Old Bond Street, which had been occupied successively by the Old Water-Colour Society and the Associated Artists. He even had the temerity to invite Turner to join him in the speculation, but met with a refusal. In 1823 he was one of the founders of the Society of British Artists and remained nominally a member till his death in 1849.

Born and bred on country soil, Glover had all the instincts of a farmer, and was a man of indefatigable energy, in spite of his club feet and his eighteen stone weight. It was his love of the land, I suggest, which led him in 1830 to envisage a large farming venture in the Swan River Colony, now called Western Australia. He was a great reader of the Bible, and no doubt saw himself as a patriarch of the Old Testament surrounded by his family and by flocks and herds. Before his departure he made arrangements for the disposal of all the finished water-colours which remained in his possession; 'consisting of many of his most magnificent and favourite productions on stretching frames and others mounted for the portfolio, hitherto reserved by him as the finest specimens of his talents'.[1] He had already disposed of his house in Montagu Square, and was now a wealthy man. According to a newspaper cutting of 1830 in the Victoria and Albert Museum, he was said to be taking £60,000 with him to Australia, and the writer could not 'understand how the emigration of men of such property can benefit this country'.

Glover did not settle after all in Australia, but in Van Diemen's Land, now known as Tasmania.[2] He took with him his entire family and had an adventurous voyage lasting six months. It began by Mrs. Glover, seventy years old, having to climb 'the common rope ladder up the whole side of the vessel, which she accomplished, without any accident'. In Tasmania, besides being actively engaged in the work of a large sheep farm, Glover and his sons continued to exercise their art. In one consignment to London, Glover sent thirty-five canvases for sale. In 1835 he sent to London, for exhibition in Bond Street, more than fifty water-colours of the scenery and birds of Tasmania, including a picture of his house in Hobart Town. Little is known about the work of Glover's son, John, who, before the migration to Tasmania, had exhibited from 1808 to 1829. In 1808 either he or his brother William had set up with Glover's pupil, Henry Allport, as a drawing-master at Birmingham. William exhibited from 1813 to 1833, and some of his pictures were shown in Bond Street, from 1820 to 1830, at the exhibitions which members of the Academy called 'Glover's annual manufactory'.

[1] Advertisement in *The Times*, May 12, 1830, of the auction on May 18–19 at Stanley's rooms at 21 Old Bond Street.
[2] For a full account of Glover's voyage and of his life and activities in Tasmania, see 'A Painter who Emigrated' in *The Times*, November 15, 1930.

John Glover was an artist of some individuality and a great deal of manual skill. His work embodied the results of a close and patient study of nature, but like Barret and others, he made the mistake of thinking that water-colour could be linked up with the grand manner in oil. Long after other painters were working with direct local colour, Glover held to the use of underlying local tints. In his early drawings, such as *The Fisherman*,[1] the style of Payne is clearly visible, and he never quite abandoned Payne's method of priming his work with warm and cool greys. Referring to his *Devil's Bridge* in the Water-Colour Society's exhibition of 1808, John Landseer wrote[2]:

> The pervading richness and truth of Mr. Glover's sunshine in this picture is admirable. No water-colour painter knows better than he how to cool or warm the greys which prevail in his middle tints and shadows to the degrees which are requisite to give the general effect of nature to his lights.

His pupil, Edward Price, left an eye-witness account of Glover's methods and materials[3]:

> I think that Mr. Glover's method with his water-colour drawings was always the same. He invariably made a finished drawing in Indigo, Indian Red, and Indian ink, and then he coloured it. He had a glass of water, and a white plate on which he mixed his tints; and he worked with a spread camel's hair pencil [i.e. brush]. With this little implement he produced a great number of drawings under a great variety of expressive effects, and there was a perfection of work which none of his pupils ever attained. With these means, and rapid handling, he could express with wonderful truth a gleam of light upon a wooded hill or passing shade across a mountain range, or any transient effect. . . . I think Mr. Glover always used the common drawing board and the drawing paper by Whatman of that description. I imagine that he never used hot-pressed paper or the rough paper. Before he commenced his neutral tint he put on the paper a gradation of warm colour, beginning at the top with water farthest from the sun and increasing the strength to the bottom of the picture, or rather till he was below the horizon. He used Yellow Ochre and sometimes Light Red. If he had a soft cloudy effect to give, he made the paper damp, and while it was in that state he put in the sky. Then, with his neutral tint of Indigo and Indian Red he put in his distances, and nearly finished his work as he came to the foreground, reserving washes of this neutral tint to complete his effect. After this he used colour. He used very few colours, and those the most simple. Mr. Glover rarely used the sponge. Neither had he occasion to practise any device to alter his work. He was not liable to mistakes. Whatever his head approved, his hand was free to execute.

Some further testimony is added by W. H. Pyne[4]:

> Who that had not seen this eminent artist at his easel could have supposed the possibility of twisting camel-hair brushes together, spreading them, to the apparent destruction of their utility, yet dipping them in jet black Indian ink, or grey, or such tints as suited his purpose, and by a rapid and seemingly adventitious scrambling over the surface of his design, prepare the light and elegant forms of the birch or willow, the graceful sweepings of the branches of trees of larger growth, and the vast masses of woods and groves sparkling in their various foliage?

[1] B.M. 1885. 6.13.88.
[2] *Review of Publications of Art*, 1808, p. 181.
[3] Roget, I, pp. 306, 307.
[4] *Somerset House Gazette*, I, 1823, p. 133.

Both Price and Pyne draw attention to the split-brush technique, which is the main feature of Glover's work. By dividing with thin wire the hair of his brush, or of two small brushes joined, he obtained several sharp points, which he used for painting foliage. This mechanical, but labour-saving and effective, device was of special value, when used with an outward flick of the brush, round the edges of his trees. It was this kind of short cut which made him, like Payne, so fashionable a drawing-master. *The Landscape with River and Cattle*,[1] the *View of Bangor*[2] and *Landscape with Waterfall*[3] (Pl. 93) are all good examples of the split-brush technique. In drawings such as these, and in his *Borrowdale*[4] (Pl. 94) he shows his worship of Claude. Though his work is uneven and at times mannered in its conventions and elaborations—only rarely is he 'rude and blotted', as Samuel Redgrave says in his *Dictionary*—he achieved broad effects which possess attraction in their spirit of classical repose. But his warm tints merely gave a glow to his careful under-painting in monochrome. It was by leaving clear spaces in his monochrome that he produced his characteristic flicks of light. He was not a colourist.

George Barret, junior (1767–1842), painted pastoral subjects like Glover, producing variations of Claude. Again like Glover, Barret was mistaken in thinking that it was in his province, or in the province of water-colour, to picture Arcadian landscapes in the grand style. Turner alone was sufficiently talented and confident to be successful in this intention. George Barret was born in Orchard Street, Oxford Street, and, when his spendthrift father died in 1784, was left to fend for himself. His brother, James Barret, exhibited landscapes in oil and water-colour between 1785 and 1800. His sister, Miss M. Barret, became a miniature painter, was an exhibitor at Somerset House in 1797–1799, and, a quarter of a century later, joined the Water-Colour Society. George was far more distinguished as a painter, but little is known about his early struggles before the appearance of his first exhibited work in 1800.

With reference to a *Wood Scene* by George Barret, executed about 1799, Pyne[5] writes: 'We have watched the progress of this artist, we may almost say step by step, from the period when he commenced his career. Mr. Barret began early to study from nature, and to copy trees, banks, weeds &c. with careful identity. His early coloured drawings were simple in effect and chaste in colouring.' He was strongly influenced at the outset by Girtin, notably in his *Windsor Castle*.[6] (Pl. 95) His habit, we are told, was to go to the same spot and watch the sunrise, morning after morning, making slight memoranda. He used to wait till the effect appeared that suited him, and go to the same sketch over and over again at the same hour on different days, working only as long as the particular effect lasted.[7] Many of his simpler landscapes, painted directly from nature in the earlier part

[1] London, Bethnal Green Museum, No. 1122–1886.
[2] Cardiff, National Museum of Wales.
[3] Manchester University, Whitworth Art Gallery.
[4] Newcastle upon Tyne, Laing Art Gallery.
[5] *Somerset House Gazette*, II, 1824, p. 47.
[6] V.A.M. 1757–1900.

[7] Roget, I, p. 177.

of his career, are sensitive and charming. In his later poetical and ideal compositions he followed Claude and his successors in his presentment of a rich expanse of landscape melting into a far horizon, a middle distance with castle or bridge, a foreground of temple and tower, slopes crowned with pine and cypress, cattle or goats browsing on shadowed lawn, and above it all a blue and amber sky. It was from these stereotyped formulae that he repeated again and again the conventions found in such pictures as his *Landscape Composition*[1], his *Classical Composition, Landscape*[2] (Pl. 96) and *Italian Landscape*.[3] Laurence Binyon aptly says that they 'remind one in their drowsy unreality of a drop-scene in a provincial theatre'. On the other hand, some of his little studies of street and coast, of sunrise and sunset, are charming in their honest observation and delicate execution. Their spontaneity was lost in his later work. C. E. Hughes rightly indicates that while there is a great deal of light and colouring which is rich and pleasing in his more showy works, there is an obvious woolliness of texture.

Barret differed from Glover in that he abandoned the old theories about monochrome underpainting. He rightly attributed the fading of early water-colour drawings to the use of thin pigment containing Indigo Blue, and maintained that water-colours are 'perfectly durable when properly applied with a liberal supply of the material, and without any previous preparation of gray'. His treatise[4] includes those opinions and gives a list of colours which may be presumed to be those employed in his own practice: (For skies) Yellow Ochre, Burnt Sienna, Light Red, Pink Madder, Cobalt and, for a final wash to give brilliancy, Indian Yellow; (For other parts of the picture, all the above and) Raw Sienna, Indian Red, Brown Madder, Vandyke Brown, Brown Pink, Gamboge and Indigo. What is noticeable in that list is the predominance of warm colours, as though he were trying to paint not merely a Claude but the golden varnish that covers a Claude.

Barret's connection with the fortunes of the Old Water-Colour Society has already been related, and nearly six hundred of his works appeared in its exhibitions. He died in 1842 and, like his father, left his widow and children destitute. Roget[5] informs us that 'he had continued, as indeed he did to the end, to wrestle with poverty, but while working thriftily to support a wife and family, he ever thought more of putting gold into his drawings, than of the amount of precious metal for which those drawings might be exchanged'. Many years after his death his works began to command his prices, e.g. £420 for *Solitude* in 1863, £330 for *Walton Bridge* in 1875, and £383 for *Classical River Scene* in 1884. His reputation at that time was much higher than it is now. Even as late as 1897 Cosmo Monkhouse[6] could write: 'Turner himself could not excel him on this ground (the 'high art' of landscape) and, indeed, it may be doubted if this greater artist ever achieved such perfect irradiation,

[1] London, Bethnal Green Museum, No. 1090–1886.
[2] Newcastle upon Tyne, Laing Art Gallery.
[3] Cardiff, National Museum of Wales.
[4] G. Barret, *Theory and Practice of Water-Colour Painting*, 1840.
[5] Roget, I, p. 299.
[6] C. Monkhouse, *Earlier English Water-Colour Painters*, 1890, p. 173.

such limpidity of sunlight, or could obtain at once such elaboration and such purity as Barret in his finest drawings.'

Closely associated with Glover and Barret, as a landscape painter and as one of the founders of the Water-Colour Society, was William Havell (1782–1857). Born at Reading he was the youngest of the group. His father, Luke Havell, is said to have been drawing-master at the Reading Grammar School, under a famous headmaster, Dr. Richard Valpy. He did not find his calling lucrative enough for the maintenance of himself and his wife and family of fourteen children, and he hoped that his sons would embark on a more prosperous career. Yet several took to art in one form or another; two became well-known engravers, but William, who was the third son, out-topped the others. With some reluctance his father gave way to the boy's persistence and allowed him to follow his bent. It may be that it was his father who then encouraged him to contemplate the high example of Girtin, Turner and Varley. Quite early work shows that he was going direct to nature, working in broad washes of local colour, and disregarding traditional precepts for correct composition. He was found sketching at Dolgelly by the Varleys in 1802 and at Ross-on-Wye by Cornelius Varley and Cristall in 1803. And he had the good fortune to sketch with David Cox at Hastings in 1812. Cox used to boast that he painted a sunrise, and then awoke his young friend by flinging pebbles at his window to show what he had done while the other slept.[1] To watch the Varleys, Cristall and Cox at work was a liberal and enviable education for a young painter. Though he was clearly influenced in his actual practice by the Varleys, as is shown by his *Kilgerren Castle*, 1806 (Pl. 98),[2] he was a devoted admirer of Turner. 'The knowledge', he said, 'which Girtin and Turner had acquired of sunlight was so completely developed in their works that it seemed to have been held in hand, and thrown into the subject at pleasure.'[3]

Havell exhibited three of his Welsh subjects at the Royal Academy in 1804 and in the same year, at the age of twenty-two, he became one of the foundation members of the Water-Colour Society. His views in Wales were superseded by others of the English Lakes, which he visited in company with Reinagle in 1807.[4] Pyne says that he lived for two years in a Cumberland village.[5] After that he devoted himself to subjects of river scenery, round about Caversham, Henley, Windsor and his native town of Reading. In 1812 he published a set of twelve coloured aquatint plates (the engraver was his brother, Robert) with the title, *A Series of Picturesque Views of the River Thames*. These aquatints, remarkable facsimiles of his water-colours, illustrate his outstanding skill in expressing the play of sunlight and the effect of atmosphere on distant hills. The breadth of vision, shown in his earlier drawings, coupled with careful retouching in detail, made his work eminently suitable for the engraver. From 1813 to 1817 his drawings furnished frontispiece and monthly headings to a small annual pocket-book known as *Peacock's Polite Repository*, and in 1823 he supplied

[1] Solly, *Life of Cox*, 1873, pp. 25, 26.
[2] V.A.M. 3057–1876.
[3] Roget, I, p. 297.
[4] Farington, *Diary*, August 15, 1807.
[5] *Somerset House Gazette*, I, 1824, p. 193.

six of the subjects for aquatints by Robert Havell in *A Series of Picturesque Views of Noblemen's and Gentlemen's Seats*.

In 1816 Havell, who had retired from the Water-Colour Society, sailed for China as official artist to the Embassy of Lord Amherst, but resigned his position and made for Calcutta, where he acquired considerable practice as a portrait-painter in water-colours on a small scale. On his return to London, after an absence of over ten years, he rejoined the Water-Colour Society in 1827, but found his position taken by younger men, and consequently began to paint in oil. This perhaps accounts for a change in his technique. One of his friends, writing about the Society's exhibition of 1827, says: 'Havell, who, excepting the loss of a few teeth and the acquisition of a *menton de galoche*, is much the same, sent some clever drawings, though I find they are not popular with the members, owing to the free use of body colour.'[1] Of his twelve exhibits, three were views at Rio de Janeiro, one in China and the rest English subjects. In 1828 Havell was in Italy, and Joseph Severn[2] wrote to Uwins from Rome: 'I have just been seeing Havell, who has taken some sketches at Albano truly sublime; there is one of the lake, beyond anything I had ever seen.' From the same pen comes a description of Havell's manner of life and work in Naples. Uwins declared that Havell's experience and criticism had rendered his friend's arrival at Naples the most important event in his own professional life. He adds that 'to see him paint is like seeing Paganini play a fiddle'; and he gives this lively sketch on July 29 1828:[3]

> Havell says the heat is as bad as Bombay. He is for driving back as fast as possible to England; he says a year in Italy is enough to kill any man.[4] The burning sun, the bugs, fleas, and mosquitoes! and then the necessity of suffering 365 unwholesome dinners! With all these evils and sufferings, of which he certainly makes the most, he is doing the most delicious sketches and most glorious pictures. This country, in truth, is just suited to his romantic genius; and notwithstanding the impossibility of living in it, I do not expect to see him leave it as soon as he talks of. Havell is like many of his countrymen, he will not adapt himself. . . . He wants a beefsteak with the gravy in it and a mutton chop that will burn the mouth. He cannot eat figs for his breakfast, and maccaroni and cucuzzi for his dinner.

Havell was back in London in 1829, but made a second retirement from the Water-Colour Society. From 1830 he was occupied almost exclusively with oil-painting. He lived for thirteen years at 16 Bayswater Terrace, and then removed to High Row, Kensington, where he died. He was somewhat embittered in his life-time by lack of the recognition which he undoubtedly deserved. Examples of his work in the British Museum and the Victoria and Albert Museum would seem, in my opinion, to set him on a higher plane than the better-known Glover and Barret. His output—for he painted in water-colour for only some fourteen years—was much less than theirs. One wonders how much of his work

---

[1] Mrs. Uwins, *A Memoir of Thomas Uwins*, 1858, I, p. 184.
[2] Uwins, *op. cit.*, II, p. 232.　　　　　　　　　　　　　　　　[3] Uwins, *op. cit.*, II, p. 124.
[4] This is in direct contrast with the Shelleys at about the same time. In her *Diary*, written in England on May 14 1824, Mary writes: 'Let me only dream to-night that I am in Italy. Mine own Shelley, what a horror you had (fully sympathised in by me) of returning to this miserable country! To be here without you is to be doubly exiled, to be away from Italy is to lose you twice.'

remains to be discovered and, more particularly, where are the results of his two years sojourn in Italy? I cannot recall ever seeing an Italian subject by Havell except a *Coast Scene, Amalfi*.[1]

We may now pass to some foundation members who were of lesser distinction, and must include in that class the two first Presidents.

William Sawrey Gilpin (1762–1843),[2] first President, was the son of Sawrey Gilpin, R.A., best known as an oil-painter of animals, though he made water-colour studies as well both of animals and landscape. William Sawrey had a good practice as a drawing-master when the Water-Colour Society was formed in 1804. It may be surmised that it was his social connection and influence rather than his painting which caused him to be elected the Society's first President in 1805. Roget[3] suggests that the inferiority of his performance as a painter became apparent in the exhibition and alienated many of his pupils. This led him to retire in 1806 and to accept an engagement as a drawing-master in the Royal Military College, Great Marlow, which transferred later to Sandhurst. Farington made the following note[4]:

> Gilpin Junr. called to-day and thanked me for my assistance to procure Him the appointment of Drawing Master at the Royal Military College.—The 5 members of the board attended and He had the *first* vote of each of them. . . . His salary is to be at present £190 a year,—8s. a week for lodging money,—7 chaldrons & ½ of Coals, & Candles—and at the end of the first & Second 5 years, at each of those periods His salary is to be encreased £30 a year.—Alexander[5] is treated with much respect & sat at the board while the merits of the Candidate was under consideration.
> Gilpin told me that His Uncle, the late Revd. Mr. Gilpin, author of the Tour of the Wye &c &c, who was many years Master of Cheam School, made in that situation a fortune of about £700 year.

After leaving the Water-Colour Society Gilpin devoted himself in his spare time (he taught at the Royal Military College in the mornings only) to the theory and practice of landscape gardening and 'obtained almost a monopoly therein'. He laid out gardens at Danesfield, Enniskillen Castle and other seats, and published *Practical Hints for Landscape Gardening* in 1832. In this art he seems to have been more efficient than in the art of landscape painting.

William Frederick Wells (1762–1836), second President, was a highly educated and intelligent man and a sound though not brilliant painter. He is now almost completely forgotten or ignored. Born in London the same year as Gilpin, he studied pencil and crayon drawing at the age of twelve under J. J. Barralet or J. M. Barralet, both of whom were working as drawing-masters in 1774, when Wells would be twelve. He exhibited two views in Scotland at the Royal Academy in 1795 and these were followed in later years, up

[1] V.A.M. E.719-1922.
[2] I. A. Williams, 'The Artists of the Gilpin Family, with special reference to William Sawrey Gilpin,' *O.W.S. Club*, XXIX, 1951.
[3] Roget I, p. 215.
[4] *Diary*, February 24, 1806.
[5] William Alexander was head drawing-master, W. Delamotte second, and Gilpin third.

132

to 1801, by landscape subjects, mostly in Wales. He made what in his days was an unusual painting tour, in Norway and Sweden. Soon after 1801 he began his endeavours to stimulate his fellow-practitioners of water-colour to form a society for the purpose of holding an independent exhibition of their paintings. At the momentous meeting in November 1804, when the Water-Colour Society was formed, Wells was elected a member of the Committee, and succeeded Sawrey Gilpin as President in 1806–1807, but withdrew from the Society after its reconstitution in 1812. In 1805 he sent twenty-two drawings to the Society's exhibition at prices ranging from two to fifteen guineas, and a manuscript in the Victoria and Albert Museum records that he sold at least ten, priced in all at £56 12s. od.

In 1813, on the foundation of Addiscombe Military College for the East India Company's cadets, Wells was appointed its first Master of Civil Drawing and held this post till his death at Mitcham, Surrey, in 1836. About 1792 Wells was introduced to Turner by Robert Ker Porter (1777–1842), a somewhat romantic figure, who began his career as a scene-painter in the Lyceum Theatre, became historical painter to the Czar of Russia, married a Russian princess, was given an English knighthood in 1813, and published in 1821 a record of his travels in the Orient. We have met him already as a member of a sketching-club in association with Girtin and Francia. Wells became a life-long friend to Turner and, as has previously been related, suggested the first idea of the *Liber Studiorum*, the five initial studies for which were made in Wells' cottage at Knockholt. Wells' daughter tells us that for Turner in his early life her father's house (then in Mount Street, Grosvenor Square) was 'a haven of rest from many domestic trials too sacred to touch upon', and describes how on three or four evenings every week her father and Turner sat drawing by the light of an Argand lamp.[1] Turner appointed Wells one of the executors of his will, and left a legacy of £100 to each of Wells' three daughters.

Wells' work as a water-colour painter is rarely found. Three of his larger drawings are in the Victoria and Albert Museum. *The Dawn*[2] (Pl. 101) shows him as a classical painter in the manner of Glover and Barret, faithfully following the tradition of Claude. Perhaps Turner's life-long devotion to Claude had its beginning when, at the age of seventeen, he first came into close contact with Wells. In *The Dawn* and other works by Wells may be noted his technical method of working with small and short parallel strokes, from the point of a fine brush, vertical or sloping, sometimes cross-hatched. He was never successful either with the drawing or the placing of figures in his landscape work.

Another unsatisfactory member of the original group, but unworthy for a different reason, was John Claude Nattes (*c.* 1765–1822). He was born in England of Irish parents and in 1781–1784 we find him exhibiting Italian scenes. He travelled in Scotland between 1797 and 1800, making views for J. Stoddart's *Remarks on Scotland*, and in 1804 published *Scotia Depicta*. In that year he became one of the founders of the Water-Colour Society, but three years later was charged with exhibiting drawings as his own productions

[1] W. Thornbury, *Life of Turner*, II, 1862, pp. 53, 55.
[2] V.A.M. 1303–1872.

which were the work of other persons, with the dishonourable intention of obtaining a larger dividend from the year's profits than his own works would have entitled him to. He was found guilty and expelled. Nattes again resorted to Somerset House for exhibition and his name appears in the Academy catalogues up to 1812. In 1820–1822 he was travelling in Italy and the South of France; he died in South Molton Street, London.

Least significant among the original Water-Colour Society group of landscape painters comes James Holworthy (1781–1841), born at Bosworth, Leicestershire. Originally a student under Glover, as we have seen, he made himself known by his Welsh views at the Royal Academy in 1803 and 1804, and then joined the ranks of the newly formed Society. He exhibited there till 1824, when he married a niece of Joseph Wright of Derby (Turner sent two of his water-colours as a wedding gift), and retired from his profession to reside on an estate which he purchased near Heathersedge, Derbyshire. Monkhouse describes him as 'an able and elegant artist, very skilful in the use of Indian ink, but not venturing far in the colour process'. Like Wells, he was a life-long crony of Turner, and received from him what Finberg[1] describes as many 'long discursive epistles'. In the Library of the Victoria and Albert Museum is a volume lettered *Exhibition. Society of Painters in Water Colour, &c.*, which contains numerous missives addressed to Holworthy.

The original members of the Water-Colour Society were mainly, as has been seen, painters of landscape. Joshua Cristall (1767–1847), on the other hand, was essentially a figure-painter, though he excelled in the combination of figures with landscape. Cristall was born in 1767 according to most accounts, though a letter of his written in 1837 suggests that the year of his birth was 1769. He was the son of a Scottish father, who married a widow of Penzance, and became master of a small Cornish trading vessel; he is also described as a shipbreaker, with yards at Rotherhithe, Penzance and Fowey. The father persistently opposed his son's wish to become a painter. He was oblivious to the fact that nothing would deter a boy who spent his scanty pocket-money on Spanish liquorice, which he used as a water-colour to adorn the whitewash of his bedroom with spirited designs, and so the boy was apprenticed to a china dealer in Aldgate. With his mother's secret assistance he practised art, perhaps profiting by some knowledge of the retail trade, became a painter upon china, and later a traveller, for Turner's manufactory near Broseley. During this period, probably about 1792, he endured all kinds of discouragement, not least an avalanche of a letter from Mary Wollstonecraft, some passages from which may well be quoted:

> I think you ingenious, yet I am afraid that you are too sanguine in your expectations of succeeding as an artist. Besides abilities, a happy concurrence of circumstances is necessary to enable a painter to earn a livelihood; and many years of anxiety and patient industry must be passed before a man of superior talents can look with any certainty for to-morrow's subsistence. . . . I only wish to caution you against the headstrong ardour of youth. Pursue your studies. Practise as much as you can; but do not think of depending on painting for a subsistence before you

[1] A. J. Finberg, *Life of Turner*, 1939, p. 250.

know the first rudiments of the art. I know that you wish to be the friend and protector of your amiable sister, and hope no inconsiderate act or thoughtless mode of conduct will add to her cares. . . . How do you come on with your Music and Drawing? You scarcely know what industry is required to arrive at a degree of perfection in the Fine Arts, and how dreadful it is to plunge into the world without friends or acknowledged abilities. I have lately made some inquiries, and I think that it would be next to madness for you to launch out before you made any preparatory steps. London is not now paved with gold, and a false step in the beginning of life frequently throws a gloomy cloud over the fairest hopes. . . . Virtue is self-denial. If you cannot bear some present inconvenience, you are a common man and will never rise to any degree of eminence in anything you undertake.

Cristall was not going to be tied to any task-work which he hated. Making for London, he went through a period of odd employments and much hardship. At one time he entered into an agreement with a Scottish comrade in a printing establishment to live, both of them, for twelve months on a barrel of salt pork and a bag of rice. They did it, and survived. When he was thirty his mother was still buying shirts for him, but he was by then within sight of success. By some means or other he managed to enter the Academy schools about 1795 and, like so many other young artists, was helped by the guidance and friendship of Dr. Monro. We find him sketching in the Lakes in 1802 and 1803. He was also taking pupils, among them George Dyer, that gentle and eccentric poet who walked out of Charles Lamb's house into the New River and was nearly drowned. In 1803 Cristall exhibited at the Royal Academy, and in 1804—but he was now over thirty-five—he joined in forming the Water-Colour Society. Of his work before this date little is known, but many of his pencil sketches made before 1805 are in the British Museum, and Lord St. Levan owns at St. Michael's Mount six water-colours of Cornish subjects, signed and dated 1794, described by Dr. Percy in his MS. catalogue, now in the British Museum, as 'very carefully done and of a prevailing blue colour'.

Cristall's early work after 1805, was akin to that of Barret, consisting mainly of classical figures in landscape, a combination of the epic and pastoral design so much in favour at the close of the eighteenth century. A *Classical Composition*[1] (Pl. 106) and a *Pastoral*[2] are good examples. Both of them have affinity with the work produced at Girtin's sketching-club, and both suggest that Cotman, in the building up of his method, may have owed something to Cristall as well as to John Varley. Then followed genre and rustic scenes, treated in a simple and natural manner, with much fuller and more direct colour than had been employed by his predecessors in this mode. He was applying to genre the large fluid washes of local colour which Girtin and his followers had brought into landscape. In the work of Richard Westall and Hamilton and in the delicately tinted drawings of Wheatley, peasant girls, with their pretty graces, had belonged to the stage rather than the kailyard. Cristall's women folk are living and robust, solid in air and sunlight, not in the artificial light of the limes. Among the nearly 500 works which he contributed to the Water-Colour Society's exhibitions between 1805 and 1847 a large proportion are single figures, of

[1] Newcastle upon Tyne, Laing Art Gallery.
[2] Once owned by Sir Henry F. Wilson.

135

fisher folk, shepherds, gleaners, peasant girls spinning, knitting, lace-making, bleaching linen, gathering fern, drawing water at the well. They are well studied sturdy figures, with a natural rather than sentimental grandeur, poised, always firm on their feet. A *Study of a Peasant Girl*[1] is an excellent example.

In 1808 Cristall had come to the notice of Farington, a sign that he was being reckoned as of some account. The *Diary* on May 11 and May 21 contains these entries:

> Ward called to invite me to dinner on the 21st instt.—He spoke of Chrystal, the Artist, who He sd. had been almost in a state of despondence which His medical attendant thought wd. endanger His life. This was owing to want of success (encouragement) in consequence several artists put down their names for 5 guineas each to make up a Sum for Him.—In consequence of Crystall's drawings made last Summer have been much admired, Ward sd. a Host of Artists are preparing to go to Hastings.
>
> West gave his opinion 'that Artists ought to *represent their own Country* as it is, and not represent that of which they could only have an idea'. He said that several of those artists who have been of late distinguished for their *water colour drawings*, have obtained their popularity by it.—Glover, Chrystal & Heaphy are of this class—while, Ward observed, Havil [Havell] & Varley run more into the ideal.

By 1808, then, Cristall had clearly abandoned his epic-pastoral subjects in order to represent his own country and its inhabitants as they are. His *Fishmarket on the Beach, Hastings, 1808*,[2] and *Fishermen on the Beach, Isle of Wight*[3] show figures well grouped and solidly drawn. With work of this kind and with studies of single rustic figures Cristall continued, becoming President of the Water-Colour Society from 1820 to 1831. He died in 1847, and the descriptive title of the sale catalogue in the year following his death aptly epitomises his achievement:

> Catalogue of the beautiful original WORKS of that highly talented Artist, Joshua Cristall, Esq., Deceased; comprising beautiful finished DRAWINGS in WATER COLOURS including Narcissus and Echo, the Premium Picture[4]; beautiful Arcadian scenes; a grand view of Snowdon, and other compositions and Rustic Scenes; numerous highly interesting SKETCHES of Classical and Rural Scenes; Views in Scotland, Wales, and the most beautiful parts of England, in Pen washed with Bistre, Chalks, and Pencil; a GRAND CARTOON[5]; a few SKETCHES IN OILS; PAINTING MATERIALS, etc., which (by order of the Executors) will be sold by Auction by Messrs. Christie and Manson . . . on Tuesday April the 11th 1848 and two following days.

There were 617 lots, most of them comprising several items, and they realised a total of only £185 13s. 0d. The highest price was for Lot 558, 'An Arcadian Scene—very fine', £5 10s. The 'Snowdon—a *grand drawing*' went for nine shillings.

There are one or two examples of Cristall's work in pure landscape in the Victoria and Albert Museum, but in view of the numerous landscapes which he exhibited, his works of

---

[1] Coll. Mr. and Mrs. Paul Mellon.
[2] V.A.M. 431–1873.
[3] Hereford, City Art Gallery.
[4] Awarded one of the first of three premiums of £30, instituted by the Water-Colour Society in 1819. Barrat and C. Varley received the other two.
[5] An unfinished cartoon, 1844, for competition under the Government Scheme for decorating the Houses of Parliament.

136

this class are so rarely found that Randall Davies was possibly justified in 'thinking that a good many of them may be masquerading under other names with a forged signature, or among that numerous class of sometimes beautiful works catalogued merely as "English School" for want of a genuine one'. I think it must have been with reference to landscape that Samuel Palmer (planning out his work for 1844, on a sheet of notes in the library of the Victoria and Albert Museum) refers to Cristall as saying, 'White, black, and grey, manifest the colours, and the colours give white, black and grey beauty as colour.' Palmer's train of thought is shown by two other notes on the same sheet: 'White in full power from the first. Remember blazing days wherein it makes mid-tint local colors in sunshine seem dark', and, 'To get vast space what a world of power does Aerial Perspective open! From the dock leaf at our feet, far, far away to the isles of ocean, and thence, far thence, into the abyss of boundless light. Oh what heavenly grays does this suggest.'

Something may be said here about Thomas Heaphy (1775–1835), who has been mentioned already in this chapter. Though he was not one of the founders of the 'Old' Society, he became a member in 1807. He was apprenticed to R. M. Meadows, the engraver, and was employed in colouring prints after Richard Westall, and others. To use the contemporary term, he became a 'soft-print toucher'. He entered the Academy Schools in 1796, and from 1797 exhibited portraits and genre subjects at the Royal Academy. In 1808, the year in which his dozen exhibits at the Old Society were sold for 629 guineas, Heaphy went off to Hastings, and in 1809 exhibited his *Fish Market, Hastings* at the Water-Colour Society. It drew the attention of Benjamin West, then President of the Royal Academy, who said of it to Pyne: 'Sir, the subject is so well treated in its way, the expression is so complete, and the colouring and harmony are so pure and perfect, that it leaves one nothing to wish.'[1] The picture was said to have been sold for 500 guineas, a sum then unprecedented in the history of water-colour prices. It was no doubt this picture to which Hearne referred in a conversation with Farington, recorded on July 5, 1809. After condemning Turner for his lack of sublimity and dignity in rural subjects, compared with the simplicity and sentiment of Gainsborough, Hearne proceeded: 'See the Public cry up Heaphy's drawings, one of which was sold for 400 guineas. Take away the Mackarel from it, which were well imitated, and what is it?' Heaphy had exhibited only forty works in all, when in 1812, the year in which he exhibited *The Wounded Leg*,[2] he retired from the Society to devote himself mainly to portrait painting in oil. He was among the originators of the Society of British Artists, and became its first President in 1823.

Paul Sandby Munn (1773–1845) was elected an associate of the Old Water-Colour Society at its second annual meeting in 1805. His father, James Munn, was a carriage decorator and landscape painter (possibly also a drawing-master) at Greenwich. He was a friend of Paul Sandby, who became godfather to Paul Sandby Munn. Sandby gave early lessons to his godson and made him a good draughtsman on traditional lines, so that in 1799 he began to exhibit landscapes at the Royal Academy. Between 1802 and 1813 he

[1] *Somerset House Gazette*, I, 1823, 194.   [2] V.A.M. 604 (A.L. 2800).

supplied drawings to Britton for eight of the plates in the *Beauties of England and Wales*. In 1799 he became a member of the Sketching Club founded by Girtin,[1] and was secretary later under the presidency of Cotman. At the meetings of the Club he was in close contact with Cotman, T. R. Underwood, W. Alexander and the Varleys, but his style was set and he remained a reactionary. His brothers, William and James, conducted a stationers' and printsellers' business at 107 New Bond St., and in the back parlour or on the upper floor Paul Sandby Munn, the artist brother, worked at drawings which were sold in the shop. Young ladies of fashion bought them as drawing-copies, and so constant was the demand that Munn called in his friend Cotman, nine years his junior, to help in maintaining the supply. It was Cotman's chief occupation during the years 1802 to 1804. To increase their stock of drawings, Munn and Cotman went off together on sketching tours, to North Wales in 1802 and to Yorkshire in 1803. Several drawings made by Munn during these excursions are in the British Museum. From a pencil and wash drawing there, inscribed *Gordale, near Malham, July 26, 1803*,[2] Munn painted a larger water-colour of Gordale Scar, exhibited at the Royal Academy in 1804. An artist seated on a rock in the middle distance, making a sketch of the waterfall, is almost certainly Cotman. Munn exhibited forty works in all at the Old Society, nearly all of them views of Derbyshire or the Lakes, but never rose above associate rank. His style became close to that of Cristall and Heaphy. He seems to have settled at Hastings as a drawing-master and three of his drawings made there in 1811 are in the British Museum. His work was sound and pedestrian. In spite of his close association with Cotman, at a time when the latter was producing some of his most brilliant work, Munn preserved an eighteenth-century character following the well-trodden path of the topographers, but he forsook their delicate precision and unpretentious clarity without quite absorbing the breadth and dignity of Girtin and Cotman. Even when he became less timid in his use of colour, he was harking back to the brown and golden notes of Girtin. His *Buttermere*,[3] made in 1804, two years after Girtin's death, is a charming blue-grey drawing still embodying the principles taught by his godfather twenty years before; and other drawings in washes of blue and grey suggest that he was strongly influenced by Dayes. A sketch by Munn, *View of Snowdon from the vale of Llanberis*, made in 1802 during his tour in Wales with Cotman, and the finished drawing, are in the Victoria and Albert Museum.[4] Though the indigo throughout has faded, the drawing is, for Munn, exceptionally powerful and romantic. He seems to have found unusual stimulus either in the impressive scenery or in Cotman's companionship.

Munn's pupil, Francis Stevens (1781–1823), was elected with him to the associateship of the Old Society in 1805, and became a full member in 1809. He was probably born at Exeter, and was known later as 'Stevens of Exeter'. He exhibited landscapes with rustic

[1] For drawings made at the meeting of September 28, 1799, including work by Munn, see reproductions in *The Connoisseur*, August 1922.
[2] B.M. 1889. 12.18.17.
[3] Cardiff, National Museum of Wales.
[4] V.A.M. P.24–1939 (sketch); V.A.M. P.8–1938.

138

buildings from 1804 to 1823 at the Royal Academy and on the walls of his own Society. His *Devonshire Cottage*,[1] (Pl. 113) an elaborate drawing in the tinted manner, was probably one of the works which he submitted as a candidate in 1805. He appears to have been teaching at Sandhurst Military College in 1816, and before this date he had published a series of *Views of Cottages and Farmhouses in England and Wales*, etched by himself from drawings by Munn, Varley, Hills, Pugin, Prout and others.

Variety of another kind was provided in the Society's early exhibitions by Robert Hills (1769–1844), a highly accomplished painter and etcher of animals. Born at Islington in the same year as his friend, James Ward, nothing definite is known about his parentage or his childhood except that he had drawing lessons from John Alexander Gresse, possibly at Mrs. Broadbelt's school in Queens Square, Bloomsbury, where Gresse was drawing-master. An interesting newspaper advertisement, of the probable date 1789 runs:—[2]

STAINED GLASS

R. HILLS, No. 4, Keppell Row, New Road, Tottenham-court, near Portland Bar, respectfully acquaints the Nobility and Gentry, that he has lately finished for sale, a great variety of subjects; consisting of landscapes, moon-lights, church-pieces, views of Vesuvius, &c. wherein the different effects of the sun, fire, &c. are introduced in such a manner as to render them far superior to any other kinds of paintings.—Also several smaller subjects, as flowers, insects, &c. which, when mounted up with coloured glass, at the same time that they greatly add to the beauty of a room, form an agreeable shade, and are therefore well adapted for summer-houses, grottos, &c. Coats of arms executed in a style of superior elegance, and on reasonable terms.

When Robert Hills first exhibited his work in 1791 he gave his address as Keppel Row, New Road, which is now the Marylebone Road. Basil Long[3] has shown that Keppel Row was only a group of houses, and it seems fairly certain that the advertiser was our Robert Hills at the start of his career. He was a student at the Royal Academy schools in 1788. It is certain, however, that 'he soon found a wiser master in the force of his own inclination, which led him to the study of animal life in the forest, the farmyard, and the pasture, sketching with untiring zeal, deer, oxen, sheep and cattle, singly and in groups, in great variety, or in observing their habits under the varied influences of the seasons. His careful studies of the heads, horns and bones of the different species testify to the pains he took to master the distinctive features and exact structure of animal form.'[4]

From 1798 to 1815 he issued a remarkably fine series of etchings of animals, a separate instalment for each type: deer 151, horses 48, asses and mules 80, dogs 55, sheep and goats 108, swine 36, oxen 200, cattle 100; making, with two frontispieces, 780 prints sold at the moderate price of £40. Hills' own collection of over one thousand proofs, many in unique states, is in the Print Room of the British Museum. They are not masterpieces of

[1] V.A.M. 441.
[2] V.A.M. *Cuttings from English Newspapers*, II, *1686–1835*, p. 527.
[3] B. S. Long, 'Robert Hills', *Walker's Quarterly*, 1923, No. 12.
[4] Roget, I, p. 137. An album of drawings by Hills belonging to the Royal Water-Colour Society, contains sketches of horns; anatomical studies of joints, skulls, skeletons with every bone named; a skeleton of a sow from bones and notes as to the positions of bones, is in the Hunterian Museum.

imaginative or interpretative etching; they were never intended to be more than faithful and accurate studies for the benefit of students or artists who wished to enliven their landscape; but they show remarkable knowledge of the anatomy, movements and habits of animals; in their rendering of actual form they are impeccable. As faithful records they are unequalled, and rank in this respect beside E. W. Cooke's etchings of shipping and craft.

Hills was a man of tremendous energy, for during these years he not only produced his 780 etchings but had some connection as a teacher and painted a large number of water-colours, many of them distinguished by a careful and minutely stippled finish. At the Royal Academy in 1791 he exhibited a *Wood Scene with Gipsy Fortune-Tellers*, in the next year a *Landscape*, and in 1800 a *Cottage Scene, with Cattle*. With his friends Nattes and Shelley, he helped to found the Water-Colour Society in 1804, and became its first secretary, his services being recognised in 1809 by a presentation of plate to the value of one hundred guineas. Between 1805 and 1844 he exhibited 573 works, including nine in which other artists had a share. He frequently added groups of animals, usually deer, to enliven landscapes by G. Barret, G. F. Robson and W. A. Nesfield; 'Animals by Hills' constantly appeared in a catalogue. Many water-colours of the period contain animals obviously by, though not credited to, Hills. He is draughtsman rather than colourist, and is at his best, particularly from about 1810 to 1825, in studies where textures are not so carefully rendered or details so closely developed as in his later work. Laurence Binyon[1] rightly draws attention to a drawing, *Village, with Rustics in a Shed*,[2] (Pl. 115) of a village in a snow shower, with rustics sheltering, which is intimate and charming.

In 1800 Hills became a member of a Sketching Society,[3] with James Ward, Samuel Shelley, James Green, J. C. Nattes and W. H. Pyne. They used to meet once a week at each other's houses to sketch and converse upon art. It was their rule to drink tea and porter and eat bread and cheese, so as to avoid competition in providing elaborate suppers. Sometimes they had thirty to forty other artists as guests. In the summer they made country excursions and spent the day in sketching. A writer in the *Library of the Fine Arts* describes how the coterie once met in the evening at the Fleur-de-Lis, a rural inn of Windsor Forest, all anxious to see the drawings of the others. Joshua Cristall had sketched groups of beeches; James Ward had produced a masterly study of the homestead of the inn, from which he subsequently painted a cabinet picture in oil; William Havell came to headquarters at the appointed hour and exhibited a coloured scrap, observing 'This is all I have done in my day's ramble'; he had spent several hours in the delineation of a portion of an old brick wall, overgrown with ivy. 'Hills, too, was of the party; who, after rambling in his accustomed haunts amongst the King's stags at Swinley, returned with a collection of studies of red deer, which for characteristic truth and beauty of execution rivalled the finest doings of the old masters.' Though Hills' pictures are mainly of animals, many have landscape backgrounds of a specific scene. Windsor Park and the Lake

[1] L. Binyon, *English Water-colours*, 1933, p. 93.   [2] Coll. Mr. and Mrs. Tom Girtin.
[3] Farington, *Diary*, March 22, 1804.

92 'A Yorkshire Road'
Coll Mr & Mrs Paul Mellon $4\frac{1}{4} \times 7\frac{1}{8}$: 108×181 *Water-colour*
John GLOVER (1767–1849)

93 'Landscape with Waterfall'
Manchester University, Whitworth Art Gallery $15\frac{7}{8} \times 23\frac{3}{8}$: 390×592 *Water-colour*
John GLOVER (1767–1849)

94 'Borrowdale'
Newcastle upon Tyne, Laing Art Gallery   16½ × 24 : 418 × 608   *Water-colour*
John GLOVER (1767–1849)

95 'Windsor Castle'

V.A.M. 1757–1900 $20\frac{7}{8} \times 28$: 530 × 710   *Water-colour*

George BARRET II (1767 or 1768–1842)

96 'Classical Composition, Landscape'

Newcastle upon Tyne, Laing Art Gallery $5\frac{1}{8} \times 8$: 130 × 203   *Water-colour*

George BARRET II (1767 or 1768–1842)

97 'View of Lancaster'
Oxford, Ashmolean Museum   13½ × 19⅛: 340 × 486   *Water-colour*
William HAVELL (1782–1857)

98 'Kilgerren Castle, Pembrokeshire'
V.A.M. 3057–1876   19⅜ × 27½: 491 × 698   *Water-colour, signed*
William HAVELL (1782–1857)

99 'Muddiford, Hants'

V.A.M. 91.D.36 $8\frac{5}{8} \times 14\frac{1}{4}$: 219 × 361   *Water-colour*

William Sawrey GILPIN (1762–1843)

100 'Coast Scene'

B.M. 1881.5.4.173   7 × 13: 177 × 330   *Water-colour*

William Sawrey GILPIN (1762–1843)

101 '"The Dawn": Ruined Castle above a River'
V.A.M. 1303–1872   20 × 28⅞: 507 × 728   *Water-colour signed, dated at the back 1807*
William Frederick WELLS (1762–1836)

102 'Boughton Hill, near Canterbury'
B.M. 1953.12.12.13   11 × 16¾: 279 × 425   *Water-colour*
William Frederick WELLS (1762–1836)

103 'Italian Ruins'
V.A.M. P.8–1949 $9\frac{3}{4} \times 14\frac{3}{4}$: 248 × 374   *Water-colour*
John Claude NATTES (1765–1822)

104 'Blunderston, near Lowestoft'
Coll. Mr & Mrs Paul Mellon $11\frac{3}{4} \times 8\frac{1}{2}$: 298 × 216   *Water-colour*
John Claude NATTES (1765–1822)

105 'Girl Peeling Vegetables'

Coll. Mr & Mrs Paul Mellon $17\frac{1}{2} \times 13\frac{3}{4}$: 444×349 *Water-colour*

Joshua CRISTALL (1767–1847)

106 'Classical Composition'
Newcastle upon Tyne, Laing Art Gallery $10\frac{1}{2} \times 16\frac{1}{8}$: 267 × 408   *Water-colour*
Joshua CRISTALL (1767–1847)

107 'Country Scene'
Coll. Mr & Mrs Paul Mellon $11\frac{1}{8} \times 18\frac{1}{8}$: 282 × 460   *Water-colour*
Joshua CRISTALL (1767–1847)

108 'Mallwyd on Dovey'

Coll. Mr & Mrs Paul Mellon   11 × 16: 280 × 406   *Water-colour, signed*

Sir Robert Ker PORTER (1777–1842)

109 'The Drawing-master'

Coll. Mr & Mrs Paul Mellon   5 × 7¾: 127 × 197   *Water-colour*

James HOLWORTHY (1781–1841)

110 'Fisherman's Cottage'

Newcastle upon Tyne, Laing Art Gallery $18\frac{1}{2} \times 24\frac{1}{2}: 457 \times 621$ *Water-colour, signed and dated*

Thomas HEAPHY (1775–1835)

III 'In Nant Franken, Carnarvonshire'

B.M. 1935.3.9.9.   8¼ × 12¾ : 210 × 323   *Water-colour, signed and dated 1805*

Paul Sandby MUNN (1773–1845)

112 'Hastings from White Rock'

B.M. 1868.3.28.329   10 × 16 : 254 × 406   *Water-colour*

Paul Sandby MUNN (1773–1845)

113 'A Devonshire Cottage'

V.A.M. F.A.441 $18\frac{3}{4} \times 25\frac{3}{4}$: 376 × 653   *Water-colour, signed and dated 1806*

Francis STEVENS (1781–1823)

114 'Budd's Green, Kent'
Coll. Mr & Mrs Paul Mellon   8 × 12⅛: 203 × 307   *Water-colour*
Robert HILLS (1769–1844)

115 'Village with Rustics in a Shed'
Coll. Mr & Mrs Tom Girtin   12¾ × 16¾: 323 × 425   *Water-colour*
Robert HILLS (1769–1844)

116 'Alderney Cows and Calves'

V.A.M. 1931–1900 $20\frac{7}{8} \times 18\frac{3}{4}$: 530 × 476   *Water-colour, signed and dated 1820*

Robert HILLS (1769–1844)

117 'An Eagle'

Coll. Mr & Mrs Paul Mellon $14\frac{5}{8} \times 13\frac{5}{8}$: 372×346 *Pencil and water-colour, varnished*

James WARD, R.A. (1769–1859)

118 'Snowdon—an Approaching Storm'

Coll. Mr & Mrs Paul Mellon $6\frac{5}{8} \times 12\frac{3}{4}$: 167 × 323   *Pen and grey wash, signed and dated 1853, on verso*

James WARD, R.A. (1769–1859)

119 'Valley Landscape with Figures at a Gate'

Coll. Mr & Mrs Paul Mellon $8\frac{3}{4} \times 12\frac{1}{2}$: 222 × 317   *Water-colour*

James WARD, R.A. (1769–1859)

120 'River Bank'

Coll. Mr & Mrs W. W. Spooner $9\frac{3}{4} \times 11\frac{3}{4}$: 247 × 298   *Water-colour, initialed*

James WARD, R.A. (1769–1859)

121 'Holy Ghost Chapel, Basingstoke'

B.M. 1885.6.13.44 $8 \times 11\frac{1}{8}$: 203 × 282   *Water-colour*

James WARD, R.A. (1769–1859)

122 'Near Cheadle, Cheshire'

B.M. 1941.12.13.714 $9\frac{1}{2} \times 12\frac{3}{8}$: 241 × 314   *Water-colour*

James WARD, R.A. (1769–1859)

District figure frequently; in 1811 and 1812 Surrey scenery about Dorking and Box Hill; from 1817 and 1818 the country round Sevenoaks. In his later life, Penshurst Park and Knole Park, and the picturesque farmyards of Kent, supplied many themes. A typical example, showing his highly skilful draughtsmanship of woodland scenery and of animals is the *Scene in Knole Park with Fallow Deer*[1] exhibited at the Water-colour Society in 1818. His charming little sketches of rural scenes, with their silvery quality of colour, are frequently annotated in shorthand, though not apparently in any of the usual methods. Two other artists of the same period, George Chinnery and James Ward, also wrote shorthand notes on their sketches. There is such similarity between some tree studies by Ward and by Hills that I think they must often have worked side by side. Finally, it may be said that Hills, like Turner, stayed with Walter Fawkes at Farnley. A very fresh water-colour inscribed *Farmyard at Leathley near Farnley, Yorkshire*, 1818,[2] together with seventeen drawings made in Kent, came from the collection of John Garle, F.S.A., who was one of the trustees appointed under Hills' will. Roget records that 179 drawings and sketches by Hills, which belonged to Garle, were sold at Christie's on April 27, 1874. These, and other works mentioned, give no indication of foreign travel, but within a month of the victory at Waterloo, Hills traversed the battle-field, recording his impressions. After his return to England he published *Sketches in Flanders and Holland*, illustrated by thirty-six aquatints made by himself from his sketches. In or before 1831 and again in 1833, with G. F. Robson as his companion, he visited Jersey.

Reference may be made here to the somewhat rare work in water-colour of James Ward (1769–1859). Son of the manager to a fruit and cider merchant, Ward was born in Thames Street, London. He became a bottle-washer at the age of nine in the cellars over which his father presided; but when he was about thirteen his father allowed him to study under John Raphael Smith. He left Smith a year later and was bound in 1783 as regular apprentice to his elder brother William Ward, then at the beginning of his very successful career as a mezzotint engraver. James also gained considerable renown by his mezzotints, mostly of landscape and animal subjects, but abandoned this side of his art in 1817 and gave to the British Museum a representative set of his prints, including many working proofs. His earlier drawings of domestic and rustic scenes are in the style of his brother-in-law, George Morland—he himself described his early pictures as 'pure Morland'—but Morland could not draw animals with the artistic skill and convincing accuracy of Ward. His *Horses and Foals*,[3] *Pigs*,[4] and *Sow and Pigs*[5] and *A Calf*[6] are typical of his work as a superb draughtsman of animals.

James Ward abandoned his imitation of Morland, turned to the Dutch School, and made his fame as a painter in oil with such vigorous and spirited works on the grand scale as his *Fighting Bulls*[7] and his *Gordale Scar*,[8] both of them strongly influenced by Rubens. A

[1] Huntington Library, San Marino, California.
[2] Formerly Coll. Sir Bruce Ingram.
[3] V.A.M. D.877–1907.
[4] Birmingham, City Art Gallery.
[5] Coll. Mrs. Eleanor Williams. Reproduced in *Some Victorian Draughtsmen*, by Hesketh Hubbard, 1944, pl. 16.
[6] Once Coll. T. Lowinsky.
[7] V.A.M. 220–1871.
[8] Tate Gallery.

141

writer in 1809 wisely said about Ward's art: 'Not the School of Morland—but the resurrection of Rubens.' Ward was elected A.R.A. in 1807 and R.A. in 1811. As a member of the Academy, he belonged to no water-colour society, and his work in the lighter medium, like that of Callcott and Constable, has been ignored till quite recent times. His landscapes in water-colour have never had their due meed of praise. The romantic outlook, as in the *Mountain Stream in Wales*,[1] is combined with search for realistic truth. Ward draws detail, but it is submerged and embodied in his large and poetic generalisation. Here, and in some of his small landscapes—the *Dunstanborough Castle*[2] is a good example— he is as romantic as in the *Gordale Scar*. Some of his early water-colours, but for the signature, might pass as the work of Girtin. The *View near Swansea*[3] shows the example of Girtin, even to the little dots and spots in the foreground. The water-colour landscapes are something of a rarity and are not often met with outside public collections. *Mountain Landscape*[4] (Pl. 122) and *Holy Ghost Chapel, Basingstoke*[5] (Pl. 121) are interesting in their grouping of certain elements which appear in Girtin and Cotman, and his study of *A Young Woman and a Boy*[6] is deftly handled, with real feeling for the water-colour medium. One of the finest of his works is the *Chiseldon, Wilts.*[7] It is drawn in ink, like the *Dunstanborough*, as if with the nervous line of an etcher, thickening and thinning and breaking into dots. The loose vibrating pen-work is washed over with warm colour of rich yellows and browns, and with colder summer greens on meadows and trees. It is curiously akin to similar work by J. F. Millet in the Ionides Collection (Victoria and Albert Museum), not only in handling but in its air of naïveté. Like the Millet drawings of this type it has the naturalistic and romantic quality of the Dutch Masters of the seventeenth century. It may be added that, in many of Ward's drawings, particularly in his earlier work, the 'W' will be found to be a monogram containing the four interwoven letters of Ward's name. His earliest signature was 'J.W.', but there is good evidence that in later years he went through batches of his old drawings, signing them 'J.W.,R.A.', often in addition to an earlier 'J.W.'. In other words, a drawing signed 'J.W.,R.A.' may have been made many years before his election to the Royal Academy. All of Ward's water-colour drawings, which I have seen, appear to belong to a period before 1830, when he had not become engrossed in oil-painting.

James Ward's fame as a water-colour painter lags far behind his merit, but he must not be confused with his namesake and contemporary James Ward (1800–1885), a pugilist who took up oil-painting and produced numerous landscape and sporting pictures, some of which were exhibited at Liverpool and elsewhere from 1840 to 1860.

1 Coll. Mr. and Mrs. Paul Mellon.
2 Once Coll. Sir Robert Witt.
3 Coll. Mr. and Mrs. Paul Mellon.
4 B.M. 1941. 12.13.714. (Near Cheadle, Cheshire).
5 B.M. 1885. 6.13.44.
6 B.M. 1885. 6.13.54.
7 Manchester University, Whitworth Art Gallery.

CHAPTER IX

The Associated Artists

John Charles Barrow   Louis Francia   William Wyld
Luke Clennell   Thomas Bewick   Alfred Edward Chalon
John James Chalon   William Marshall Craig   James Holmes
Joseph Clarendon Smith   Sir Augustus Wall Callcott
Thomas Sidney Cooper   Joseph William Allen   Joseph Powell

The preceding chapter dealt with some of the founders of the 'Old' Water-Colour Society, and similar attention must be paid to early members of the Associated Artists in Water-Colours, founded four years later. The Associated Artists formed an Opposition although their methods and policy were the same as those of the older Society. The two exhibitions could, apparently, have been interchanged without anyone being aware of the fact. There was not room at the time for two Societies which were so identical, and both began to run into stormy waters. In 1812, as has been related, the Associated Artists died, while the older Society, survived under a new name and constitution.

The catalogues of the Associated Artists during the four years of the society's existence contain many well-known names.[1] Blake, Cotman, Cox, De Wint, Prout, Samuel Owen, all exhibited under its auspices, and Cox was President in 1810. These and other prominent members or exhibitors will figure in later chapters, but some account may be given here of others who are by no means negligible, particularly Francia and Clennell. François Louis Thomas Francia (1772–1839), generally known as 'Louis Francia', was born at Calais. He came to England at an early age, and about 1794 was an assistant in J. C. Barrow's drawing-school. J. P. Neale, the topographic draughtsman, described him, while working at the school, as 'a conceited French refugee, who used to amuse the party with his blundering absurdities'.[2]

Little has been known about John (or Joseph) Charles Barrow[3] (*fl.* 1789–1802), under whom Francia worked, but W. T. Whitley,[4] who discovered a biographical memoir of Barrow contributed by Francia to the *General Chronicle*, wrote as follows:

[1] For a full list of members and exhibitors, see Roget, I, pp. 271–273.
[2] Roget, I, p. 99.
[3] Roget gives his first name as Joseph, but Francia speaks of him as John.
[4] Whitley, 1800–1820, p. 219.

'Francia, who had a great opinion of Barrow, expresses his surprise in the opening passage of his memoir that none of the drawing master's many pupils have given his memory the deserved meed of praise, instead of leaving this last act of duty to a man who is a stranger to his blood and an alien in his country. Barrow, says Francia, was the son of a wealthy oil merchant in Thames Street, and brought up in luxury at his father's country house at Twickenham. He succeeded to the parental estate and business, the last of which he abandoned to follow art, and was engaged by Henry Pars in 1791 as assistant in his drawing school in the Strand.[1] Later he conducted an academy in Great Queen Street, Lincoln's Inn Fields, in which, says Francia, some of our best architects acquired their knowledge of geometry and perspective. But unlucky speculations led him to a debtors' prison, and he died in a state of destitution.

When Francia first came to this country, and before he could speak a word of English, he made the acquaintance of Barrow at a school at Hampstead, and was so strongly attracted by his charm of manner that he joined him and shared his fate through all the vicissitudes of the last thirteen years of his life. "Had he been fortunate," says the French artist, "he was qualified by his mental powers for the first situations in the state. In short he was a man such as we seldom see. He formed two pupils, Louis Francia and John Varley."'

To that account may be added that Barrow also, at one time, held an evening drawing-school twice a week at his house, No. 12 Furnival's Inn Court, Holborn; was a member of the Old Incorporated Society of Artists; published *Picturesque Views of Churches and other Buildings*, 1790; and was employed by Horace Walpole, for whom he painted views of Strawberry Hill. Two of these, drawn in 1789, were in the collection of the late John Lane. His *View of Croyland Abbey* and *View of the Thames in the Great Frost of 1789* (Pl. 123) are in the British Museum[2] and two drawings, one an interesting monochrome, *Scene in a Classical Temple*,[3] dated 1800, are in the Victoria and Albert Museum.

Francia, while still an assistant to Barrow, was apparently a fellow student with Girtin at Dr. Monro's, and was secretary of Girtin's Sketching Club in 1799. His drawings made at the Club's meetings are almost indistinguishable from those of Girtin. The texture, the washes, the little spots, the broad treatment of masses, are entirely in the Girtin manner. Each may have influenced the other, though Girtin's breadth of style and harmony of colour were essentially his own contribution to British art. I have never seen any water-colour by Francia, at any rate among his earlier drawings, which did not possess a strong analogy with Girtin. A *Landscape with Cottages*,[4] resembles an early Girtin so closely that someone in the past was encouraged to superimpose a forged signature of Girtin over that of Francia: cleaning revealed the original signature, but traces of the forged one are still visible. His *Landscape with Trees*[5] is very close to Girtin, though it does not show quite his dignity of composition; and the fine drawing of *Transports returning from Spain, February,*

[1] The School originally started by William Shipley.
[2] B.M. 1890. 5.12.9 and 1891. 5.11.32.
[3] V.A.M. P.6–1956.
[4] Cardiff, National Museum of Wales.
[5] Coll. Herbert Powell (N.A.–C.F.)

144

1809[1] (Pl. 124) again testifies to the value of Girtin's example and inspiration. The *Lane and Cottages*[2] in the Victoria and Albert Museum, once held to be one of Girtin's finest water-colours, is now thought to be a pastiche by Francia after a sepia and pencil drawing by Girtin in the British Museum.[3]

Francia exhibited eighty-five landscapes at the Royal Academy between 1795 and 1821, and is said to have been 'Painter in Water-Colours' to the Duchess of York. In 1810 he published *Studies of Landscape*, a series of forty remarkably fine soft-ground etchings after drawings by himself and other painters, among them Gainsborough, Hoppner and Girtin. These are the more interesting because they show Francia's trend towards the romantic, and because they are by no means literal transcripts but, in the words of the title, are *Imitated from the originals by L. Francia*. The complete set of these prints is extremely rare. Francia was a member of the Associated Artists from 1810 to 1812, and their Secretary during the last two of these years.[4] In 1817 he returned to his native Calais, and thereafter was mainly occupied in painting coast scenery and shipping in the Channel; he died there in 1839. More important almost than his own work at this period is the fact that he met, and helped to form, Bonington. Francia came across him, when Bonington was not more than fifteen, sketching on the quays at Calais. Francia gave him some lessons, which were certainly free, continued and started Bonington upon his career with a knowledge of what was best in English water-colour, i.e. the value of drawing and of clean washes of direct colour. William Wyld (1806–1889), at some time Secretary to the British Consul at Calais, was also a pupil of Francia. He became a close friend of Bonington, and was his executor. In 1839 he published twenty lithographic views of Paris; exhibited from 1849 to 1882 at the Royal Academy and the New Water-Colour Society (now the Royal Institute), of which he became an associate in 1849 and a member in 1879. He spent most of his life in Paris, frequently contributing to the Salon, where he was awarded two medals, and was made a member of the Legion d'Honneur in 1855. He is said to have played a large part in the development of water-colour painting in France. It was Bonington, and not Francia, whose influence is most apparent in Wyld's work. How near Wyld may come to Bonington is apparent in his drawings of the *Rue Royale*,[5] *Place Royale*[6] and *Palais Royal*.[7]

Francia's work, whether it be of landscape or marine subject shows a consistent level of quality with rare taste, refinement and skill and latent power beneath its untroubled surface. His colour, though subdued and low in tone, is far from monotonous. He deserves credit as one of the first to discover that there could be beauty in sombre landscape themes which, before his time, were thought ugly, grim or trivial, and may be compared with the

[1] B.M. 1890. 5.12.82.
[2] V.A.M. P.68–1919.
[3] B.M. 1855. 2.14.50, 51; see T. Girtin and D. Loshak, *Thomas Girtin*, 1954, p. 202, no. 497.
[4] He was not Secretary of the Old Water-Colour Society, as stated by Redgrave, Monkhouse, Binyon in the B.M. catalogue, D.N.B., etc.
[5] Coll. H.M. The Queen.
[6] Coll. H.M. The Queen.
[7] Coll. H.M. The Queen.

poet Crabbe, whom Byron described as 'Nature's sternest painter, and the best', and who produced similar effects in verse.

> *Far to the left he saw the huts of men,*
> *Half hid in mist that hung upon the fen,*
> *Before him swallows gathering for the sea,*
> *Took their short flights and twittered o'er the lea;*
> *And near the bean-sheaf stood, the harvest done,*
> *And slowly blackened in the sickly sun.*
> *All these were sad in nature, or they took*
> *Sadness from him, the likeness of his look,*
> *And of his mind—he pondered for a while,*
> *Then met his fancy with a borrowed smile.*

That poetic description, with its feeling of gloom and melancholy, struck a new note in English appreciation of landscape, and it is a note which is echoed again and again by Francia. It was a novelty for a painter to find beauty in the bleak far-flung stretches of moor and marshland, in muddy estuaries whence the tide had ebbed, in shadows cast by grey and gloomy skies. Girtin and Francia found a lyrical beauty in loneliness, desolation and silence. It seems probable that much of Francia's early work, plausibly or even with honest intent, has been accredited to Girtin (I have seen many so-called Girtins which are probably by Francia), and much of his later work by Bonington.

The work of Luke Clennell (1781–1840), in its consistency and in its ordered restraint of low tones, is not far from that of Francia. Clennell was born at Ulgham, near Morpeth, where his father was a farmer. In 1797 he was apprenticed in the craft of wood-engraving to Thomas Bewick at Newcastle, and became one of his most distinguished pupils. He had the rare advantage of serving his apprenticeship during the seven years, 1797 to 1894, which saw the publication of *British Birds*, and is said to have cut the tail pieces of the *Water Birds*. In the autumn of 1804 he came to London, and set up as an engraver on his own account, showing a skill which soon won him many commissions from publishers. In 1806 he was awarded the gold palette of the Society of Arts, and in 1809 a gold medal for his large engraving, from a design by Benjamin West, for the diploma of the Highland Society. He is best known for his remarkable reproductions on wood, exact and yet sympathetic, of Stothard's charming pen-and-ink designs for Roger's *Pleasures of Memory*, 1810. But at this time Clennell began to forsake engraving for water-colour painting, and became a member of the Associated Artists, exhibiting in their Bond Street gallery from 1810 to 1812. In 1812 he was elected, together with David Cox and C. Barber, an associate of the Old Water-Colour Society, where his drawings were chiefly figure groups of contemporary life in picturesque aspects, soldiers, smugglers, fishermen, country folk, or a crowd at a fair. He was following Francis Wheatley, but with a more vigorous and impulsive style. At this period of his life he was making projects for oil-paintings, and his cartoon for *The Charge of the Life Guards at Waterloo* gained the premium of 150 guineas offered by the British Institution. In 1814 he received a commission from the Earl of

146

Bridgewater to paint a large picture of a dinner given to the Allied Sovereigns at the Guildhall. Unfortunately in 1817, before the picture was finished, Clennell lost his reason, was never wholly himself again, and died in a lunatic asylum at Newcastle upon Tyne in 1840. A newspaper of August 1819,[1] appealed for support on behalf of a print, to be engraved by W. Bromley after the *Life Guards* design, in aid of the artist's three young and motherless children. Another contemporary notice says:

'The Earl of Bridgewater, on hearing of the melancholy situation of the ingenious young artist, CLENNEL, and his infant family, immediately determined to have the picture upon which the artist had been employed, in its unfinished state. His Lordship was to have given fifteen hundred pounds for it when completed. It contains nearly four hundred portraits of the Royal personages, their suites, and other distinguished characters, who were present at the grand civic dinner in Guildhall. From this picture, another upon a very large scale was to have been painted by the same artist for the Corporation of London, to be placed in Guildhall.'

From all this it would appear that, though Clennell was an artist of signal accomplishment, his work in water-colour may be taken as having been confined to about ten years, 1807 to 1817. In a long and appreciative notice in the *Dictionary of National Biography*, Austin Dobson writes: 'As a water-colour artist, it is probable that he had not reached his highest point when his faculties failed; but he had already exhibited a distinct ability for landscape and rural scenes. Fineness and delicacy are less conspicuous in his work than breadth, spirit and rapidity of handling.' It is not surprising that Clennell's paintings are difficult to find; but the British Museum has his *Newcastle Ferry*[2] (another version belonging to Mr. and Mrs. Paul Mellon is shown Pl. 129) and a *Portrait of Sir William Domville*,[3] as Lord Mayor of London, 1814—the latter in pencil with flesh tints admirably touched; and in the Victoria and Albert Museum are his *Wayside Inn*[4] and *The Sawpit*,[5] 1810. The Laing Art Gallery, Newcastle, owns over a dozen of his drawings. Among these the *Lanercost Priory* and the *Mitford Manor House* (made as an illustration to Scott's *Border Antiquities*, 1814) show his close adherence to the school of Girtin and Francia. The spirited sketch *On the Tyne, Bill Point*[6] (Pl. 130) (*c.* 1804) is of special interest as being a study (5 × 8 inches) for the larger picture (16 × 25 inches) in the Powell Collection.[7] The sketch in particular approaches very close to De Wint in its rich but sombre colouring, its dragged paint, its big masses enlivened by sparkling lights. One feels that if Clennell's career as a painter had not been cut short by mental failure in 1817, he would have revealed the qualities of De Wint.

Mention has been made of Thomas Bewick (1753–1828), as Clennell's teacher and that

[1] V.A.M., *Cuttings from English Newspapers*, IV, *1686–1835*, pp. 1174, 1195.
[2] B.M. 1885. 11.14.94.
[3] B.M. 1861. 11.9.510.
[4] V.A.M. 980–1901.
[5] V.A.M. 586.
[6] Newcastle upon Tyne, Laing Art Gallery.
[7] Coll. Herbert Powell (N.A.–C.F.). Catalogued as *Coal Barges on the Medway* when exhibited at the Tate Gallery, 1930.

must be the excuse for introducing him at this point, though he never exhibited a water-colour or belonged to any society. Though Bewick was, first and foremost, a wood-engraver—the greatest of English wood-engravers and a master of the 'white line'—he must not be ignored as a painter in water-colour. As he was essentially an engraver, not much need be said here about his training and practice. He was born at Cherryburn House, near the hamlet of Eltringham, on the south bank of the Tyne, a few miles from Newcastle. In a letter to John Chambers,[1] in which he sketches the principal events of his life, Bewick refers to his birthplace and adds: 'My father, John Bewick, who farmed the collieries there, was of a lively and cheerful temper of mind, and was much noticed by the whole countryside for his witty sayings, his droll stories, and his facetious remarks.' The inheritance of that drollery and facetiousness is shown in Thomas Bewick's vignettes. He was apprenticed to Ralph Beilby, an engraver at Newcastle upon Tyne, visited London in 1776, but hated its 'extreme riches, extreme poverty, extreme grandeur, extreme wretched-ness—all of which were such as I had never contemplated before'.[2] So he returned to Tyneside, entered into partnership with Beilby, and never left the district again. He stuck to his craft of engraving, and when his *History of Quadrupeds* was published in 1790 he was astounded by what he describes as 'a glut of praises bestowed on the book'. Those who know the *Quadrupeds*, the *Select Fables*, 1784, the *History of British Birds*, 1797–1804, and his large wood-cut of *The Chillingham Bull*, 1789, may not realise that Bewick often used colour in finishing his tiny drawings before their translation into the fascinating wood-cut vignettes which form the tailpieces in his books. Those vignettes, so quiet and unpretentious, are little masterpieces of observation, humour, technical skill and imaginative insight. Leslie,[3] Constable's biographer, wrote that they 'abound in incidents from real life, diversified by genuine humour as well as by the truest pathos. There is often in these little things a deep meaning that places Bewick's art on a level with styles which the world is apt to consider as greatly above it. The student of landscape can never consult the works of Bewick without improvement.'

Bewick's use of water-colour was entirely hidden during his lifetime and remained almost unknown till Miss Isabella Bewick, in 1882, made an extensive gift of his original drawings to the British Museum. Two small water-colour studies of birds and a larger *Flying Fish*[4] (Pl. 132) are in the Victoria and Albert Museum, but outside of those two collections examples of his work in colour are extremely rare. At the British Museum lovers of Bewick's wood-cuts will find the original studies, in colour over Indian ink, of many of their favourites—the fisherman with bent rod against a background of river, rock and foliage; the boys, playing at soldiers, astride some tombstones; the monkey roasting a fowl on a spit; the man holding on to his cow's tail as he fords a stream; the woman in a farm-

[1] Quoted in Maggs' *Catalogue of Autograph Letters*, 1924, No. 449.
[2] *Memoir*, his autobiography, written in 1822, published first in 1862, and republished, with an introduction by Montague Weekley, 1961. Ruskin, as Slade Professor in Oxford, used to counsel all of his pupils to acquire this book.
[3] C. R. Leslie, *Autobiographical Recollections*, 1860.
[4] V.A.M. 253–1904.

148

yard beating off a gander; the boy falling from a broken branch into a stream; the snow man; the old woman and the swarm of bees; the suicide hanging from a tree. Those subjects—and there are many others equally good—which are so familiar in the wood-cut versions, entitle Bewick to his place among water-colour painters of renown. In *The Water-Colour Drawings of Thomas Bewick*, 1930, by D. Croal Thomson, drawings of birds and landscape tail-pieces are finely reproduced in colour.

Other artists who, like Francia and Clennell, began their career as water-colour painters by exhibiting with the Associated Artists were Alfred Chalon, W. M. Craig and James Holmes. Alfred Edward Chalon (1780–1860) and his elder brother John James belonged to a French family long settled in Switzerland. Both were born at Geneva, and were brought to London at an early age by their father, who became Professor of French at the Royal Military College, Sandhurst. Alfred became a student at the Royal Academy in 1797, exhibited there from 1801, and in 1807 and 1808 was a member of the Associated Artists. He became the most fashionable painter of his day of women's portraits in water-colour, of a size usually about ten or fifteen inches high. His work of this type had a dash and dramatic vigour which lent special interest to his portraits of opera singers, actresses and dancers, many of which were engraved. He drew, for instance, a most charming group of four famous ballerinas, Grisi, Taglioni, Grahn and Cerrito, reproduced in Serge Lifar's *Carlotta Grisi*. His interest in the stage and his wit are shown by the series of brilliant caricatures which are in the Victoria and Albert Museum. The caricatures, no doubt, were only circulated in private, for it was by his more serious work that he won his fame. After Queen Victoria's accession, he painted a full-length in water-colours showing Her Majesty in robes worn at the dissolution of Parliament. He was appointed Painter in Water-Colour to the Queen, and sent another portrait of her to Paris in 1855. C. R. Leslie writes[1]: 'To my mind Alfred Chalon has long been the first among painters in water-colours; and yet, though his beautiful drawing of the Queen was in the great Paris Exhibition in this year (1855), the prize for water-colour art was given to Cattermole!'

Alfred Chalon was elected A.R.A. in 1812, and R.A. in 1816. In 1833 the brothers Chalon were living with their father and sister at 42 Great Marlborough Street. 'The love and harmony in that family', wrote Leslie, 'was such as, were it universal, would make this world a paradise.' Mrs. Newton, living next door, provides another glimpse of this artist in a letter written on May 12, 1833[2]:

'Next door to us are the Chalons. Alfred Chalon is the famous and fashionable water-colour painter; so fond of painting ladies in flowing silks and airy laces that some of the artists published an advertisement in one of the morning papers to the effect that "muslins and laces would be done up equal to new at 19, Berners Street", which was his residence before he became our neighbour'.

John James Chalon (1778–1854), should rightfully have had his place in the preceding chapter, but has been withheld till now so as to place him in association with his brother. He

[1] *Op. cit.*, 1860.   [2] Whitley, 1821–1837, p. 262.

was born two years earlier, and became a student at the Royal Academy in 1796. He was elected an associate of the Old Water Colour Society in 1805, and a member in 1807, but retired after the disruption of 1812. In the Victoria and Albert Museum are two or three water-colours of this early period of his activity, notably *Street Scene, Erith, Kent*,[1] 1808, which bears a close resemblance in style and subject to the contemporary work of Cornelius Varley. His themes in general comprise landscape studies, many of them on the Thames or the Wye, pleasantly diversified by skilfully grouped figures, and some marine views and animal subjects. After 1812 J. J. Chalon took to oil-painting, and was elected A.R.A. in 1829 and R.A. in 1841.

The two Chalons, both of them clearly sociable men, were the founders, with Francis Stevens, of a Sketching Society which followed the lines of Girtin's sketching club. The new club started in 1808 under the pompous title of 'The Society for the Study of Epic and Pastoral Design', following a classification adopted by Turner in his *Liber Studiorum*, which began to appear in 1807. It is now generally, and more conveniently referred to as 'The Chalon Sketching Society'. Hesketh Hubbard[2] has given a full account of its history and work, based upon its Minute Books. The members, who were not to exceed eight in number, met every Wednesday evening in rotation at one or another's house. The host chose a subject for illustration; the members worked on it from six till ten: then, as in other similar societies, they had a supper of bread, cheese and beer, after which they proceeded to inspect and criticise the evening's output. The host of the evening retained the drawings, but was not allowed to sell them.

Besides the two Chalons and F. Stevens the foundation members (making seven in all) were M. W. Sharp, William Turner of Oxford, Cornelius Varley and Thomas Webster. Thirteen later members (the last election apparently took place in 1832) were H. P. Bone, R. T. Bone, Joshua Cristall, J. S. Hayward, C. R. Leslie, George Lewis, John Partridge, C. J. Robertson, G. F. Robson, Clarkson Stanfield, J. Stephanoff, S. J. Stump and Thomas Uwins. How much the Society centred round the Chalons is shown by the fact that J. J. Chalon attended 971 meetings and A. E. Chalon 874, while the next highest were S. J. Stump 796, Clarkson Stanfield 446, Robert Bone 412 and J. Cristall 406. Many leading artists were invited as visitors; among them, Constable, De Wint, William Havell, John Varley, Robert Hills and Edwin Landseer. John Sheepshanks, Washington Irving and Captain Marryat were among guests. Queen Victoria and the Prince Consort took a personal interest in the affairs of the Society, so much so that in 1842 John Partridge, who was then painting a full-length portrait of the Queen, arrived from Windsor bearing an envelope sealed with the arms of the Queen and Prince Albert, and enclosing a command, in the Queen's own hand, that the subject for the evening should be 'Desire'. Within three months the Queen set another subject 'Elevation'. Her Majesty expressed a wish to pur-

---

[1] V.A.M. 137–1890.
[2] *O.W.S. Club*, XXIV, 1946. Earlier references to the Society will be found in Roget, I, pp. 279–281, and Mrs. Uwins, *Memoir of Thomas Uwins*, 1858, pp. 163, 164.

chase a drawing by each member, but the Society (unwilling to infringe their early regulation against sales) unanimously resolved to offer a presentation set, which the Queen was pleased to accept.

For thirty-two years, up to 1840, the sketches made at the weekly meetings were always in monochrome, like those of the Girtin sketching club; and I think that the obvious explanation is that the drawings had to be made by the light of candles or oil lamps. In 1840 the experiment of making coloured drawings was tried. At first it was considered satisfactory, but in May 1840 a minute records: 'Finish of the unsuccessful experiment of colouring'. Thereafter at intervals colour was retried. The last meeting on record was held at 10 Wimpole Street, the home of the Chalons, on February 25 1851. The two veteran brothers, staunch supporters of the Society from its foundation forty-three years before, were now in their seventies, and the only other two surviving members, C. R. Leslie and Clarkson Stanfield, were both nearing sixty. The subject was 'What you Will'; and 'Everybody very tired', says the brief and final minute.

Returning to the members of the Associated Artists we come to William Marshall Craig (c. 1765–c. 1828).[1] His first known exhibit was at Liverpool in 1787, and he seems to have lived at Manchester from 1787 to 1790. About 1791 he came to London, and from that date onwards was a prolific exhibitor of water-colour drawings, portraits, rustic figures, landscapes and domestic scenes. At the Royal Academy between 1788 and 1827 he exhibited 152 works, including miniature portraits; and he became a member of the Associated Artists in 1810. He was evidently a man of good birth and education, for he was tutor in his younger days to the third Viscount Courtenay; and, later, he produced several pedagogic works, *An Essay on the Study of Nature in Drawing Landscape*, 1793; *Instructions in Drawing Landscape*, 1814–1815 and *Drawing and Understanding the Human Figure*, 1817. He was determined that 'the object of the pencil is to imitate nature', and in his books he makes violent assaults upon the Rev. W. Gilpin for such 'vicious' precepts as that it is admirable 'to add altitude to mountains, to manufacture trees and foregrounds where necessary and even to turn the course of rivers'. Craig, however, did not always follow his own precepts, and certainly abandoned them when he produced the *Landscape*, in monochrome, owned by Mr. L. G. Duke. That romantic scene, with its gnarled tree and massive boulders in the foreground, and its ruined castle on a mountain behind—obviously a manufactured composition—would seem to be entirely after Gilpin's own heart. In his exhortations about the payment of scrupulous regard to objective truth, Craig emphasises that: 'Whatever is beautiful in Nature will also be beautiful in Art if faithfully represented', and 'Copy exactly what you see that you may copy exactly what you imagine.' He hated what he calls 'shorthand kinds of representation', and is entirely true to his own principles in *The Wounded Soldier*[2] and in two genre subjects, *The Penalty of Breaking a Hedge*[3] and *Boy and*

[1] In writing about Craig I am indebted to Mr. Ralph Edwards, whose article on 'Queen Charlotte's Painter in Water Colours', in *The Collector*, December 1930, contained hitherto unrecorded information.
[2] V.A.M. 1750–1871.
[3] B.M. 1857. 11.14.31.

Girl with Cattle[1] (Pl. 134). The British Museum catalogue, contrary to its usual method of giving merely the method, describes the last two as 'water-colours; highly finished'. They are certainly remarkable for the way in which every intricate detail is wrought with minute fidelity. Birket Foster, William Hunt and the Pre-Raphaelites did not surpass Craig in the painstaking rendition of the realities of every blade of grass, every leaf, every wrinkle in a tree-trunk. Redgrave's safe comment that 'his water-colours have much careful finish, and though frequently tame and mannered, some of his illustrations are not without merit' hardly does justice to a craftsman who brought supreme skill to bear on trivial and sentimental themes. He certainly does not do justice to the painter of that white cow, belaboured by a farmer as it breaks through a hedge.

Craig systematically cultivated the great, and became Painter in Water-Colours to Queen Charlotte; was drawing-master to the Princess Charlotte, of whom he made the delicately tinted portrait now in the British Museum[2]; and was Miniaturist to the Duke and Duchess of York. His portraits in water-colour are in the nature of miniatures, frequently of oval shape, and have considerable merit, though not possessing John Downman's graceful elegance. Two such drawings of the artist's daughter and son, dated 1797 and 1798 respectively, which belonged to Sir Algernon Tudor Craig, K.B.E., show that W. M. Craig could deal truthfully and sympathetically with the fresh colour and charm of childhood.

James Holmes (1777–1860), exhibited with the Associated Artists in 1808 and became a Member in 1809. Till their break-up in 1812 he showed twenty-two pictures, about half of which were portraits. Like Samuel Shelley, he was a fashionable miniature-painter, varying his portraits with subject pieces. In this latter part of their output Shelley and he were very different. Whereas Shelley sought the ideal and the sublime, Holmes liked the plain humour and pathos of domestic scenes, as shown by such titles as *Hot Porridge, The Married Man* and *The Doubtful Shilling*. The last of these is said to have 'drawn a tear from the appreciative eye of the Duchess of York, and was not only bought by Beau Brummel, himself a proficient amateur painter of miniatures, but led to a lasting friendship between the artist and the king of fashion'.[3] Holmes continued with the same kind of work after his election to the Old Water-Colour Society in 1813 in its temporary phase as the 'Society of Painters in Oil and Water-Colours'. His *Michaelmas Dinner* in 1817, bought by King George IV, then Prince Regent, illustrated a verbal sketch by Lord Chesterfield of a bad carver of goose: 'He cannot hit the joint, but in his vain efforts to cut through the bone, splashes the company.' He ceased to be a member of the Old Society in 1821 and afterwards exerted the whole of his influence in the foundation of the Society of British Artists. Holmes was a popular teacher, and had to raise his tuition fee from a guinea to two guineas an hour, so as to reduce the number of pupils. Not the least remarkable thing about him is Gilchrist's statement that Blake was indebted to Holmes and to Richter for

---

[1] B.M. 1895. 6.17.407.   [2] B.M. 1906. 5.15.1.   [3] Roget, I, p. 380.

123 'The Thames in the Great Frost of 1789'

B.M. 1891.5.11.32 $13\frac{3}{4} \times 19\frac{1}{8}$: 349 × 485   *Water-colour, signed and dated J. C. Barrow, 1789*

Joseph Charles BARROW (fl. 1789–1802)

124 'Transports Returning from Spain 1809'

B.M. 1890.5.12.82 $11\frac{1}{8} \times 15\frac{7}{8}$: 283 × 402   *Water-colour*

François Louis Thomas FRANCIA (1772–1839)

125 'Mousehold Heath'

Coll. Mr & Mrs Paul Mellon   12½ × 9¼: 311 × 234   *Water-colour*

François Louis Thomas FRANCIA (1772–1839)

126 'Interior of a Church'

V.A.M. 623 (E.5658–1910)   9¾ × 7¾: 247 × 197   *Sepia*

François Louis Thomas FRANCIA (1772–1839)

127 'The Seine at Bas Mendon'
Coll. Mr & Mrs Tom Girtin $6\frac{1}{8} \times 8\frac{3}{4}$: 156 × 222   *Water-colour, signed*
William WYLD (1806–1889)

128 'Venice'
Newcastle upon Tyne, Laing Art Gallery $11 \times 17\frac{1}{4}$: 280 × 438   *Water-colour*
William WYLD (1806–1889)

129 'Baggage Wagon in a Thunderstorm'
Coll. Lord Eccles   16⅛ × 24⅜: 410 × 620   *Water-colour*
Luke CLENNELL (1781–1840)

130 'On the Tyne; Bill Point'
Newcastle upon Tyne, Laing Art Gallery   5 × 7¾: 127 × 197   *Water-colour*
Luke CLENNELL (1781–1840)

131 'Newcastle Ferry'
Coll. Mr & Mrs Paul Mellon   5¾ × 8: 146 × 203   *Water-colour*
Luke CLENNELL (1781–1840)

132 'Flying Fish'
V.A.M. D.253–1904   Oval, 7⅝ × 10⅛: 194 × 258   *Water-colour, signed and dated 1822*
Thomas BEWICK (1753–1828)

The eye a little high & bright
The Body a little more plump

The Natural size

Thomas Bewick

133 'A Starling'
Courtauld Institute of Art, Witt Coll.   6½ × 8½ : 165 × 216   *Water-colour*
Thomas BEWICK (1753–1828)

134 'Boy and Girl with Cattle'
B.M. 1895.6.17.407   6½ × 8½: 166 × 216   *Water-colour*
William Marshall CRAIG (fl. 1788 d. 1828)

135 'The Opera Box'

B.M. 1886.2.16.2 $18\frac{1}{2} \times 13\frac{5}{8}$: 469 × 346   *Water-colour, signed and dated 1838*

Alfred Edward CHALON, R.A. (1780–1860)

136 'Landscape with Water-mill'

V.A.M. 319–1900   24½ × 21 : 621 × 533   *Water-colour, signed*

John James CHALON (1778–1854)

137 'Ruins of Nether Hall, near Royden, Essex'
V.A.M. 329–1895   20½×16½: 520×419   *Water-colour, signed*
Joseph Clarendon SMITH (1778–1810)

138 'The Bridge of the Old Palace at Eltham'

Coll. Mrs Cecil Keith $15\frac{7}{8} \times 19\frac{7}{8}$: 403×505 *Water-colour*

Joseph Clarendon SMITH (1778–1810)

139 'Dordrecht'

V.A.M. P.130–1931 $8\frac{5}{8} \times 13\frac{5}{8}$: 219 × 345   *Water-colour*

Sir Augustus Wall CALLCOTT, R.A. (1779–1844)

140 'Landscape with a Cottage'

V.A.M. 1945–1900 $9\frac{1}{4} \times 13\frac{5}{8}$: 236 × 346   *Water-colour, signed, and dated 1836*

Joseph William ALLEN (1803–1852)

141 'Cows on River's Edge'

V.A.M. 513   15¼ × 21⅛ : 386 × 526   *Water-colour, signed and dated 1849*

Thomas Sidney COOPER, C.V.O., R.A. (1803–1902)

142 'Watermill, Tintern, Monmouthshire'

B.M. 1875.10.9.13 $10\frac{3}{4} \times 8 : 273 \times 203$ *Water-colour, signed and dated 1805*

Joseph POWELL (c. 1780–1834(?))

143 'West View of Worcester Cathedral'

V.A.M. 1759–1871 $23\frac{1}{4} \times 18$: 590 × 457   *Water-colour, signed and dated 1798*

Joseph POWELL (c. 1780–1834(?))

'a greater fullness and depth of colour in his drawings than he, bred in the old school of slight tints, had hardly thought could have been developed in water-colour art'.[1]

A minor but not insignificant member of the Associated Artists was Joseph Clarendon Smith (1778–1810). Born in London, the son of a builder, he ran away to sea at an early age and after serving before the mast for three years entered Christ's Hospital with a view to studying mathematics and navigation. He developed skill in drawing and was apprenticed to an engraver. Subsequently he became a member of the Associated Artists in 1809. Attacked by consumption, he went to Madeira, but died on the voyage home. His working life as a painter in water-colour was only some five or six years, and his drawings are rare. Those which exist prove him to have been a topographical painter of high merit and ability. A *Tintern Abbey*[2], shows him as a disciple of Girtin, falling not so far short of the master in colour and design.

In this chapter may be included Sir Augustus Wall Callcott (1779–1844), a contemporary of the artists above mentioned, though he was not a member of any Water-Colour Society. Like Turner and James Ward, however, he would no doubt have taken active participation in the new movement if he had not been debarred by his membership of the Royal Academy. Callcott, who was born in Kensington, was a younger brother of John Wall Callcott, musician and composer. Augustus himself had musical leanings, and for six years sang as a chorister at Westminster Abbey. In 1797 he became a student in the Royal Academy schools and, after being a pupil of Hoppner, began his career as a portrait painter. That he had a partiality for water-colour is shown by his membership of Girtin's Sketching Club; and the congenial friendship of Girtin and John Varley no doubt encouraged his liking for landscape art, which soon began to exercise a greater sway than portraiture. It was as a painter of landscape and coast scenes that he made his name. He was elected A.R.A. in 1806, and R.A. in 1810, as a painter in oil; and was knighted in 1837. As an oil-painter he won high praise from contemporary critics. 'We know of no landscape painter, with the exception of Turner,' says one of them in 1831, 'who has so much poetry and air in his views as Mr. Callcott, and he excels Turner in finish'; and the critic of the *Morning Post* advised Turner 'to look to him as a model for truth and purity in landscape'.[3] Though his work was mainly in oil he was highly proficient in water-colour, and used the method for his sketches in England and on his travels in France, Holland and Italy. At his first meeting with Farington in 1805 he discussed the demand for water-colour drawings, but had set his heart on becoming an associate of the Royal Academy. Referring again to Callcott in 1806, Farington[4] says: 'He told me He was born at Kensington gravel pits in the House in which He now resides. He sd. He has found an advantage in residing a little way from London as He is not now so liable to have His time invaded by Loungers who in London were accustomed to call upon Him to look over His Portfolios.' In 1811 Callcott

---

[1] A. Gilchrist, *Life of Blake*, I, 1863, p. 247.
[2] Coll. Mr. and Mrs. Paul Mellon.
[3] Whitley, 1821–1837, pp. 211, 235.
[4] *Diary*, October 24, 1806.

spoke to Farington about 'the great changes in the disposition of the public to purchase Water Colour drawings at the Exhibitions . . . , said it showed How temporary public opinion is; How much of fashion there is in liking any particular kind of art; and added that He believed Sir George Beaumont had done much harm to the Water Colour painters by His cry against that kind of art'.

In 1827 Callcott married Maria (1785–1842), the widow of a Captain Thomas Graham. She wrote several works on travel, and was known to countless children of past generations by her famous educational work, *Little Arthur's History of England*, first published in 1835 as by M. C. (Maria Callcott). Turner, in a letter of 1827, described her as 'a very agreeable Blue Stocking'. A woman of vigorous intellect, she once remarked in John Linnell's presence that 'she would rather be called a bitch than a female'. She was, moreover, a painter in water-colour. She died in 1842, and in 1845 Sir A. W. Callcott bequeathed some hundreds of drawings by her to the British Museum. They are mainly sketches made in 1809 and 1810, when she was in India with her first husband, and on tours in Italy in 1819 and in South America from 1821 to 1823.

Thomas Sidney Cooper (1803–1902) was another painter who, like Callcott, was determined to enter the Royal Academy and so was barred from membership of any water-colour Society. Born of humble parentage at Canterbury, Cooper began work as a coach-painter, coupling this occupation with some scene-painting at the local theatre. Sir Thomas Lawrence helped him to enter the Royal Academy Schools in 1824, and after nine months' tuition Cooper returned to Canterbury as a teacher of drawing. He became friendly with William Burgess, who lived at Dover and who exhibited landscapes at the Royal Academy and Suffolk Street from 1838 to 1856. In 1827 they went to Brussels together. Cooper remained there for four years, paying his way by teaching and portrait-painting, and studying under Eugène Verboeckhoven, the famous Flemish animal painter. That was the turning-point in his career, and coming to London in 1831 he settled down to the production of highly finished pictures and drawings of cattle and sheep. His work of this nature won him election as A.R.A. in 1845 and R.A. in 1858. His pastorals, with their sleek and prosperous kine, were eminently suitable as backgrounds in the homes of prosperous Victorians. He continued to ring changes on the same subjects until his death in 1902. Such examples of his water-colour work as *Bull and three Cows in a Stable*,[1] 1838, and *Cows on a River's Edge*[2] 1849 (Pl. 141), belong to his best period, and show his accurate draughtsmanship, his painstaking realism of form and colour, and his sound instinct for good grouping.

Joseph William Allen (1803–1852), was born at Lambeth the same year as Sidney Cooper and was educated at St. Paul's School. For a time he followed his father's profession and became an usher in a school at Taunton, but finding that he had a bent for painting returned to London, and worked for a time under a picture dealer. He then

[1] F. J. Nettlefold, Catalogue I, p. 110 (plate).
[2] V.A.M. 513.

154

obtained employment as a scene-painter at the Olympic Theatre, where he came into contact with Clarkson Stanfield and Charles Tomkins. He exhibited oils and water-colours from 1826 at the Royal Academy, the British Institution and the New Water-colour Society. Then he joined the newly formed Society of British Artists, becoming its Secretary and in 1838 its President. He was drawing-master at the City of London School from its foundation. His various occupations and his large practice as a painter in oil left him little time for water-colour, but his rare drawings, such as *Landscape with Cottage*,[1] 1836 (Pl. 140), and *A Cottage*,[2] *c.* 1830, link up with the earlier work of Cox and Prout, and show a pleasing quality of warm colour.

Joseph Powell[3] (*c.* 1780–1834 or after) was a regular exhibitor at the Associated Artists from 1808 to 1812, and became the first President of the New Water-colour Society when it was formed in 1832. Samuel Redgrave, who was his pupil, made the grave error of entering him in the *Dictionary of Artists* as 'Powell, John, landscape painter', and Redgrave's misnomer was followed by Thieme-Becker, *Lexicon* and the *Dictionary of National Biography*. The ghost of John Powell was finally laid by Mr. Jonathan Mayne in 1948,[4] and Joseph was re-established in his rightful place. All of the water-colours and drawings in the Victoria and Albert Museum, the British Museum and elsewhere (some of them signed 'J. Powell', but none with a full Christian name) can now be definitely assigned to Joseph. The exact date of his birth, given by Redgrave as 'about 1780', is unknown, but he was a pupil of B. T. Pouncy and exhibited at the Royal Academy from 1796 to 1833. His *West View of Worcester Cathedral*[5] (Pl. 143), dated 1798, and now in the Victoria and Albert Museum, is almost certainly the drawing shown at the Royal Academy in that year. After the New Society's exhibition of 1834 all trace of him is lost and it may be assumed that he died in the latter part of that year, or soon after.

This and the preceding chapters have been planned to include a fair cross-section of painters whose work in water-colour had won for them an established reputation before the year 1820. At that time a new, younger, generation—Cox, De Wint, Prout and others—born later than Turner and Girtin, and most of them in the years 1780 to 1790, was beginning to come to the fore and to add new lustre to water-colour art. They form the theme of subsequent chapters.

[1] V.A.M. 1945–1900.
[2] F. J. Nettlefold catalogue, I, p. 4 (plate).
[3] See also Vol. I, p. 179.
[4] J. Mayne, 'Joseph Powell', *Burlington Magazine*, XC, 1948, pp. 267–268.
[5] V.A.M. 1759–1871.

CHAPTER X
Samuel Palmer

John Linnell   Edward Calvert   Francis Oliver Finch

By way of approach to Samuel Palmer something should be said about John Linnell, who was a dominant influence in the making and shaping of Palmer's early career and in the marring of his later years. He introduced Palmer to Blake; and Linnell's daughter became Palmer's wife. Linnell was very much the Victorian father, devout but eccentric in his religion, secure in his own prosperity, a despot and not always a benevolent one, with an overpowering love of authority and for giving advice whether about conduct, economics or art. About his relationship with Blake much has been said in an earlier chapter.

John Linnell (1792–1882) was the son of James Linnell, carver, gilder, picture and print-seller of Streatham Street, Bloomsbury. At the age of twelve he was making copies from Morland's pictures, which his father sold for as much as ten pounds each. Later his father was induced to pay £100 premium to John Varley. Linnell lived for a year at Varley's house in Broad Street, Golden Square, as a pupil, and had William Hunt as a comrade. Another of the pupils was William Mulready, and the trio frequently sketched together on the banks of the Thames. Under the patronage of Benjamin West (possibly Linnell senior made frames for him) young Linnell entered the Academy schools in 1805, and became one of the group who enjoyed the help and encouragement of Dr. Monro. He was a member of the Old Water-colour Society from 1812 to 1820, when he resigned in order to give his whole attention to oil. From about 1810 to 1820 he was painting portraits and also made many water-colours in the outskirts of London and in Windsor Forest, with a few in Wales and the Isle of Wight. Though he resorted to water-colour occasionally during his later life (in the Victoria and Albert Museum and elsewhere are pleasant landscapes painted by him after 1860) his reputation was acquired through his landscape painting in oil.

In 1824 Linnell was residing at Collin's Farm,[1] North End, Hampstead, a fifteenth-century building. It was to this farm that Charles Dickens carried off his wife in 1837 after the death of her sister, Mary Hogarth: 'Young, beautiful and good, God in his mercy numbered her with his angels at the age of seventeen.' About 1818 Linnell had introduced

[1] Now known as Wylde's Farm.

156

Varley to Blake, and after 1824 the three had frequent meetings at Collin's Farm: it was a favourite resort of Blake on Sunday afternoons. Palmer became another intimate and owed to Linnell the 'memory of hours spent in familiar converse' with Blake, whom he cherished to his dying day.

For many years after Linnell became Palmer's father-in-law, the two men were in constant touch, but of Linnell's influence upon Palmer's style there is comparatively little trace. Linnell, however, liked to paint ripened corn-fields and great snowballs of cumulus clouds, closely packed and seeming almost tangible; and this type of field and cloud predominates in Palmer's early water-colours and the imaginative landscape drawings which he made at Shoreham in bistre, sepia and Indian ink. In 1828 Samuel Palmer wrote to Linnell[1]: 'Those glorious round clouds which you paint, I do think inimitably, are alone an example how the elements of nature may be transmuted into the pure gold of art.' There speaks the disciple. Palmer was living in Broad Street, Bloomsbury, at the time, and his son paints this happy 'conversation piece':

> Fortunately for my father, Broad Street lay in Blake's way to Hampstead, and they often walked up to the village together. The aged composer of the *Songs of Innocence* was a great favourite with the children, who revelled in those poems of the lovely spiritual things and beings that seemed to him so real and so near. Therefore, as the two friends reached the farm, a merry troop turned out to meet them led by a little fair-haired girl of some six years old. To this day she remembers cold winter nights when Blake was wrapped up in an old shawl by Mrs. Linnell, and sent on his homeward way, with the servant, lantern in hand, lighting him across the heath to the main road.

Nearly fifty years ago my friend and teacher Sir Frank Short lent me *The Life and Letters of Samuel Palmer*, published in 1892. It seemed to me that just as he reverenced the etchings of Samuel Palmer, so he regarded this book as a sort of Bible for the young student eager for knowledge not only of etching but of art in general. And he was right. The book is full of wise thoughts, the revelation of an artist's inner mind. Palmer's touches of idiosyncrasy, his bursts (in notes and correspondence) into italics and capitals and still larger capitals, serve to make him all the more endearing. His son, the late A. H. Palmer, who was its author, wrote to me much later from his home in British Columbia saying that the 1892 biography of his father was out of date and incomplete. He pointed out the absence of all the letters from Palmer and his wife in Italy to the Linnells in Bayswater, and the great interest of matter revealed by his research among unknown papers of Linnell. Some of that added information he generously gave in the catalogue of the exhibition of Samuel Palmer's work at the Victoria and Albert Museum in 1926. There was hope that he might publish a new and amplified biography but he died some years ago, and I do not know what became of the mass of material which he had accumulated. In order to find Samuel Palmer placed in his right age and surroundings; to realise his ambitions, perplexities and despondencies; to know some of the chief circumstances of his life, his character and personal appearance, his whims and foibles, his essential greatness and his little flaws and

[1] A. H. Palmer, *Life and Letters of Samuel Palmer*, 1892, p. 176.

157

unamiable failings, we must read the biography published in 1892 together with Geoffrey Grigson's *Samuel Palmer: The Visionary Years*, published in 1947.

Samuel Palmer (1805–1881) was the elder son of a bookseller who lived in Surrey Square, in the Parish of St. Mary's, Newington. Something of his mentality the boy, no doubt, owed to his father, and to his grandfather and great-grandfather, both clergymen of repute. He seems to have owed much also to his nurse, Mary Ward, one of those faithful, thoughtful, affectionate servants—simple, yet deeply read in their Bible, like Stevenson's 'Cummy'—who especially belong to the nineteenth century. When he was between three and four years old, Mary and he stood watching the full moon rising behind the branches of a great elm, casting a maze of shadows on the opposite wall. As the shadows changed, Mary repeated the couplet:

> 'Fond man! the vision of a moment made.
> Dream of a dream, and shadow of a shade.'

Samuel Palmer never forgot that incident and the chiaroscuro of light and shadow became the dominant motif in all his later work. And he never forgot Mary Ward. In the Victoria and Albert Museum, as a gift from his son, are a copy of Milton's Poems in two volumes, given to Samuel Palmer by his nurse, and a little memorandum which he wrote on the day of her death, as a record of their farewell, after she had kissed him good-bye and blessed him with her last words. Mary read the Bible and Milton to the boy. His father, who not only sold books but read them, encouraged his son at an exceptionally early age to study Latin and a wide range of English literature. He passed what A. H. Palmer later described as 'a sedentary and precociously grave' childhood. Sensitive and delicate, the boy developed a taste for art. At the age of twelve he had, in his own words, 'a passionate love for the traditions and monuments of the Church; its cloistered abbeys, cathedrals and minsters, which I was always imagining and trying to draw; spoiling much good paper with pencils, crayons, and water-colours'.

In 1819, at the age of fourteen, he exhibited two landscapes at the British Gallery, Pall Mall, and three at the Royal Academy. By 1822 he had become acquainted with Stothard, John Linnell, John Varley and Mulready. Of Linnell, he wrote: 'It pleased God to send Mr. Linnell as a good angel from Heaven to pluck me from the pit of modern art.' And to Linnell he owed the most notable event of his early life, his meeting with Blake.

> On Saturday, 9th October, 1824, Mr. Linnell called and went with me to Mr. Blake. We found him lame in bed, of a scalded foot (or leg). There, not inactive, though sixty-seven years old, but hard-working on a bed covered with books sat he up like one of the Antique patriarchs, or a dying Michael Angelo. Thus and there was he making in the leaves of a great book (folio) the sublimest designs from his (not superior) Dante.[1] He said he began them with fear and trembling.

[1] A. H. Palmer pointed out, in a letter to me, that his father was wrong in this recollection. Blake's *Job* was published in 1826, and he was at work upon this at the time of the first interview. Later, Palmer may have seen him at work on *Dante*, but A. H. Palmer could prove from unpublished Linnell-Blake accounts that the *Dante* scheme had not been thought of in 1824. Mr. Geoffrey Grigson, however (p. 142), thinks that Blake may well have been designing from Dante before the actual commission from Linnell, and Gilchrist (I, p. 332) says the Dante drawings were begun in 1824, while Blake was still working on the *Job*.

I said, 'O! I have enough of fear and trembling.' 'Then,' said he, 'you'll do.' He designed them (100 I think) during a fortnight's illness in bed! And there, first, with fearfulness (which had been the more, but that his designs from Dante had wound me up to forget myself), did I show him some of my first essays in designs; and the sweet encouragement he gave me (for Christ blessed little children) did not tend basely to presumption and idleness, but made me work harder and better that afternoon and night.

A little later, in 1825, he writes in his sketch-book: 'I sat down with Mr. Blake's Thornton's *Virgil* woodcuts before me . . . They are visions of little dells, and nooks, and corners of Paradise; models of the exquisitest pitch of intense poetry. . . . Depth, solemnity, and vivid brilliancy only coldly and partially describe them. There is in all such a mystic and dreamy glimmer as penetrates and kindles the inmost soul.' Blake's visionary, mystic teaching had already sunk deep into the student's mind. Mary Ward—Linnell (who added to his keen appreciation of Dürer and Michelangelo)—William Blake—Virgil and Milton—all of these were external sources and influences which served to call forth the genius in Palmer. The fine flowering and quintessence of that genius is something elusive which evades analysis. Palmer was no imitator. The spark from Blake seemed but to kindle the fuel which flamed in early drawings such as *Ruth* and in the later designs for Milton and Virgil.

Palmer's Royal Academy pictures were probably subjects found at the little village of Shoreham in Kent. He certainly went there with Frederick Tatham in the spring of 1826 'to design from Ruth', and in 1827 settled there with his father and Mary Ward.

Much of the work done by Samuel Palmer at this period was so little appreciated or understood that he himself kept it hidden away during his lifetime. If Blake and Fuseli met with mockery from their contemporaries, it was not likely that Palmer, still under twenty, obviously a rebel, should receive credit for pictures and drawings which were entirely out of key with the popular art of his time. He had exhibited at the Royal Academy when only fourteen, and in 1825 he sent there two small landscapes, *A Scene from Kent* and *A Rustic Scene*, probably the works mentioned by him as being commissioned at seven guineas each by a patron named Bennett. They were ridiculed by the critic of the *European Magazine*, who, after mentioning the landscapes of Turner, Constable and others, continues:

> And there are two pictures by a Mr. Palmer so amazing that we felt the most intense curiosity to see what manner of man it was who produced such performances. We think if he would show himself with a label round his neck, *The Painter of A View in Kent* he would make something of it at a shilling a head. What the Hanging Committee means by hanging these pictures without the painter to explain them is past conjecture.[1]

Among constant visitors to what he called his 'valley of vision' at Shoreham were other enthusiasts who in London had flocked to 'The House of the Interpreter', as they described Blake's dwelling. Among them were George Richmond, Edward Calvert, H. Walter and Francis Oliver Finch, who called themselves 'The Ancients'[2]; not that they were ancient

[1] Whitley, 1821–1837, pp. 90, 91. The two paintings are not mentioned in A.H. Palmer's *Life*.
[2] For the 'Ancients' and their relationship with Blake see A. H. Palmer, *op. cit.*, p. 42; L. Binyon, *The Followers of William Blake*, 1925, p. 13; G. Grigson, *Samuel Palmer*, 1947, p. 86.

themselves, they were very young, but because much of their talk focused upon the ancient poets and painters. Despising the fashions and schools of their day, immersing themselves in romantic visions of the past, searching Virgil's *Eclogues* and Milton's earlier poems for records of primitive life and husbandry, dreaming their dreams, and tiring the sun with talking, they curiously anticipated the Pre-Raphaelite group of a generation later. They were not visionaries in the sense that Blake was a visionary. Their aim was to reconcile creative imagination with a literal, almost scientific representation of nature's facts and appearances. Their visions were not supernatural, but entirely natural, down to the last jot of faithful veracity. It must have been a great day for them all when Blake, in company with Calvert and his wife, journeyed to Shoreham from Charing Cross in the vast carrier's van drawn by eight or ten horses with hoops and bells jingling on their heads. The group who gathered round Palmer at Shoreham were known to the village as 'Extollagers'—so A. H. Palmer relates in his biography. It is a curious word which has the appearance of being invented by themselves, and seems to combine an idea of wild enthusiasm and exaltation with the fact of their being astrologers to the extent of wandering in a band on summer nights to watch the stars and the Northern glimmer in the sky. A drawing of a walnut tree made in 1826 by Robert Hills and signed 'Extollager'[1] not only confirms the queer word but shows, what has not hitherto been known, that Hills may have been an intimate member of the company.

In a letter of 1879 Palmer writes of 'that genuine village where I mused away some of my best years', and one feels that when he said best years he meant the years of his best work. There, in the silence and the solitude, withdrawn from the dust and tumult of the town, he embarked on a period of rare inspiration and enrichment. With Blake, the visible world and the invisible were one; 'nature put him out'. Young Palmer with all his visionary thoughts, clung to the earth, and made constant detailed studies of the pastoral countryside where he lived and worked, but he wrote that, 'I will, God help me, never be a naturalist by profession'. The very skies, dawnings, sunsets, gloamings, moonlights, over the Garden of England, the orchards and the barns of Shoreham village, filled Palmer's mind and were echoed in his work all through his life. In 1824, he notes: 'I will begin a new sketch-book and, I hope, try to work with a child's simple feeling and with the industry of humility.' That is an important note, for if his work of this time is archaic and simple, it is naturally and not self-consciously primitive, as is the case with much recent art. Palmer was still unsophisticated, and still retained his 'eyes of youth'. And, like Blake, Palmer was working at this period with the inward eye as well as the outward gaze, painting in his own words 'the visions of the soul' in complete indifference to the spirit of his age and contemporaries. There is a tangled wild-flower beauty in these earlier works that is lacking in the more forced productions of his later days.

In some cases his drawings of this period depend upon colour. The study, *In a Shoreham Garden*[2] (Pl. 145), is singularly modern in its outlook, in the stark directness of its methods,

[1] Coll. Mr. and Mrs. Paul Mellon.   [2] V.A.M. P.32–1926.

in its arbitrary schematisation, and even in its use of the bare toned paper. There is no attempt at literal representation. The figure is theatrical and some of the blossoms are the size of toy balloons. But that scented wealth of flowering in an old garden embodies all the sunshine and magic of the countryside, and is more real than literal realism could have made it. Blake and Fuseli may be behind it, but the blazing colour is Palmer's own. One has only to think of what was being produced at that date in water-colour to realise the individuality, the independence, almost the defiance, not only in spirit, but in the prodigal use of loaded paint, that characterise this work.

This applies to other remarkable water-colours of this period—*The Magic Apple Tree*[1] (Pl. 146), *The Timber Waggon*,[2] the *Golden Valley*[3] and *The Orange Twilight*.[4] *The Magic Apple Tree*, like *In a Shoreham Garden*, is a tribute in a way to Blake. In the exaggeration of leaf, blossom and branch is the exaggeration with which Blake distorted and magnified human limbs with such noble purpose. Palmer described the apples as 'a tremendous and utterly abnormal crop' and says, 'The whole is a conflagration of colour.' In the *Orange Twilight* the pomp of sunset, the intensity of light where the sun sinks behind a range of hills, is almost blinding to the eyes, so bright that the shadowed slopes seem black, as at first sight in nature. Yet they, too, are luminous and glowing. One must also refer to that long series of black-and-white drawings, including *Ruth returned from Gleaning*[5] (Pl. 147) and a vast number of romantic, visionary studies of landscape, which were a feature of the Exhibition at South Kensington in 1926. That Palmer was in advance of his time is shown not only by drawings like these but by the mixture of poetry and realism in his superb water-colour, *The Barn*[6] and its companion *Tow-bridge with a Mossy Pool*[7] or by his straightforward representation of nature in *Hailsham; Sussex; Thunderstorm*[8] (Pl. 144)—when the artist was only sixteen. This is a surprising drawing, both because it is by Palmer, and because it is dated 1821. *The Barn* and other Shoreham water-colours seem to have defied the years; they are as fresh, the colours as glowing, as if they had been painted yesterday.

A typical example of Palmer's work of this early period is *Lane and Shed, Shoreham*[9] (Pl. 148). Beginning from a loose sketch in pencil particularised and amplified with free pen drawing, it is finished with washes of colour mixed with Chinese white. Being painted thus on a grey Creswick card it has not the brilliance of *The Barn* or *In a Shoreham Garden*, but both in technique and spirit it helps to illustrate an important phase of Palmer's art.

At this early stage of his career you feel already that Palmer is telling you not what he has seen but of his thoughts—his thoughts of the glory of the sun, the magic of moonlight, the

[1] Cambridge, Fitzwilliam Museum.
[2] Present whereabouts not known; repr. Binyon, *Followers*, pl. 23.
[3] Present whereabouts not known; repr. Binyon, *Followers*, pl. 33.
[4] Mr. Michael Maclagan.
[5] V.A.M. E.3449–1923.
[6] Coll. Mr. and Mrs. Paul Mellon.
[7] Coll. Colonel B. Buchanan.
[8] Coll. Mr. L. G. Duke.
[9] V.A.M. P.88–1937.

161

mystery of the stars; thatched cottages couched under immemorial trees; the enigmatic beauty of lanterns swinging in the night; lamplight giving gold to a window-blind; the goodness of harvest and ripe fruitage; men that drive the plough and scatter the grain; all the bounty and beauty that make the history and happiness of rural England. This Shoreham period represents what for long was the least known side of his career, because there was little market for these drawings at the time of their production when to use Palmer's own word, they seemed 'outrageous'. A. H. Palmer told me that his father treasured the Shoreham drawings throughout his life but was reluctant to bring out the portfolios containing them except for some rare individual who might understand their purpose and their meaning. The Shoreham drawings, the later Milton and Virgil drawings, and the etchings, show his individual outlook and exalted imagination at their best.

In 1835, with health improved, he settled in London ('the great national dust-hole', he described it), in a house of his own, 4 Grove Street, Lisson Grove, near the homes of Calvert and Linnell. In 1836 he painted in Devonshire, and then, in company with Calvert and Henry Walter, went on a sketching tour in Wales. In 1843, after his return from Italy, he made a second Welsh trip. During the 1836 visit he met Crabb Robinson, who noted Palmer's 'eye of deep feeling and very capacious forehead', and thought him 'probably a man of genius for the arts', but disliked his views: 'He is so much behind on moral subjects as to disapprove of the Corporation and Test Acts. He believes in Witchcraft'.[1] It was on the 1836 journey that he made two impressive drawings, *Snowdon*[2] and *Mount Siabod from Tyn-y-Coed*.[3] This is the more probable because, in a letter of August 19, 1836, written from Tintern to George Richmond, he mentions a visit to Snowdon, and asks for a loan of three pounds because he had 'not enough cash to carry me to London. . . . If you've a mangy cat to draw, christen it Palmer.' These drawings may well have been a payment or a thank-offering for the loan. They possess, but in a modified degree, the qualities which were so remarkable in the Shoreham work. The waterfalls and mountains are more naturalistic, and the colour instead of being loaded is cool and pure. He was becoming more eclectic, but there his outlook was still imaginative. It was at this time that he quoted what he describes as one of the very deepest sayings he had met with in Lord Bacon: 'There is no excellent beauty that hath not some strangeness in the proportion', and he wrote himself: 'Excess is the essential vivifying spirit, vital spark, embalming spice . . . of the finest art.' This excess, and strangeness of proportion, had appeared in his drawings of fruit trees. Beauty and strangeness were offered to him again, though in a different form, by the scenery of Wales and he took advantage of it in these drawings, which express the structural essence of his theme with dominant notes of grey heightened with body-colour.

A new period in Palmer's career began in 1837 with his marriage to Hannah, the eldest

---

[1] Unpublished entry in Crabb Robinson's *Journal*, December 1836, quoted by G. Grigson, *Horizon*, IV, 1941, p. 322.
[2] Once in Coll. Mrs. Arthur Davey.
[3] Coll. Mr. and Mrs. Paul Mellon.

daughter of John Linnell, who, a dozen years older than his son-in-law, was well on the way to distinction and prosperity. Linnell is described by Mr. Grigson as 'the eccentric, ruthless, quarrelsome, talented and detested artist . . . who developed into a suspicious, tyrannical, cruel egotist'.[1] From what A. H. Palmer told me, that is a true portrait of Linnell, which he intended to paint in detail in the revised *Biography*. It was decided that the young couple should spend some time in Italy, Palmer painting from nature, and his wife executing commissions given by Linnell for copies of old masters. Within four weeks of his marriage Palmer was in Rome; and in Italy he found the visions of fruitfulness, grandeur and beauty that his reading and thought had led him to expect. It was a 'golden and glittering' Italy that, at any rate for his finished drawing, he sought—and found. 'You can only look', he wrote, 'at dazzling palaces, blazing in Italian sunshine, with your eyes half shut. Indeed, Italian air and Italian light, and the azure of an Italian sky, can scarcely be imagined in England.' He had forgotten that, not much earlier, he had written: 'The weather for months was very rainy, and (we being without a fireplace) so cold that I wore a waistcoat lined with flannel, and Mrs. Palmer wrapped up like a mummy.' The greyness, sadness and monotony that are well known to anyone who has lived throughout a year in Italy were disregarded or unseen, except in his studies, though fortunately in some of these he remained true to his Shoreham memories. His *Civitella, near Subiaco*,[2] is a fine example of his studies; almost in monochrome, very modern in its design and its use of spots and shapes. Other Italian studies, quiet and cool in colour, with his characteristic memoranda dotted all over them, are in the collection of Mr. and Mrs. Paul Mellon. From Rome he wrote: 'The outline I believe to be the only first step and great accomplishment of art.[3] When pure and expressive outline is on the paper, the prey is caught. The rest is like cooking and garnishing it.' And so he began a long series of faithful, careful drawings, ranging from studies of trees to panoramic views of Rome and Florence. Of the tree studies, Ruskin wrote later,[4] after speaking of Creswick and Linnell:

A less known artist, Samuel Palmer, lately admitted a member of the Old Water-Colour Society, is deserving of the very highest place among followers of nature. His studies of foreign foliage especially are beyond all praise for care and fullness. I have never seen a stone-pine or cypress drawn except by him; and his feeling is as pure and grand as his fidelity is exemplary. He has not, yet, I think, discovered what is necessary and unnecessary in a great picture; and his works, sent to the Society's rooms, have been most unfavourable examples of his power, and have been generally, as yet, in places where all that is best in them is out of sight. I look to him, nevertheless, unless he lose himself in over reverence for certain conventionalisms of the older schools, as one of the probable renovators and correctors of whatever is failing or erroneous in the practice of English art.

Of his 'cooked and garnished work' of this date *The City of Rome and the Vatican from the Western Hills*[5] is a splendid example; and the Victoria and Albert Museum possesses a fine

[1] *Horizon, op. cit.*, IV, 1941, p. 324.
[2] Manchester University, Whitworth Art Gallery.
[3] It was surely about this time that Ingres uttered his sound and much discussed, 'Le dessin, c'est la probite de l'art.'
[4] *Modern Painters*, 1846, 1, pt. 2, sec. 6, chap. i, p. 604.
[5] Ill. in *O.W.S. Club*, IV, pl. XI.

drawing of the same type and period in *The Villa d'Este*,[1] 1837 (Pl. 152), largely painted with body-colour, whose cypresses are elaborated from a study (one probably seen by Ruskin, and now in Mr. and Mrs. Paul Mellon's collection), which surely served later for the finest of all his etchings, *The Early Ploughman*. The *Florence*,[2] probably painted in 1838, is a pure water-colour, and gives an admirable example of the results of fading. It appears to represent a sunset effect in red and yellow tones, but when the old mount was removed in 1919, the strips of the drawing hidden by the mount on each side were a deep blue. They showed that the entire background and sky had been painted largely with indigo, which had disappeared so completely as to leave in some places little but the bare surface of the paper, and in others, notably on the mountain just behind the town, a wash of Indian red.

Full of plans for exhibiting and for teaching, Palmer returned to London in 1839, and spent a considerable period of difficulty and misgiving. In an entry in one of his notebooks for 1840 is the significant passage: 'Supposing lessons stop, and nothing more is earned—avoid snuff, two candles, sugar in tea, waste of butter and soap. . . . But it is more difficult at present to get than to save. Query, Go into the country for one month to make little drawings for sale?'

A. H. Palmer[3] pictures him as he set out on one of the sketching tours, loaded with paraphernalia, like the first Alpine climbers.

> The sketching expeditions were not made in at all a luxurious manner. The apparatus carried was as simple as it was complete. A deal case or a portfolio slung round the shoulders with a strap held a good supply of paper, together with two large but very light wooden palettes coated with home-made white enamel and set with thick clots of colour so prepared as to be readily moved by the brush or the finger. A light hand-basket held a change or two of linen, reserve colours, an old campstool which had seen service in Italy, and, when necessary, the lunch or dinner. The coat was an accumulation of pockets in which were stowed away the all-important snuff-box, knives, chalks, charcoal, coloured crayons, and sketch-books, besides a pair of large round, neutral-tint spectacles made for near sight. These were carried specially for sunsets and the brightest effects of water; and, together with a small diminishing mirror, completed the equipment. The minimum of the plainest clothes and boots heavily nailed furthered the sketcher's object, which was to travel on unfrequented tracks or mountain paths, in any company or none, and utterly unfettered. A good constitution and the training of his youth made him indifferent to rough quarters and rough diet.

With regard to the all-important matter of technique, I may draw again on A. H. Palmer[4] for a description of his father's procedure when working out-of-doors from Nature[5]:

> He sketched rapidly, though not so rapidly as in after years; while to save time he used a great deal of warm middle-tint paper and body-colour, a practice he eschewed in most of his finished drawings. Many of the sketches show a more or less advanced preparation in black chalk or pen-

[1] V.A.M. P.29–1919.   [2] V.A.M. P.27–1919.   [3] *Op. cit.*, p. 75.   [4] I, *Op. cit.*, p. 76.
[5] In one of the finest of his drawings, of about 1850, the *Landscape with Mill* (Dixon Bequest, Bethnal Green Museum), it is noteworthy that all the highlights on the trees to the left, innumerable flecks of white, are got by scrapings; all the similar lights on the trees to the right by the use of Chinese white. At a short distance the difference is not noticeable. It seems as though he were deliberately testing one method against the other in the same picture, just as one notices again and again in Turner's practice.

cil, or in a colour such as bistre, used with a pen. Pens, indeed, of all sizes were resorted to as at Shoreham, from the little crow-quill to the reed. His execution varied from delicate stipple or most minute draughtsmanship to the bold sweep of a brush two inches broad, filled from the thick masses of colour on the wooden palettes. These large clots of easily-moved colour were a distinguishing peculiarity in his practice, both in and out of doors; and he had many small china saucers which he filled to the brim with the pigments of which he used the most, so prepared as to set, without becoming hard. He recommends an advanced pupil to take out 'whole saucers full of colour, great reed pens, vast brushes, and bottles of brown ink', but he takes care at the same time to reiterate his watchword—'Exactness'. He seldom attempted to attain in one sketch more than the pith or kernel of the subject; but upon a separate paper, or on the margin, he made memoranda of appropriate figures, cattle, or clouds which happened to appear, together with notes explaining the deficiencies of the sketch in peculiarly subtle or exquisite passages. The immense mass of material and knowledge he accumulated therefore is not to be measured so much by the actual sketches, as by the system of shorthand notes (as we may call them) in pen, brush, and pencil, which almost invariably accompanied them. These notes he was able to read and make use of many years afterwards, and in a peculiar manner.

These sketching tours, no doubt, came as pleasant interludes in the toil and depression of picture-making and teaching in London; but, as his biographer has pointed out, they were annual *campaigns* and in no sense holidays. He was living thus when new encouragement and exhilaration came, with the news of his election in 1843 as an Associate of the Old Water Colour Society. He was now passing through what may be called his middle period, when he looked away from that Virgilian atmosphere which, however, he never cleared from his inner vision and showed in unaffected drawings his intense love and admiration for the simple countryside. In his Shoreham period he made many close and searching studies of nature, but in his work of that time he was depicting the secluded recesses rather than the clear spaces of landscape. He had resorted to the subconscious, rather than the conscious experience. Now, in this 'transition stage', as A. H. Palmer describes it, the visions were being forgotten, and the simple aspects of nature presented. He writes of 'Ground soft for pasture or repose. The accident which most quickens such beauty is LIGHT.' In his *Treatise on the Principles of Landscape Design*, 1816–1821, John Varley, Palmer's first teacher, had written: 'Great principles of unity compel us to consider the effect of sunny daylight as constituting the subject, landscape acting here as a second consideration and a vehicle for the light.'

The drawings such as *Farm-yard Princes Risborough*[1] (Pl. 151), 1845, and *A Harvest Field*,[2] both in the Victoria and Albert Museum, or *Carting the Wheat*,[3] exhibited at the Old Water Colour Society in 1848, the linear work on which Palmer laid stress is set down with fine structural foundation; the colour is simple and unemphatic, but the coolness of silvery light is his aim; combined with the mellowness of incipient autumn. He was devoting himself to what he called 'a batch of imitation'—unaffected studies from nature, English scenery in its sober and gentle aspects. He was, however, still exhibiting Italian

[1] V.A.M. P.23–1919.
[2] V.A.M. P.26–1919.
[3] Present whereabouts unknown; ill. O.W.S. Club, IV. Pl. XVI.

drawings in a high, sometimes forced key, with a rich impasto of body-colour while he was producing these far more sensitive and subtle works in clean and transparent washes. The truth seems to be that in his continuous struggle against adverse circumstances he was wrestling with some way of satisfying his own aims and pleasing the public at once. Again and again his books of memoranda and accounts contain notes such as (in 1846): 'I must, D.V., strike at once a NEW STYLE. SIMPLE SUBJECT; BOLD EFFECT; BROAD RAPID EXECUTION'; and later (1850): 'Try something like the solid BLOCKS of sober colour in De Wint. . . . Why do I wish for a NEW STYLE? 1st, To save time. 2nd, To govern all by broad, powerful chiaroscuro. 3rd, TO ABOLISH ALL NIGGLE. THE MEANS: 1st, To work from a bold sepia sketch carried on so far that figure and everything should be already decided. 2nd, Not to be solicitous about the brightness of little specks of light, so as to hinder the full sweep of a great brush by which should be attained the full and right at a distance.'

In 1848 he removed to 1a Victoria Road, Kensington, to be near Kensington Gardens and the still half-rural Brompton. On the death of his father he migrated, but not far, to 6 Douro Place, and there produced the flow of his contributions to the Old Water Colour Society. In the eleven years of his Associateship he contributed seventy works to the Society's exhibitions in Pall Mall. In the first three years there was a large proportion of Italian subjects, but the drawings that followed, and those that succeeded his election as a full member in June, 1854, were of pastoral scenery in Great Britain. North Wales, Cornwall and Devon (the 'heaped-up richness' of Devon always inspired him) supplied many of his themes. 'I mean never to do a landscape without some little figure story', he wrote in 1859; and certainly well-placed figures and cattle add to the liveliness and effect of his landscape work.

His letters still speak of 'summers literally wasted', while he struggled with pupils; of 'patient well-doing, unappreciated and ridiculed'; of taxing his 'strength to the utmost to benefit my family'; of his work as 'a yoke and a burden'. Yet, amid all his troubles and doubts and perplexities, he retained an unabated enthusiasm, a constant delight in Nature and in his memories of Nature, as when he refers to 'that first flush of summer splendour at Shoreham', which had entranced him more than twenty years before. But all this enthusiasm and delight were darkened by the loss in 1861 of his eldest son, More, whose progress and brilliant promise were his father's greatest consolation through all his times of stress. Though it is not my purpose to give a detailed account of Palmer's life, the death of his son has been mentioned because it profoundly affected the outlook of his later years. Of the water-colours of his last twenty years I hesitate to write fully because they do not compare with those of his Shoreham period or of his middle period. The real Palmer of those last twenty years is the Palmer who produced the etchings—things of a lasting poetic beauty, like *The Early Ploughman* and *The Belman*—and the monochrome drawings in illustration of Virgil and of Milton. The last, in particular, combine the Shoreham spirit with a mature knowledge and experience. Palmer had lived in 'the valley of vision', but he had also passed through the valley of the shadow of death. The result, as achieved in the monochrome drawing, *The Eastern Gate*,[1] is splendid and memorable. This is a work which deserves to be compared with Cotman's *Breaking the Clod*. But while he was producing the etchings and the Milton drawings, some of his exhibition pictures bore too close a relationship (an economic relationship in fact) to the solid furniture and expensive carpets of his villa drawing-room at Furze Hill House, Reigate, where he moved in 1862. How he scoffed at his 'GENTEEL RESIDENCE, with a BUTLER'S PANTRY', and the spring-cleanings, and the prim visitors in the drawing-room. The real Palmer cultivated convolvulus and other weeds in a corner of the garden, and shut himself up in the room, sacred to himself, with its wooden tables, its simple chairs, its mugs, saucers and gallipots, and the portfolios labelled 'Shoreham' and 'Milton'. There, amid the silence and the flickering light of candle or lamp, the stars shouted again in the heavens; again he watched, as with Mary Ward, the dancing chequer of light and shade. The old spirit shone out once more in the drawings that embodied the visionary landscapes of Virgil and of Milton. But the handsome furniture, and Mary, the housemaid who pulled up the harebell roots that he had been coaxing for three years, all demanded an expenditure which could only be met by exhibition work in which he was too consciously aiming at something which would be gorgeously romantic in its chromatic and sentimental appeal. He was far too honest to produce deliberate pot-boiling work, but the exigencies of villa life did undoubtedly lead him to consider the public taste, and the popularity of Linnell's forced chromatic effects in that artist's oil-paintings may have induced emulation. Hence a cohort of pictures gleaming with purple and gold, purple pools reflecting golden leaves glittering, and ruined Gothic windows made to quiver in the slanting rays of the setting sun. Whether we like them or not, they compel us to realise his extraordinary knowledge, his forceful technique, his intense response to the beauty of sunset. Blake had condemned oil-painting because you could not use real gold in it. Palmer, too, would have liked to paint in gold. 'Shell gold' was always among his pigments. But no shell gold and no combination of lemon-yellows and madders in water-colour will make a true gold, such as he saw at Shoreham in evening skies and autumn foliage and lighted windows beneath the thatch.

As a *tour de force* of his later period may be mentioned *Emily and Valancourt at the Château le Blanc*[2] (from *The Mysteries of Udolpho*). The castle glows in the concentrated evening light, in contrast with the shadowed foreground (in which the figures are a mere excuse for the subject) and the tall dark trees whose edges are tipped with golden light. Here, and in the large *Towered City*,[3] 1880, (both were at the Fine Art Society in 1941), he secured a brilliant blaze of colour by working with body-colour upon a ground of white. Some of this later work has almost the solid impasto of oil-painting, and attains an effect which even oil can scarcely surpass. Exactly the same method was used in *The Waters Murmuring*,[4]

[1] V.A.M. E.1317–1925.
[2] Whereabouts unknown.
[3] V.A.M. E.1318–1925.
[4] V.A.M. E.1320–1925.

167

1877, an illustration to *Il Penseroso*. This, too, is executed with fully-loaded body-colour, in jewelled opulence of emerald, ruby and gold. It gives a brilliant effect of sun glinting through foliage and touching some of the figures with light, while others are in shadowed recesses by rock and stream.

His last period may be said to have begun in the 'fifties, when he abandoned transparent colour and worked with an impasto of opaque colour or on a board prepared with a wash of Chinese white. He sought brilliance, particularly in his skies, and if Turner and others painted a rainbow, he must outvie them with a comet. Hence, *The Comet*,[1] 1858, seen from the skirts of Dartmoor. It is a highly stippled, but daring and impressive drawing.

Much more may be said in extenuation of the man who was producing highly-wrought exhibition work, while unprofitable Milton drawings were occupying his thoughts and encroaching on his time. Palmer, his eyes blinded by sunlight, was, I feel, not only trying to hold his own beside his contemporaries but to attempt the impossible. However much one may dislike the colour in some of his later pictures, they are superb in tone and composition. A. H. Palmer pointed out again and again that the pictures were made in the dim light of a small room—he described it in a letter to me as 'a miserable, cramped, ill-lit, little bedroom studio'—often by lamp light, and could never look their best in the fierce light of an exhibition gallery. Seen in a subdued and diffused light, such as that of the room in which they were painted, they have a different refined appeal.

Looking at his work throughout his long career, with its mixture of research, actuality and imagination, one feels that it has the quality of certain classic poetry. It is Gray's *Elegy* in terms of paint. 'Now fades the glimmering landscape on the sight', with every one of the opening lines of the *Elegy* is a Palmer drawing described in verse. His thoughts were nearly always of twilight and sunset. A drawing such as *Sunset through the Trees*[2] shows the intensity of his knowledge. That his is great and enduring art is proved by the fact that Palmer—the Palmer of the Shoreham drawings and the etchings—has influenced profoundly many artists of today. Like Thomas Hardy he makes us feel a sense of the physical world, of the deep and solemn beauty of landscape not only as an environment but as part of human life. He realised with extraordinary intensity his pastoral vision, the blur of dusk, the gold and purple bars of light over the western hills, the warmth and comfort and lazy peace of the hamlet nestling in its peaceful hollow, the lights gleaming in cottage windows, the largesse of the ripening year, the fields and pens 'loud with the lowing of cattle and the bleating of sheep'. In the words of his son: 'Old age crept gently upon him, inexorable, but not unkind. He looked forward with no dread to the approaching change, for he believed it would enable him to enjoy, in a more perfect manner than was possible in this short life, a state of intellectual light and vigour.'

Among Palmer's close associates, the 'little band who reverenced Blake as their chief,

[1] Whereabouts unknown.
[2] Ill. *O.W.S. Club*, IV 1926–1927, pl. XVIII.

and very sincerely loved art for its own sake', were Edward Calvert and F. O. Finch. Edward Calvert (1799–1883) was born at Appledore, Devon. The son of a naval officer, he entered the Navy, and in the dim light of the midshipman's cabin exercised his artistic talent as best he might. Like the French etcher Meryon, shocked by seeing a companion killed, he left the Navy and took to art as his profession. After a course of study in Plymouth he came to London in 1824, worked in the Royal Academy schools with the encouragement of Fuseli, and exhibited at the Academy from 1825 to 1836. In 1826 Palmer met him at the Academy exhibition, looking like 'a prosperous, stalwart country gentleman, redolent of the sea and in white trousers'. Calvert constantly destroyed his work before completion and, in the words of his friend and fellow student George Richmond, was 'always stretching out his hand to grasp that which he could not attain'. Calvert found in Claude what he described as 'the freshness of an early age—midst seeming pathways, threading the mysteries of retreat to seclusions of blessedness'. That saying of his might have been written by Samuel Palmer, and shows how completely he was imbued with the same spirit as Palmer and Blake. It was but natural that, when about 1826 he made their acquaintance through Palmer's cousin, John Giles, he should yield to their mystic Christianity. Like Palmer and Richmond he succumbed to the spell of Blake. He found in Blake's woodcut illustrations to Virgil's *Eclogues*, a source which led him to take up woodblock and graver for the expression of his own poetic imaginings.

Like Blake and Palmer he was a pastoral painter, but while they show religious feeling, Calvert was apt to respond to the feasts of Dionysus and the rustic loves of Daphnis and Chloe. While Palmer followed in the footsteps of Virgil, Milton and Bunyan, Calvert's path led into the pagan idylls of Theocritus. His changing thoughts and aspirations are reflected in the series of exquisite engravings on wood and copper—each one a gem— which he produced from 1827 to 1829. One of the first was *Christian Ploughing the Last Furrow of Life*, with the inscription, 'seen in the Kingdom of Heaven through Jesus Christ our Saviour'. It was probably *The Bacchante* (known to Samuel Palmer as *The Prophet*) of the next year, 1828, and *The Chamber Idyll*, the finest of the Calvert prints, which caused Palmer to speak of Calvert's 'naughty disobedient heresies', but by September Calvert was 'finishing with surprising rapidity, the effect of prayer, a beautiful and luxuriant design of the cider pressing', inscribed 'by the Gift of God in Christ'. And Palmer said in a letter: 'Your *Cider Press* in poetic richness, beats anything I know, ancient and modern.' *The Bride* was perhaps saved from a charge of paganism by its inscribed confession (and surely Calvert had his tongue in his cheek) 'O God. Thy Bride seeketh Thee: A stray lamb is led to Thy folds.' But in 1834 Palmer was anxiously writing that Calvert was 'in deliberate hostility to the gospel of Christ', and Calvert cut away the Christian sentences from *The Cyder Feast* and other prints in their third states. There were whispers among his friends of sacrificial ceremonies in his garden, and Sir William Richmond, who stayed with him as a boy, 'not without a thrill saw in his little back garden an altar erected to the honour of the great god Pan'. But he remained always 'My dear Friend' to Palmer, who wrote to

169

him from Devonshire in 1848: 'I have been thinking much lately of the shortness of life; and when I passed through your youthful haunts and "ancient neighbourhood", every turn of which seemed to speak to me of you and Mrs. Calvert, I could not help remembering how great and important an addition to the happiness of my life had been your united friendship.'

Closely associated with the engravings and particularly with *The Bride* is a little masterpiece in water-colour, *The Primitive City*[1] (Pl. 159). It is a veritable jewel, faceted, prismatic, only three by four inches in size. Drawn with pen, and tinted slightly except for the intense blue of the sky, it is like an illumination in a medieval missal. Far from being an imitation of medieval work, it is essentially Calvert, having the same spirit, the same delicacy and poetry of imagination as his small woodcuts and line engravings. The half-draped figure, the slender fruit trees, the shepherd and his flock, the waggon drawn by oxen, the husbandman leading his ass with laden paniers, the ancient buildings beneath a crescent moon, are all portrayed with closest detail and loving care. In this exquisite drawing Calvert conveys 'infinite riches in a little room'. Both Roget and Laurence Binyon have pointed out that *The Primitive City* is half-way between the creations of Blake and the sensuous imaginations of Rossetti. To that extent Calvert is a precursor of the Pre-Raphaelites, and it is strange that the engravings and this lovely water-colour came in a moment and were merely a brilliant phase in his development. This felicity soon deserted his hand and mind.

It is not without interest to note that Palmer came to reverence Calvert even more than Blake. In proof of this I may quote from a letter written to me by A. H. Palmer on April 9, 1920:

> My father valued these Calverts more highly than he did his Blakes. At one time three of Blake's finest panel pictures were stored away in the basement with a lot of rubbish; and it was barely possible to see that they were pictures. But the little Calverts were in the special portfolios which my father toned his mind withal, every day. They brought back to him, like Finch's little oil picture of Peter Wilkins, the days of his boyhood. Calvert's *Cyder Press* he referred to sometimes as the acme of what he loved best. One little gem (*The Chamber Idyll*) was always kept in a paper chemise, hard to pull off, lest Mrs. Grundy should one day poke her snout into the sacred room.

It has usually been assumed that *The Primitive City* was contemporary with the engravings of 1827 to 1830, but when it was presented by the National Art Collections Fund to the British Museum in 1947, a pencil inscription *Edward Calvert 1822* was found.[2] This writing had been covered by the mount when the drawing was exhibited at the Royal Academy exhibition of British Art in 1934. If the signature and date are authentic (and there seems to be no reason for doubting this), they show that Calvert was already working in his early Plymouth days under the influence of Blake and that in spirit at least he was one of 'The Ancients' before ever he met Linnell, Richmond and Palmer. The truth of

[1] B.M. 1947.2.17.1.
[2] N.A.C.F., 44th Annual Report, 1948, p. 15.

170

this is confirmed by what the artist's third son, Samuel Calvert, says: 'At the age of twenty-two, Edward Calvert commenced painting those minute and beautifully finished works in full scale of colour, of which we now only possess a few, among which are the illuminated idyll Mr. Richmond refers to as *The City*, and the small adaptation from Baring's Claude—*Sunrise*.'[1] It must be accepted, then, that Calvert made the drawing when he was twenty-three and that it antedates the engravings.

Calvert's last exhibit at the Royal Academy was in 1836. Possessing a sufficient patrimony, he lived a life of ease and dignified retirement till his death. We may well wonder whether in his last fifty years he was conscious that in his past there had been a transcendent glory and gleam. During those fifty years he became more of a realist; he spent evenings beside Etty studying the nude; he was trying, in his own words, to 'transform physical truth into musical truth'; he became lost in a maze of theory; he wrote to his son, 'I coveted the mastery over colour, and it has eaten up the bulk of my life.' He continued to paint sketchy but sensitive fragments in oil—in the British Museum are many of the oil studies made during his later life—dealing with pastoral legend and the myths of ancient Greece. If I find these later works appear vague, woolly and anaemic, let it be said that to the poetic instinct of Laurence Binyon they appealed as having rare beauty in their temperate colour and as a mirror to Calvert's brooding mind.[2]

With Linnell, Richmond, Calvert and Palmer, Finch was one of 'The Ancients' who sat at the feet of Blake in the closing years of the poet-painter's life. Blake struck him 'as *a new kind of man*, wholly original, and in all things'. Finch himself was described by Sir Henry Cole as 'a painter, a poet, a musician, a humourist, and a gentle and kindly spirit',[3] and by Samuel Palmer as 'the last representative of the old school of landscape painting in water-colours'. After Finch's death in 1862 Palmer said that 'he had imagination; that inner sense which received impressions of beauty as simply and surely as we smell the sweetness of the rose and woodbine'.

Francis Oliver Finch (1802–1862) was born in London and in 1814 or 1815 was a pupil for three years under John Varley and remained as his articled pupil for an additional two years. It is interesting to note that Varley at this time could claim a premium of £200 for an articled pupil. Finch matured rapidly and became an exhibitor at the Royal Academy at the age of fifteen. Working for a time at Sass' Academy, he studied figure painting and portraiture, but after his election to the Old Water-Colour Society in 1822 he gave himself entirely to landscape.

Finch's works were of a poetic nature, usually a classical composition with a temple or castle in the middle distance. He was a worshipper of Claude, but his own romantic imagination appears in his *Castle in a Hill-girt Wood*[4] and in *Landscape with Stormy Sky*,[5]

---

[1] Samuel Calvert, *Memoir of Edward Calvert*, 1893, p. 12.
[2] 'Followers'. *Op. cit.*, pp. 27–29.
[3] Eliza Finch, *Memorials of F. O. Finch*, 1865.
[4] Cardiff, National Museum of Wales.
[5] Dixon Bequest, Bethnal Green Museum.

where he breaks away from conventional classicism. His work is easily confused with that of George Barrett II, so alike are they in subject, sentiment and method. Finch on the whole is even more concerned with detail and finish; it is recorded that he was unusually slow in execution. Like Barret he constantly used the trick of wiping out leaf-shaped spots of high light in his foliage. In April 1862, just four months before Finch's death, G. P. Boyce records in his diary that he: 'Bought a little moonlight drawing, *Tranquility*, by F. O. Finch. Was more glad that I had done so when James Holland informed me that the painter had been a second time struck by paralysis and that the money would be useful to him.'

144 'Hailsham, Sussex, Thunderstorm'
Coll. Mr Leonard G. Duke   8¼ × 12½: 209 × 318
Water-colour, signed with monogram, dated 1821
Samuel PALMER (1805–1881)

145 'In a Shoreham Garden'

V.A.M. P.32–1926   11 × 8¼: 280 × 209   *Water-colour and body-colour*

Samuel PALMER (1805–1881)

146 'The Magic Apple Tree'
Cambridge, Fitzwilliam Museum   13¾ × 10¼: 349 × 260   *Water-colour*
Samuel PALMER (1805–1881)

147 'Ruth Returning from Gleaning'
V.A.M. E.3449–1923 $11\frac{1}{2} \times 15\frac{1}{2}$: 293 × 392   *Chalk and wash*
Samuel PALMER (1805–1881)

148 'Lane and Shed, Shoreham, Kent'
V.A.M. P.88–1937 $11 \times 17\frac{3}{4}$: 279 × 450   *Water-colour, signed*
Samuel PALMER (1805–1881)

149 'A Shepherd Leading his Flock under the Full Moon'
Coll. Mr Leonard G. Duke $5\frac{7}{8} \times 7$: 149×178 *Sepia*
Samuel PALMER (1805–1881)

150 'Dark Trees by a Pool'
Cambridge, Fitzwilliam Museum
$4\frac{1}{8} \times 2\frac{5}{8}$: 105×67
Sepia
Samuel PALMER (1805–1881)

151 'Farmyard, Princes Risborough, Bucks'
V.A.M. P.23–1919   15½ × 21¼: 394 × 539   *Water-colour, signed*
Samuel PALMER (1805–1881)

152 'The Villa d'Este'

V.A.M. P.29–1919 $10\frac{3}{4} \times 14\frac{3}{4}$: 273×374 *Water-colour and body-colour*

Samuel PALMER (1805–1881)

153 'Tintagel'

B.M. 1910.7.16.17 $10\frac{1}{4} \times 14\frac{1}{2}$: 260×368 *Pencil and water-colour*

Samuel PALMER (1805–1881)

154 'Moonlight Scene with a Winding Stream'
Coll. Mr & Mrs Paul Mellon
$10\frac{1}{2} \times 7\frac{1}{8}$: 267 × 181
Sepia heightened with white
Samuel PALMER (1805–1881)

155 'Wimletts (? Ormletts) Hill, Kent'
Coll. Mr & Mrs Paul Mellon $10\frac{7}{8} \times 15$: 276 × 381   *Water-colour*
Samuel PALMER (1805–1881)

156 'Collecting the Flock'

V.A.M. 136–1892 $10\frac{1}{4} \times 13\frac{1}{4}$: 260 × 336   *Water-colour, signed and dated 1862*

John LINNELL (1792–1882)

157 'View in the Fens'

Coll. Mr & Mrs Paul Mellon $6\frac{3}{8} \times 9\frac{1}{8}$: 162 × 232   *Water-colour, signed*

John LINNELL (1792–1882)

158 'Underriver, near Sevenoaks, Kent'

Coll. Mr Leonard G. Duke $8\frac{1}{4} \times 12\frac{5}{8}$: 210 × 320   *Pen and brown wash*

John LINNELL (1792–1882)

159 'The Primitive City'
B.M. 1947.2.17.1
$3\frac{1}{8} \times 4\frac{1}{2}$: 80 × 114
Water-colour, signed and dated 1822
Edward CALVERT (1799–1883)

160 'Landscape Study'
B.M. 1890.4.15.401   6 × 10: 153 × 254   *Water-colour*
Edward CALVERT (1799–1883)

161 'Landscape with Castle'

Coll. Mr & Mrs Paul Mellon $6\frac{1}{4} \times 8\frac{1}{4}$: 158 × 210   *Water-colour*

Francis Oliver FINCH (1802–1862)

162 'Composition'

Coll. Mr & Mrs Cyril Fry $9\frac{1}{4} \times 12\frac{1}{4}$: 234 × 311   *Water-colour*

Francis Oliver FINCH (1802–1862)

CHAPTER XI

Richard Parkes Bonington

Thomas Shotter Boys   Ambrose Poynter
Henry Liverseege   Alfred Elmore   John Scarlett Davis
William Roxby Beverly

Water-colour painting in Britain was kept alive by its continuing capacity for change and development. Bonington and others showed that fresh life could be grafted upon the old stock; his particular contribution was a new luminosity and a lyric gift of colour.

In the first half of the nineteenth century water-colour was a medium very rarely used by French painters, and British water-colour painting was almost unknown across the Channel. When the influence occurred it was almost accidental. By chance Bonington as a boy was taken to live at Calais; by chance he fell in with a teacher who had worked beside Varley and Girtin; and he grew up to become a practitioner of water-colour in the English manner in Paris. Long before he was recognised in this country he was held in honour by the French and exercised an important influence upon French painting. He was the first painter in France to reproduce the limpid simplicity of sky, water and sea-coast, the infinite depths and subtleties of light and shadow playing upon landscape and architecture.

The student of Bonington is faced with a variety of problems. Besides his own replicas or virtual replicas there are innumerable imitations, forgeries as well as those works by other artists whose style can only be distinguished from Bonington with difficulty.

Richard Parkes Bonington (1802–1828)[1] was born at Arnold, near Nottingham. His father held a post as governor of the Nottingham County Gaol, but lost his appointment in 1797, the year one of his pictures was hung at the Royal Academy. His local prestige enabled him to start again as a drawing-master in Nottingham, with a side-line as print-seller and stationer. He married in 1801, and Mrs. Bonington opened a school for young ladies in that year and thus had a resident drawing-master, but by 1816, perhaps owing to her husband's restless nature and the prevailing economic conditions, the school was

---

[1] The *Dictionary of National Biography* and other works of reference have given his birth-date as 1801. But in 1909 Robert Mellors of Nottingham discovered an entry in the register of baptisms at the High Pavement Chapel, Nottingham, showing that Bonington was born on October 25, 1802, and was baptized on November 28, 1802. (*See* Nottingham, Thoroton Society, *Transactions*, XIII, 1909.)

closed and though both parents struggled on with teaching work, their lessons were thinning out. At the end of 1817 or early in 1818 Bonington Senior migrated to Calais with his family and set up a lace-factory with himself as designer. The lace business supported the family life both at Calais and later in Paris. After their son's death the father and mother returned to London, where they were able to live at ease on what they had inherited by way of money or of pictures and drawings yet unsold.

It stands to his father's credit that young Richard received some careful instruction in drawing, even if it was firmly intended that he should become a breadwinner by making lace designs in the family factory. But nothing could stop him from playing truant and from making sketches in the streets and on the quays of Calais. Francia, then resident in Calais, watched the youthful artist at work, and took him under his wing. That accident of circumstances started the potential lace designer on the road to fame as a painter. For some months Francia gave secret help to the promising beginner. Under the skilled tuition of an artist who had been Girtin's friend in London, Bonington absorbed the traditions of English water-colour art. He learned how to lay in his washes, how to render the shape of clouds and the movement of a sky, and above all how to secure breadth while remaining sensitive to detail. From Francia he perhaps learned also the virtue of simplicity in method. Francia had been a friend of Girtin and it is not unreasonable to detect something of the Girtin touch in Bonington's pencil work. It was probably owing to Francia, who had published twelve plates of tree studies in 1814, that Bonington's foliage in his water-colours is so well and freely handled.

The head of the family had no patience with his son's landscape work and he did his best to thwart the boy's progress in this direction. The story told by Dubuisson[1] may be a picturesque accretion upon Bonington's biography and not entirely in accord with accounts given many years after the event by Delacroix and others, but it has graphic possibilities. Dubuisson relates that a climax came when the father burst into Francia's house, defying him to give more lessons to his wastrel son. Richard was hiding upstairs while the storm was breaking below. Though he was not yet sixteen, he determined to cut and run, and armed by a letter from Francia to his friend and patron, M. Morel, a rich ship-owner and mayor of Dunkirk, he set off immediately from his home. The story continues that Morel read Francia's letter, presumably saw examples of Richard's work, and sent him off to Paris (either Morel or Francia must have provided the necessary funds) with an introduction to the young Eugène Delacroix.

Bonington lived frugally and worked untiringly as a student. He spent much time in making copies in the Louvre, and many years later Delacroix recalled a memory of the 'tall youth in a short coat who was silently making water-colour studies, for the most part from Flemish landscapes. Already he had a surprising skill in this method, which was in those days an English novelty.'[2] Bonington joined the Ecole des Beaux Arts in 1819 and

[1] A. Dubuisson and C. E. Hughes, *Richard Parkes Bonington*, 1924.
[2] André Joubin, *Correspondence Générale d'Eugène Delacroix*, IV, 1936–1938, p. 286.

174

also worked in the studio of Baron Gros, paying his fees of 20 francs a month. Gros insisted that, 'Drawing comes first, colour second', but on one occasion at least he admitted the importance of colour. You do not give sufficient attention to colour, he said to his class. 'Colour, let me tell you, is poetry, charm, life; without life there is no work of art.' The story goes that he was referring particularly to some water-colours 'streaming with light' which he had seen in a shop window, not knowing that Bonington was their author. Corot in his old age related that in his boyhood, working as a draper's assistant, the sight of a water-colour sketch by Bonington in L. Schroth's window determined his future career.

The time came when Gros, in recognition of the high merit of Bonington's water-colours, advised the young painter to *marcher seul*, but gave him the freedom of his studio. Bonington with his ambitions not satisfied by landscape work alone, continued his studies under Gros till his mastery of figure work was complete. Wherever he went, both then and later, he pursued his study of figures in their natural surroundings as well as in the studio, filling his sketch-books with pencil notes such as those of French fisher-folk, peasants, and labourers.[1]

The brilliant water-colour sketches which Gros had admired were sold at 15 to 20 francs apiece and brought in a small but regular income. Bonington could afford to hire a fiacre, as Girtin had done, and sketch from it undisturbed by the crowd of grown-up onlookers and fidgety urchins by whom painters are so often harassed. Soon he had made enough money to justify in 1821 a sketching tour in the Seine Valley with visits to Mantes, Rouen and Havre. By 1822 his reputation was rising and he made his first appearance at the Salon. His water-colours of *Lillebonne* and *Havre*, both of which have since disappeared, were acquired by the Société des Amis des Arts for 430 francs. The road to fame was open for a young artist who had won the recognition of this distinguished body of connoisseurs.

Every summer until his death in 1828 Bonington was on the road, 'his knapsack on his back over his long blouse, a flat cap on his head like that of a grand vizier and his stick in his hand',[2] painting, making sketches, looking for decorative designs in landscape and architecture. He followed many of his French friends in exploiting the possibility of lithography.[3] Then in the famous Salon of 1824, so often spoken of as having given a new impetus to French painting and as the starting-point of the Barbizon School, Bonington showed three oils and a water-colour, *Vue d'Abbeville*. His work was favourably noticed and secured for him a gold medal, Constable and Copley Fielding receiving a like honour. The novel technique of these English painters, the sparkling effect of open air in their landscapes, the purity and brilliance of their colour,[4] seemed a startling innovation to the

---

[1] Two sketch-books in B.M. 201.a.1 and 200.b.2.

[2] Virgile Josz, in *Mercure de France*, 1901.

[3] Lithographs from many of his landscape drawings were to appear in Baron Taylor's *Voyages Pittoresques dans l'ancienne France*, 1823–1847. His well-known lithograph of the Rue du Gros Horloge and other Normandy subjects are in the second volume.

[4] Delacroix, *Journal*, I, 1932, p. 234, wrote: 'Constable dit que la supériorité du vert de ses prairies tient à ce qu'il est composé d'une multitude de verts différents. Le défaut d'intensité et de vie à la verdure du commun des paysages, c'est qu'ils font ordinairement d'une teinte uniforme. . . . Ce qu'il dit ici du vert des prairies peut s'appliquer à tous les autres tons.'

representations of the classical tradition with its dependence upon tone rather than colour and upon studio composition.

By 1824 Bonington was on close terms of friendship with Delacroix, Gericault, Isabey and other leaders of romanticism in France. To what extent Bonington influenced this movement or how far he was swept along in the stream it is difficult to determine. Like his French companions, he was steeped in Shakespeare and was fascinated by the romances of Sir Walter Scott. Costume and armour, the glitter of silk and satin, the pomp of palaces and courts, appealed to his dramatic sense. Drawings of 1822 and 1823 in the British Museum show how keenly interested he was in medieval and renaissance armour and costume, and in its historical authenticity. These studies were preparations for such pictures as *Lady and Page* and *Lady and Cavalier*, now in the Wallace Collection. He never ceased to paint landscape, but figure groups, masterly in composition and rich in deep brilliance of colour, provided a new theme added to the architectural subjects and the coast and river scenes which had hitherto occupied his mind and hand. Landscape began to take second rank in his ambitions.

Probably in this new side of his work Bonington was influenced by Delacroix not merely in subject, but in handling. The two of them were sharing a studio when Delacroix wrote to Soulier in 1826: 'Il y a terriblement à gagner dans la société de ce luron-là, et je te jure que je m'en bien trouvé.'[1] All the same one feels that Bonington, in his romantic figure subjects, showed the greater indebtedness. They reveal a fuller and more solid impasto, a deeper and more romantic sense of colour, than his landscape work. On the other hand, however stirring the figure subjects may be in colour and tone, they are more exotic and artificial. They lack the fresh immediacy of his landscapes. In his fancy subjects he is more derivative. Not only had he watched Delacroix at work, but he had copied Dutch and Italian masters in the Louvre. Rubens, with his dramatic colour, influenced him and his contemporaries in France just as he influenced many artists in England. Bonington's aim was to achieve in a single picture 'la finesse des Hollandais, la vigueur des Venétians, et la magie des Anglais'. He did not live long enough to weld and to blend all these influences.

In 1825 Bonington came over to England, with Delacroix in his company for at any rate part of the time. One of their main occupations was making numerous studies of the Samuel Meyrick collection of armour. They were in touch with the Fieldings and with Prout, beside whom Bonington had painted at St. Omer in 1823. He had a quiet and retiring nature, which caused him to shun social encounters. He made no attempt, for instance, to gain personal contact with Turner, but he was tremendously impressed by Turner's work which on this and later visits he probably saw at the Academy and else-where. Though he was dazzled by its poetry and technique, he remained a realist. In some of his later landscapes his colour, always having a clean, tonic, astringent freshness and already at times high in key, took on a fiery iridescence, which may have been bor-

[1] Joubin, *op. cit.*, I, p. 173.

rowed from Turner. But in Bonington's drawings which deal with domestic interiors, his characters are flesh and blood, his rooms hold solid tapestries and furniture, unlike Turner's later interiors of Petworth House.

As a result perhaps of his visit to England he sent to the British Institution in 1826 two oil landscapes, *French Coast* and *French Coast with Fishermen*; and his power was at once recognised. The *Literary Gazette*[1] said:

> Who is R. P. Bonington? We never saw *his name* in any catalogue before, and yet here are pictures which would grace the foremost *name* in landscape art. Sunshine, perspective, vigour, a fine sense of beauty in disposing of colours, whether in masses or mere bits—these are extraordinary ornaments to the room.

At the beginning of 1826 he met Frederick Tayler, who was born in the same year as himself and was later to become President of the Old Water-Colour Society. This connection provides an interesting episode in Bonington's life, not recorded until Whitley quoted a letter written by Tayler to F. G. Stephens, the art critic.[2]

> It was at the hotel at Calais that I first met R. P. Bonington. He was with the French landscape painter, Francia, and at the same hotel was S. W. Reynolds, the engraver, who reproduced many of Sir Joshua's works. Bonington had been making studies in the neighbourhood of Calais, and so, finding myself so warm an admirer of his talents, we struck up a friendship and agreed to take lodging together in Paris. This we did, and studied together in the Louvre and at home, painting night and day.
>
> After a time we took a house with a painting-room for horses, which had belonged to Horace Vernet. Here we had not been long before Bonington was seized with a longing to see Rome and make some studies in the Vatican, and I was left to take care of the house and his pictures, when an accident occurred which placed them in considerable danger. I was painting a portrait of a horse for Lord Henry Seymour, when suddenly the French cook entered the room bearing a set of *couverts* on his head. This so frightened the horse that he broke from the lad who held him and dashed at full speed round the room, kicking out in all directions, to the great danger of Bonington's pictures which were placed on the ground. A favourite pointer dog of mine left the room, also at full speed, and I never could hear any tidings of it afterwards. Some time, after this Bonington returned from Rome[3] bringing some fine studies made in the Vatican, etc., and I left Paris and went to Scotland. While there I heard to my great regret that Bonington had had a sunstroke while painting in a boat on the Seine, and from this, alas! he never recovered.

In the spring of 1826 Bonington made the pilgrimage of two months to Italy which is mentioned by Tayler. It seems probable that Bonington's visit to Venice was largely inspired by Samuel Prout, who had made an extensive tour in Italy during 1824. He definitely suggested particular Venetian subjects to Bonington before his departure. It is interesting to note that Sir David Wilkie was in Venice at the same time as Bonington. As a travelling companion Bonington had Delacroix's friend Baron Rivet, whose diary shows that Bonington was frail, gloomy and depressed. Already he seems to have had the

---

[1] Feb. 4, 1826, no. 472, p. 76.
[2] Whitley, 1821–1837, pp. 150, 151.
[3] A. P. Oppé (review of 'Bonington' by Hon. Andrew Shirley in *Burlington Magazine*, LXXIX, 1941, pp. 99–101) distrusts Tayler's memory and is very doubtful whether Bonington ever visited Rome.

melancholy air of a doomed man. He spent a brief time at Bologna and Milan, but time enough to provide us with the superb water-colours of *The Church of S. Ambrogio, Milan*[1] (Pl. 167) and *The Leaning Towers, Bologna*[2] (Pl. 166). In Italy he made many pencil notes, and several sketches in oil and water-colour, all of them serving for studio work during the following year. On his return to Paris, with all this material in hand, he found himself in possession of a capital sum of 7,000 or 8,000 francs earned since January. With collectors such as Lewis Brown, Capt. W. Webb and M. Paul Perrier, and with various dealers in Paris and in London, his work was in strong demand.

In 1827 and in the spring of 1828 he visited England again.[3] On the third visit he presented a letter of introduction to Sir Thomas Lawrence, who was to attend Bonington's funeral later in the year. In 1828 he was overworking, and his fragile body was visibly wasting; he painted whenever he had strength to lift a brush, but by July, after his return from England, he was a complete invalid. His parents took him to London for advice from St. John Long, a quack specialist in consumption. Visiting the studio of his engraver, George Cooke, he lay stretched out on two or three chairs. Sir Edmund Bacon owns a sketch of a *Coast Scene* with a label on the mount inscribed:

> Original Sketch by R. P. Bonington. John Sadler, one of the last of the old Line Engravers, sold me this sketch along with 2 others in 1891. He said that when a youth of 15 he was articled to George Cooke, the well known engraver of many of Bonington's Pictures. In 1828 Bonington called about the Plate of one of his pictures for he seemed very ill and depressed, to amuse him Cooke gave him a bottle of Walnut Juice and with this he made 2 or 3 drawings and then threw them into the waste paper basket. Sadler rescued them and preserved them until they became mine. Bonington died in the following week and this is probably one of his last works. George H. Shepherd 1906.

On September 23, 1828, not long before his twenty-sixth birthday, Bonington died.

Bonington's friends and associates must have known him as a prolific worker; but how prolific became clear only after his death. With Bonington, as with Girtin, one is compelled to consider how far pathology accounts for certain types of genius. There is a quality of radiance and the exaltation of ecstatic youth in Bonington's work, as there so often is in the work of those whom the gods love.

In 1826, in spite of his large output, it may be said that in England Bonington was almost unknown. Shortly after his death, however, he came to sudden fame in London, Of this there is contemporary evidence in a newspaper of 1829.[4]

> Bonington, the ingenious artist, whose premature death at the moment his fame and talents began to be appreciated, every lover of genius must deplore, like Burns the poet has been most honoured since his death. The whole tribe of R.A.'s who scarcely deigned to notice him while living, and in their annual Exhibition placed his brilliant works in holes and corners, now that he is no more chaunt requiems to his memory, and give even 'twenty, thirty, aye forty ducats for his pictures in little.'

[1] London, Wallace Collection.
[3] For the third visit in 1828 see Oppé, *op. cit.*

[2] London, Wallace Collection.
[4] V.A.M. Library, Cuttings, vol. VI, No. 1550.

Perhaps that last sentence was a gibe at Sir Thomas Lawrence, P.R.A., who bought *The Turk* at the British Institution and acquired several pictures by Bonington at the Sale of 1829?

As early as 1831 the market was flooded with imitations of Bonington. 'It has happened with Bonington', says a writer of that date,[1] 'as it has never done with all those who dare to think for themselves, that their works, while living, do not pay them half so well as the imitations of their style do the servile herd who crowd in upon their fame after their death.' 'The cupidity of dealers has been so great that caution and perception are now necessary in buying a Bonington. As in the case of Girtin, imitation is daily at work to ensnare the collector.'[2] That forgeries were plentiful by 1834 is again shown by a note in the *Morning Chronicle*[3]: 'He died, and fashion made him an idol; and simpleheaded collectors have humoured folly-fashion to the top of her bent, but the rage did not and has not yet stopped within its legitimate bounds. We could have excused the extravagance had it spent itself on Bonington himself, but his empty shadow has come in for a vast share. Copies and imitations have been multiplied and spread in all directions.'

Bonington's remaining works were sold at Sotheby's on June 29, 1829. Lord Lansdowne, the Duke of Bedford, Sir Thomas Lawrence, Samuel Rogers and William Seguier, Keeper of the King's pictures, were among the bidders. 'The sale', said *The Athenaeum*, 'produced altogether £2250, and the avidity which was shown to possess the simplest work left by the deceased, and the prices to which his most important productions were raised by competition, were quite remarkable. Memoranda for his own use, the mere tracings of the artist, were anxiously bid for and run up to extravagant prices.' Actually, the nominal purchaser of forty lots, including the large oil-painting *Henry the Third of France*, was Colnaghi, acting probably in several instances on behalf of Bonington's father.[4] In 1834 the father felt that time was ripe for a further unloading of his stock and arranged an exhibition at the Cosmoramic Gallery in Regent Street, borrowing several works from noble owners and interspersing his own property. Such pictures as were not on loan were then offered at Christie's in a two days' sale, May 23–24, 1834. After the father's death there was another sale at Foster's in 1836, and the residue of the family collection was dispersed at Sotheby's on February 10, 1838, after Mrs. Bonington's death.

By the end of 1838 over 160 oil paintings, over 300 water-colours, and more than 900 sketches in black-and-white or with slight tint, had passed under Bonington's name through the sale-rooms in England and France.[5] Hundreds more must have still remained in private hands. Even allowing for the fact that his father may have inserted other copies by himself than those openly described as such, Bonington's output must have been prodigious for a

---

[1] Letter on Artists and Dealers, *Library of the Fine Arts*, I, 1831, p. 58.
[2] *Magazine of Fine Arts*, 1833, p. 148.
[3] *Morning Chronicle*, February 21, 1834.
[4] Whitley, 1821–1837, pp. 167, 168.
[5] Catalogues of Sales are given in Dubuisson and Hughes, *op. cit.*, pp. 126–206, and by Shirley, *op. cit.*, pp. 121–158. In the former work the sales are priced.

working life of about eight years; and if he were the author of all the works accredited to him from 1828 onwards he would seem to have been superhuman. The sum total includes palpable forgeries, copies, and imitations, and sometimes the genuine work of such painters as Louis Francia, James Holland, William Wyld, William Callow, W. R. Beverly and others, executed in a close similarity to the Bonington manner. The exhibition of *Pictures and Drawings by Richard Parkes Bonington and his Circle* held by the Burlington Fine Arts Club in 1937 was startling and instructive in its juxtaposition of originals, counterfeits, imitations and similarities. In his admirable introduction to the catalogue A. P. Oppé points out that Bonington was so well known both in France and England that great caution is necessary before accepting as Bonington's any work to which his name has not been traditionally attached. He allows that this may not apply to slight sketches; and innumerable slight sketches in the Bonington manner offer a constant and continued puzzle as to their precise authorship. A good instance is the *Dordrecht*,[1] one of the most attractive and accomplished among all the water-colours in the Victoria and Albert Museum. It could be firmly attributed to Bonington on stylistic grounds if there were any evidence that he ever visited Holland; and none exists. And it is unlikely that, if he ever went to Holland, so rapid a worker should have brought back a single subject from a country where so much would have made an instant appeal. Once attributed to Bonington, that brilliant drawing now appears in the catalogue under the heading of 'Unknown Painters'. The *Bridge of St. Maurice, Valais*[2] shows how mystifying and unexpected Bonington can be. Many would have assigned that drawing to Harding or Callow, if it were not on paper watermarked 1823 and authenticated by W. J. Cooke's engraving, published in 1828. Then there is *The Quay*,[3] once catalogued as Bonington, and honoured by a colour reproduction in Dubuisson's book. It is now assigned to Holland or Roberts.

If we now look more closely into the technical aspects of Bonington's work, we find that he began by following Girtin and Francia, or Girtin through Francia, in the use of low tones. Typical of his early period is *The Church of S. Gilles, Abbeville*.[4] He continued to follow Girtin and Francia in choice of subject, Girtin in the combination of architecture and landscape, Francia in coast and shipping themes. At the outset of Bonington's career there is no trace of the brilliant colour and individual brushwork which were to become so characteristic, but from the start his work depends upon breadth and directness. In most of his landscape work Bonington tried to preserve the crystal clarity of his first washes. There is an enviable sureness in his work. He possessed, in Huet's words, 'le génie de l'aperçu—un aperçu fin et juste de la Nature'. He took a delight in his actual surroundings, without any wish to delve below the surface or elicit any hidden meaning.

When Bonington passed beyond the immediate influence of Francia, his colour became thinner and more fluid as he adopted a more picturesque naturalism. In his later phase he

[1] V.A.M. 1808–1900.
[2] V.A.M. P.27–1934.
[3] V.A.M. C.A.I.–14.
[4] V.A.M. P.26–1928.

180

began to use stronger colour, to employ body-colour, and to adopt more technical devices. Those steps can be seen if we compare his *Church of S. Gilles, c.* 1820, his grey *Fishing Boats*[1] a year or two later perhaps painted with more fluid colour, and his *Sunset in the Pays de Caux*, 1828,[2] rather florid in colour, and worked largely in body-colour, with high lights scraped out.

In his later landscapes and in his figure work it was his emotional appeal as a colourist which won the admiration of the French. His colour notes have a resonance and translucency which in other hands might have come perilously near to crudity. Alike in his architectural drawings, e.g. the *Institut from the Quays, Paris*,[3] and in his landscapes, e.g. *Sunset in the Pays de Caux*, he searches for an opportunity to introduce a touch of red or crimson. What saves him from the charge of overstatement or facile picturesqueness is that he knows how to combine cold notes of grey with his warmer and more positive tones, crisp and flickering strokes with his steady washes. Bonington is a master of soft undertones. Where others put a touch of vermilion in an emerald setting, Bonington used rose madder in subtle contrast with a pearly lucency like that of platinum or old pewter, a glowing ash in a fire gone cold, achieving his purpose by few devices. His singing touches of colour, diffuse their effect throughout the design. Oppé[4] has said that, 'If a picture is merely vaguely atmospheric, it is most probably a copy or an imitation. Bonington at his best is a master of instinctive detail, giving each incident its proper tone and position for light and life and rhythm.' In all of his figure subjects it will be noted how the white high lights are perfectly placed and how the figures are often partly shadowed so that there may be eloquent patches of light and warm tints.

The life and rhythm of the form depend also upon Bonington's brushwork. For architecture, landscapes and figures alike, from about 1824 he uses the fine point of a brush in quick bold strokes of line or hatching, as other artists use pen or pencil, to give structure and accent. The method was not his own invention, for we find it in Turner, Holland, Callow, J. F. Lewis and others. Those brush lines—lines rather than strokes—used with consummate skill, are eminently characteristic of Bonington, and it is the deliberate use of this method which makes his work so easy to imitate. All the same, no other painter has approached Bonington in the use of what has been aptly described as his *touche coquette*.

Another technical device—again not his own invention, but used by him with superlative effect—is his manner of laying a broken granular wash of coruscating colour. The brush is charged with almost dry colour, and the side of it is dragged broadly across the paper. Sometimes, in Bonington's case, it is lifted at the end of a stroke so as to leave a comet-like shape of colour, becoming more and more broken till it ends in a series of clustered points. No one has known better how to use the rough surface of paper to catch these glittering points, and how to scumble a stipple of dry colour so as to leave innumerable

---

[1] London, Wallace Collection.
[2] London, Wallace Collection.
[3] B.M. 1910, 2.12.223.
[4] Burlington Fine Arts Club, *Bonington and Circle*, Exhibition, 1937. Introduction by A. P. Oppé, p. 10.

gaps or interstices of white paper. He used this device for his clouds, his waves, his landscape foregrounds, for the texture of a building or a costume.

The use of line-drawing with a brush and the dragging of colour are the two main characteristics of Bonington's technique. Another feature is his constant practice, from about 1824 onwards, of applying gum (probably gum arabic) as a varnish. It is interesting to note that in 1824 Varley began his practice of varnishing his drawings with copal. In both cases the thin coating of gum was used for the purpose of giving depth and transparency to shadows. Typical examples by Bonington will be found in the Wallace Collection, notably *The Antiquary* and *The Letter*, both painted in 1827. It may be suggested that this use of a gum varnish and his increasing use of body colour were consequent upon his growing attachment to oil-painting. When, in his water-colours, he obtained his high lights by leaving bare paper or using transparent colour, and then worked with lavish body-colour on his darker passages and shadows, he must have found that the result was jumpy, as such a combination must inevitably be. And so he strove to restore transparency to the heavy and opaque darks by touching them with gum. The process had been barred as far back as 1809 by the Old Water-Colour Society, and by 1824 Bonington should have known—or Copley Fielding and other English friends should have warned him—that gum, so applied (his own drawings are proof) tends to darken, blister and crackle.[1] But, like so many other artists of his period, Bonington was trying to key up his water-colours, particularly his figure subjects, so that they might vie with oil-paintings. Possibly his segregation in Paris and his close contact with artists working in oil, induced him to abandon the purity of his native tradition and to pile up colour and obtain glitter by means of varnish. In his historical subjects he unites transparent washes and touches with the more solid impasto obtained by body-colour and by scumbling and glazing. While he may put in a head with touches of pure colour—always with clean brushwork and never stipple— he loads costumes and background with a rich potency of body-colour enhanced by gum. To express pomp his colour had to be high-flavoured and Rubens-like. A picture such as *The Antiquary* shows a hybrid and meretricious result that is certainly very near to oil-painting.

In his architectural drawing Bonington's pencil line is sparkling and brilliant, full of verve, finely expressive of detail; his crowds and single figures, dashed in with skilful economy of touch, display an animated piquancy. On the other hand, his work shows throughout a weakness of perspective, which is one of the characteristics which distinguish his drawings from those of Prout, Holland, Pritchett or Scarlett Davis, all of whom were far more conscious of the rules of perspective and their importance in a drawing of a street scene. When the authenticity of drawings ascribed to Bonington is a matter of dispute, one can almost argue that if the perspective is without flaw, then some other draughtsman should be considered. Bonington in 1828 and Callow in 1864 made water-

---

[1] For the full text of the O.W.S. resolution and the disadvantage of varnish in water-colours, see Vol. I, part I, p. 38.

colour drawings of the *Leaning Tower, Bologna*[1] almost from the same spot. Though the Bonington drawing is infinitely finer than the Callow subject it is distinctly weaker in its treatment of perspective. Admirers of the lovely architectural drawings made by Bonington in France and Italy are apt to ignore what is an obvious failing. Ruskin went straight to the point when he said that if the young genius had learned the first rules of perspective, and never seen either Paris or Venice, it had been extremely better for him. Bonington excels as a colourist, with a colour sense supported by brilliance of execution and by knowledge of the value of sudden contrasts and subtle combinations. It is an error, however, to place his pencil drawings of architecture above those of Holland, David Roberts or Callow. An architectural sky-line in a Bonington drawing is vastly inferior to a sky-line by Prout.

Thomas Shotter Boys follows close, and with no great interval, in the wake of Bonington. More than any other painter he absorbed and developed Bonington's manner both in drawing and colour. How close he comes is proved by the fact that a drawing of *Rouen*,[2] which was catalogued as a Bonington at the Royal Academy Exhibition of British Art in 1934 and at the Burlington Fine Arts Club exhibition of *Bonington and his Circle* in 1938, has now been firmly assigned to Boys. Although I feel the *Rouen* may be taken as an outstanding example of Bonington's brilliance and dulcet clarity of colour, his fine manipulation of a grey sky and the shadows which it casts, the figures, singly or in groups, being put in with the apparent minimum of effort which is characteristic of his work, yet it is so close to the signed drawing by Boys of *The Seine and Tuileries*[3] that the new attribution to Boys may well be right. This difficulty arises with other drawings, particularly when, as is so often the case, they repeat a Bonington subject. One could be justified in giving the authorship to Bonington of *Town in Normandy* (St. Omer) assigned to Boys in the catalogue of the F. J. Nettlefold collection.[4] In the same collection was the *Garden of a French Chateau*, 1832, by Camille Roqueplan.[5] This and two drawings by him in the Whitworth Art Gallery show the powerful imprint made by Bonington on the work of French artists of his day.

Thomas Shotter Boys (1803–1874), was born about nine weeks later than Bonington, at Pentonville, Islington. At the age of fourteen he was articled to George Cooke, the engraver, and in 1825 went over to Paris, where he found extensive employment from French publishers for his engraved work. According to the account (apparently based on information given by the artist himself) in Henry Ottley's *Dictionary*,[6] he 'formed an intimacy with Bonington, who persuaded him to leave engraving and take to painting. Accordingly he studied under this distinguished painter till his death blow, a *coup de soleil* received while

[1] Bonington–Wallace Collection; Callow–V.A.M. F–52.
[2] Manchester University, Whitworth Art Gallery.
[3] Coll. Alfred Powell (N.A.C.F.).
[4] F. J. Nettlefold Catalogue, I, p. 26 (plate).
[5] F. J. Nettlefold Catalogue, IV, p. 266 (plate).
[6] 1866 Supplement to Bryan's *Dictionary*.

sketching one day on the Seine.' Callow, who was closely associated with Boys in Paris between 1831 and 1834, denies that Boys was Bonington's pupil, saying that if this had been the case he would certainly have known.[1] Callow's memory may have been at fault; his autobiography was written nearly seventy years later. He allows, however, that Bonington and Boys were acquainted, and though the word 'pupil' need not be stressed, it seems obvious that Boys not only knew Bonington but, during a friendship of three years, must have constantly watched him at work and assimilated his methods.[2]

From 1832 to 1873 Boys exhibited at the New Water Colour Society and at the Royal Academy in 1847 and 1848. He became an associate of the former body (now the Royal Institute) in 1840, and a member in 1841.[3] While producing a steady annual output of water-colours he retained his early interest in reproductive work. Like Bonington, he saw the possibilities of lithography, and from 1835 onwards contributed many lithographs to Baron Taylor's grandiose publication of the *Voyages pittoresques et romantiques dans l'ancienne France*. On his own account he made full use of the lithotint process discovered or improved by C. Hullmandel. Joseph Nash,[4] in his *Architecture of the Middle Ages*, published in 1838, acknowledged his own obligation to Hullmandel and added that 'by the introduction of the stump in place of the point for making large tints, the Artist has an instrument placed in his hands, which for freedom and rapidity of execution, admitting at the same time both of the greatest delicacy as well as force of tint, nearly equals the pencil (i.e. brush) in colour—indeed it may almost be called painting on stone'. When Boys published in 1839 his *Picturesque Architecture in Paris, Ghent, Antwerp and Rouen*, with its twenty-six superb colour-plates, he dedicated it to Hullmandel; and certainly the lithographs, with their cool, simple and direct colouring are remarkable facsimiles of Boys' drawings. The clear transparency of the artist's colour, and in particular the sparkle of white in the blue sky, are admirably rendered. No wonder that a writer in the *Quarterly Review* at the end of 1839 expressed surprise that twenty-six prints, equal in effect to water-colour paintings, could be bought for so small a sum as eight guineas.

Boys followed up the success of this volume by publishing in 1842 his *Original Views of London As it Is*. In the London series the plates were not printed in colour from several stones, but were coloured by hand in close facsimile of the artist's own colour washes. The main part of the edition was in monochrome, and the coloured sets are extremely rare. His colour lithographs touch the high-water mark of reproduction. Each of them is potentially a water-colour, so cleanly is it finished, so sparkling is its appearance. In his later years Boys suffered so much neglect as a water-colour painter that he was driven to the production of hack work as an engraver. Among other work of this nature, including woodcuts for Blackie's *History of England*, he etched two plates for Ruskin's *Modern Painters*, and in

[1] *William Callow, an Autobiography*, 1908. Callow's own association with Boys is referred to in another chapter.
[2] The B.M. has a drawing on tracing paper by Boys of Bonington's studio, 1952. 5.10.9.
[3] H. Stokes, 'Thomas Shotter Boys', *Walker's Quarterly*, No. 18, 1925, gives a list of water-colours exhibited by Boys.
[4] Joseph Nash, *Architecture of the Middle Ages*, 1838.

184

Stones of Venice was responsible for all the lithographs after Ruskin's drawings and for the etched outlines of some of Lupton's mezzotint plates. Ruskin wrote of 'copies from my pen drawings etched by Mr. Boys with a fidelity for which I sincerely thank him', but though in *Modern Painters* he lavished praise upon Prout he ignored Bonington and Boys, whose water-colours he must have known. His word was law, and as Stokes[1] says, 'the word was not given, and Thomas Shotter Boys passed slowly into oblivion'.

Of his technique little need be said, except that he followed Bonington's manner, even to the use sometimes of body-colour and of touches of red which give an effective accent in conjunction with greys and greens. He was masterly in his draughtsmanship, quite on a level in this respect with Holland, Stanfield and Roberts, and in perspective drawing was far superior to Bonington. His figures, singly or in crowds, have liveliness and truth but individually are not so spirited as those of Bonington. They conform harmoniously with his buildings, making spots of rich colour, and costume details are as carefully studied as the little details of hanging lamps that swing above the Paris streets. He enjoyed the play of light on porches and façades and steeples of Portland stone and on the flat surface of stucco, white or yellow. If we look at the best of his work with its close resemblance to Bonington in subject and style, and if we remember that Boys' working period covered fifty years as against Bonington's eight, it seems impossible to account for the comparative rarity of water-colours by Boys except by assuming that very many, particularly his earlier drawings, have been absorbed and submerged in Bonington's *œuvre*. Nevertheless there is a reasonable number of authentic works by Boys in our public galleries. In the Victoria and Albert Museum are nine drawings including the *Paris: View near the Pont Royal*[2] and *The Pont Neuf, Paris,*[3] which show his atmospheric sense and his extreme ability in handling architectural themes. The British Museum has five water-colours, among them two exceptionally large drawings of *Paris from the Seine*[4] and *Boulevard des Italiens, Paris*[5] (Pl. 174). It is interesting to note that all the drawings in these Museums bear dates from 1829 to 1838, and that the best of Boys' drawings in the Musée Carnavalet, Paris, are of the same period. Obviously the immediate influence of Bonington stirred Boys to his finest efforts such as the *Hotel de Ville, St. Omer*[6] (Pl. 171) of 1832. It may be added that Boys signed his drawings T.B. as well as T.S.B., and in many cases his full name may be found on boxes, carts, mural advertisements and other unexpected places in his drawings; once, like Turner, he puts it on a pavement tomb.

Here may be mentioned Ambrose Poynter (1796–1886), who studied water-colour painting under Thomas Shotter Boys. Born in London, Poynter entered the office of John Nash, the architect, in 1814 and remained with him for about five years. From 1819 to

---

[1] *Op. cit.,* p. 37.
[2] V.A.M. A.L.5745. } A study of these drawings was made by E. Beresford Chancellor, 'Boys in Paris', *Archi-*
[3] V.A.M. P.25–1922. } *tectural Review,* LX, 1926, pp. 89–91.
[4] B.M. 1870. 10.8.2363.
[5] B.M. 1870. 10.8.2364.
[6] Newcastle upon Tyne, Laing Art Gallery.

1821 he travelled in Italy and elsewhere, and on his return set up as an architect in Westminster. He became a foundation member of the Royal Institute of British Architects, and first provincial inspector to the Government School of Design. He was the architect of many government schools and several London churches. As an accomplished draughtsman and as a pupil of Boys, he was naturally a close adherent of the Bonington school; indeed, he may well have been more influenced by Bonington himself than by Boys. It may be said in evidence for this that three of his water-colours, lent by C. F. Bell, were included in the Burlington Fine Arts Club's exhibition of pictures and drawings by Bonington and his Circle in 1937. These attractive drawings bore dates from 1834 to 1836 and in the Victoria and Albert Museum is *The Church of St. Gervais, Paris*,[1] 1836. Ambrose Poynter was the father of Sir E. J. Poynter, P.R.A.

Reference may also be appropriately made at this point to Henry Liverseege and Alfred Elmore, who closely followed their contemporaries, Bonington and Delacroix, in the painting of history and romance. Their work deals almost entirely with genre scenes or with the portrayal of characters from Shakespeare and Scott. Henry Liverseege (1803–1832) was born at Manchester a year later than Bonington. In 1827 he came to London and exhibited at the Royal Academy, the British Institution and Suffolk Street. He liked a spice of humour in his subjects, *Brigands at a Table in a Cave*, 1831,[2] is typical of his not very lofty style. He died at Manchester and a series of mezzotints from his works was published in 1832–1835 with the title, *Recollections of Liverseege*.

Alfred Elmore (1815–1881), a much better artist, was born at Clonakilty, County Cork. Coming to London he entered the Royal Academy Schools. He completed his training in Paris and Munich, spent two years at Rome, exhibited at the Royal Academy from 1834, and in due course won membership as a painter in oils. His oil-paintings of historical and genre subjects, by which he is represented at Dublin, Birmingham and other public galleries are dull and uninspired. In spite of his Academy rank he would have passed into oblivion if a large number of his water-colours had not come to light through the dispersal of a family collection in 1933. These drawings probably represent his early work in Paris, where he must have arrived soon after Bonington's death. They are not signed or dated, and as Oppé cynically remarks, have 'now enriched the cabinets of France, England and, no doubt, America with many a "Bonington" and "Delacroix"'. Several of them, however, remain under their authentic name, having been secured by the British Museum and the Victoria and Albert Museum.

Elmore's figure subjects of knights and fair ladies, pages and dwarfs, kings and priests and troubadours, show the extent to which he had absorbed Bonington's treatment of similar themes. As in Bonington's case, a study of Italian Masters, of Titian, Tintoretto and Veronese, contributed towards his love of rich colour and of rhythmical design. His *Two women on a balcony*[3] or *Lady and Troubadour*[4] are sufficiently akin to Bonington's *On the*

---

[1] V.A.M. 256–1894.
[3] V.A.M. E.881–1933.

[2] V.A.M. 101–1894.
[4] Once in the author's collection.

Balcony, Venice,[1] and might almost suggest an attribution to Bonington if Elmore's other work in water-colour had remained unknown and unidentified. His drawings are swiftly executed in bold washes with a full brush, and nearly always with a slight admixture of body-colour. He seems to have had a liking for unusually tall upright subjects, the height about twice the width. Though in his figure subjects Elmore aims at Bonington's lusciousness of colour, his church interiors, such as *Worshippers*,[2] are often worked in a most pleasant harmony of greys and grey-greens. His landscapes, such as *Landscape: river and water-meadows*[3] and *Landscape with Terrace and Fountain*[4] are brilliant impressions, snatched from nature with a clear eye for the values of tone and atmosphere. If Elmore's romantic medievalism is sometimes sentimental, it is never cheap, like Cattermole's, and it reveals a sincere emotional quality. His figures are not just puppets like those of Liverseege; if he is not quite a Bonington, he takes a high place in our Water-Colour School.

A painter of the Bonington circle, whose work in water-colour has become somewhat obscure, is John Scarlett Davis (1804–1845). Many of his drawings have been attributed to Bonington, A. W. Callcott, David Roberts and others. Exhibitions in the Hereford Public Library, 1926, the Cotswold Gallery, 1933, and the Burlington Fine Arts Club, 1937, did much to distinguish his work and to revive his reputation. Scarlett Davis (or Davies) was born at Leominster and was the second son of James Davis, silversmith and watchmaker. There is in existence a small drawing of Leominster by Scarlett Davis, in which a porter carries a bale inscribed, 'James Davies, Watchmaker, Lemster'. In 1816 he was sent to school in London and won a silver palette from the Society of Arts for a pen drawing of *The Coronation of Henry VI*. He studied painting under W. P. Witherington and mezzotint-engraving under Charles Turner, and in 1820 became a student in the Royal Academy schools. For several years he was occupied in painting oil portraits, landscapes and architectural interiors, and published some lithographs of Bolton Abbey in 1829. In 1830 he went to Paris to paint an interior of the Louvre for Lord Farnborough, and remained in France for nearly two years. His first journey to Italy was made in 1833; for the greater part of 1837 he was at Amiens, painting views in the Cathedral; from there he went to Munich and travelled through the Tyrol to Venice; the winter of 1840 was spent at Amsterdam; in 1841 he went to Rome, and returned by way of Florence, Genoa and Lyons. On some of his earlier journeys he was accompanied by James Holland; a *French Peasant Woman*[5] by Davis once belonged to Holland. Redgrave's tale that David 'married early in life, became drunken and of demoralised habits—got into prison and died before the age of thirty' is both cruel and false. He was a well-educated man, abstemious in his habits, married happily at the age of twenty-eight, and when travelling abroad in his later years was invariably accompanied by his wife and his two daughters; he died in 1845, largely through overtaxing his strength in painting a nine-foot canvas.

[1] Liverpool, Lady Lever Art Gallery.
[3] V.A.M. E.882–1933.
[5] Coll. Mr. D. L. T. Oppé.

[2] Once in collection of the author.
[4] Once in collection of the author.

Judging from the few water-colours which can be definitely assigned to him, Davis is one of the closest followers of Bonington both in technique and subject. His exquisite draughtsmanship is shown in pleasantly tinted drawings such as *Porte St. Martin, Paris,* 1831[1] (Pl. 179), *The Louvre,* 1836,[2] and a charming little interior, *French Monastic Church.*[3] Other interiors, showing admirable fusion of architectural and atmospheric interests, are *North Transept, Canterbury,* 1836,[4] and *St. Eustache, Paris.*[5] The latter, in itself complete, is a study for part of an oil painting which was exhibited at the Society of British Artists in 1834. How brilliant, how Rembrandtesque, Davis could be in his draughtsmanship is shown by an *Interior of St. Michael, Munich*[6] (Pl. 180), in pen and sepiaw ash. Through the mixed pattern woven by the later topographers the work of Scarlett Davis shines like a thin streak of gold.

W. R. Beverly painted coast scenery and seascapes in the fluid luminous manner of Bonington and occasionally used the dry and dragged brushwork which is a prominent feature in Bonington's technique. It seems not unlikely that some work by Beverly lies hidden among the vast number of drawings impossibly ascribed to the greater man. William Roxby Beverly (*c.* 1811–1889), artist, scene-painter, actor, actor-manager and theatre proprietor, was born at Richmond, Surrey. William Roxby, his father, was a north-country actor and theatrical manager, who assumed the surname of Beverly in honour of the minster town in Yorkshire. The son, judging by his varying signatures, was uncertain whether his name should be spelt Beverley or Beverly. In his quite early days young Beverly lived in a stage-atmosphere and among scene-painters; as a boy, he was often taken out to sketch by Clarkson Stanfield. His first engagement as a scene-painter was at the Theatre Royal, Manchester, in 1830. He was in London from 1839 to 1842 at the Old Coburg (later the Victoria) Theatre, where his brother-in-law was manager. In 1842 he returned as principal scenic artist to the Theatre Royal, Manchester. Then we find him as principal artist at the Olympic in London, and after some years at the Princess' from 1846, he moved with Charles Matthews and Madame Vestris to the Lyceum. In 1853 he was appointed scenic director at Covent Garden, and in 1854 started on his thirty years of artistic successes at Drury Lane. He was the real inventor of the transformation scene, a thrilling feature of all Pantomimes in Victorian days. When at the Princess he took on, as an assistant, George Augustus Sala, then eighteen years old and a budding artist, afterwards to be described as the Prince of Special Correspondents and the First Journalist of Europe.[7] Sala remained with him through 1846, and followed him to the Lyceum.

All through the crowded years of his theatrical work Beverly found time for paint-

[1] V.A.M. 2944–1876.
[2] Cardiff, National Gallery of Wales.
[3] Cardiff, National Gallery of Wales.
[4] Manchester University, Whitworth Art Gallery.
[5] Once belonging to C. E. Hughes.
[6] Coll. Mr. D. L. T. Oppé.
[7] R. Straus, *Sala; the Portrait of an Eminent Victorian,* 1942, pp. 48–50.

163 'Rouen from Bon Secours'
Coll. Mr S. Cope Morgan $5\frac{1}{4} \times 8\frac{5}{8}$: 133×219 *Water-colour*
Richard Parkes BONINGTON (1802–1837)

164 'Fishing'
Coll. Dr W. Brockbank $6\frac{1}{2} \times 9$: 165×228 *Water-colour*
Richard Parkes BONINGTON (1802–1837)

165 'Dives—Procession outside a Church'

Liverpool, Walker Art Gallery   12¾ × 15⅛: 323 × 384   *Water-colour*

Richard Parkes BONINGTON (1802–1837)

166 'The Leaning Towers, Bologna'
London, Wallace Collection   9¼ × 6¾ : 240 × 170   *Water-colour*
Richard Parkes BONINGTON (1802–1837)

167 'The Church of S. Ambrogio, Milan'
London, Wallace Collection   8⅝ × 11¼: 220 × 290   *Water-colour*
Richard Parkes BONINGTON (1802–1837)

168 'Coast Scene with Shipping'
Aberdeen, The Art Gallery and Regional Museum   5¼ × 7¼: 133 × 183   *Water-colour*
Richard Parkes BONINGTON (1802–1837)

169 'On a Venetian Balcony'
Glasgow, Art Gallery and Museum
$6\frac{3}{8} \times 4\frac{3}{8}$: 162 × 111
Water-colour with some body-colour
Richard Parkes BONINGTON (1802–1837)

170 'Odalisque'
Paris, Musée Du Louvre
$7\frac{1}{2} \times 5\frac{1}{8}$: 190 × 130
Water-colour
Richard Parkes BONINGTON (1802–1837)

171 'Hotel de Ville de St Omer'
Newcastle upon Tyne, Laing Art Gallery $20\frac{1}{2} \times 16\frac{1}{4}$: 520 × 412   *Water-colour*
Thomas Shotter Boys (1803–1874)

172 'L'Institute de France'

Coll. Mr & Mrs Paul Mellon $13\frac{3}{4} \times 10\frac{1}{4}$: 349×261 *Water-colour*

Thomas Shotter Boys (1803–1874)

173 Church of St. Alphage, Greenwich

B.M. 1944.10.14.23   8⅛ × 6½: 207 × 166   *Water-colour*

Thomas Shotter Boys (1803–1874)

174 'Boulevard des Italiens, Paris'

B.M. 1870.10.8.2364   14¾ × 23⅝ : 374 × 398   *Water-colour, signed and dated 1833*

Thomas Shotter Boys (1803–1874)

175 'Church of Larchant, near Fontainebleau'

B.M. 1942.10.10.8 $7\frac{7}{8} \times 4\frac{7}{8}$: 200 × 125   *Water-colour, signed and dated 1834*

Ambrose POYNTER (1796–1886)

176 'Don Quixote'

B.M. 1900.8.24.522 $12\frac{5}{8} \times 9\frac{1}{8}$: 320 × 231   *Water-colour*

Henry LIVERSEEGE (1803–1832)

177 'A Peasant with his Cart and Horse'
B.M. 1933.7.11.8 $6\frac{7}{8} \times 8\frac{3}{8}$: 174 × 213   *Water-colour*
Alfred ELMORE (1815–1881)

178 'Landscape and Trees'

B.M. 1933.7.11.5 $5\frac{1}{2} \times 8\frac{1}{4}$: 140 × 210   *Water-colour*

Alfred ELMORE (1815–1881)

179 'Porte St. Martin, Paris'

V.A.M. 2944–1876 $10\frac{3}{4} \times 11\frac{7}{8}$: 273 × 302   *Water-colour, signed and dated 1831*

John Scarlett DAVIS (1804–c. 1844)

180 'Interior of St. Michael, Munich'

Coll. Mr D. L. T. Oppé $10\frac{1}{4} \times 14\frac{1}{4}$: 260 × 363   *Pen and wash*

John Scarlett DAVIS (1804–c. 1844)

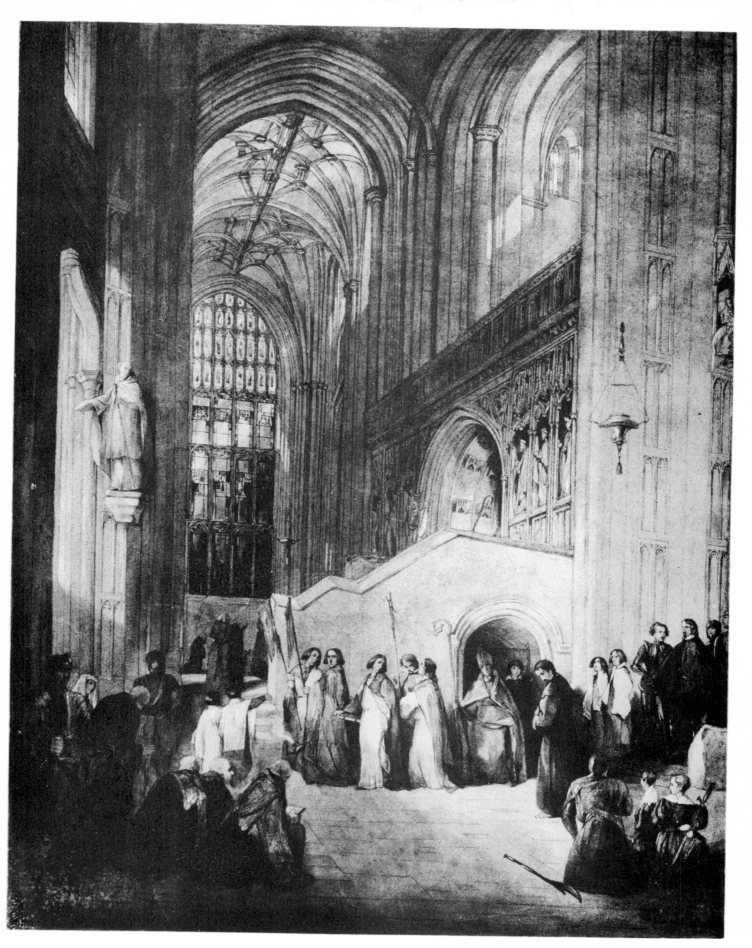

181 'North Transept, Canterbury Cathedral'
Manchester University, Whitworth Art Gallery   15¼ × 11½ : 387 × 292   *Water-colour*
John Scarlett DAVIS (1804–c. 1844)

182 'The Ravine'

V.A.M. P.16–1919   14⅜ × 10½: 374 × 267   *Water-colour*

William Roxby BEVERLY (c. 1811–1899)

ing outdoor landscapes in water-colour. He believed firmly that the scene-painter's studio provided the best possible training for any artist, and pointed out that he himself was the last of the group of men bred and trained in the painting-room of the theatre, a group which included De Loutherbourg, Clarkson Stanfield, David Cox, Jock Wilson, David Roberts, G. Chambers, D. F. Tomkins and J. O'Connor. It was a training which cultivated breadth, atmosphere and directness of touch. Between 1865 and 1880 Beverly exhibited twenty-eight works at the Royal Academy, and the same number at the Dudley Gallery. His subjects were found on the English coast, notably at Scarborough, Sunderland, Eastbourne and Hastings; the Thames and the Lake District, Paris and Switzerland, also provided occasional subjects for his brush. His pencil sketches of architecture, shipping and coast scenery exhibit a deftness and assurance of touch, which brings him into close alliance with Bonington, Callow and Holland. His output as a painter was limited owing to his busy professional life. Examples of his art will be found in the Victoria and Albert Museum and in the Galleries at Bristol, Rochdale and Birmingham. Much of his work must be in private collections, and rarely comes into the sale-room. There can be no doubt that if there were wider knowledge of his radiant and limpid water-colours, with their structure of crisp and finely descriptive drawing, Beverly would have a much higher place than he has hitherto occupied in any history of water-colour. At the moment he is almost forgotten. Nowhere is his training as a scenic artist better used and better shown than in his excellent and original *The Ravine*[1] (Pl. 182), a drawing which alone entitles Beverly to a higher rank than he has ever held.

[1] V.A.M. P.16–1919.

CHAPTER XII
David Cox

David Cox II   William Evans of Eton
Harry John Johnson   William Evans of Bristol

On June 1, 1808, as has already been related, Farington records in his *Diary* that Sir George Beaumont 'reprobated the rage for water colour drawings, but it was said that the passion is subsiding. Haydon said that a gentleman had laid a wager of 20 guineas that in *three years* there will be no Water Colour Exhibition.' That bet was lost, for in the succeeding years water-colour painting flourished as never before or since.

In that year, 1808, the Water-Colour Society had been firmly established for four years, and a new group of artists was coming to the fore. Already Turner and Girtin had extended the possibilities of water-colour far beyond the earlier methods employed by Sandby and his contemporaries. John Varley, as we have seen, had shown the value that lay in powerful washes, in solid blocks of colour. By 1808, then a man of thirty, he held a firm position as a teacher, leader and adviser. The men who were coming of age just before and just after 1808 were promoters of a more unhampered use of colour, more flexibility of method, more understanding of technique. The ways lay open for still further innovations and varieties in approach and in handling; and, as so often in history, the movement and the men coincided. It is of importance to look at the birth-dates of artists whose work is considered separately in this book but who, immediately following after Varley, as a group, helped to make the reputation of our Water-Colour School:

J. S. Cotman	1782	Copley Fielding	1787
David Cox	1783	W. H. Hunt	1790
Samuel Prout	1783	J. Linnell	1792
P. De Wint	1784	C. Stanfield	1793

It is no wonder that, at the beginning of the nineteenth century, with Turner as the leader, water-colour began to exhibit a fresh originality and variety. And it is important that seven of the artists who names appear above were born in the decade 1782–1792, and that Cotman, Cox, Prout and De Wint came into the world within a period of two years.

David Cox (1783–1859), was born in Heath Mill Lane, Deritend, a south-eastern suburb of Birmingham. His father was a worker in iron, a blacksmith and whitesmith, making among other things horse-shoes, gunbarrels and bayonets. It was intended that the son should follow his father's trade, and John Pye, the engraver, made a note: 'When I first knew David Cox he was employed to wield the great hammer at a blacksmith's shop in Windmill Yard, Digbath, Birmingham.'[1] But Cox was not destined for long to see the sparks flying and the glowing metal yield under his blows. Owing to an accident by which he tripped over a door-scraper in the evening dusk, his leg was broken, and while in bed took to copying prints with pen and pencil, and, having a box of paints given to him by a cousin, began to experiment with colour. He was too delicate in any case for manual labour, and his natural proclivity becoming clear he was sent to a drawing-school kept by Joseph Barber. Among fellow-pupils were Charles and Joseph Vincent Barber, sons of the artist, and Samuel Lines. Cox was fortunate in having an excellent master, who could teach him the value of sound composition and the use of clean washes of colour. Making good progress under Barber's instruction, he was apprenticed in 1798 to one Fielder in what was called the 'toy trade', his employment being to make miniature paintings upon lockets, snuff-boxes and similar trifles of fancy work, which called for some ingenuity of design and taste in execution. His term of apprenticeship being abruptly closed by his master's suicide in 1800, young Cox at the age of seventeen got an engagement at the Birmingham Theatre, helped thereto by the same cousin, Henry C. Allport, who had endowed him with his first box of paints. Like David Roberts, who made a similar debut some twenty years later, he even took a small part on the stage now and then. Many other well-known landscape painters besides Cox and Roberts had experience in scene-painting; it is sufficient to mention Sam Bough, De Loutherbourg, G. Chambers, Clarkson Stanfield, W. R. Beverly and W. H. Hunt. At the back of the stage Cox washed brushes and mixed colours for the scene-painters and afterwards spoke of their chief, James De Maria, as being an artist of considerable talent. In the evenings he was still assiduous at Barber's drawing class.

Allowed to try his prentice hand on some side scenes at the Theatre, Cox won favour with his employer, the elder Macready, father of the well-known tragedian, W. C. Macready. There were other provincial theatres under Macready's management at this time, and for about four years young Cox travelled on circuit to Bristol, Leicester, Sheffield, Manchester, Liverpool and other places. A tiff with Macready and the prospect of better employment under Astley, the circus proprietor, brought him to London in 1804. Astley had suffered from several disastrous fires, and in 1804 opened a new and splendid circus at Lambeth, with some scenes painted by Cox. London not only provided him with opportunity, but gave him a wife in the person of his landlady's daughter. Although Mary Agg[2] was twelve

[1] Roget, I, p. 331.
[2] Ragg is the name given by all of Cox's biographers, but Gordon Roe, *Cox the Master*, 1946, quotes evidence that her maiden name was Agg.

191

years older than her husband, their partnership was ideal, and in her sympathetic understanding of her husband and his art she remained a faithful helpmate till her death in 1845.

It was not long before Cox found himself reduced to the painting of scenery for provincial theatres at Swansea and Wolverhampton at four shillings the square yard. He also produced small studies in Indian ink or sepia for sale, through a dealer named Simpson in Greek Street, Soho, to country drawing-masters as 'copies' for their pupils. For these early drawings he found material in sketches made in the outskirts of London and Birmingham, and in 1805, in company with Charles Barber (1784–1854), Joseph Barber's son, who later became President of the Liverpool Academy, he made a journey to North Wales. There he added a mountain scenery to his subject matter, working all the time in outline or with a tint of Indian ink. In 1806 he returned to Wales and tried a little colouring on the spot with 'indigo, gamboge, purple lake and sepia, dissolved in bottles'. The results were 'low in tone but truthful, and somewhat in the manner of Barret and Varley'.[1] About this time he was learning to appreciate the old masters, and bought Pond's chiaroscuro facsimiles of Poussin, Claude and Salvator Rosa; moreover, out of slender means, he was one of the earliest subscribers to Turner's *Liber Studiorum*, the first part of which appeared in 1807. Very happily, too, he resolved to get some lessons from John Varley, to whom he was introduced by Palser, the picture-dealer.[2] After giving him a few lessons, at ten shillings apiece, Varley heard that his pupil was an artist by profession—though Cox modestly declared that he was only trying to become one—and refused to take more of his money.

In 1808, after his marriage, Cox settled in a small cottage at the corner of Dulwich Common, and began the teaching which was to develop into an important means of livelihood. With a vague idea that perspective was covered by his scene-painter's tricks of deceiving the eye of a sitter in the dress-circle, he began by hanging out a card: 'Perspective taught here.' But when an aspiring carpenter and builder came for lessons, Cox discovered that 'perspective' was more scientific than he thought. Deciding that Euclid must be mastered, he bought a copy but was bewildered by the diagrams, and hurled the volume right through the lath-and-plaster wall of his fragile home. Henceforth his drawings contained such perspective as most artists acquire by ocular observation without the aid of science. So severely did he judge himself in his Dulwich days that many a sketch, made while his wife sat beside him reading a book aloud, was put down a convenient grating in the gutter lest she should save it from destruction. In after life he once pointed to a grating in the street, saying: 'Look there. That was the spot where I used to send the

---

[1] N. N. Solly, *Life of David Cox*, 1875, pp. 17 and 18.
[2] Palser was then in Westminster Bridge Road, near Astley's Circus. Later he migrated to King Street, St. James's. Soon after I wrote this, early in 1941, the Palser Gallery was hit by a German bomb and became a gaping cavern. For some years the gallery had been owned by Douglas Thomson, who had a keen and sound knowledge of the early water-colour drawings in which he specialised. Thomson died in March 1941, his death probably accelerated by the shock, on his arrival one morning, of finding his premises and all their contents destroyed.

fragments of my drawings floating down into the Thames.' When out sketching in later days he would sometimes sigh, 'Nature beats me.' But though he was dissatisfied with many of his Dulwich drawings, some of the best were exhibited by Palser and caught the eye of Col. the Hon. H. Windsor, afterwards Earl of Plymouth, who not only took lessons himself but found for his teacher several aristocratic pupils in the West End of London. Before long Cox's charge for an hour's instruction was ten shillings.

Cox exhibited at the Royal Academy from 1805. In 1809 he sent ten drawings to the exhibition of the Associated Artists in New Bond Street. A contemporary critic finds in his work 'a careless haste and sketchiness of finish which betrays the coarseness of scene-painting . . .. There is much truth and force in his pictures; but his skies seem to be composed of the same material as the landscape, and assimilate so exactly with the ground that it is hard to tell where one leaves off and the other begins.'[1] Much the same criticism was repeated by A. J. Finberg,[2] more than a hundred years later, when he wrote that 'Cox's way of slithering over the individuality of objects, of making his rocks as rounded and as soft as his trees and clouds, and his trees and clouds as sharp and hard as his rocks, is irritating to anyone who has learned to use his eyes.' At the time, however, when Ackermann's critic was writing about Cox, his work, though it contains the seed of his later prowess, appears nowadays rather laboured than sketchy; and knowing now what a material element in his work the union of sky and earth was to become, we realise that there was prophetic and unconscious praise in what the critic wrote. If there was one point at which Cox and Constable surpassed even their forerunner, Girtin, it was in their recognition that land and water reflect and echo the sky's gaiety or gloom.

In 1810 Cox was President of the Associated Artists, and exhibited thirty-seven drawings, but held the chair for one year only; the Society collapsed in 1812. In the spring of that year Cox took his wife and his three-year-old son to Hastings, and made many studies on the foreshore, where generations of artists have painted boats and net-sheds against their background of cliffs, as well as inland views of Battle Abbey and other places in the neighbourhood. In June, together with Luke Clennell and his friend C. Barber, he was elected a member of the Old Water-Colour Society, and was a constant exhibitor there till 1859. According to Graves' *Dictionary of Painters*, he showed no less than 849 works. The total may seem large but, as Basil Long points out, 'it was eclipsed by the indefatigable Copley Fielding, whose exhibits numbered 1671, and by Henry Gastineau with a score of 1310, while William Collingwood Smith passed the thousand mark with 1064. Cox holds the fourth place.'[3] Varley was a runner-up with 739, and Prout with 560. Up to the last year of his life Cox made an annual visit to London, to see this and other exhibitions, even when in 1847 he found that: 'London is quite Babylon; the WHIRLING of carriages quite bewilders me and makes me giddy.'

[1] R. Ackermann, *Repository*, I, p. 493; III, p. 433.
[2] A. J. Finberg, *English Water Colour Painters*, 1905, p. 143.
[3] B. S. Long, 'David Cox', *O.W.S. Club*, X, 1932/1933.

In 1814, Cox, judging by the figures given by Solly, must have been making a few hundreds a year, but the prospect of a fixed post and an assured income led him to accept an appointment at the Military College, Farnham, where Sir William Napier, author of the *History of the Peninsular War*, was one of his pupils. 'Farmer Cox', as Turner called him, liked neither his courtesy title of Captain, with a servant to wait upon him, nor his irksome duties largely concerned with map-work, nor the fact that residence in college separated him from his wife and his son. He threw up his job within twelve months, and at the end of 1814 took a post in Miss Croucher's seminary for young ladies, in Widemarsh Street, Hereford. His pay was £100 per annum for teaching twice a week during term time, and he was required to instruct his pupils not only in landscape drawing but drawing of heads and hands, and 'bronzing on white wood in Chinese fashion', apparently some form of lacquer work. He taught at the Hereford Grammar School from February 1815, at Miss Croucher's from October 1814 to the end of 1819, and also at another similar establishment kept by Miss Poole. As a drawing-master he profited by the long holidays which schools enjoy, took private pupils at 7s. 6d. to 10s. 6d. an hour, among them Joseph Murray Ince, and found time to paint landscapes among the lovely scenery of the rivers Lugg and Wye, and to tour in Wales and other parts of the country.

Part of his time was employed in the preparation of a practical book for his own and other students, *A Treatise on Landscape Painting and Effect in Water-Colours*, published as a folio volume by S. and J. Fuller, of Rathbone Place, in 1814; there were several subsequent editions, one at least as late as 1841. Besides twenty-five plates of soft-ground etchings the volume contains fifteen aquatints in colour, so highly finished by hand as to give almost the effect of an original drawing. In the accompanying text he indicated the principles of close touch with Nature to which he adhered throughout life in his own practice. 'The principal art of Landscape Painting', he said, 'consists in conveying to the mind the most forcible effect which can be produced from the various classes of scenery; which possesses the power of exciting an interest superior to that resulting from any other effect; and which can only be obtained by a judicious selection of particular tints, and a skilful arrangement and application of them to differences in time, seasons and situation.' The *Treatise* was followed by a smaller oblong quarto, *A Series of Progressive Lessons in Water-Colours*, published in 1816. By 1823, this had reached a fifth edition, with larger and improved aquatint illustrations. The list of pigments which are recommended for the student's use may afford an indication of the master's own practice. They are: 'Gamboge, Light Ochre, Light Red, Lake, Vermilion, Burnt Sienna, Vandyke Brown, Prussian Blue, Indigo, Black and Sepia'. The success of these books caused their author to follow them with another 'drawing-book of studies and landscape embellishments', *The Young Artist's Companion*, issued by Fuller in 1825. In this there is a coloured frontispiece and, at the end, twelve colour aquatints of still-life and landscape, engraved by T. Sutherland and R. Reeve; these too are highly finished in water-colour. A revised *Progressive Lessons* was issued in 1845; and it is interesting to note that the pigments are varied by the addition of Indian Red and Brown Pink and the substitution of Cobalt for Prussian Blue.

Though he ceased to teach at Miss Croucher's in 1819, Cox continued to reside at Hereford till 1827, when, feeling the insistent call of London, he removed to 9 Foxley Road, Kennington Common. One of his first pupils here was Henry Cole, afterwards Sir Henry Cole, K.C.B., first Director of the South Kensington, now Victoria and Albert, Museum. In the Museum, with many other drawings by Sir Henry, is a copy of a Cox drawing made by him about 1827. An article on 'David Cox as a Drawing Master',[1] by H. M. Cundall, throws valuable light on Cox's methods at this period and on his proficiency and zeal as a teacher. During his residence at Kennington one of his pupils, Miss Frances Carr, was about to make a sketching tour on the Rhine, and for her benefit Cox made a series of sketches, accompanied by notes, dealing with possible compositions and with arrangements of light and shade. Cox had never seen the Rhine, but he judged from paintings by various artists that 'there is mostly a tameness and littleness in the foregrounds of Rhenish scenery; perhaps the hills and castellated knolls are too fanciful in form to be picturesque and not sufficiently large or distant to possess grandeur, unless under extraordinary effects of light and shade. It will, therefore, be desirable to lessen their distinctness against the sky in some parts and to throw the strongest emphasis upon the foreground. Under morning and evening effects this will meet the case in nature, but at mid-day you will need to watch and avail yourself of every passing shadow and every happy combination of objects rich and powerful in colour, to contrast strongly with the detail and variety of forms in the distance.' Cox's drawings of purely imaginary scenes and effects, made for Miss Carr, display all the sparkle and brilliance with which he could render his ideas in a small rapid sketch. Eight of these sketches are reproduced in the *Art Journal*, three of them extremely well, in colour. Cox's accompanying notes on contrasts of light and dark, the placing of the main masses, the fixing of points of interest, the importance of giving breadth instead of dwelling upon insignificant objects, the value of foreground shadow to throw interest upon the distance, and so forth, are sound on theory and full of enlightenment as to his own methods.

Both from Hereford and from his new home at Kennington, though much of his time was occupied in teaching, Cox contributed to the Old Water-Colour Society drawings of subjects found in the home counties and their southern coast, and especially on the Thames from Battersea to the river's mouth. With these are a considerable number of views in North Wales, and a few of Bolton Abbey, Kenilworth, and Lynmouth in Devon. In 1826 he made his first trip to the Continent, making sketches in Holland and Belgium, chiefly in pencil as he glided along canals, the colours being sometimes noted in writing. His brilliant sketch, dated 1830, of *Dort Boats*,[2] his *Dort, from the Sea*,[3] 1831, and *Ghent*[4] are

---

[1] *Art Journal*, 1909, pp. 177–179.
[2] Manchester, City Art Gallery.
[3] Once belonging to Mr. Frank Gaskell.
[4] Manchester University, Whitworth Art Gallery.

among the fruits of this journey. In 1829 he took his son with him on a visit to Paris, calling upon Francia, Bonington's teacher, at Calais, and also sketching at Boulogne. James Holland related how Cox, not knowing any French, made himself understood by the aid of his pencil. 'If he desired an egg, he drew one; and in order to make a waiter understand that he wanted it boiled, he represented the shell broken, and put a touch of colour to indicate the yolk.' In Paris, with a sprained ankle, he sat in a cab and made drawings of the Tuileries, Palais de Justice, the Church of Saint Eustache, Chambre des Députés, Rue St. Honoré, Montmartre, the bridges over the Seine, and many other subjects. His final visit to Paris was in 1832, and memorable among drawings made on this occasion or on his earlier visits to France are sketches of pier and harbour, of stormy skies and tossing seas, at Calais, Boulogne and Dieppe. Some of his most fresh and sparkling drawings were the vintage of these French tours, and of the thirty-six drawings which he exhibited in 1833, thirteen were of French subjects, views at Calais predominating.

During these years he had also paid constant visits to Windsor and to North Wales, made an excursion to Yorkshire in 1830 (Bolton Abbey called for further visits), was in Derbyshire with his son to make drawings of Haddon Hall in 1831, and in after years was to stay again at the 'Peacock' in Rowsley. Then, from 1835 to 1847, he produced an important series of drawings made round Lancaster and the neighbouring district, mostly of the Ulverston Sands, with market folk, some on foot, others on horseback or in carts, crossing the wet sands at low tide among varying effects of rain and cloud, mist and sunshine.[1] A third group, belonging to this culminating period, consists of drawings made from sketches on the Wharfe, of Bolton Abbey and Park, Barden Tower, and the neighbourhood.

The year 1836 is of note because Cox then discovered a special kind of paper, which he used afterwards for so many of his drawings. Getting some sheets by chance (it was an ordinary wrapping paper) he found from the Excise mark that it was manufactured at Dundee, and ordered a ream of it. A paper of similar nature and quality, produced today, is always known as 'David Cox paper'. Solly gives the following account:

It was in the year 1836 that Cox first met with the rough Scotch wrapping paper which on trial turned out to be very unabsorbent of colour when used for water-colours, producing a powerful effect. The surface is hard and firm, the paper being made from old linen sailcloth well bleached. Cox obtained the first few sheets by chance at Grosvenor and Chater's, and on showing it to S. and J. Fuller, their traveller ascertained from the Excise marked stamped upon it, 84B, that it was manufactured at a paper-mill at Dundee, North Britain. There a ream was ordered for Cox, and it was some time before it could be obtained. On its arrival he was rather surprised to find that it weighed two hundred and eighty pounds, and cost eleven pounds. However, Mr. Roberts was willing to share in the purchase, and after some years Cox rather regretted that the quantity ordered had not been larger, as he was never able to obtain the same quality of paper again. . . .

---

[1] One of these drawings was *Crossing the Sands*, exhibited in 1835, and sold at Christie's in 1876 for £1732 10s. 0d. The largest price, it may be said here, ever paid for a drawing by Cox was £2950 at the Quilter Sale in 1875, for his *Hayfield*. This, with seven other water-colour drawings and twelve oil-paintings by Cox, was sold at Christie's on November 9, 1945, from the collection of Edward Nettlefold. The price dropped to £630.

Some of Cox's most powerful studies and drawings after this period were painted on the rough Scotch paper. It gave the texture he required, and suited his peculiar mode of rapid work with a large brush, charged as full as possible with very wet though rich colour. It enabled him to obtain *power* at once. The paper was very thick, not quite white, with here and there little black or brown specks. In the landscape parts these specks were of no consequence, but they looked out of place in the sky. On one occasion being asked what he did to get rid of them, he replied, 'Oh, I just put wings to them, and then they fly away as birds!'[1]

This is supplemented by Hall[2] who constantly watched Cox at work. On one occasion he saw several unusually large and prominent specks in the sky of a drawing, and said: 'Whatever will you do with these great specks, Mr. Cox? I can see them half across the room! "Specks! Specks!" he replied. "Why, put a couple of wings to them and turn them into birds." And soon a breeze was whirling and tossing the rooks above the tree-tops.' Cox rightly took it as a high compliment when a lady said: 'How fond you are of painting *wind*, Mr. Cox!'

The raw material used for the paper varied very much from time to time. The main ingredients were ropes, sail-cloth, bagging and similar waste matter, and it was made on machines long since scrapped.[3] The chief features were that the fibres composing the pulp were unbleached, making the paper tend towards a warm grey in tone, and that the surface was rough, and therefore helpful to Cox in his broken colour and high lights. As the paper was only intended by the makers for the purpose of wrapping, little attention was paid to a regular sizing or to the elimination of mineral and other foreign matter which found their way into the pulp; hence the specks. On one point, but an important one, I must differ from Solly, and suggest that he was entirely wrong in stating that the rough Scotch wrapping paper, was 'very unabsorbent of colour'. The paper, being lightly sized or half-sized, though not so absorbent as blotting paper or so-called 'plate' paper, must have absorbed colour much more freely than the highly sized Whatman and other papers which were in vogue. On sized paper, especially on the popular 'hot-pressed' paper, unless it is well soaked in water, colour will remain to a large extent on the surface, with a hard edge to the washes. Cox paper, on the other hand, absorbs the colour without first being made damp, and if the washes are put on with a full brush there are no hard edges. Another point is that colour laid on Cox paper in a full wash soaks at once into the paper and dries out much lighter than, without experience, the painter would expect. That was realised by Cox when he worked on this paper 'with a large brush, charged as full as possible with very wet though rich colour'. And the fact must not be overlooked that, before his discovery of the Scotch paper, Cox preferred what he called 'my old favourite cartridge' to a hard sized paper,[4] and cartridge paper is fairly absorbent, though not to

[1] Solly, *op. cit.*, pp. 80, 81.
[2] W. Hall, *Biography of David Cox*, 1881, p. 148.
[3] Some of my information has been kindly given by Mr. H. L. Dixon, of Messrs. L. S. Dixon & Co., Liverpool, makers of modern 'David Cox' paper, to which they have tried to give all the characteristics of the original, with greater purity and regularity of the materials used. Unfortunately their office at Liverpool, which contained valuable records about the paper used by Cox, was destroyed by enemy action in 1940.
[4] Letter to his son in 1845, quoted by Solly, *op. cit.*, p. 131.

the same degree as 'Cox paper'. Solly says little about the colour of the paper, but its warm, greyish tone, as well as its absorbency, is conducive to quick rendering of atmospheric effects, and gives an artificial 'quality' which has enabled many users of modern Cox paper to disguise their own shortcomings and to win credit beyond their deserts. More than one critic has described its effect as 'flattering'. It is astonishing how a space of Cox paper, of quite grey tone, can look a pure white when surrounded by colour, especially by blue.

About 1839 Cox was drawn to oil-painting. A strong impression was made upon him by the work of W. J. Müller, a painter equally effective in water-colour and in oil, who had just returned from the East with a freight of pictures. Müller was nearly twenty years his junior, but the veteran did not hesitate to place himself under the younger man's tuition and to watch him at his easel. Müller's rapidity and breadth of execution made a special appeal to a painter who had come to believe in taking short cuts. Cox, who saw Müller wipe out a small picture with which he was dissatisfied and get well on the way with another inside twenty-four hours, was amazed at his dexterity. After watching Müller's brilliant handling in oil, Cox was heard to murmur: 'You see, Mr. Müller, I can't paint.' But he understood the ease of Müller's work in oil. 'There is not half the trouble with oils as with water-colours', he wrote to his son in 1843. 'I should never again touch water-colours only for my honour and duty to the Society I belong to. I have had more plague with two of my large drawings this year than I should with twenty in oil.' From then onwards Cox painted still more frequently in oil, selling his pictures at low prices from £5 upwards. Here it may be added that, out of seven water-colours sold by him in 1837, the largest was priced at 35 guineas, but none of the others exceeded 6 guineas. Though he never obtained high prices for his work (only once did he obtain £100 for a painting, his large oil of *Rhyl Sands*) he made a regular and steady income by his teaching, and in the course of his long life managed to save £12,000, a substantial sum in those days.

His desire to devote himself to oil-painting was one main reason for his determination to leave London again and to hand over much of his teaching work to his son. So in 1841 he leased Greenfield House in the village of Harborne, then about two miles from his native Birmingham. He had won a modest competence by forty years of earnest work and was now able to get free of pupils, to paint without intermission in water-colour and in oil, and to make sketching tours among his favourite haunts in Yorkshire, Derbyshire, Lancashire and Wales. From 1844 to 1856 he made an almost annual visit to Bettws-y-Coed. This little village, then almost unknown to the tourist, became his Mecca, and the district round about was as dear to him as Barbizon to Millet and Dedham to Constable. His biographers give a detailed and anecdotal account of Cox's life at Bettws and of the episodes and incidents shared by him and his cronies at the Royal Oak Inn. 'For a long succession of summers', writes Hall[1], 'the famous artist might have been seen—with ruddy complexion, a figure by no means slight, and clad in a suit of sober grey—lounging before

[1] Hall, *op. cit.*, p. 80.

198

the Royal Oak, smoking a cigar, or issuing from its then humble portal, sketch-book in hand, after an early breakfast, to jot down with rapid strokes the leading features of some lovely "bit" near at hand, or to trace the lines of some more extensive subject, more distant, in the Lledr valley, or by the side of the beautiful Conway river.' In 1847 Cox painted a sign-board for the Royal Oak. This sign, a fine oil-painting of a noble tree, was framed in 1861 and inset over a fireplace indoors. To so much value did it once attain, that n 1880 it became the subject of a lawsuit carried finally to Sir J. Bacon, the Chief Judge in Bankruptcy. The landlady, for whom Cox painted the sign, claimed it as her own property, and Lady Willoughby D'Eresby, owner of the freehold, held that it was a fixture of the house.[1] On a final appeal in 1881 the freeholder won, and the sign still hangs within the hotel for all to see.

In 1850 Cox produced one of his most celebrated works, *A Welsh Funeral, Bettws-y-Coed*, the scene being one which he witnessed after the death of a consumptive girl in the village. Cox made many studies for this picture, painting several versions in oil and in water-colour.

In 1855, on his attaining the age of 72, friends and admirers raised a subscription for presenting him with his portrait, and he was persuaded to make a journey to Edinburgh and give sittings to Sir John Watson Gordon. It is a fine portrait, even if the President of the Royal Scottish Academy did contrive to make Cox look more like an Elder of the Kirk than 'Farmer Cox', the genial landscape painter. The portrait ultimately came into the possession of the Midland Institute at Birmingham and is on permanent loan to the Corporation Art Gallery, which possesses the largest collection of works by Cox. An excellent portrait of Cox, by W. J. Wainwright, more intimate and friendly than the ceremonial one, belongs to the Royal Water-Colour Society.[2] On September 22, 1856, a year after the Watson Gordon portrait was painted, Cox signed his name for the last time in the visitors' book at the Royal Oak. In G. P. Boyce's *Diary*, under the date November 17, 1857, is the following entry[3]:

> Burt and I went round to see poor old Mr. Cox at Harborne. I found him not much altered in the face, but much pulled down and enfeebled and his breathing very difficult. He did not recognize me at first sight, but recalled me to mind after a few words had passed. He asked me several questions as to when I had been to Bettws, whether I was continuing painting and where I had been to. He still continues painting, mostly in oil, and in idea and in colour often his present things are as fine as the old. He showed me several things he had in hand. One a reach of the Thames with a whole rainbow in a grey sky, very true and effective; another a mountain and lake scene, etc. He was very warm and friendly in parting, saying ,'God bless you', several times. He pointed out the portrait of himself by Watson Gordon, which was presented to him and which hung on the wall, saying he had to go to Edinburgh on purpose.

Cox became feebler year after year, till there came a night in 1859, when he looked round his sitting-room studio and, as he mournfully shut the door, said: 'Good-bye,

[1] *The Times*, September 17, 1880, etc.
[2] Reproduced in *O.W.S. Club*, X, 1932/1933, pl. I.
[3] *O.W.S. Club*, XIX, 1941, p. 26.

pictures! Good-bye, I shall not see you any more.' He died, a few days later, on June 7, 1859. As E. V. Lucas wrote[1]: 'Cox may have been disappointed to receive so little praise, but he was a sensible and sincere man who found his chief joy in serving art, both by day and night (painting much by lamplight) and what time was over he spent in cheerful, equable quietude. His nature was sweet and kindly, and his heart the abode of a simple, deep piety.'

In teaching water-colour painting Cox impressed upon his pupils the value of the preliminary drawing, and in looking at his own swift and fluent work in colour we are apt to overlook the structural basis of his work in pencil or charcoal. In his *Treatise* he urged his pupils to attain proficiency in the art of pencilling, saying that 'he who devotes his time to the completion of a perfect outline has more than half finished his piece'. In his drawing, as in his colour work, he arrived at what he wanted with directness, speed and purpose. He works with a flickering, jerky line, broken still more by the roughness of the paper; his trees, his mountains, his foregrounds of rocks or heather, are drawn with crisp, angular touches that suggest movement and vibration, the flutter of light and shade. It is never a flowing line. Whether he uses pencil or brush strokes, Cox's work displays the same dynamic flutter. How near he comes to Constable, when working in black-and-white, is shown by a series of his monochrome drawings in the Ashmolean Museum, particularly one with a water-mill on the left and a waggon entering a pool.

As to his technique when using colour we have the contemporary evidence of those who watched him at work. From Hall's biography, we learn that for many years he used colours made up in hard cakes, washing them out into large or small saucers. Later he adopted the moist colours of modern invention. In the course of time he increased the three or four colours used on his excursion into Wales in 1806, adding cobalt, vermilion, light red, yellow ochre and brown-pink. Emerald green (Cox was a little apologetic about it) was kept for an occasional touch on draperies or the mossy coating of a stone or tree trunk. Hall describes how, on a wet day, Cox mixed saucers of colour, and worked on three or four drawings at once, painting with great rapidity and with large sable brushes. Many of his outline sketches, he adds, were drawn with charcoal or black chalk, which was absorbed by his colour or allowed to show through. Body-colour he studiously avoided, except perhaps for a sharp touch on figures and for bright lights in a foreground. G. P. Popkin supplied to Solly his recollections of Cox's method of work, and particularly a demonstration which Cox gave of 'how I always sketch'.[2]

He worked with a large swan quill brush, and *slopped* his colours with water (he used the old-fashioned *hard* cake colours, but of extra size, in the usual japanned tin sketching box). He was jealous of wearing his brush, and if any colour was obstinate from having been baked in the sun, he rubbed it with his finger. His tints were very fluid, but not watery, and he explained that, by working with a full brush, the colours never dried *dark*, as they would do if the brush were half dry. I noticed that tints which looked very dark dried quite light. His system was constant *repetition of touches* till the effect was produced, being very careful that the preceding touches

[1] E. V. Lucas, *The British School*, 1913, p. 42.
[2] Solly, *op. cit.*, p. 174.

200

were dry. He seldom washed his tints after laying on, as he liked to see each touch defined, not softened off; he said it gave spirit and character to the sketch. 'But mind,' he said, 'I am only showing you how *I* sketch. These are three sketches I have just done for you, they are not *drawings*. I have done the same thing for other people, and they have sold them afterwards as my drawings.'

In 1851 G. P. Boyce, sketching at Bettws, was proud when Cox came up and shook hands. During some days of August Boyce watched Cox at work, and records in his diary[1] that 'Mr. Cox uses cobalt for blue sky, French blue and black for shadows of distant ones [clouds?] and black for do. of those at higher angles, cobalt and light red for distance, indigo, gamboge and purple lake for middle distance; brown-pink is merged into foregrounds. He uses Prussian blue in bright greens. . . . Mr. Cox uses purple lake and gamboge for foliage in middle distance, and indigo, gamboge and burnt sienna for do. in foreground.'

In a letter of advice to his son, written on November 14, 1842, Cox himself speaks of his methods of working in water-colours[2]:

Try by lamplight a subject in charcoal, and don't be afraid of darks, and work up to the subject throughout with charcoal in the darks, middle tint and half, with some very spirited touches in part to give a marking. When you have done all this, have your colours quite soft, and colour upon the charcoal. Get all the depth of the charcoal, and be not afraid of the colour. When you look at it by daylight, and clean it with bread, you will find a number of light parts which have been left where the colour would not exactly adhere over the charcoal. For a distant mountain I have used cobalt and vermilion; and in the greyer part I mix a little lake and a small quantity of yellow ochre with the cobalt. In the middle distance I work each part separately; in fact, something like mosaic work. The foreground the same, taking care to leave the reflected lights clear for a distant cool or bluish tint. I use very similar colours for the middle distance—for green, indigo, lake and gamboge, with its varieties; occasionally, for the rocks, cobalt, vermilion, or yellow ochre, and sometimes lake instead of the vermilion. In the foreground I use indigo and vandyke brown, and indigo and brown-pink—sometimes add sepia to the indigo and brown-pink. I use for the grey in the sky cobalt and vermilion; and for the more neutral grey, cobalt and light red.

These contemporary accounts may be supplemented by the admirable analysis which C. E. Hughes[3] makes of Cox's manner as shown particularly in the important collection left by John Henderson to the British Museum, consisting mainly of Cox's more carefully elaborated works:

The Henderson collection consists almost exclusively of these, and as the majority of the spurious Cox drawings which one sees in sale-rooms are attempts in this manner, a somewhat minute analysis of it may not be out of place here. The effect of the greater part of a typical drawing in this class seems to have been produced by the rapid manipulation of brush strokes, averaging about one inch in length. Distant mountains were put in with long, sweeping lines, broadly horizontal, laid over a preliminary wash, but in the parts of the picture which lie nearer to the spectator the lines become shorter and more varied in their direction, until a magnification of

[1] 'Extracts from Boyce's Diaries 1851–1875', *O.W.S. Club*, XIX, 1941.
[2] Solly, *op. cit.*, p. 119.
[3] C. E. Hughes, *Early English Water Colour*, 1950, p. 64.

the middle distance would reveal a series of curving touches which marvellously combine to form the rounded surfaces of trees and hills. High lights on these would be carefully rubbed out. The foreground shows the same treatment on a larger, more defined and more intelligible scale, and the strokes are frequently put over irregular washes. Here the high lights, despite Solly's statement to the contrary, are quite often in body colours. A good Cox drawing of this sort, though it has a great appearance of being dashed off, contains a very large amount of brush-work. It is done quickly and spontaneously, but it is no matter of just a few minutes. There is evident rapidity of handling, but there is no carelessness.

It is important to note the extent to which Cox managed to keep his touches of different colours pure and separate in what he described as 'a sort of mosaic work'. In this he differs entirely from Varley and Cotman who worked in even, flat washes, and from De Wint who mixed his colours, running one into another. Cox's wandering, straggling, but harmonious touches, moving with constant rhythm like ripples on the sea, bring him into close companionship with Constable as a forerunner of the French Impressionists. Cox and Constable anticipated them in seeing the value of 'broken colours', of irregular, vibrating touches to suggest the palpitation of light, the movement of the wind, the glint of the sun. Cox's close kinship with Constable has never been fully realised, but we have only to look at his *Rhyl Sands* (*c.* 1850)[1] (Pl. 188) and then pass to Constable's seashore sketches to realise how parallel they are in spirit, outlook and actual handling. In *Rhyl Sands* Cox plants you on the shelving shore among dumpy figures buffeted by the blustering wind; you smell the tang of the sea and hear the splash of the waves while you watch the horseman venturing into the surf. It is a drawing in which he has gathered together and piled up all his suggestions of nature by adding image to image, detail to detail, in a multiplicity of crisp telling touches that seem to trip lightly off the end of his brush. It is pure impressionism leading right away, like a Constable painting, from the ordinary conceptions and conventions of the time. In *Lancaster Sands*[2] (Pl. 189) (it was once in the collection of W. S. Ellis, sold at Christie's in 1877) there is less vibration of touch, but the same spirit of outdoor freedom and freshness. The two figures bend to the wind as they hurry across the wet sands before the lowering clouds burst into rain.

The figures in *Rhyl Sands* and *Lancaster Sands* are characteristic of Cox and the wide appeal of his work undoubtedly depended upon his acceptance of human interest as an integral part of his landscapes. He filled what he called his 'hand-books' with endless memoranda and sketches of incidents and people. His figures are always lively, well placed, and appropriate to their environment; but it may be noted that they are almost invariably squat and rather legless; his women, dumpy, beshawled, many-petticoated; he loved a touch of bright colour on fluttering kerchief or shawl; his men, short, stunted, bandy-legged; his horses and ponies low and sturdy. In this respect he never threw off the influence of Varley, whose figures are always thick-set and dumpy. Children and their pleasures afforded great delight to Cox. Both of them loved the young and loved also their

[1] V.A.M. P.30–1930.
[2] Coll. Mr. and Mrs. Paul Mellon. The *Rhyl Sands* in the Manchester Art Gallery treats the same subject in oil with slight variations.

flicker of movement, their bright faces and gay clothing, flying kites or gathering black-berries, or listening to the song of a lark, the boys fishing or bathing in shady streams.

Cox's work as a whole may be said to show three broadly marked and distinctive manners.[1] His early style was hard and dry, based on the work of the topographers in its neutral colour and tight handling; and then from Barber and from Varley, he learned the value of clean washes and of thoughtful design; and his painting began to show more freedom and facility, though it was still heavy and low in tone. In his second or middle period, roughly from 1820 to 1840, he showed a broader outlook and greater command of his materials. After his initial yielding to Varley he never looked to right or left for aid in his art and painted with unaffected singleness of purpose. His colour was more powerful; he was more buoyant in his manner and in his use of broken colour for the rendering of transient effects. Solly[2] describes the drawings of this middle period as pure in colour, with a considerable amount of finish:

Those especially painted for albums are highly finished, and, although they have perhaps less breadth than those very early works which, in their neutral low tones and flat washes, resemble the works of John Varley and the early efforts of Prout, they gain on the other hand in brilliancy and atmosphere. . . . Cox objected, even when finishing highly, to the use of body colour, and on the rare occasions where he transgressed this rule, it was merely for small and sparkling touches of light. He worked with a large swansquill brush, full of colour, putting on his tints very wet, so that they dried full and powerful, but without blackness. To give richness he hatched over again with repeated touches, but he avoided washing over the tints when once applied, as he considered that the plan of washing made the effect weak and poor. The range of his colour-box was of the simplest description, and the rarer pigments sometimes used by artists were unnecessary to him. When half-finished or even when more advanced, his sketch or drawing would sometimes look flat and tame as he reserved the full power of his pallet for the finishing, when his consummate knowledge enabled him with a few powerful touches on the figures, and a rather dry brush dragged over the foreground, to give point and force to the whole, and clear up the half-shadows, putting everything into its right place.

During this middle period he produced hundreds of works which won for him his greatest popularity, which possessed the elements of realistic finish which appealed to patron and dealer in Cox's own time.

In these days we are inclined to find Cox's chief contribution to water-colour art in his third period, when he was producing with mercurial ease, often on his rough-toned paper, large generalised aspects of nature, with vigorous and intrepid execution, an easy sweep and variety of touch. In such works he saw only breadth and simplicity, and was never distracted by multiplicity of detail. His figures are less defined and have greater movement and action. He was working, as he put it, 'in my own clumsy way', producing drawings which his contemporary critics described as 'coarse' or 'blotty': to quote one of

[1] Gordon Roe's (op. cit., p. 93) expansion into nine 'periods' is of great interest to the student of Cox, but one feels that it is unduly subtle and analytical. Roe has to admit 'overlapping' between one period and the next. On a similar system, Turner's art could be divided into some twenty 'periods'.
[2] Solly, op. cit., p. 75.

them, his 'blurred and imperfectly realised execution was a severe lesson to the lovers of the neat and conventional'. Thackeray was more understanding when he wondered 'where the secret is, and how, with strokes so rough, and on such small pieces of paper, air and distance, storm and sunshine should be described so lucidly'.[1] It is upon the large impressionism of these later drawings, with their imagination and racy vigour, that the real reputation of Cox will rest. But what we have to remember is that those three periods are not strictly defined; they dovetail into each other. Cox did not abandon one manner when he took up another somewhat different. Mood, paper, daylight, lamplight, hurry, leisure, a hundred reasons, made him shift his ground and vary his procedure. In the case of many of his drawings it would be rash to assign them, without evidence, to a definite period of his life. Some of his sketches made in France, for instance, would be unhesitatingly accepted as work of a more mature period, if we did not know their date. Such drawings are timeless; they were made at fever heat, with an intensity of awareness, from the scene before his eyes. By these, too, he will be remembered. All that having been said, we may consider more closely the progress of his work as shown by individual examples.

As an example of Cox's early drawings in his first period may be taken a very delicate *Old Westminster*,[2] 1805, not unlike a Girtin in its sensitive touch. One of the finest, his *Scene In Windsor Park*[3] (Pl. 184), signed and dated 1807, shows his kinship, at this early stage of his career, with Varley and with Turner of Oxford, another of Varley's pupils. The dominant note throughout, in sky and trees, is blue; and the drawing has probably been preserved in a portfolio, for there is no sign of fading in the indigo used for the trees. In many drawings made by Cox in later years, while he was at Hereford, the blues have faded out, leaving prevalent tones of brown and russet grey. Few drawings, in which indigo have been used have so kept their freshness as the *In Windsor Park*. This brilliant and surprising drawing has a depth of colour, a close-knit compactness, which is in strong contrast with the loose, feathery, atmospheric work of his later drawings. It follows closely an earlier drawing of *Kenilworth*, made about 1807; there is a sketch for it in the Birmingham Gallery, and a larger version, dated 1830, in the Lady Lever Art Gallery. All of them are based on a landscape by Gaspar Poussin which Cox copied in Simpson's shop. The disposal of the trees and the curving flock of sheep, is the same in each. The Windsor drawing is less constrained in its treatment of foliage; there is more movement in the figures; the foreground shows a typical brook; the beginnings of the later Cox are coming into view. What is of special interest is that the whole treatment of the distant trees and of Windsor Castle shows clearly the influence of Varley and proves that the Varley lessons were probably given in 1807 or 1808. Some of Cox's earlier works of this period, which remained unsold, were simply covered up with fresh pieces of paper so that he might save the cost of a new stretching-frame. Several of his most characteristic productions have been found hidden

[1] W. M. Thackeray, *Sketches after English Landscape Painters* (*c.* 1850).
[2] Birmingham, City Art Gallery, 347–07.
[3] V.A.M. P.24–1948.

in this way; sometimes three or four were stretched one over the other on the same board.[1]

Still dark and heavy in its treatment, and careful in its finish, but a powerful drawing in the early manner, is *The Old Bridge, Bridgenorth*,[2] of 1809. The *Lugg Meadows, near Hereford*,[3] may be dated about 1817 and shows a similar solidity and closeness of study. Cox has still not abandoned his heavy treatment of foliage in the classical manner of Poussin. Though he was no imitator of Turner, his friendship and close contact with him about 1820 were, I think, factors in the loosening of his style and his adaptation of a higher key of colour. Solly also records that he was an admirer of Bonington and copied two of his drawings; this, again, together with his association with Bonington's master, Francia, may have persuaded Cox towards a greater clarity of colour. There is bolder colour in his *Water-Mill, North Wales*,[4] presumably the *Water-Mill at Festiniog* exhibited in 1821, but it still suggests Varley in its direct washes, its forcible contrast of light and shade, its conventional tree breaking the skyline of hills. Cox was actually not using more than the ten or so colours which he recommended in 1823, but he was becoming less heavy-handed and getting more power from his colour.

Soon after 1820 Cox entered his second period. He achieved detachment and developed his own style with broken colour, repetition of short swift touches, concern with rapid changes of light and atmosphere, sense of the earth spinning underfoot and dizzy clouds racing in the sky. Girtin and Cotman and De Wint filled their drawings with things that have the beauty of time, aged trees, and churches, buildings and barns, rich in a mellowness inherited from the past, warm with the patina spread over them through long cycles of years. But whereas gravity and calmness and serenity brought out the best in these artists, it was the change and caprice of Nature which inspired Cox to his happiest efforts. He was at his best on one of those days when the wind makes the kites fly, and the sails of windmills go merrily spinning, and birds seem to be tossed by gusty winds. Cox enjoyed the movement of clouds above his head, the stream of sunshine in April showers, the fleeting gleam and shadow chasing across the heath. It is of this middle period that Ruskin wrote, over a hundred years ago.[5] After a dictum that 'style is the saying of a particular thing in the only way in which it can possibly be said', he adds: 'The recollection of this will keep us from being offended with the loose and blotted handling of David Cox. There is no other means by which his object could be attained; the looseness, coolness and moisture of his herbage, the rustling crumpled freshness of his broad-leaved weeds, the play of pleasant light across his deep heathered moor or flashing sand, the melting of fragments of white mist into the dropping blue above; all this has not been fully recorded except by

[1] A *Windsor Castle* by Cox was purchased by Mr. J. Allnut in 1812 at a sale of works belonging to the ill-fated Associated Artists, and when his collection was being prepared for sale in 1861 two other drawings were found underneath it attached to the sketching-board. De Wint's *Cricketers* was discovered in the same way by Vokins.
[2] Once belonging to W. Craig Henderson.
[3] V.A.M. 74–1885.
[4] V.A.M. 3028–1876.
[5] *Modern Painters*, vol. I, sec. I., chap. VII.

him, and what there is of accidental in his mode of reaching it, answers gracefully to the accidental part of nature herself. Yet he is capable of more than this, and if he suffers himself uniformly to paint beneath his capability, that which began in feeling must necessarily end in manner. He paints too many small pictures, and perhaps has of late permitted his peculiar execution to be more manifest than is necessary. Of this, he is himself the best judge. For almost all faults of this kind the public are answerable, not the painter.'

That is a perfect contemporary summary of Cox's greatness, and his weakness, and the cause of it. During much of this middle period Cox toiled in his studio to please the public, with scores of drawings made from conventional ingredients—the wind on the heath, the foreground pool fringed with burdock and reeds. Or he was teaching, when his method was to sit down and, in one or two lessons, demonstrate the making of a water-colour to a pupil. At first, the pupil retained the drawing; later, Cox kept it himself to sell. Or, as we have been told, he would work indoors, on a wet day, at three or four drawings simultaneously. 'I keep on at my water-colours', he wrote in 1845, 'a little each morning while my room is getting warmed, and then work at my oil until dark. At lamplight at my water-colours again.' He was unable to hold in check the onward sweep of productive mechanism, Cicero's *motus animi continuus*. Like Varley, he was never able just to rest and meditate, awaiting the instant spur, the sudden flash, that seems to come from some outward source of compulsion to the artist. Samuel Butler[1] in his *Notebooks* expresses it with enviable simplicity of statement: 'Do not hunt for subjects, let them choose you, not you them. Only do that which insists on being done and runs right up against you, hitting you in the eye until you do it. This calls you and you had better attend to it, and do it as well as you can. But till called in this way do nothing.' No wonder that as a result of all the humdrum cogency, there were days when the fine edge of Cox's knowledge and perception became dulled and tarnished by habit. No wonder that at times his work was hackneyed and commonplace. Not that his work was ever downright bad, being saved by his gift of picturesque painting, his comprehensive and ubiquitous knowledge. The huge collection at Birmingham is permanent witness that he produced for his patrons and clients a mass of trite though accomplished drawings, and that only a limited number have the thrust of insight, the moment of penetration, which can make his work so individual and so delectable. Outstanding are some of the drawings made on the Ulverstone sands, where he found subjects that gave him freedom to enjoy the bigness of skies, the movement and reflection of figures in shallow water. Fine examples are *Crossing the Lancaster Sands*[2] or *Lancaster Sands*.[3] *River Scene with Anglers*[4] (Pl. 186) remains in my memory as a drawing which is radiant, sunny, alive, possessing all the dewy freshness and vigour of Cox at his best. There are the same qualities of freshness, fine design and vibrant life in the large *Hayfield*.[5] Among many

[1] Samuel Butler, *Notebooks*, 1930, chapter VII, p. 105.
[2] Burnley, City Art Gallery.
[3] Coll. Mr and Mrs. Paul Mellon.
[4] B.M. 1958, 7.12.335.
[5] F. J. Nettlefold cat., op. p. 146.

206

moorland scenes *Near Carnarvon*[1] is memorable. The *Barden Tower, Yorkshire*,[2] 1836, and *Dryslwin Castle, Vale of Towy*,[3] of about the same date, are typical drawings of high quality.

These and many other exhibition pieces, as opposed to sketches, help to build up Cox's high reputation, but he was a much better artist in his outdoor sketches and in the dashing products of his final period, when he achieved his full importance as a stylist and proved his power. Many of the small sketches were probably made in Cox's 'hand-book'. A good example is *Dieppe Pier*,[4] only seven by nine inches in size, with its dashing waves, its wet pier almost part of the sea, its stormy sky, its figures and ships and the birds above them all fluttering and tossing in the wind. Closely akin to it in subject and treatment is *The Old Pierhead, Liverpool*.[5] There are many architectural studies which compare with those two sketches in their spirit and brilliance, some of them made during Cox's visit to Paris in 1829. A perfect example of this type is *The Porch of St. Philip's Church*,[6] 1836, crisp and brilliant in drawing, simple and glowing in colour, masterly in what it says and in what it leaves unsaid. Cox could have had no sale for this kind of drawing in the 1830's, though we, with our knowledge of the Impressionist School, can appreciate the merit of this happy shorthand of dots and dashes, with light atmospheric washes of colour, giving so much more life to the scene than the more pretentious methods of so many of his exhibition pieces.

In such sketches and in a few of his more finished works we find the cream of Cox up to about 1840. After that date, and especially, though not exclusively, when he used his rough toned paper, he not only produced still better work, but was more consistent in well-doing. He was free from the drudgery of teaching; he had never suffered from the private chagrin, the actual anxieties of living, which preyed upon the mind of his friends, Samuel Palmer and Cotman; he was free to give rein to his intuitions and better instinct; he was free to flout the public. The man of sixty threw off the shackles when he retired to Harborne in 1841, and for more than fifteen years, until his eye-sight began to fail, worked and painted as though he were living again through a period of untrammelled, adventurous youth. He settled down to those simplifications which, in art, are so much more difficult, and more rare, than serried complexities. With passionate zeal he embarked upon bold ventures which, as Roger Fry[7] says about *Rhyl Sands*, were 'right outside the conventions of his day and prophetic of a quite modern outlook'. He painted the hills of Wales (his *Stone Bridge, Wales* in the Birmingham City Art Gallery is typical) with a new intensity and vigour, as if he were seeing them for the first time. When his friends on the Committee of the Old Society complained that his works had become too rough, Cox made the truthful rejoinder that 'they forget that these are the work of the mind, which I consider very far before portraits of places'. He found other things than the mere traditional and accepted beauty which make the water-colour of the drawing-room. He found in Wales, to quote Sir Frederick Wedmore,[8] 'the truer characteristics of that remote scenery and of its

[1] Once belonging to Mrs. C. P. Allen.
[2] B.M. 1900. 8.24.497.
[3] B.M. 1878. 12.28.52.
[4] Coll. Mr. and Mrs. Paul Mellon.
[5] Manchester University, Whitworth Art Gallery.
[6] Birmingham, City Art Gallery, 557'04.
[7] R. Fry, *Reflections on British Painting*.
[8] F. Wedmore, *Studies in English Art*, 2nd. Series, p. 89.

207

desolate life: the wild woods heavy with rain, the stone-walled fields, the dogged tramp of the cloaked peasant woman over the wet path, the blown shepherd and huddled flock on the mountain sheep-walk. Cox entered into the spirit of that lonely landscape, simple and humble even in its grandeur.'

Apart from Welsh subjects there are many other notable drawings dating from this period. *Flying the Kite*,[1] 1853, in the Manchester Art Gallery was shown at the R.A. Exhibition of British Art in 1934, and it was interesting to compare it with the larger version belonging to Mr. R. R. Leatham of Belfast, for which it was probably a study. Fine though the larger painting is, the sketch with its looser, wetter touches, has a freedom and concentration that suffer a certain decline in the more 'important' studio picture. One could be very happy with either, but I feel that Cox's real heart was in the sketch. *The Frightened Flock*,[2] is one of several versions, dating from 1846 to 1855, of a scene in Old Sherwood Forest. Perhaps the best is that called *Skirts of the Forest*,[3] which once belonged to David Cox junior, having been bought back by his father from Messrs. Agnew. It is swift, direct, expressive in every touch. But all of Cox's later work may be said to culminate in *The Challenge*,[4] (Pl. 190) of 1853. In this noble drawing all the wide moor, the tumbled sweeps of bracken and matted heather are dulled by a flurry of cloud and rain. A lonely bull stamps and with lifted head roars his challenge, as though defying the threatening elements. It is a work which moves us by its power and sincerity. Sir Charles Holmes,[5] a severe critic of Cox's 'raw, brilliant blots and splashes', allowed that in *The Challenge* Cox had his 'moment of real grandeur'. Close beside it, for similarity of concept and for real grandeur, might be placed *The Night Train*, 1849. Under a lurid evening sky the flash and rumble of a train which rushes past the edge of a wild heath have startled a group of horses into a wild gallop. A last flicker of sunlight through the dark clouds is dramatically focused upon the two nearest horses, whose plunging movement is superbly realised. Once owned by F. J. Nettlefold,[6] and there are two smaller versions in the Birmingham City Art Gallery.

Few painters have ever been the victim of so many forgeries and imitations. In 1905 Sir Whitworth Wallis,[7] Director of the Birmingham Art Gallery, drew attention to the most barefaced sales of spurious works by Cox. A young lady used to call at a house, with a pitiful story of being compelled to sacrifice treasures acquired from Cox himself by her grandmother. The swindle was successfully worked all over the West and North of England from Crewe and Hull to Carnarvon and Taunton. Fortunately, within a year the daughter and the father, who was the 'artist', were arrested at Huddersfield and, on

1 Manchester, City Art Gallery.
2 Birmingham, City Art Gallery, 276'25.
3 Once owned by J. M. Harvey.
4 V.A.M. 1427–1869.
5 Sir Charles Holmes, *Constable and his Influence on Landscape Painting*, 1902, p. 208.
6 Catalogue op. p. 138.
7 Letters to *The Connoisseur*, XII, 1905, pp. 55, 186.

208

183 'Westminster from Lambeth'

Coll. Mr & Mrs Tom Girtin $5\frac{5}{8} \times 11\frac{1}{4}$: 143 × 286   *Water-colour*

David Cox (1783–1859)

184 'In Windsor Park'

V.A.M. P.24–1948 $14 \times 19\frac{7}{8}$: 355 × 504   *Water-colour, signed and dated 1807*

David Cox (1783–1859)

185 'Handsworth Old Church, Birmingham'

V.A.M. P.23–1948 $17\frac{5}{8} \times 25: 446 \times 634$ *Water-colour, signed and dated 1828*

David Cox (1783–1859)

186 'River Scene with Anglers'

B.M. 1958.7.12.335 $10\frac{3}{4} \times 14\frac{1}{2}: 273 \times 371$ *Water-colour*

David Cox (1783–1859)

187 'Tour d'Horloge, Rouen'

Coll. Herbert Powell (N.A-C.F.)   13½ × 10: 342 × 253   *Water-colour*

David Cox (1783–1859)

188 'Rhyl Sands'
V.A.M. P.30–1930 $10\frac{1}{4} \times 14\frac{1}{4}$: 261×361 *Water-colour*
David Cox (1783–1859)

189 'Lancaster Sands, Low Tide'
Coll. Mr & Mrs Paul Mellon $10\frac{1}{8} \times 14\frac{1}{2}$: 257×368 *Water-colour*
David Cox (1783–1859)

190 'The Challenge'

V.A.M. 1427–1869 $17\frac{1}{2} \times 25\frac{1}{2}$: 444 × 646   *Water-colour*

David Cox (1783–1859)

191 'A River with Rapids'

B.M. 1923.7.16.14 $12 \times 17\frac{1}{4}$: 304 × 438   *Water-colour*

David Cox II (1809–1885)

192 'The Keeper's Lodge, Hyde Park (Old Cake House)'
V.A.M. D.412–1899 $8\frac{1}{4} \times 11\frac{1}{2}$: 210 × 292   *Water-colour, signed and dated 1835*
William Evans of Eton (1797 or 1798–1877)

193 'Mill at Droxford'
V.A.M. 2990–1876 $13\frac{1}{4} \times 17\frac{3}{4}$: 336 × 450   *Water-colour*
William Evans of Eton (1797 or 1798–1877)

194 'Autumn Landscape, North Wales'
B.M. 1890.5.12.74 $8\frac{5}{8} \times 13\frac{1}{2}$: 220 × 342   *Water-colour*
William EVANS of Bristol (1809–1858)

195 'Jedburgh Abbey'
V.A.M. 585–1870   12½ × 20 : 316 × 507   *Water-colour, signed and dated 1846*
Henry John JOHNSON (1826–1884)

196 'Aloes and Prickly Pears'
Coll. Mr & Mrs Paul Mellon   10¼ × 15 : 260 × 380   *Water-colour*
Henry John JOHNSON (1826–1884)

conviction, received severe sentences of imprisonment. Hundreds of those drawings are probably still accepted as genuine by their present possessors.

About David Cox junior (1809–1885) little need be added to what has been already said of him above. He was instructed in art by his father, was his constant companion, and imitated his father's style. The superficial resemblance of manner calls for the exercise of caution by collectors. He became an Associate of the New Water-Colour Society (now the Royal Institute) in 1841 and a Member in 1845, but resigned in 1846. In 1848 he was elected an Associate of the Old Water-Colour Society, and was a frequent exhibitor. He died at Chester House, Streatham Hill.

Among many painters who in manner were close followers of Cox may be mentioned William Evans (c. 1797/8–1877), known as 'Evans of Eton'. Born at Eton he was educated at Eton College, and studied medicine, but abandoned it for art. He received lessons from De Wint and W. Collins, and in 1818 succeeded his father, Samuel Evans, who had been drawing-master at the College since 1796, and became a house-master in 1840. He was elected an associate of the Old Water-Colour Society in 1828, and a member in 1830. He painted much in Scotland and on the Thames; and among generations of pupils he encouraged good drawing and stimulated taste for landscape. For over a century and a quarter and for four generations, an Evans was drawing-master at Eton. Another Samuel Evans, William's son, held the post from 1854 to 1903, and his son, William Sidney Vernon Evans, from 1893 to 1922, working as his father's assistant from 1893 to 1903.

The cognomen 'of Eton' appears in the Water-Colour Society's catalogues from 1845, when William Evans (1811-1858), known as 'Evans of Bristol', or 'Welsh Evans', became an associate. The latter produced large mannered drawings showing every device of sponging and abrasion.

Harry John Johnson (1826–1884), born at Birmingham, calls for mention in a chapter dealing with David Cox. Johnson was a close friend of his fellow-townsman, and accompanied him on his first visit to Bettws-y-Coed and on other sketching expeditions in North Wales. In his young days Johnson had lessons in the Birmingham Studio of Samuel Lines, a most able teacher. Later he studied under William Müller, and when Müller joined the Lycian expedition in 1843 Johnson, then seventeen, went out in his company. Three volumes of sketches by Johnson,[1] contain drawings made in Lycia, showing his skill in absorbing his master's method—a method of faithful drawing and fluent wash, which, like that of Varley, supplied an ideal course of instruction for any beginner. On his return to London he used to work in the Clipstone Street Studio in Müller's company. Both in his pencil and colour work, Johnson retained the influence of Cox, but still more that of Müller, throughout his life. He was an admirable draughtsman; his studies of boats in particular have high merit; and his sketches in general have a force and vitality not always displayed in his exhibition pieces. From 1845 he exhibited foreign views at the Royal Academy. He was elected an associate of the Institute in 1868 and a member in 1870.

[1] Once in the author's collection.

CHAPTER XIII

Peter De Wint

Every morning of his life, even when on his sketching tours, Peter De Wint read the Scriptures and learned a text by heart or wrote out a prayer before breakfast. We also learn from De Wint's grand-daughter that he suffered from postprandial fits of ill-temper, and Sir Walter Armstrong[1] relates that De Wint was so irritable that all but his most intimate friends used to address him with caution, putting themselves in an attitude of mental defence in preparation for his attack. De Wint lived an even and uneventful life as is shown in a memoir written by his widow,[2] in tribute to her husband and her brother, William Hilton, which is the main source of knowledge about the actual events in De Wint's career.[3]

Peter De Wint (1784–1849) was descended from an old Dutch family of De Windts, who were merchants of wealth and position in Amsterdam. Their coat of arms, consisting of 'Four heads proper blowing four winds', was appropriate, not only to merchant-adventurers who migrated to foreign lands, but to their descendant who was essentially an artist of the open air. Among those forebears a John Peter De Wint won a considerable fortune in New England, and sent his son Henry to Leyden and London to be trained as a physician. In his medical career Henry, having become estranged from his father, drifted in 1781 or thereabouts to Stone in Staffordshire, and there Peter, his fourth son, was born.

From his boyhood Peter De Wint was passionately devoted to drawing, and, in spite of the narrowness of the family means, was allowed to take lessons from a local drawing-master Rogers, who resided near Stafford. His father, with some misgiving, surrendered to his son's desire to abandon the intended study of medicine, and sent him to London in 1802 as an apprentice to John Raphael Smith, the famous mezzotint-engraver, who was the close friend and companion of George Morland. De Wint was following in the footsteps of the

---

[1] Sir Walter Armstrong, *Memoir of Peter De Wint*, 1888.
[2] Harriet De Wint, *A Short Memoir of Peter De Wint and William Hilton, R.A.*, 1900 (privately printed by Miss H. H. Tatlock, the artist's grand-daughter).
[3] Mrs. Tatlock in 1872 gave several important water-colours by De Wint to the Victoria and Albert Museum. By the bequest of her daughter, Miss H. H. Tatlock, six more fine drawings were added to the collection in 1921. The rest of Miss Tatlock's collection was inherited by her friend, Miss Bostock, and on Miss Bostock's death was sold at Christie's in September 1941.

210

great, for both Turner and Girtin, it may be recalled, were employed in their boyhood on colouring prints for John Raphael Smith. In Smith's house in King Street, Covent Garden, he found, as his fellow apprentice, William Hilton, and the two were scarcely ever separated until Hilton's death in 1839. Their work was entirely different in character and subject, but their habits and ideas were very close, and a further bond between them was De Wint's marriage in 1810 to Hilton's sister Harriet. Hilton's parents lived at Lincoln, and it was to be expected that De Wint, marrying into the family, formed an attachment for the city and surrounding countryside. After the marriage Hilton lived with the De Wints at 10 Percy Street, Bloomsbury, until in 1827 he took up his residence at Somerset House as Keeper of the Royal Academy.

In 1806, four years before the marriage, De Wint and Hilton had left the studio of J. R. Smith and lived together in Broad Street, Golden Square. Here they were neighbours of John Varley, six years senior to De Wint, and from him De Wint received much counsel and instruction that must have been most profitable to the younger man. From Varley, no doubt, De Wint absorbed some of his breadth and boldness of technique, and he was fortunate, about the same time, in becoming one of the group of students who frequented Dr. Monro's house in Adelphi Terrace. There he found his chief inspiration in the drawings of Girtin, whose restraint and self-command were the basis of De Wint's earlier work and became the lasting fabric to which he applied later his own superb ornament of colour.

In 1808 he exhibited with the Associated Artists in Water-Colours, and in 1809 became a member. In the same year he worked as a student in the Royal Academy Schools. He exhibited occasionally at the Academy, but most of his work was shown with the Old Water-Colour Society, of which he became an Associate in 1810, and a Member in 1811. The rest of his life is merely a story of domestic happiness, work with pupils, and the yearly visits to his chosen sketching districts. 'I do so love painting', he used to exclaim. 'I am never so happy as when looking at Nature. Mine is a beautiful profession.'

He paid one short visit to Normandy in 1828 but, unlike Cotman, he was disappointed. His subject is always the English scene. Castles, high above valleys and winding rivers; cottages, barns and haystacks nestling comfortably under trees; the rich red of old bricks; cattle pasturing in lush meadowland; church spire or cathedral tower rising above ancient roofs; the illimitable spaciousness of the fens; in all this De Wint found satisfaction.

He began with Lincoln, and anyone visiting the cathedral city and looking at its characteristic admixture of red bricks and russet tiles, with weather-worn grey and yellow stone, will understand its appeal to De Wint, and will recognise how he found there the scheme of colour which runs through all his work.

According to his wife, 'he was partial to river scenery and studied much on the borders of the Trent about Newark and Nottingham; with the Thames too he was familiar and frequently remarked on the different characters of the two rivers, one so bright and sparkling, the other soft and silvery. Rapid streams delighted him much, and the Wharfe, the Lowther, the Dart and others were studied with the greatest intensity. He preferred the North of England, and spent much time in Yorkshire, Cumberland and Westmorland. He was frequently at Lowther Castle. . . . Lancaster was also a place which he greatly admired, and he made many sketches of distant views of the fine old Castle. Bolton Abbey he visited many times and always with increased delight.'[1] He did not visit Wales till 1829 or 1830, but then declared that it was a painter's country. He returned to Wales several times and his last visit was in the autumn of 1835. The castles of Powis, Carnarvon, Conway and Harlech were the subjects of several drawings, as were Gloucestershire and Gloucester Cathedral. The Wye rather disappointed him, though he was much pleased with Goodrich, Chepstow and especially with Tintern Abbey. In Norfolk he spent many happy weeks at Castle Rising, where Colonel and Mrs. Greville Howard in several autumns lent him their house. We hear also of his delight in Ludlow, of visits to Matlock and Haddon Hall in Derbyshire, of an autumn tour in Hampshire in 1843, and of his last excursion to Devonshire in 1848. He was a constant and untiring worker, as we realise from the fact that between 1807 and 1849 he exhibited 326 pictures, and that his remaining works, which were sold at Christie's in 1850 (excluding the hundreds retained by his widow), came to a total of 493.[2]

As a water-colour painter he obtained modest but adequate reward, and never had to complain of a lack either of pupils or patrons. As a painter in oil he received neither credit nor reward, and even now his mastery of oil is too little appreciated. It is all to the honour of John Raphael Smith that from the first he showed belief in De Wint's power of painting in oil. At the end of four years Smith waived his legal rights and cancelled his pupil's indentures on the sole condition that for two years he should paint in oil nine subjects a year, of stipulated size, 'all of which several pictures are to be landscapes and to be delivered into the hands and be the absolute property of the said John Raphael Smith'. And faithfully delivered they were. But in the years to come De Wint's oil landscapes, sent to the Royal Academy, were rejected or skied, and after the artist's death, William Vokins, the dealer, climbing to a loft at 40, Upper Gower Street, which had been boarded, plastered, whitewashed and fitted with ledges to hold canvases, was astonished to find it full of fine things quite unknown. From that loft came the *Woody Landscape*[3] and *The Cornfield*,[4] now in the Victoria and Albert Museum, and which without his water-colours would establish De Wint as one of the great English landscape painters.

It is difficult to attempt a chronological survey of De Wint's work, because it has no definitely separated periods and styles, like that of Cotman, and because he never dated or signed his drawings.[5] *Beach Scene* (Lincoln, 39)[6] is unique in bearing a signature which on

[1] H. De Wint, *op. cit.*, p. 20.   [2] *O.W.S. Club, I*, 1923–1924.
[3] V.A.M. 261–1872.   [4] V.A.M. 258–1872.
[5] Mr. Peter Rhodes suggested divisions in style and periods in his introduction to the Exhibition Catalogue at Reading, 1966. (Eds.)
[6] In 1937 the Usher Art Gallery, Lincoln, held a comprehensive exhibition of the works of Peter De Wint which owed much to the knowledge and enthusiasm of Sir Geoffrey Harmsworth. Numbers in brackets refer to those in the catalogue of this exhibition.

212

comparison with De Wint's letters proved to be authentic. De Wint himself, when asked why he never signed his work, replied: 'My pictures are signed all over.' The collector, therefore, should be careful in accepting as genuine a drawing which purports to bear a signature by De Wint, for many artists have produced imitations, or drawings in the De Wint manner, which are uncannily deceptive.

Though the dating of his work offers complex and intricate problems, it may be taken that most of his sepia drawings and his still-life studies, belong to an early and formative stage of his career. It is a period of disciplined restraint in contrast with the freedom of his later art. One of these early works illustrates a Victorian drawing-room scene, a most unusual subject for De Wint (Lincoln, 19). Many still-life studies, mainly of earthenware pots and pans, e.g. *Tub, Vase and Green Cloth*,[1] show the development of his colour sense. The lovely quality of their greys, the ivory or amber of cloth or background, with warmer notes of ochre and indian red on the vessels, is the key which runs all through his better-known drawings of architecture and landscape. These still-lifes reveal a distinct side of De Wint's genius, and until recent years were little known. One of them depicting in sombre colours two kitchen pots, one black, the other reddish brown, and a basket partly covered with cloth, all on the green cloth of a table, is on the back of a *View of the Thames, looking towards Cookham* (a sketch for the larger work in the Victoria and Albert Museum). It was probably at an early stage of his career that he made his careful study of *Weeds in Water*[2] (Lincoln, 217) and his *Dock Leaves*[3] (Lincoln, 216), which Sir Walter Armstrong[4] reproduced in his *Memoir*. De Wint probably kept these for reference all through his life when painting his foregrounds, just as Samuel Palmer retained for constant use his study of cypresses at the Villa D'Este.

A drawing which may be ascribed to an early date, possibly before 1815, is the *Farmyard, Pool in Foreground*[5] (Lincoln, 190). It is strongly influenced by Girtin and is made in a scheme of delicate greys and ochres. Another drawing of much the same period is the *Landscape with Churchyard*[6] (Lincoln, 7), 5 × 19 inches, on the type of paper which was adopted later by Cox, and has superb quality in its reticent greys. A definite date (it was exhibited in 1808) can be given to *Westminster Palace, Hall and Abbey*[7] (Lincoln, 100). The contemporary *Examiner*[8] gave a notice of the exhibition of the Associated Artists, where this picture appeared, and which is the earliest known criticism of De Wint's work. It records that his view of Westminster Hall and Abbey from the Bridge, 'has an agreeable simplicity of effect'. In its discipline and simplicity the drawing again shows his inheritance from Girtin, and there is more than a hint of Girtin's *White House* in the distant river-bank and reflections on the left.

By 1809 De Wint was beginning to make his mark. With reference to the second exhibition

[1] Lincoln, Usher Art Gallery.
[3] Lincoln, Usher Art Gallery.
[5] Manchester, City Art Gallery.
[7] V.A.M. P.61–1921.

[2] Once Coll. Sir Edward Marsh.
[4] *Memoir, op. cit.*, pl. 8.
[6] Coll. Sir Geoffrey Harmsworth, Bt.
[8] Whitley, 1800–1820, p. 141.

of the Associated Artists in that year, the critic of the *Beau Monde*[1] selects for particular commendation De Wint's large landscape, *View of Lincoln, effect of early hour of morning*, with boats and shipping in the foreground, and says:

> Mr. De Wint has nothing to fear from the boldest and bravest of his predecessors in water colour landscape. He has manifested in the present exhibition that professional skill which can only be founded on accurate—by which we do not mean minute—observation, confirmed and rendered familiar by habit. He has opened a road for himself not far wide of those in which Turner and Callcott are travelling through the landscape of life, and may proceed with a steady face towards the ultimate object of his ambition, where he will find a niche prepared for his reception.

Cookham[2] (Lincoln, 31), possibly the *Cookham* exhibited in 1814, is another early drawing, made on the double-page of a sketch-book. Here the example and teaching of Varley are clearly followed. It is a perfect example of De Wint's most direct approach to nature, set down in bold blots and washes, without any second touching, from a very full brush. The sky, except on the lower horizon, is untouched paper, giving an effect of great space and luminosity. The influence of Varley, to a lesser extent and in the washes rather than the colour, is seen in two versions, varying slightly, of *Old House on the High Bridge, Lincoln* (Lincoln, 12, 28). One, belonging to the Victoria and Albert Museum,[3] is possibly the *Old Bridge in Lincoln* exhibited in 1812; the other (Pl. 197) belonging to Colonel P. L. M. Wright, may be a year or two later. Both are superb in their colour, and in their massive solidity, akin to that of Cotman's *St. Luke's Chapel, Norwich*.[4] I have mentioned the *High Bridge* because it must be allowed that in his architectural themes De Wint was surpassed by many painters. He was never very curious or exact about structure, whether in architecture or in trees. The shape and mass interested him far more than the details. In his suggestion of the spirit of historic buildings he fell far short of Girtin and Cotman.

Another early drawing which can be dated, for it is probably that exhibited as *A Cricket Match* at the Old Water-Colour Society in 1815, is *The Cricketers*[5] (Pl. 199) (Lincoln, 98). W. Shaw-Sparrow[6] relates that De Wint, finding that he could not sell it, strained another piece of paper over its surface to save the outlay on a new stretcher. After his death, when preparations were being made for the sale at Christie's, the hidden water-colour was found. After Cox's death, as has been mentioned, several of his drawings were also found buried beneath others from a similar motive of economy. If *The Cricketers* really is *The Cricket Match* of 1815, the period during which it lay hidden must have been one of nearly thirty-four years. It is said to represent Ockley Green, with Leith Hill in the distance.[7]

[1] Whitley, 1800–1820, p. 153. Similar high praise was given by the critic, probably Thomas Uwins, in the *Repository of Arts*, 1809, I, 493, who speaks of De Wint's 'correct observation of nature, fine selection of form, truth and simplicity of colour'.
[2] Once coll. W. Craig Henderson, K.C.
[3] V.A.M. 179–1898.
[4] Norwich, Castle Museum.
[5] V.A.M. 515.
[6] W. S. Sparrow, 'Masters of English Landscape Painting', *The Studio*, 1903.
[7] R. Redgrave, *David Cox and Peter De Wint*, 1891, p. 72.

In the Bodleian Library, Oxford, are some water-colour drawings by De Wint, which were made as illustrations to the *History of Cheshire* by George Ormerod, published in three volumes in 1819. The Bodleian possesses a large-paper copy of the three volumes, later extended by the author to ten by the addition of about 800 extra illustrations, among them the drawings by I. Jackson, G. Pickering, Copley Fielding and De Wint, from which the engravings were made.[1]

Fairly early in date must be many of the small sketches which were pasted into albums by Mrs. De Wint after her husband's death. The *Landscape with Churchyard*[2] is made up of two pieces found in separate albums. The albums were inherited by her grand-daughter, Miss Tatlock, and by her bequeathed to Miss Bostock. Their pedigree is beyond question, and they are all the more interesting because several are not immediately recognisable as the work of De Wint. One of the most attractive is *Windmill and Boatmen*[3] (Lincoln, 40), an unfinished sketch, with just a wash of delicate colour, grey and green, melting into rose, with one note of deep indigo in the centre setting two figures into relief. There is similar freshness and bloom in *Old Post Mill*[4] (Lincoln, 132), a slight but masterly sketch.

In De Wint's work during the last thirty years of his life we find a variety of method from drawings where landscape is swiftly recorded with slight washes of colour, to a more solid manner with a full range of glowing colours, like the *Cottage at Aldbury*[5] and beside them both, the meticulously finished picture on the grand scale. Those large pictures—*Canterbury*[6] (Lincoln, 18) and *Cookham on Thames*[7] (Lincoln, 32) are excellent examples—show all the knowledge, skill and subtle resource of which De Wint was capable, but, like the big drawings by Cox, represent days of toil in a studio. They seem to be a little over-dressed, lacking the naturalness and simplicity of his outdoor work. The easy, unstrained vigour of his smaller sketches, their unity, achieved by perfection of form and colour, is lost by enlargement and by forced methods of elaboration. Those complex works had to be painted in pieces and patches. And though De Wint would have been a great artist had he painted nothing but these, one feels his finest water-colour is always one in which the painter can get from side to side of his paper with one stroke of a wet brush.

De Wint was essentially an outdoor painter, avidly seeing his subject, eagerly setting it down with swift strokes of his brush, heedless if the foreground was but a casual suggestion, as long as the main masses, the central interest, were right. Probably most of his drawings, except the large exhibition subjects, were begun, at any rate, in the open air. A good example is *Glastonbury* (Lincoln, 47),[8] which remains incomplete, an obvious out-door work, done at one sitting, with swift washes merely suggesting form and colour. Other examples

---

[1] Roget gives details of De Wint's drawings for engraved illustrations, as well as many other facts of his life.
[2] Coll. Sir Geoffrey Harmsworth, Bt.
[3] Coll. Sir Geoffrey Harmsworth, Bt.
[4] Once coll. Miss Bostock.
[5] Lincoln, Usher Art Gallery.
[6] Coll. Lord Ashton of Hyde.
[7] University of Liverpool.
[8] Coll. Sir Edmund Bacon, Bt.

are an unfinished study of *Lincoln Cathedral from Drury Lane*,[1] and *Lincoln from South East*[2] (Lincoln, 37) where there is still a bare patch to the right with pencil indication of a waggon and of figures. Still slighter than these, but very attractive for their delicate flush of colour are *Mountain and Lake*[3] (Lincoln, 184) and the *View in the Lake District*[4] (Lincoln, 211) and *Landscape with Rainbow, Caerphilly Castle*[5] (Lincoln, 108). *Eel Traps, Goring on Thames*[6] (Lincoln, 185) is a perfect example of a quick out-door seizure of the essentials of a scene.

In the last ten years of his life De Wint was painting with complete boldness of summary execution. There is a remarkable vigour and expressiveness in his handling of trees in such drawings as *Lowther*[7] of 1839 (Lincoln, 91) or the *Landscape with Cliff and Pool*.[8] And it was in 1847, within two years of his death, that he painted the superb *Cottage at Aldbury*[9] (Usher Art Gallery, Lincoln), with its warmth of sun-filled colour, so spontaneously and freely handled that it must have been carried without halt to its finish. Akin to it, and known to have been painted in 1845, is *St. John's Hospital Canterbury*,[10] 1845 (Lincoln, 8), typical in its intermingling of glowing colour with passages of grey, all dashed in with supreme vigour and rapidity. Probably of the same period, and certainly of the same type in its richness of mellow colour, is the *Potter Gate, Lincoln*[11] (Lincoln, 135) in the Victoria and Albert Museum. It must have been completed indoors, but it shows no signs of labour.

De Wint was often at his best in drawings which show by their shape, or by a crease down the middle, that he worked over a double page of his oblong sketch-book. His natural scheme of composition was horizontal. Perhaps his Dutch ancestry gave him a special feeling for the wide sweep and far-flung recession of the fenlands. Girtin alone, in the British School, has the same power of giving not only depth and height, but lateral immensity, yet even he does not excel De Wint in the suggestion of flat lands stretching endless to the dim horizon. A fine example is the *Fen Country*.[12]

If we were to choose one drawing to demonstrate De Wint's masterly composition and robust handling, it might be that brilliant achievement, *A Road in Yorkshire*.[13] At first sight it is radiant with light like a water-colour by Constable. But in fact, like a Girtin, it is formed of sombre and neutral colour, with two passages of light, and a brilliant, almost untouched sky. This sombre work is in complete contrast with the sunlit *Cottage at Aldbury*. Together they show the full scope of De Wint's genius.

[1] Lincoln, Usher Art Gallery.
[2] Coll. Sir Geoffrey Harmsworth, Bt.
[3] Coll. Sir Edmund Bacon, Bt.
[4] Cambridge, Fitzwilliam Museum.
[5] Cambridge, Fitzwilliam Museum.
[6] Nottingham, City Art Gallery.
[7] Lincoln, Usher Art Gallery.
[8] V.A.M. P.64–1921.
[9] Ill.'*Masters of English Landscape Painting*', Studio 1903 pl. w. 19.
[10] Coll. Brigadier E. R. Kewley, D.S.O.
[11] V.A.M. P.59.1921.
[12] V.A.M. P.135.1929.
[13] London, Tate Gallery (3484).

216

And at this point it may well be emphasised that De Wint gained his impression of radiant heat and sunshine much more by careful balance and juxtaposition of light and dark than by any high pitch of colour. A harvest field, fringed by trees and hedgerows is a subject shared by De Wint and Cox. But a De Wint is tones lower than a Cox; it is worked with deep washes of ochre, burnt sienna, umber and indigo, instead of with flickering touches of high colour with white paper showing transparently between. Even in a sunny drawing like *Cottage at Aldbury* De Wint is painting with a deep Indian red where another artist would use crimson lake or rose madder. But, sombre though De Wint's scheme is, the result is always brilliantly radiant. Cox perhaps may be more qualified to suggest the glittering atmosphere of early spring and summer; De Wint is unsurpassed in his rendering of an autumnal wood and the feeling of glow and heat is obtained by cunning contrast of intense colour.

For his water-colours, through the earlier part of his life, De Wint felt himself fortunate in getting a guinea or two; and at the very height of his career, twenty to thirty guineas was about his average demand. At the same time, it is clear that, at a period when Cotman was poor and neglected, De Wint was comparatively prosperous. The reason, no doubt, was that where Cotman was vague and abstracted in his way of life, De Wint was definite and orderly. In 1831 his work was 'so congenial to the general feeling of the collectors of water-colour painting that not only his larger works, but every scrap from his ingenious pencil is sought with avidity'.[1] The 100 guineas at which, late in his career, one of his exhibits was priced at the Old Water-Colour Society's show in 1841, was much above the average.[2] His patrons, asking why he should charge guineas instead of pounds for his drawings, received the charming reply: 'The pounds are mine, the shillings are Mrs. De Wint's.' This and many tales are told of his shrewdness as a business man, and it is even related that on finding it necessary to sketch some cows in a pupil's drawing, he raised his hour's fee from a guinea to five-and-thirty shillings. His attitude was very different from that of David Cox, who wrote to a patron, on January 10, 1850: 'After you left my house yesterday evening I was thinking of the price I had charged you for the six sketches you purchased, and I am sorry to say that I have charged you more than in my conscience I ought. I have therefore sent you three more to make the deal more agreeable to my feelings. Trusting you reached home safely, I remain, dr Sir, Yours most truly, David Cox.'[3]

That De Wint's work did not command any fanciful or even high prices is proved by the sale of his remaining works at Christie's, May 22–28, 1850. The 493 lots realised £2364 7s. 6d. The highest price was £31 10s. od., the lowest 8s., and the average a little under £5 each. Within thirty years of his death, at the Quilter Sale of 1875, his *Southwell, Notts* sold for £1732 10s. od. Of his brother artists, Constable, who bought a water-colour

---

[1] *Library of Fine Arts*, I, 1831, p. 410.
[2] This was the *West Front of Lincoln Cathedral, from the Castle Hill*, V.A.M. 1021–1873.
[3] Adrian Bury, *Thomas Collier*, 1944, p. 57.

by De Wint in 1827, alone seems to have recognised his worth. He praised his work, and in 1830 he gave De Wint a presentation copy, now in the British Museum, of the first number of *English Landscape Scenery*, with mezzotints by David Lucas after his own pictures. There is pleasure also in recalling that in the same year one of those who apparently understood De Wint best was the poet John Clare, who wrote about his own work:

> '*I found the poems in the fields*
> *And only wrote them down.*'

During his brief flash of success and notoriety, Clare made a descent upon the society of London, just as Burns had done in Edinburgh, and there made the acquaintance of the artist. After his return he wrote a charming and diffident letter begging for 'a bit of your genius to hang up in my cottage. What I mean is one of those scraps which you consider nothings after having used them, and that lie littering your study. For nothing would appear so valuable to me as one of those rough sketches, taken in the fields, that breathe the living freshness of the open air and sunshine, where the harmony of earth, air and sky form such a happy unison of greens and greys, that a flat bit of scenery on a few inches of paper appears so many miles.' It is characteristic of De Wint, the man of prayer and the man of business, that the poor poet's pleading won no response. Again, to show how De Wint struck his contemporaries, we may quote from Samuel Palmer's notebook of 1850. Palmer speaks of seeking a 'new style', of an endeavour 'instead of aiming at finish to aim at executing the mental vision with as little manipulation and as much inventive energy as possible'. And he adds, with one of his characteristic burst into capitals: 'Try something like the solid BLOCKS of sober colour in De Wint.'

While it is satisfying to know that artists so different in outlook as Constable and Samuel Palmer could appreciate De Wint's power, the fact remains that throughout his life he prospered on an income gained chiefly from teaching amateurs. Even at a late period of his career De Wint gave lessons all through the London winter, beginning his day at nine and ending at six, with but an hour's rest all day. By 1827—he was then over forty and a full member of the Old Water-Colour Society—his price for lessons had risen from five shillings to one guinea an hour. That he had many aristocratic ladies as his pupils is shown by inscriptions in some of his sketch-books. One of these books in the Victoria and Albert Museum contains notes with each sketch indicating pupils to whom he had supplied this or a similar subject for copying, and it is always stated whether the copy is to be in colours or in sepia. A pupil more noteworthy than the ordinary amateur was Samuel Austin (1796–1834), the well-known painter of sea and coast subjects. Austin was a poor clerk with a keen love of sketching; and some charitable person gave him the means of receiving three precious lessons from the great De Wint. When the last lesson came to an end, the young student burst into tears, and it is vain to search for any record that the great De Wint gave him three more lessons without fees. But even in his three lessons, Austin absorbed much of De Wint's quality and style, as was seen in a group of his works lent from

218

1928 to 1930 to the Victoria and Albert Museum at that time belonging to a Mr. George Hornblower.

With regard to De Wint's influence on amateurs whom he taught, Randall Davies[1] supplies notes of his patrons and pupils, none of whom except Austin became a professional artist. At Belton House, Lincolnshire, where De Wint gave instruction to Lord Brownlow's family, Davies found a drawing with a mass of shipping on the right foreground and a single boat on the left, inscribed: *Venice, about 1848, by Mr. Cheney, De Wint's best pupil.* It had been sent in 1887 to a well-known firm in London for framing, and came back with their expert's note that 'but for the un-Venetian little boat it might have been by De Wint'. But the boat was by De Wint! Perhaps he charged 5s. extra for that boat!

I was once shown a Lincoln subject which seemed, without any doubt, to be a superb De Wint. It displayed his rich sombre colouring with indisputable hints of the Indian red which figures in his severely limited palette. But on the back was an autograph note showing that the drawing was by Frederick Nash, an artist with a totally different outlook and style. Yet it was found that De Wint and Nash were working together at Lincoln in 1810, and that both exhibited their Lincoln drawings, of which this could be definitely identified as one, at the Old Water-Colour Society in 1811.

De Wint's palette has been mentioned, and there is no doubt that his wise limitation of pigments accounted for much of the simplicity and directness of his work. While Girtin used fifteen colours, De Wint's palette was confined to the following ten pigments: Indian red, vermilion, purple lake, yellow ochre, gamboge, brown-pink, burnt sienna, sepia, Prussian blue and indigo. All of these pigments were in hard cakes. To these, for occasional use, he added four others in half cakes: orange ochre, Vandyke brown, olive green cobalt and emerald green. He employed brushes of two sizes, both large: one with a fine point, the other round and well-worn. He used a thickish paper, usually "old Creswick" or Whatman, and no one knew better than De Wint how the roughness of a paper can be used to give luminosity to an even wash. He had immense skill in dragging his brush over his granular paper so as to utilise the grain for sparkles of light and variety of texture. He was at his best when every part of his work was laid in with a full, flowing brush, and a rich mosaic of added colour was floated in to avoid all second touching on a dry ground. Thus we get the untroubled freshness and the full richness of bloom that lend so much charm and distinction to his art. While he rarely washed down any mass of colour to obtain gradation, he may occasionally have put a second wash over a dry ground, but his best pictures, and especially his sketches, were carried out entirely in undisturbed colour. A close examination of his work shows how skilfully he used a sharp pen-knife, first to gain a broken effect in his trees by scraping irregularly across his colour; and next to gain sparkle by flicking out high lights where the sky gleams through foliage. A good example of his use of knife or razor is found in *Lake Hewell, Worcestershire*[2] (Lincoln, 11), where a high

---

[1] R. Davies, 'Peter De Wint', *O.W.S. Club*, I, 1923–1924.
[2] Coll. The Hon. Mrs. Doggett.

light across the water and the shapes of tree trunks have been obtained by the use of a sharp point. Another characteristic of De Wint's technique is his use of the brush, filled with colour and then pressed down on the paint-box till the hairs split apart, to give the suggestion of foliage, the sharp broken edges of trees. This use of the brush, in which he followed Glover, is clearly seen in the *View near Oxford*.[1]

It may well be emphasised that the outstanding feature in his work is his amazing faculty for avoiding the application of a second wash or the addition of finishing touches, over a dry underpainting. In all his happiest work he had the art of keeping large passages wet, leaving light spaces here and there, and running in rich warm colour to give his darks; then letting it all dry out quite undisturbed. That is why his dark tones are so fresh and luminous, so different from darks produced by two or more washes of superimposed colour. He had the courage to leave spaces that many painters would have sought to complete by further work. It was of his swifter method that Ruskin wrote: 'Supposing that we had nothing to show in modern art, of the region of the raincloud, but the dash of Cox, the blot of De Wint, or even the ordinary stormy skies of our inferior water-colour painters, we might yet laugh all efforts of the old masters to utter scorn.'[2]

Very rarely, except in his large works, did De Wint use body-colour, and then with the false and cheapening effect that body-colour is apt to give. His large *West Front of Lincoln Cathedral*[3] is marred by staring touches of Chinese white, which are all the more 'jumpy' because of the general fading of the whole drawing.

Owing to his free use of perishable indigo, many of De Wint's drawings, like those of Samuel Palmer of the same date, have so faded that the entire subject has a red evening glow instead of a noon-day effect. In the National Museum at Dublin are four drawings by him of great interest as demonstrating stages of his work on the same subject, but exposure long ago to light in the art school of the Royal Dublin Society has destroyed their full value. The old heresy that Indian red 'eats up' the blue was repeated in the introduction to the Lincoln catalogue. The truth is that for his warm summer skies, his cloud shadows, the grey tones of his foregrounds, De Wint mixed with his indigo not only yellow but also a certain quantity of Indian red. The fugitive indigo and the yellow with it have disappeared, owing to the action of light. The red, slightly used in the sky, more strongly used elsewhere, has remained fast. In his love of blue distances, of great masses of foliage, where blue is necessary for the production of green, De Wint employed indigo perhaps more than any other colour. A De Wint water-colour requires even more care than other contemporary drawings, and should never be exposed to sunlight. Direct sunlight will bleach the yellow of a canary's feather (when not on the living bird) to a pure white in about a week. Exposed to sunlight the life of the indigo which De Wint used would not be much longer.

[1] V.A.M. 2.N.G.
[2] *Modern Painters*, pt. II, sec. III, chap. IV, para. 7.
[3] V.A.M. 1021–1873.

220

IV 'Lincoln'

B.M. 1958.7.12.341   26⅜ × 39½ : 670 × 1113   *Water-colour*

Peter DE WINT (1784–1849)

197 'Lincoln, Old Houses on the High Bridge'
Coll. Col. P. L. M. Wright $17\frac{1}{2} \times 20\frac{3}{4}$: 444×526 *Water-colour*
Peter De Wint (1784–1849)

198 'The Foss Dyck near Lincoln'

Coll. Mr & Mrs Paul Mellon $9\frac{3}{4} \times 16\frac{1}{2}$: 247×420 *Water-colour*

Peter DE WINT (1784–1849)

199 'The Cricketers'

V.A.M. 515 $22\frac{1}{2} \times 34\frac{3}{4}$: 571×882 *Water-colour*

Peter DE WINT (1784–1849)

200 'Chester'

Coll. Mr and Mrs Tom Girtin $10\frac{3}{4} \times 16\frac{3}{4}$: 273×425 *Water-colour*

Peter De Wint (1784–1849)

201 'Gloucester, 1840'

V.A.M. P.62–1921 $18\frac{1}{8} \times 24\frac{1}{2}$: 460×622 *Water-colour*

Peter De Wint (1784–1849)

202 'House among Trees'
Coll. Mr & Mrs W. W. Spooner   12¾ × 19: 323 × 482   *Water-colour*
Peter DE WINT (1784–1849)

203 'The Harvesters'
Coll. Mr & Mrs Paul Mellon   6¼ × 10½: 158 × 266   *Water-colour*
Peter DE WINT (1784–1849)

204 'The Wayside'
Coll. Mr & Mrs Paul Mellon $7\frac{1}{4} \times 9\frac{1}{2}$: 184 × 242   *Water-colour*
Peter De Wint (1784–1849)

205 'Girl with Bucket, and a Boy'

Coll. Mr and Mrs Cyril Fry $8\frac{1}{2} \times 7: 216 \times 178$ *Water-colour*

Peter De Wint (1784–1849)

206 'Still Life'

Coll. Mr & Mrs Cyril Fry $8\frac{3}{4} \times 7\frac{1}{4}$: 223 × 184   *Water-colour*

Peter De Wint (1784–1849)

207 'Bruges, Church of Notre Dame'
Coll. Mr & Mrs Paul Mellon 15½ × 20¾ : 394 × 527 *Water-colour*
Samuel AUSTIN (1796–1834)

When we view De Wint's work as a whole—and the Lincoln Exhibition made this possible[1]—we realise that he was always at his best when his work was done quickly and at one sitting; in drawings where he knew when to stop, though parts were literally un-finished; when he left the foreground to look after itself, just covering the paper with suggestive hints of form and colour, seeking no adventitious aid from clumps of burdock or mounds of stone or earth. In the slightest and most spontaneous of his drawings, the *Cookham*, the *Lane with Cottages*, the *Cottage at Aldbury*, he is infinitely greater than when he introduces delicate and elaborate ingenuities of form and style. It is with regard to such work alone that one can forgive the criticism of Ruskin who had great respect for De Wint. He says that, 'De Wint makes me feel as if I were walking through the fields.' He speaks of his admirable truth of tone; his knowledge of lowland rivers; his effective painting of winter scenes. But his summary—again because he was the major prophet preaching the gospel of Turner—damns De Wint with faint praise. 'There is much that is instructive and deserving of high praise', he writes,[2] 'in the sketches of De Wint. Yet it is to be remembered that even the pursuit of truth, however determined, will have results limited and imperfect when its chief motive is the pride of being true; and I fear that these works testify more accuracy of eye and experience of colour than exercise of thought. Their truth of effect is often purchased at too great a loss of all beauty of form, and of the higher refinements of colour; deficiencies, however, on which I shall not insist, since the value of the sketches, as far as they go, is great: they have done good service and set good example, and whatever their failings may be, there is evidence in them that the painter has always done what he believed to be right.'

De Wint, like Constable, has survived Ruskin's patronising criticism and now the warm tribute paid by Thackeray, the year after De Wint's death, is to be preferred. 'Our well-beloved De Wint has gone like one of those calm summer days he used to depict. He spent his life in one revel of sunshine. . . . Fuseli, who wanted an umbrella to look at Constable's showers, might have called for a pot of porter at seeing one of De Wint's hay makings.'

De Wint is one of the great technicians of water-colour, one of those who can make colour luminous and keep his darks transparent and sparkling. No artist has interpreted the rich-ness of English landscape with a more sympathetic mind and a more responsive hand. He paints, in Edmund Blunden's words, 'the landscape that we have lived'. He never showed any high degree of fidelity or care in his drawing of detail, but he never lost his feeling for weight and mass, his sense of the solidity of a building, the vastness of skies and the big sweep of landscape. No other painter has ever put on paper with more effect that touch of fine colour from a full-flowing brush, which, as it dries out, transparent and rich in bloom, is the essence of the art of water-colour. As Thackeray pointed out, he never confined his work to morning or evening, when long sweeping shadows make easier pictures; he was

[1] The permanent collection in the Usher Art Gallery contains about forty examples of De Wint's water-colours. An illustrated catalogue was published in 1947.
[2] *Modern Painters*, I, part II, sec. I, para. 23.

221

not frightened by the sun in its meridian. Thackeray also noted that De Wint was a keen observer, rather than an inventor. It is evident in all his work that he never invented the smallest figure; his harvesters and haymakers are never artificially grouped as pictorial adjuncts to enliven his scene. They seem to belong to the fields, to have grown from the soil as surely as his trees. And to De Wint's credit we may remember that this most conventional of men in his daily life, was daring and unconventional in his art; that he brought into the art of water-colour something new, something unknown to Turner and Girtin and Cox. He is not an echo: he is a voice. He had 'a beautiful profession', and out of it he produced things of lasting beauty.

De Wint died in London on June 30, 1849, and was buried in the Chapel Royal of the Savoy. Against the south wall of the south aisle in the beautiful Angel Choir of Lincoln Cathedral is an elaborately carved stone sarcophagus, commemorating William Hilton, R.A., and De Wint, 'erected as a tribute of affection by the bereaved sister and widow Harriet de Wint 1864'. It is decorated with bas-reliefs of subjects taken from Hilton's pictures and with *Lincoln Cathedral from the West*, from the picture by De Wint now in the Victoria and Albert Museum.

CHAPTER XIV
Copley Fielding

The Fieldings   The Richardsons
The Rowbothams   The Fripps
G. F. Robson   William Turner of Oxford
and other artists

Constable in his youth called upon the great Farington and complained that his critics looked 'only to the surface and not to the mind. The mechanism of painting is their delight. Execution is their chief aim.' What Constable said to his mentor, though he was presumably speaking of oil, might apply to many water-colour painters in the first half of the nineteenth century. The public appreciated dexterity and understood laborious finish. The painters, to earn their living, supplied what their patrons demanded. For this reason it is often in their early work and in their unexhibited sketches, made for their own satisfaction, that we find true art and genuine emotion instead of mechanised formula. Of those who came to be supreme in execution Copley Fielding is a good example.

Anthony Vandyke Copley Fielding (1787–1855) was a considerable artist, but not such a great one as is suggested by the high-sounding names bestowed by his god-parents in the church of East Sowerby, near Halifax, Yorkshire.[1] His father, an indifferent portrait-painter, wished to indicate his respect for one of the greatest painters of his own calling and for his friend, John Singleton Copley, R.A. His four sons were all dedicated to art as their profession. Copley was the second. His elder brother, Theodore Henry Adolphus (1781–1851), and his younger brothers, Thales (1793–1837) and Newton Limbird Smith (1799–1856), all had some success as painters. Theodore exhibited landscapes and portraits at the Royal Academy, taught drawing at the Military Academy at Addiscombe, and published a treatise on painting. Thales became an Associate of the Old Water-Colour Society in 1829, and for many years taught drawing at the Woolwich Military Academy. Newton

---

[1] In token of Fielding's association with Halifax, a typical drawing by him of *Robin Hood's Bay* was presented to the Bank-field Museum, Halifax, by the National Art Collections Fund in 1940.

painted animals and was well-known as an engraver and lithographer. He enjoyed considerable reputation in France, where he taught the family of Louis Philippe; he died in Paris. Examples of the work of these brothers may be seen in the Victoria and Albert Museum. In both quality and quantity of artistic output they were far surpassed by Copley.

Soon after Copley's birth his father removed to London, and in the boy's sixteenth year migrated to the Lakes, taking a cottage first at Ambleside and afterwards at Keswick. Four miles away, at Troutbeck, lived Julius Caesar Ibbetson. Young Copley was sent out by his father early each morning to draw from nature, and although the boy was lacking in originality, it proved an effective form of training. By 1807 his drawings were having some sale in Liverpool, and he seems to have given lessons there for a time. A Welsh tour in 1808 by way of Flint and the Vale of Clwyd to Chester enlarged his experience of the mountain scenery which was to become his main theme in the following years. In 1809 he was attracted by the magnet of London, where he derived great benefit from the teaching and advice of Varley, and in order to be near him (Varley was in Broad Street, Golden Square) took a lodging in Wells Street. In 1813 he married Varley's sister-in-law, Susannah Gisborne, and in the historic year 1815 they took possession of a little house in Judges' Walk, Hampstead, the previous tenant having been Mrs. Siddons. Under Varley's guidance Fielding had acquired proficiency enough to obtain his election as an associate of the Old Water-Colour Society in 1810. The exhibition of 1811 bore witness to tours in Cumberland, Northumberland and Scotland, and another visit to Wales gave him fresh subjects for the exhibition of 1812. Soon he became launched on his stupendous traffic in drawings. In the eight years from 1813 to 1820 he exhibited at the gallery of the Water-Colour Society 327 works, an average of over forty drawings a year, and he maintained this average for forty-three years in all. His complete list of exhibits during his life-time reached the total of 1748, apart from works which he exhibited at the British Institution and at the Royal Academy. He became a full member of the Water-Colour Society in 1812, Treasurer in 1817, Secretary in 1818, and President, on Cristall's retirement in 1831. Together with Constable and Bonington he was awarded a gold medal at the famous Paris Salon of 1824.

Up to 1816 Fielding's exhibits were almost exclusively subjects found in North Wales and the Lakes, with a few in the neighbourhood of London. In 1817 his wife's health demanded permanent residence for her at the seaside. Sandgate was chosen, and in her company Fielding spent as much of his time as was possible. In 1819, for instance, we find among his exhibits many views on the coast of Kent from Dover to Romney Marsh, as well as his usual Welsh subjects. The sea thus became his second theme. He lived at Brighton from 1829 to 1847, first at 41 Regency Square and then at 2 Lansdowne Place, but always retained a studio in London. His residence in Sussex led him, about 1830, to begin his studies of the South Downs, from which in his later years he developed the most popular type of 'Copley Fielding'. His stock-in-trade consisted, as has been seen, of three subjects and, as was caustically suggested, Fielding painted 'one sea, one moor, one down, one lake, one misty gleam'. And it is true that in such a vast output of work there can rarely have been such small variety, Ruskin, speaking of his landscapes, says:

> It is impossible to pass by his down scenes and moorland showers, of some years ago, in which he produced some of the most perfect and faultless passages of mist and raincloud which art has ever seen. Wet, transparent, formless, full of motion, felt rather by their shadows on the hills than by their presence in the sky, becoming dark only through increased depth of space, and light only through increased buoyancy of motion, letting the blue through their interstices, and the sunlight through their chasms, with the irregular playfulness and traceless gradation of nature herself, his skies will remain as long as their colours stand, among the most simple, unadulterated, and complete transcripts of a particular nature which art can point to. Had he painted five instead of five hundred such, and gone on to other sources of beauty, he might there can be little doubt, have been one of our greatest artists.[1]

Roget and others who have written about Copley Fielding make no mention of Girtin as an early influence upon his art. Varley recognised that Fielding had no great originality, and I suspect that part of his teaching was to make his pupil study Girtin's work. In Fielding's earlier pieces, notably the *Flintshire, Rhuddlan Bridge*[2] (Pl. 209), 1809 and the *Cottage and Pool*[3] there is much more of Girtin than of Varley. Features, lineaments, trappings, are those of Girtin. Varley, and perhaps Turner, are reflected in a drawing of the following year, 1810, *Castle on a Cliff: Fishing Smacks*[4] (Pl. 210). It has the qualities of a fine mezzotint; in other words, it is exactly right in the placing of its heavy masses and its gradations of tone. Perhaps the mezzotints of Turner's *Liber Studiorum* impressed Fielding, as they impressed Cox and many others? The drawing is of special interest also because here, probably for the first time, Fielding is concerned with an effect of luminous mist, such as was later to absorb so much of his attention and skill. In 1811 he exhibited *Newark Castle: The Minstrel Boy*,[5] a grandiose composition, akin in outlook to what Cox and Turner of Oxford were producing at the time, with much wiping out of foliage and of lights against darks in the foreground. That he could, like Cox and William Turner, imitate Varley is shown clearly in the *Cader Idris*[6] of 1810, which in composition and colour is pure paraphrase of that artist. In the best of his early drawings, especially in *Rhuddlan Bridge* and *Castle on a Cliff*, he was following Girtin and Varley in the search for the simple but significant masses and lines. They are genuinely artistic with none of the swaggering *panache* which later he was to wear. In after years his art became facile, dexterous, but not always sincere. He lost his sense of subdued tone and began to search for colour that was pretty and sonorous rather than simple and expressive; and, in consequence, there was a lack of an essential infinity and repose.

[1] *Modern Painters*, pt. II, sec. III, chap. IV, para. 8.
[2] V.A.M. P.2972–1876.
[3] Manchester University, Whitworth Art Gallery.
[4] V.A.M. 2973–1876.
[5] Later in Coll. Samuel Naylor, Bettwys-y-coed.
[6] Coll. Herbert Powell (N.A.C.F.).

Soon after 1812 he developed more individuality when he settled down to an increasing range of sources for his favourite landscapes of mountain and lake. *Loch Lomond*[1] (Pl. 211), 1814, is a good example. His colour sense was greater, but, as Ruskin allowed, he indulged too much in the use of crude tints, pure cobalt, violet, rose and purple, in his distances, pure siennas in the foreground. These Highland landscapes have a tendency to a suave flimsiness and prettiness of design, particularly of the vignette type. They are full of resemblances and repetitions, of careless and slurred invention. His was always a popular art, a little commonplace in comparison with what Cox and De Wint were producing at the same period. All through his career, however, the public preferred Fielding's smooth and flattering methods to the brusque rough manner of Cox and the boldness of De Wint. It used to annoy Cox sometimes that Fielding had a much readier sale. In 1846 he said in a letter about the Old Water-Colour Society's exhibition: 'My own drawings are tolerably well hung, and the members say how well they like them. They certainly are very unlike anyone else's . . . I have at present sold only two ten-guinea drawings. . . . Fielding has sent more than forty drawings, some large, and a great number appear to be sold.'[2]

The kindest things that could be said about Fielding's mountainous landscapes were said by Ruskin.[3] One quotation has been given. Here is a second:

> Some six years ago, the brown moorland foregrounds of Copley Fielding were very instructive. Not a line in them was made out, not a single object clearly distinguishable. Wet broad sweeps of the brush, sparkling, careless, and accidental as nature herself, always truthful as far as they went, implying knowledge, though not expressing it, suggested everything, while they represented nothing. But far off into the mountain distance came the sharp edge and the delicate form; the whole intention and execution of the picture being guided and exerted where the great impression of space and size was to be given. . . . I do not know anything in art which has expressed more completely the force and feeling of nature in these particular scenes.

Ruskin makes frequent references of this nature to Copley Fielding, but admits that he alludes to him 'more especially as my own sympathies and enjoyments are so entirely directed in the channel which his art has taken'. His praise, often immoderate, is tempered by qualifications and reservations. 'As far as they went', in the passage quoted above, is one of them. He criticizes also Fielding's 'particular tricks of execution, labour somewhat too mechanical to be meritorious', 'the monotonous grey of his storm tones', his lack of careful and constructive drawing.

After 1816, when he was living for part of the year at Sandgate or at Brighton, Fielding never abandoned moor, mountain and lake, but the sea supplied a second motif. He painted misty sunset scenes from beaches of the south coast—his *Sands at Ryde*[4] is typical— and more often the open sea, with ships tossing, the white flash of gulls against a dark cloud and lowering skies, the black hollows of white-crested waves. His method, in either case,

[1] Manchester, City Art Gallery.
[2] W. Hall, *Biography of David Cox*, 1881, pp. 157, 158.
[3] *Modern Painters*, pt. II, sec. II, chap. IV, para. 4.
[4] V.A.M. 564–1882.

was the same. Instead of painting with direct washes like Varley, or running fresh colour into wet colour like De Wint, or using interlacing tints and juxtaposed touches like Cox, he produced his effects by frequent washings and by laying very gentle tones of colour one over the other. With great labour he worked, and re-worked. His storm tones and wave shadows are washed down to an even monotony of grey and indigo. By that method nothing unpremeditated or unpredictable occurred. He did manage to obtain a particular type of atmospheric suggestion, but with a resulting hint of artificiality and a lack of vigorous expression. In some of his sea-pieces, impressive though they are, the violent contrasts of tone and denial of colour are apt to degenerate into mere blackness. He was emphatically not a colourist. Kaines-Smith,[1] in writing about his marine paintings, says:

> Occasionally we find him honestly tackling the problem of marine composition, but in ninety-nine out of a hundred he merely reduces it to a formula, and this formula is one which gives the fullest possible range to that slovenly and childish weakness, the empty corner, which merely shirks one of the greatest problems of composition within rectilinear boundaries, by vignetting the design. His handling of wave-forms is superficially convincing, but careful analysis reveals that it is wholly arbitrary. The long sweeping curves converging to the compositional climax, at a point in the design selected without the smallest reference to anything but dramatic effect, and the feeble reiteration of these curves from the centre of the design outwards, become irritating: and it is only the sympathetic rendering of atmospheric effect, which does indeed approximate to truth, which redeems many of these drawings from the quality of mere hack work.

Fielding never preserved his early freshness like Cox, who in his last decade was still making new and effective use of his power. Like Tennyson and Swinburne in their later years, Fielding went on imitating himself. The picture collecting magnate of his day could commission a Copley Fielding without qualms, as the product was invariably standardised. And that is true not only of Fielding but of his compeers. A summary of the Water-Colour Society's exhibition, in 1839 by the *Athenaeum* critic gives an interesting contemporary view: '"Grove nods to grove, each alley has his brother" is the motto most appropriate to this exhibition. The same admirable Copley Fieldings, and faithful Prouts, and homely humorous Hunts, and picturesque Cattermoles and pretty Sharpes[2] and Claude-like Barrets . . . year after year hang on the walls of the same chamber in Pall Mall.'

Fielding, however, did change his subject, though his method remained the same. From about 1830 till his death at Worthing in 1855 he enhanced his reputation by the new material which he added to his stock-in-trade. With extraordinary skill he painted the swelling curves of the Downs, seen in the lazy cool shimmer of a peaceful day. In these pictures of the Downs there is a serenity which is in subtle contrast with the sooty clouds and waves of his sea-pieces. In that, at least, he showed a conscious artistry.

His downland subjects convey the suggestion of dew and vaporous mists filling the hollows, the haze of receding distance bathed in blue light, the hills undulating towards a

---

[1] S. C. Kaines-Smith, 'Copley Fielding', *O.W.S. Club*, III, 1925–1926, pp. 11, 12.
[2] Louisa Sharpe (Mrs. Seyforth). See Roget, I, pp. 547, 548.

hint of remote sea. There is no human activity in his landscape, save perhaps that of a shepherd among his flock; and what appeals is a certain timelessness, as if the hot stillness had hung for centuries over the scene. And with similar feelings one considers *Morning Mists*.[1] On a large scale, 25 × 38 inches, it says everything but tells little that is new.

Both Copley Fielding and G. F. Robson began their career as workers in the Varley vein. Under Varley's influence they developed methods of composition and colour which they carried to a high degree of somewhat uninspired efficiency. Both of them painted, very skilfully and impressively, what the ordinary man thought he saw, or wanted to see, in the mountain landscapes of Scotland, Northern England and Wales. Each of them rose to high honour as President of the Old Water-Colour Society. George Fennell Robson (1788–1833), the eldest son of a wine-merchant, was born at Durham a year later than Fielding. As a boy he hovered about artist visitors to Durham; he copied the cuts in Bewick's *History of Quadrupeds*; received some lessons from a local teacher; and then was allowed by his father to set off and try his fortune in London, with five pounds in his pocket. At the age of nineteen he exhibited at the Royal Academy, established his independence, returned the five pounds, and replenished his pocket by the successful publication of a print of his native town. This enabled him, about 1810, to pay a prolonged visit to Scotland, where he acquired a taste for the wild and rugged vastness of highland scenery; and from this time Scottish views are predominant among his exhibited works. It was probably the success of his first Scottish subjects which won his election as a member of the Associated Artists in 1810; and, after the break-up of that body, he was welcomed as a member of the Old Water-Colour Society in 1813. In the following year he published the results of his Scottish tour in a volume entitled *Scenery of the Grampian Mountains* containing forty soft-ground etchings. A reprint, with the plates attractively coloured, appeared in 1819.

During the years 1813 to 1820 Robson was a prolific contributor to his Society's exhibitions, showing 161 works, of which by far the greater number were scenes in the Grampians and the Perthshire highlands. The immense popularity of Sir Walter Scott's *Lady of the Lake*, published in 1810, must clearly have encouraged a popular response to Robson's romantic views. If the stag at eve that drank his fill on the shore of Loch Katrine was put in later by Robert Hills, this merely enhanced the attraction, for not even Landseer could paint deer, or dogs, or cattle, with the fidelity of Hills. Robson and Hills seem to have worked constantly in partnership, for many exhibits bear the joint names; sometimes, Hills putting deer into Robson's forests or driving cattle to his lake side; sometimes Robson filling in a landscape background to Hill's portraits of animals.

Robson's prowess as a painter and his zeal in the Water-Colour Society's service brought him in triumph to the Presidential chair for 1820. He was the youngest artist to hold this appointment, and was succeeded by Joshua Cristall in 1821. His water-colours were praised by his contemporaries for their 'depth of repose', their 'largeness and illusive

[1] Birmingham, City Art Gallery.

228

reality', their 'natural gradations' and their 'luminous skies'. Ruskin[1] speaks of his landscapes as 'serious and quiet in the highest degree; certain qualities of atmosphere and texture in them have never been excelled, and certain facts of mountain scenery never but by them expressed; as, for instance, the stillness and depth of the mountain tarns, with the reversed imagery of their darkness signed across by the soft lines of faintly touching winds; the solemn flush of the brown fern and glowing heath under evening light; the purple mass of mountains far removed, seen against clear still twilight'. One feels that Ruskin, when he wrote this, had just been looking at Robson's *Loch Coruisk and the Cuchullin Mountains, Skye*[2] (Pl. 215). But Ruskin has to qualify his praise by speaking of 'much bad drawing, much forced colour, much over-finish'. He found Robson unaffected but uninventive, and therefore by his canons to be excluded from the first rank of artists. Roget seems to go astray when he finds a reflection of Girtin in Robson's work and especially when he sees in Robson an inheritance of 'the solemnity and repose that pervade the simple drawings of John Cozens'. Robson was almost as far from Cozens as Vesuvius is from Ben Venue. I agree entirely with C. E. Hughes[3] that there is strong reason for assuming the Varley influence on Robson's technique, on his broad transparent washes and treatment of tree forms in the mass. In their different ways, Robson and De Wint are branches from the Varley tree. And both of them were a little mercenary in their methods. It was Robson who started the practice of holding a domestic private view of drawings before they went to an exhibition, and putting upon a picture a blue ticket with the word 'Sold', when he induced a visitor to make a purchase.

Harriet Martineau's *History of the Thirty Years Peace, A.D. 1816–1846* contains a reference to Robson:

> In 1833 we lost, by a sad accident, Robson, whose landscapes were amongst the most eagerly looked for at the Water-colour Exhibition every year. The cause of his death was the bursting of a blood-vessel in sea-sickness. His life was happy from the devotedness in the study of nature which is not subject to the disappointment to which most human pursuits are liable. His eagerness about his first earnings was that they might carry him into the Scotch Highlands, where, with his plaid about his shoulders, and the *Lay of the Last Minstrel* in his pocket, and the dusky fells and rolling mists before his eyes, he was happy to his heart's content. The spirit of those early seen Scotch mountains is in his pictures to the last. The frequenters of the Water-colour Exhibition must have been struck by the frequent appearance of Durham and its cathedral. It was because Durham was Robson's native city. He took care that its fine aspect should be nearly as familiar to others as to himself, though they had not, as he had, feasted their eyes upon it from four years old, and crept to the shoulder of every wandering artist who sat down to sketch anywhere in the environs. One of Robson's last pictures was judged to be one of his best— *London from the Bridge, before Sunrise*.

Following Copley Fielding, as another painter of the Downs and the Sussex coast was Henry George Hine (1811–1895). Son of a coach proprietor, he was born at Brighton and

---

[1] *Modern Painters*, 1888, I. p. 94.
[2] V.A.M. 1426–1869.
[3] C. E. Hughes, *Early English Water-colour, 1950*, p. 71.

was influenced from boyhood by Fielding. He was apprenticed as a youth to Henry Meyer, a stipple engraver of the Bartolozzi school, in London. After spending two years at Rouen, he returned to Brighton and took up wood-engraving and marine painting. In his earlier years he contributed illustrations to *Punch* and the *Illustrated London News*. His work, dealing mostly with scenes in the south of England, followed Fielding closely in manner and subject. He exhibited almost exclusively at the Royal Institute, becoming an Associate in 1863, a Member in 1864, and Vice-President in 1887. At the start of his career he had painted figure subjects, but afterwards turned entirely to landscape, and found his favourite themes on the Sussex coast and among the South Downs. Far less dramatic than Copley Fielding, he studied with loving care and observation the swelling contours of the downs with gashes of chalk quarry or cliff, their dry cropped turf, their structural modelling. His work was faithful, but not very inspired and confined to a narrow sphere.[1] He died at Hampstead and was buried in Highgate Cemetery.

In the track of Copley Fielding, as a painter of landscape, followed dozens of other artists, less significant perhaps, but not to be ignored. And so, if all such minor artists cannot be mentioned, it does not mean that there may not be some passage of skill and liveliness to be found in their work. That is true of the work of Thomas Miles Richardson, father and son, W. L. Leitch, and their group, who anticipated the crude ideals of the coloured picture-postcard in their sentimentalised version of nature. Thomas Miles Richardson, senior (1784–1848), was born at Newcastle upon Tyne and was apprenticed to an engraver and later to a cabinet-maker, but in 1806 succeeded his father as master of the St. Andrew's Grammar School. From 1813, however, he devoted himself entirely to painting in oils and in water-colour, exhibiting at the Royal Academy from 1814 to 1845, and was the founder in 1831 of the Newcastle Water-Colour Society. Though he occasionally painted figure subjects, most of his work dealt with landscape, coast scenes, seascapes and stormy skies. His *View of the Old Fishmarket, Newcastle*, exhibited at the Royal Academy in 1814, and other scenes and subjects in the northern counties, won him a wide reputation. In 1822, with Thomas and Robert Bewick, the wood engravers, and John Dobson, the architect, he inaugurated the first Fine Art Exhibition in the North of England.

His son, Thomas Miles Richardson (1813–1890), junior, also born at Newcastle, worked for a time with his father. From 1832 he exhibited at the British Institution and elsewhere, and after his election as Associate of the Old Water-Colour Society in 1843 he moved to London. He became a full member in 1851, and till his death was never unrepresented, summer or winter, in the Society's gallery, where 702 of his works appeared. His subjects

---

[1] In 1931 Sir George Clausen gave me a note about the work of H. G. Hine, whom he knew in his own young days: 'He painted the Sussex Downs very finely. His son, Harry, told me years ago, a little thing about his father's methods that greatly impressed me. He (H.G.H.) always used cake colours; they got a second grinding by rubbing on the slab, and were finer. Then when he had mixed a tint in a sauce, he would let it stand a while and then pour off the top and use *that* for his skies, which were of extreme delicacy. He used to say that it was as difficult and subtle to model the shapes of the Downs as it was a human body.'

were found in the Border country and in the Highlands of Scotland and later in Italy and Switzerland, beginning with views on the Lake of Como in 1843. Of Richardson's *Scene in Glen Nevis*, exhibited in 1857 at the Water-Colour Society, Ruskin wrote in his *Academy Notes*:

> Mr Richard is gradually gaining in manual power, and opposes cobalt and burnt sienna very pleasantly. But he seems always to conceive a Highland landscape only as a rich medley of the same materials—a rocky bank, blue at one place and brown at another; some contorted Scottish firs; some ferns, some dogs, and some sportsmen: the whole contemplated under the cheering influence of champagne, and considered every way delightful.

Richardson liked a panoramic aspect, and often extended the field of vision laterally by the use of paper of widely oblong proportions. His deft sketches have more charm than his larger exhibition pieces, which reveal a rather monotonous similarity in their composition and in their foreground groups of figures and animals. His continental scenes, in Germany, Switzerland, Italy and Sicily, with their turquoise brilliance of sea, lake or sky, are mannered and over-elaborated. Despite Ruskin, he is more at home, a little more genuine, in his Highland scenes such as *In Glencoe*, *Ben Muich-Dhui* and *Entrance to the Pass of the Awe, Argyllshire*. These three, with forty-one other pictures by him, many of them 26 × 39 inches in size, were sold at Christie's on September 17, 1943, in the collection of the late Sir William Thomlinson. The Richardsons knew all the tricks for certain definite effects to be gained by a free use of body-colour, often garish and over-accented. They certainly enjoyed popular success. *Como* by T. M. Richardson, jun., realised £315 in the sale-room in 1876, and *Sorrento* £310 in 1878, both during his lifetime; but there was a sad decline of value in 1943 and 1945.

To the same class belongs Thomas Leeson Rowbotham (1823–1875), born at Dublin. His father (1783–1853), of the same Christian names, lived at Bath and Bristol, and subsequently became drawing-master to the Royal Naval School at New Cross. The son, T. L. Rowbotham, exhibited from 1840 to 1875, contributing to the exhibitions of the Royal Academy and Society of British Artists, but most often to the New Water-Colour Society (later the Royal Institute), of which he became Associate in 1848 and Member in 1851. In 1847 he visited Wales, and subsequently made tours in Scotland, Germany, Normandy and Italy. He succeeded his father as drawing-master at the Royal Naval School. In his earlier days, judging by a *Rouen*[1] of 1843, assigned to him by credible tradition, he did pleasant work in the Callow manner. Then he seems to have followed the Richardsons in subject and manner, gaining popular effects by a free use of body-colour. His Swiss and Italian subjects are crude productions. In *Academy Notes*, 1858, Ruskin blames Rowbotham for 'defrauding himself of the very picturesqueness he delights in, by painting out of what he supposes to be his head, but is, in reality, only his habit'.

Here finally are some brief notes about a few more painters who may be said, in some cases perhaps rather indirectly, to belong to the same group as Copley Fielding. They

[1] V.A.M. 1504–1869.

painted the same sort of subject, often in a similar way, and typify the ordinary practice in the middle period of last century.

George Arthur Fripp (1813–1896), born at Bristol, was a grandson of Nicholas Pocock. He received his art education in his native town, taking lessons from J. B. Pyne and from Samuel Jackson, the founder of the Bristol school. A tour through Belgium and Switzerland to Italy in 1834 with his fellow townsman William Müller, resulted in a strengthening of Fripp's technique in water-colour. It was George Fripp who took Cox to see Müller painting.

Fripp himself certainly learned from Müller the value of accurate, unostentatious draughtsmanship, as is shown in the *Via Mala*[1] while with Müller in 1834.

In 1841, having moved to London, Fripp was elected an associate of the Old Society and became a full member in 1845. Apart from views of foreign scenery, chiefly in Switzerland and North Italy, his work is locally and characteristically British. His many drawings of the Thames are of high quality, with delicate atmospheric effects. Other subjects, similarly treated, were found in Wales, Yorkshire, Kent, Sussex and Dorset, the last two counties providing many careful studies of cliffs and rocky coasts.

A whole series of his drawings dealt with mountain scenery in Scotland many of them made by Royal Command in the Balmoral district in 1860. Roget[2] sums up his work by saying: 'The artist's water-colour drawings, particularly of his middle and later time, are characterized by refined delicacy and tenderness of aerial effect, by truth of colours, and by the learned breadth and scrupulous balance of their composition.' He is fully represented in the Victoria and Albert Museum, and I recall seeing a large collection of drawings by G. A. Fripp and A. D. Fripp at the house of the latter's son, Sir Alfred Fripp, a distinguished surgeon.

Alfred Downing Fripp (1822–1895), George's younger brother, was born at Bristol and came at an early age under the influence of Müller. In 1840 he joined his brother in London and was admitted to the Royal Academy Schools in 1842. In 1843 he made the first of three visits to the West of Ireland, and studies of Irish figures and scenes of peasant life are prominent in his early work. In 1844 he was elected associate and in 1846, full member of the Old Society. From 1850 to 1858 he lived in Italy, painting Roman, Neapolitan, Venetian and other themes. From 1859 he was living in Dorset and forsook the richness and force of his earlier work in an attempt to paint the delicate greys and mist-laden atmosphere of our native shores. What is perhaps his best work was done during summer sojourns at Swanage and Lulworth. I quote from an article written at the time of his death in 1895 by F. G. Stephens[3]:

These works especially the later ones, attest that Fripp was a subtle chiaroscurist, a good colourist, a poet in painting with a rare and delicate sense of what is peaceful and idyllic in

[1] Once Coll. H. S. Thompson.
[2] Roget, II, p. 268.
[3] *Magazine of Art*, 1895, p. 470.

Nature . . . while his later, or post-Roman mood, illustrated his taste for opalescent greys, delicate harmonies of low tints, and tones of great refinement, and an almost Stothard-like grace inspired the expressions and attitudes of his rustic figures.

In a sketch made by Sir John Gilbert, of the hanging committee at work before the opening of the Old Society's summer exhibition in 1870, Fripp is seated smoking a clay pipe beside T. M. Richardson.[1]

William Collingwood Smith (1815–1887) was born at Greenwich. He began to practise as an artist before he was seventeen, and received some occasional instruction from J. D. Harding. He contributed an oil-painting to the Royal Academy in 1836, but became exclusively a water-colour painter, being elected associate of the Old Society in 1843 and full member in 1849. Roget records that his total exhibits during his forty-five years of membership amounted to about 2000. He was Treasurer of his Society from 1854 to 1879, and we find him saying in a letter that, 'Dante's Inferno is deficient in not having depicted the miseries of a poor wretch casting up his accounts for the annual meeting.' His earlier subjects before 1849 were mainly marine pieces, but afterwards he painted landscape extensively in the British Isles and in France, Switzerland, Belgium, Germany and especially in Italy. At an early period of his career he began to take pupils and in his day was perhaps the most popular of drawing-masters. Among his pupils were Samuel Read, William Collingwood, W. Matthew Hale, W. Eyre Walker and J. W. Whymper. His own work is marked by breadth of effect, firmness of drawing and precision of touch, even when it lacks the finer finish in form and the subtler qualities of colour.

In the latter half of the nineteenth century there was a whole group of painters in the main line of descent from Copley Fielding. Charles Davidson (1824–1902) was born in London, of Scottish parents. Left an orphan at an early age, he spent a year as an apprentice to a seedsman and market-gardener at Brompton. For some years he studied under John Absolon. In 1844 he began to exhibit, and was elected an associate of the New Water-Colour Society in 1847 and a member in 1849. Resigning in 1853, he became associate of the Old Society in 1855 and a member in 1858. The Varleys, John Linnell and Samuel Palmer were his friends, and for many years he was a neighbour of Palmer at Redhill. After Palmer's death he settled in 1882 at Trevena, where he remained till his own death. He seems never to have travelled far from the places of his residence and was largely content to paint, with level accomplishment, homely landscapes and hay-making scenes in Surrey. Two typical subjects by him are in the Dixon Bequest, Bethnal Green Museum. He rarely signed his work, and in view of the fact that he had 800 exhibits at the Old Water-Colour Society alone, I suspect that a good deal of his output has been assigned to other artists.

Robert Thorne Waite (1842–c.1933) was born at Cheltenham and received his art education at South Kensington. In 1876 he won election as an associate of the Old Society, and became full member in 1884. His pleasant pastorals render freely and accurately land-

---

[1] Drawing, belonging to the Royal Water-colour Society, reproduced in *O.W.S.*, I, pl. III, 1923–1924.

scape in both Yorkshire and Southern England, grouped mainly round that small district in Sussex where the Downs hold up the Southern Weald from the sea and clouds from the English Channel cast shadows over sun-warmed slopes of chalky soil. *Calling the Cattle Home*,[1] 1876 (Pl. 226), is a downland scene where the Fielding influence is clearly apparent, and another good example of his work is a *Gap in the Downs*.[2]

Ernest Albert Waterlow (1850–1919), son of a lithographer, was born in London. After studying art at Heidelberg and Lausanne, he returned to London and entered the Royal Academy schools in 1872, winning in the following year the coveted Turner gold medal. Like Sir Alfred East, he worked throughout his life in oils as well as in water-colour. He was elected associate of the Royal Water-Colour Society in 1880, member in 1894, and President in 1897. As a painter in oil he became A.R.A. in 1890 and R.A. in 1903. He was knighted in 1902. His somewhat idyllic landscapes, found mainly in southern England, are marked by harmony of colour and quiet refinement. His *Westmeston, Sussex Downs*[3] (Pl. 227) is typical of his gentle art; there are three good examples of his work in the Laing Art Gallery, Newcastle, and *A Suffolk Heath*[4] in Birmingham.

Somewhat attached in sentiment and subject to the same school was H. Sutton Palmer (1854–1933), though his work showed a more exact refinement of detail, which might make one equally well associate him with Birket Foster. He became one of the leading members of the Royal Institute. Surrey furnished him with many of the subjects in which he excelled, a stretch of country seen from among the trees, a church spire to show where a village lies in the woodland, and in the distance a range of downs. It is a pleasing but a conscious and sophisticated art, depending upon recipe and very skilful technique. His work is well represented in the Whitworth Art Gallery, Manchester University.

William Turner was one of the first of a series of painters who were apprenticed to John Varley, and found in him a guide and friend. He lodged under his master's roof, just as two years before De Wint had come to London as a resident apprentice to John Raphael Smith. William Turner (1789–1862) was born at Black Burton, near Bampton, in Oxford-shire, and on the death of his father was brought up by an uncle who, in 1804, had pur-chased the estate and manor-house of Shipton-on-Cherwell, near Woodstock. William Turner came to London as a young landscape painter at a time when his greater namesake was already finding fame, and so the younger man became known as 'Turner of Oxford'. His early promise was so great that on January 29, 1808, just after his eighteenth birthday, he was elected an Associate of the Old Water-Colour Society, together with J. A. Atkinson, who was fourteen years his senior. Two days before this election Farington[5] records that: 'Varley spoke violently of the merit of a young man who has been his pupil learning to draw in water colours & Reinagle said "He had never before seen drawings equal to

[1] Dixon Bequest, Bethnal Green Museum.
[2] Birmingham, City Art Gallery.
[3] V.A.M. P.64–1920.
[4] Birmingham, City Art Gallery.
[5] *Diary*, January 27, 1808.

234

them". His name Turner.' Hazlitt wrote that the man of genius spends his whole life in telling the world what he knew himself at the age of eighteen. The *latens deitas* was in William Turner to cause his election to the Water-Colour Society at eighteen, but the altar fire burned down. Turner was not a man of genius, but his work, particularly his earlier work, has not generally received the acknowledgment which it assuredly deserves.

The Varley influence shows strongly in the earliest drawing by Turner which I have seen, *Waddon Wood and the Village of Waddington, Lancs*,[1] signed and dated 1808. Simple washes are admirably used in low tones of dark green and grey, with light and shade finely balanced under a well-studied, moving sky. The drawing does not seem to have been exhibited, and it was probably bought from the artist by its original owner, Samuel Naylor, who acquired drawings by Cox and others in this way.

Three of Turner's first exhibits on joining the Water-Colour Society (*Cornfield near Woodstock; Ottmoor, near Oxford;* and *Wychwood Forest, Oxfordshire*) won the praise of John Landseer, who in writing a criticism of the exhibition found in them the 'wide range of capacity and contrivance of a veteran landscape painter to whom nature has become familiar. . . . By the dint of his superior art he has rolled such clouds over these landscapes as has given to a flat country an equal grandeur with mountain scenery, while they fully account for the striking and natural effect of light and shade which he has introduced. His colouring is grave, subdued, and such as properly belongs to landscapes of a majestic character.'[2]

It says much for Varley, as well as for William Turner, that one of those three drawings, the *Wychwood Forest, Oxfordshire*[3] (Pl. 229), which is now in the Victoria and Albert Museum, does indeed look like the work of a veteran, yet the artist was only nineteen when he painted it. On the back is written 'A scene where a pleasure fair was formerly held in Wychwood Forest, Oxfordshire. William Turner, Shipton on Cherwell Oxon 1809.' The composition of this beautifully preserved drawing, shows a classical grandeur, like a landscape by Poussin, the centre being occupied by dark masses of trees and involved foliage. But the sky on the upper right, and the landscape below the cumulus clouds, and that glimpse of distant woodland on the left are pure Cotman, in colour, form and the superimposition of two tones of grey or green. Cotman's *Greta Bridge* and other drawings show that his style was fully formed by 1806, and by then he had certainly arrived at his superb simplification of foliage and use of a second flat wash of another similar tint, very little darker in tone, over his first light wash. But had he in 1809 quite achieved, as Turner had in this drawing, the clean-edged splendour of white clouds that, later, so often added to the deliberate pattern of his design? If Turner, when painting his *Wychwood Forest*, had learned much from Varley and Cotman, did Cotman himself learn something from Turner of Oxford? And there is real merit in another water-colour which must belong to the same early period,

[1] Present whereabouts unknown.
[2] *The Review of Publications in Art*, p. 288, 1808.
[3] V.A.M. P.136–1929.

the *Sea Marsh*,[1] a drawing full of dramatic intensity in its rendering of sunlight and storm without the mechanical conventions of his later work. Another fine work of this period is a *Landscape*[2] and the De Wint influence, added to that of Varley, appears very strongly in *London from Greenwich*[3] and *Bamborough Castle*.[4] In the case of the former, I am inclined to think that Turner was sitting beside De Wint when he made it. De Wint made more than one drawing from this very spot. The *Bamborough Castle* seems to combine a De Wint aspect of the castle with a foreground reminiscent of Varley. The silhouette of the group comprising a man and cattle, dark in the foreground, repeats the silhouette of the sunlit castle, a conscious repetition which has been referred to as a feature of Varley's art.

After this magnificent beginning, the youthful ardour, promise and innocence were to be spoiled by experience and sophistication. One likes to think that he might have become coequal with the greater Turner, but William Turner seems to have settled down to be a 'country member' of his Society, content with his provincial title, and satisfied with domestic life varied by teaching numerous pupils in Oxford and by completing in his studio the landscapes made on his sketching tours. With all his devotion to his art, and all his gifts of craftsmanship, he lacked the temperament that leads the greater man to invention or to adventure. You cannot see William Turner of Oxford making any attempt to fling his hat over a windmill. Worthy and dignified, looking like a parson of the old school, dressed in black and wearing a white tie, he lived a humdrum life at his house, 16 John Street, near Worcester College, where he resided from 1833 till his death on August 7, 1862. He became the type of the ordinary 'clever' artist, who passes an honourable day like any man of business, polishing his multitudinous sketches of picturesque material, and in due time passing honoured to his death, without having added much to the world's artistic resources.

His later drawings are extensive views, realistic and painstaking; the sense of pattern and composition in sky and landscape is lost; there is a striving for 'effect'; interest is given, not through design, but by the introduction of shepherds and their flocks; verses by Mrs. Hemans and others are added to his titles; again and again the same 'blest shepherd on the turf reclines'. More than once he described the Cherwell as, 'where the white water-lilies grow abundantly'. All of this is summed up in his *Kingly Bottom*,[5] attractive enough in its wide prospect, in its cunning splash of sunlit yellow among all the misty blue, but depending on calculated colour and fidelity of detail, instead of showing the force of inspiration that marks the *Wychwood Forest*. Kingly Vale was the subject again of his *View from the side of Bow Hill*, exhibited at the Old Water-Colour Society in 1851. It shows the usual shepherd and sheep scattered across the foreground, the same effect of sunlight and blue distance. In the *Kingly Bottom* and many similar works, such as his *Vale*

[1] Coll. H. Powell (N.A.C.F.).
[2] Coll. Mr. D. L. T. Oppé.
[3] Oxford, City Library.
[4] Oxford, City Library.
[5] V.A.M. 546.

236

208 'Richmond Hill'

Coll. Mr & Mrs Paul Mellon $6\frac{5}{8} \times 11\frac{7}{8}$: 168 × 302   *Water-colour*

Anthony Vandyke Copley FIELDING (1787–1855)

209 'Flintshire, Rhuddlan Bridge'

V.A.M. 2972–1876 $10\frac{1}{4} \times 19\frac{1}{2}$: 267 × 495   *Water-colour, signed and dated 1809*

Anthony Vandyke Copley FIELDING (1787–1855)

210 'Castle on a Cliff: Fishing Smacks'

V.A.M. 2973–1876 $10\frac{1}{4} \times 13\frac{1}{2}$: 260×342 *Water-colour, signed and dated 1810*

Anthony Vandyke Copley FIELDING (1787–1855)

211 'Loch Lomond'

Manchester, City Art Galleries $12 \times 17\frac{1}{4}$: 304×437 *Water-colour, signed and dated 1847*

Anthony Vandyke Copley FIELDING (1787–1855)

212 'House by a Pond'

B.M. 1949.8.6.1 $10\frac{1}{4} \times 13\frac{1}{4}$: 260×337 *Water-colour, signed and dated 1832*

Newton Limbird Smith FIELDING (1799–1856)

213 'Old Breakwater, Plymouth'

B.M. 1890.5.12.76 7×11: 178×280 *Water-colour*

Thales FIELDING (1793–1837)

214 'Windsor Castle, from the Thames'
B.M. 1890.5.12.77   4¼×6½: 108×165   *Water-colour*
Theodore Henry Adolphus FIELDING (1781–1851)

215 'Loch Coruisk, Isle of Skye'
V.A.M. 1426–1869   25½×44: 646×1115   *Water-colour*
George Fennel ROBSON (1788–1833)

216 'Kyles of Bute'

V.A.M. 412–1891 $10\frac{3}{4} \times 27\frac{5}{8}$: 273 × 700   *Water-colour*

Henry George HINE (1811–1895)

217 'Peverill Point, Dorset'

V.A.M. 111–1891 $9\frac{5}{8} \times 28\frac{1}{8}$: 243 × 712   *Water-colour*

Henry George HINE (1811–1895)

218 'The Lion Bridge, Alnwick'
Newcastle upon Tyne, Laing Art Gallery $9\frac{3}{4} \times 14\frac{1}{4}$: 248×361 *Water-colour*
Thomas Miles RICHARDSON I (1784–1848)

219 'Mount Parnassus'
Coll. Mr D. L. T. Oppé $13\frac{3}{8} \times 9\frac{1}{4}$: 340×235 *Water-colour*
Thomas Miles RICHARDSON II (1813–1890)

220 'Rouen, from St. Catherine's Hill'
V.A.M. 1504–1869 $12\frac{1}{2} \times 18\frac{7}{8}$: 317 × 479   *Water-colour*
Thomas Leeson ROWBOTHAM II (1823–1875)

221 'A Mountain Hamlet'
V.A.M. P.29–1921 $20\frac{3}{4} \times 29$: 526 × 735   *Water-colour, signed and dated 1852*
Thomas Leeson ROWBOTHAM II (1823–1875)

222 'Children of the Mist'

V.A.M. 401–1891   14⅛ × 25 : 358 × 633   *Water-colour*

George Arthur FRIPP (1813–1896)

223 'The Monastery of San Rocco at Olevano'

V.A.M. P.10–1932   12 × 17¾ : 304 × 450   *Water-colour, signed*

Alfred Downing FRIPP (1822–1895)

224 'The Otter's Haunt'

V.A.M. 3034–1876   16¼ × 23¼: 412 × 590   *Water-colour, signed*

William Collingwood SMITH (1815–1887)

225 'Ramsgate Pier'

Oxford, Ashmolean Museum   8⅛ × 12⅝: 207 × 328   *Water-colour*

Charles DAVIDSON (1824–1902)

226 'Calling the Cattle Home'

V.A.M. 1216–1886 $22\frac{5}{8} \times 35\frac{3}{4}$: 578 × 906   *Water-colour, signed and dated 1876*

Robert Thorne WAITE (1842–c. 1933)

227 'Westmeston, Sussex Downs'

V.A.M. P.64–1920 $13\frac{1}{4} \times 21\frac{1}{4}$: 336 × 539   *Water-colour, signed*

Sir Ernest Albert WATERLOW, R.A. (1850–1919)

228 'Stream and Meadow'

V.A.M. P.49–1917 $13\frac{7}{8} \times 20\frac{5}{8}: 352 \times 523$ *Water-colour, signed*

Sutton PALMER (1854–1933)

229 'Wychwood Forest, Oxfordshire'

V.A.M. P.136–1929 $23\frac{7}{8} \times 31\frac{1}{4}: 605 \times 792$ *Water-colour, signed*

William TURNER of Oxford (1789–1862)

230 'Landscape with Village and Windmill'
Coll. Mrs Cecil Keith $8 \times 12\frac{1}{4}$: 203×310 *Water-colour*
William TURNER of Oxford (1789–1862)

231 'Goodrich Castle'
B.M. 1867.4.13.669 $11\frac{5}{8} \times 16\frac{1}{4}$: 296×412 *Water-colour*
William TURNER of Oxford (1789–1862)

of Gloucester from Birdlip,[1] he gives with singular skill the effect of an illimitable expanse of flat country seen from a height, but he is merely following Copley Fielding in manner and method, and he lacks Fielding's genuine grasp of natural character, and his perception of space and colour.

William Turner, like his namesake, was a prolific and indefatigable worker. A large portion of his time was occupied in making the sketching tours required for his landscapes, some of which he describes as 'painted on the spot'; and those were always the best. Others he worked up in his studio, often finishing the same subject in different sizes, with varying foregrounds and atmospheric effects. He never seems to have left Great Britain, but is known to have made some Swiss and Italian drawings from sketches by other people. In his early years, as has been seen, he was working within a radius of a few miles from his Oxfordshire home, and for several years seems to have remained within the immediately adjoining counties. He visited Bristol, Cheltenham, Chepstow, the valley of the Wye, and Windsor. The Old Water-Colour Society's catalogue of 1815 indicates a visit to the Lakes. In 1817 he was in the Snowdon district, and in the following year in Derbyshire. For several years after this his sketching ground was in the midland counties with an excursion or two to Salisbury Plain and North Devon. The New Forest appears for the first time in the catalogue of 1827, and between that year and 1836, he seems to have made more than one tour in North Wales, besides revisiting the New Forest, Salisbury Plain and North Devon. By 1835 he had got to know the Isle of Wight and the West Sussex Downs, and in 1836 he sketched on the Cornish coast. He was nearly fifty when, in 1838, he made what was apparently his first trip to Scotland, passing through Glencoe, parts of Ross-shire and the Isle of Skye. In the Highlands of Scotland he found a fascination which made him almost entirely abandon North Wales, and a long series of Scottish drawings made in Skye and among the Lochs of the west coast (especially Loch Duich) show that he must have paid several visits to the North to accumulate material. The catalogues of 1841 to 1853 suggest that his route to the north must have lain sometimes through Northumberland (Bamborough, Dunstanborough and the Cheviot country), sometimes through the English Lake district (especially Ullswater and Derwentwater). The West Sussex Downs always held his affection, and during the last twenty-five years of his life, Scotland, the Lake District, Northumberland and West Sussex, together with Oxford and its neighbourhood, cover more than three-quarters of his exhibited work.[2]

In the Victoria and Albert Museum are Turner's own annotated copies of the catalogues of the Old Water-Colour Society from 1808 to 1854. The artist's notes on his own exhibits and their buyers are of special value, and his comments on his contemporaries have much interest. That he was not entirely complacent about his own work is shown by

---

[1] Present whereabouts unknown.
[2] For this account of Turner's sketching-ground I am indebted to the catalogues of the Royal Water-Colour Society and to the admirable record of Turner's work and life in the Introduction to the catalogue of a *Loan Exhibition of the Work of William Turner*, at the University Galleries, Oxford, 1895.

the fact that he notes the destruction, by his own hand, of no less than twenty-nine of his exhibited works.

William Turner's long connection with the Old Water-Colour Society may be regarded as the central feature in his uneventful life. Roget says that Turner exhibited four hundred and fifty-five works at the Water-Colour Society in the fifty-five years from the date of his admission as an Associate in 1808 to that of his death in 1862, and most of them were of large size. His remaining works, in some two to three hundred lots, were sold at Christie's on March 9, 1863. A Loan Exhibition of his works was held at the University Galleries, Oxford, in 1895, and about forty-four water-colours by him, belonging to the Rev. L. R. Phelps, were sold by auction in 1929, at the Provost's Lodgings, Oriel College. Oxford is naturally rich in drawings by William Turner. His work can be seen at the Ashmolean, and also—by a gift from Sir Michael Sadler—in the City Library. The late Mr. C. H. Wilkinson, formerly Dean of Worcester College, had some fine examples, among them a dramatic *Tintagel*.

William Turner was one of the many artists whose early promise remained unfulfilled; but lest our estimate be unfair, let it be said that Ruskin speaks of him as a 'patient and unassuming master' that he is 'sorry not to have before noticed the quiet and simple earnestness, and the tender feeling, of the mountain drawings of William Turner of Oxford'. In his *Notes on some of the Principal Pictures for the years 1856–1859*,[1] Ruskin speaks of the *View from Quiraing*, 1858, as 'a very impressive and precious drawing, full of truth in its far-off Highland hills, and glowing sky, and low floating mists', and in 1859 says, 'Look at the rolling clouds in Mr. Turner's *Ben Cruachan*, which are the truest clouds in the whole room.'

In Oxford Turner had great popularity as a teacher. His method, like that of Nicholson and other earlier men, was to take one of his studies and to paint a picture from it, stage by stage, each successive stage constituting a lesson. After each lesson the pupil took the painting home and copied what the master had done. It was a dull and uninspiring method, but no doubt it impressed on the student a definite technical procedure. His palette was simple—gamboge, Indian yellow, Prussian blue, rose madder, with cobalt and brown madder for sky, and Smith's warm grey, a colour which he regularly employed for the rocky foregrounds of his Scottish landscapes.

From 1810 to 1812, while he was a young member of the Old Water-Colour Society, Turner's prices averaged £27; and, later, they must have been much higher. His *Wychwood Forest* remained unsold in 1809 at £21. His highest price of the period 1808 to 1812 was £42 for the *View of Oxford*, from Botley Hill, in 1811. It is not without interest that De Wint's highest price in this year was £31 10s., Glover's £52 10s., and those of Havell, John Varley and Barret £42 each.

[1] *Modern Painters*, I, 327, ii, p. 28.

INDEX

of Artists Mentioned in the Text

The numerals in *Italics* refer to the principal entries relating to each artist and those in **Bold** type refer to the *Figure Numbers* of the Illustrations.